THE NEW DIALECTIC:
CONVERSATIONAL CONTEXTS OF ARGUMENT

Because developments in informal logic have been based, for the most part, on idealized and abstract models, the tools available for argument analysis are not easily adapted to the needs of everyday argumentation. In this book Douglas Walton proposes a new and practical approach to argument analysis based on his theory that different standards for argument must apply in the case of different types of dialogue.

By refining and extending the existing formal classifications of dialogue, Walton shows that each dialogue type, be it inquiry, negotiation, or critical discussion, has its own set of goals. He goes on to demonstrate that an argument can best be evaluated in terms of its contribution, positive or negative, to the goals of the particular dialogue it is meant to further. In this way he illustrates how argument can be brought into the service of many types of dialogue, and thus has valuable uses that go well beyond the mere settling of disputes and differences.

By reaching back to the Aristotelian roots of logic as an applied, practical discipline and by formulating a new framework of rationality for evaluating arguments, Douglas Walton restores a much-needed balance to argument analysis. This book complements and extends his *Argument Structure: A Pragmatic Theory*.

(Toronto Studies in Philosophy)

DOUGLAS WALTON is Professor in the Department of Philosophy, University of Winnipeg.

DOUGLAS N. WALTON

The New Dialectic: Conversational Contexts of Argument

UNIVERSITY OF TORONTO PRESS
Toronto Buffalo London

© University of Toronto Press Incorporated 1998
Toronto Buffalo London
Printed in Canada

ISBN 0-8020-4143-4 (cloth)
ISBN 0-8020-7987-3 (paper)

Printed on acid-free paper

Toronto Studies in Philosophy
Editors: James R. Brown and Calvin Normore

Canadian Cataloguing in Publication Data

Walton, Douglas N. (Douglas Neil), 1942–
    The new dialectic : conversational contexts of argument

(Toronto studies in philosophy)
Includes index.
ISBN 0-8020-4143-4 (bound)   ISBN 0-8020-7987-3 (pbk.)

1. Reasoning.   2. Logic.   I. Title.   II. Series.

BC177.W34 1998   168   C97-932464-5

University of Toronto Press acknowledges the financial assistance to its
publishing program of the Canada Council for the Arts and the Ontario Arts
Council.

This book has been published with the help of a grant from the Humanities
and Social Sciences Federation of Canada, using funds provided by the Social
Sciences and Humanities Research Council of Canada.

For Karen,
With love.

Contents

ACKNOWLEDGMENTS   ix

Chapter 1: Introduction   3
1 Statement of Purpose   4
2 Informal Logic and Fallacies   7
3 Aristotle's Five Types of Arguments   11
4 The Waning of Dialectic   14
5 Locke's Four Kinds of Arguments   16
6 Fallacies of Relevance   21
7 Other Important Fallacies   25
8 The New Approach to Dialectic   28
9 Types of Dialogue   30
10 Dialectical Relevance   34

Chapter 2: Persuasion Dialogue   37
1 Main Characteristics   37
2 Argument in Persuasion Dialogue   41
3 Commitment   43
4 Critical Discussion   46
5 Nonexplicit Commitments   49
6 Rigorous and Permissive Persuasion Dialogue   53
7 Maieutic Function   57
8 The Problem of Enthymemes   60
9 Relevance in Persuasion Dialogue   63
10 Evaluating Criticisms of Irrelevance   65

Chapter 3: The Inquiry   69
1 Main Characteristics   70
2 Advancing States of Knowledge   72
3 Aristotelian Demonstration   76
4 Is Scientific Argumentation an Inquiry?   78
5 Other Subtypes of Inquiry   81
6 Argument and Explanation   85
7 Black and Beardsley on the Inquiry   87
8 Cases of Public Inquiries   91
9 Profiles of Dialogue in the Inquiry   94
10 Relevance in the Inquiry   97

Chapter 4: Negotiation Dialogue   100
1 Main Characteristics   100
2 Subtypes   103
3 The Game-Theory Model of Negotiation   104
4 Commitment in Negotiation Dialogue   106
5 Relevance and Irrelevance   109
6 Threats as Arguments   113
7 Dialectical Shifts from Negotiation   116
8 Solutions for Deadlock   119
9 Bias and Advocacy   121
10 Advocacy Advertising   122

Chapter 5: Information-Seeking Dialogue   126
1 Main Characteristics   126
2 The Interview   130
3 Searching a Database   132
4 Position to Know   134
5 Classification of Questions   136
6 Presuppositions of Questions   140
7 How Can a Question Be a Fallacy?   141
8 Expert Consultation Dialogue   143
9 Peirastic and Exetastic Dialogues   145
10 Relevance in Information-Seeking Dialogue   147

Chapter 6: Deliberation   151
1 Main Characteristics   151
2 Practical Reasoning   153
3 Argument from Consequences   157

4 The Dilemma 160
5 Stages and Dynamic Aspects of Deliberation 161
6 Aristotle's Account of Deliberation 166
7 The Town Hall Meeting 169
8 Public and Political Deliberation 171
9 Relevance in Deliberation 173
10 Relevance Across Joined Dialogues 175

Chapter 7: Eristic Dialogue 178
1 The Quarrel as Paradigm 178
2 Eristic Dialogue 181
3 Stages of the Quarrel 183
4 Closed Attitude of Eristic Dialogue 186
5 Plato on Eristic Argument 187
6 Aristotle on Contentious Argument 189
7 Modern Revival of Eristic Argument 191
8 Relevance in Eristic Dialogue 193
9 Subtypes of Eristic Dialogue 194
10 Identifying Characteristics of Eristic Dialogue 196

Chapter 8: Dialectical Shifts 198
1 Types of Shifts 198
2 Licit and Illicit Shifts 200
3 Licit Shifts to and from Expert Consultation Dialogue 203
4 Illicit Shifts and Fallacious Arguments 205
5 The Infomercial 206
6 Deceptive Format 208
7 Success and Evolution of Infomercials 210
8 Educational and Print Formats 212
9 Contextual Evidence for Retrospective Evaluation 214
10 Obstruction of Goals by Dialectical Shifts 215

Chapter 9: Mixed Discourse 218
1 The Case of Question Period 218
2 The Problem of Fallacies in Political Discourse 221
3 Political Debate as Mixed Discourse 223
4 Evaluating Arguments in Political Discourse 224
5 The Case of Sales Dialogue 227
6 Evaluating Fallacies in Sales Dialogue 230
7 Argumentation in a Legal Trial 232

8 Pedagogical Dialogue   235
9 Aristotle's Five Types of Arguments Revisited   237
10 Aristotle on Dialectical Argument   240

**Chapter 10: The Dialectical Method of Evaluating
Arguments**   245
1 Argument Evaluation   246
2 The Four-Step Method   249
3 Evaluating Dialectical Relevance   252
4 Evaluating a Case for Relevance   254
5 Fallacies, Blunders, and Errors   257
6 Fallacies and Dialectical Shifts   261
7 Fallacies Reconceptualized in the New Dialectic   265
8 Dialectical Advice for Using These Arguments   269
9 Evidence Required to Support a Dialectical Evaluation   272
10 Prospects for the New Dialectic   275

NOTES   279
REFERENCES   285
INDEX   295

Acknowledgments

My thanks are due to the Social Sciences and Humanities Research Council of Canada for a research grant that made the work on this project possible. For discussions that have helped to shape the ideas in the book, I would most emphatically like to thank Erik Krabbe, whose collaboration with me over the past several years on a related research project has been a great source of maieutic inspiration in all my work in the field of informal logic and argumentation studies. As well, I would like to acknowledge the help contributed by discussions with other colleagues and collaborators in recent years: Tony Blair, Alan Brinton, Maurice Finocchiaro, Jim Freeman, Dov Gabbay, Michael Gilbert, Rob Grootendorst, Hans Hansen, David Hitchcock, John Hoaglund, Sally Jackson, Scott Jacobs, Ralph Johnson, Henry W. Johnstone, Jr, Christoph Lumer, Hans-Jürgen Ohlbach, Bob Pinto, Michael Scriven, Chris Tindale, Frans van Eemeren, Mark Weinstein, Victor Wilkes, John Woods, and Mike Wreen.

For word-processing the first draft, I would like to thank Louise Lepine, and for the subsequent and final drafts, I would like to thank Amy Merrett. Also, I would like to thank the University of Winnipeg for providing encouragement, support, and facilities for my research work.

I would like to thank the editors of two of my previously published articles for allowing me to use parts of them here (in chapters 1 and 10): 'Types of Dialogue, Dialectical Shifts and Fallacies,' in *Argumentation Illuminated*, edited by Frans H. van Eemeren, Rob Grootendorst, J. Anthony Blair, and Charles A. Willard (Amsterdam: SICSAT, 1992) and 'New Methods for Evaluating Arguments,' *Inquiry: Critical Thinking across the Disciplines* 15 (1996). Finally, I would like to thank Harry Simpson for help with proofreading and Rita Campbell for doing the index.

THE NEW DIALECTIC

1

Introduction

This book formulates a new framework of rationality for thinking, and in particular that part of thinking that has to do with accepting arguments as instances of good reasoning or criticizing arguments as instances of bad reasoning. The new standard advocated here is pragmatic in nature: arguments are evaluated as correct or incorrect insofar as they are used either to contribute to or to impede the goals of dialogue. Six basic types of dialogue are described: persuasion dialogue, the inquiry, negotiation, information-seeking dialogue, deliberation, and eristic dialogue. Each of these types of dialogue is put forward as a normative model which specifies broadly how an argument should be used in order to be correct or to be defensible against the criticism that it is incorrect, erroneous, or fallacious.

A dialogue (to use our generic term) or a conversation (to use an everyday term) is defined as a goal-directed conventional framework in which two speech partners reason together in an orderly way, according to the rules of politeness or normal expectations of cooperative argumentation for the type of exchange they are engaged in. Each type of dialogue has distinctive goals as well as methods that are used by the participants to achieve these goals together. Thus the view of rationality expressed here is highly collaborative. In addition, this work has a novel way of explaining the adversarial or contentious aspect of argument which is so important to our understanding of it.

The new framework is, in certain respects, also old. It goes back to the Aristotelian roots of logic as an applied, practical discipline, and brings out and formulates – in modern terms that are adequate for state-of-the-art argumentation theory – many of the leading ideas expressed in Aristotle's works on dialectical argument and fallacies, or sophistical refutations.[1] By reaching back to these early roots of the subject, this new approach restores the long-lost balance between the semantic, formal study of logical inferences and the practical study of the uses of arguments in everyday conversational exchanges. It has the effect of liberating logic from its current status as a subject of limited practical importance by counterbalancing the longstanding dominance of the exclusive and one-sided influence of Aristotle's enormously successful works on deductive syllogistic reasoning. With this approach it will be possible to apply logical standards in a systematic way to conversational arguments on controversial topics where real conflicts of opinions exist.

1. Statement of Purpose

The purpose of this book is to give a new theoretical basis for logic which can be used to evaluate arguments that arise in everyday conversational exchanges. In the twentieth century, and for most of its history, logic has concentrated mainly on evaluating arguments according to an abstract semantic model that centrally emphasizes certain deductive forms of reasoning, like syllogistic and propositional forms of reasoning. Judging arguments pragmatically, in relation to how they are used in a conversational context, has had a very low priority through the history of logic, even though Aristotle did provide a foundation in his practical works on argument – the *Topics* and *On Sophistical Refutations* – and in parts of his other works. This tradition continued in the logic textbooks, especially in the chapters or sections on fallacies, but overall this part of logic has been marked by the lack of any serious or sustained attempts to ground it on a theoretical basis (Hamblin, 1970).

In recent years this very significant gap has been filling up with a growing body of literature on argumentation theory and informal logic.[2] Several of my past contributions to this literature have framed the place of this book in the development of informal logic. In *Informal Logic* (1989a), I showed that the major informal fallacies are based on types of arguments that are, in some instances, reasonable kinds of argumentation but that can nevertheless be fallacious in other instances. In *Argumentation Schemes for Presumptive Reasoning* (1996b), I identified schemes or characteristic forms of these common types of arguments. In *A Pragmatic Theory of Fallacy* (1995), I presented a theory of fallaciousness and demonstrated how and why these argumentation schemes can be misused in certain types of cases and result in the kinds of fallacies that tradition has identified as significant.

In 1970 Hamblin moved into the vanguard by proposing a framework for the analysis of fallacies that involves placing an argument in the framework of a dialectical system that models the context of its use. He advocated studying dialectical systems descriptively, by looking at 'rules and conventions that operate in actual discussions,' and formally, by 'setting up of simple systems of precise but not necessarily realistic rules' that regulate argument exchanges between two parties (1970, p. 256). Hamblin sketched a general framework of how such systems should be set up and gave several examples, but did not provide any detailed accounts of systems that would apply directly, in a very useful way, to arguments in everyday conversation of the kind associated with the traditional fallacies. He was not very clear about the purpose of a dialectical system that models any conventional types of argumentation used in conversational exchanges, and did not seriously attempt any classification of such types of dialogues.

An outline of other formal theories of dialogue argumentation is given in Fritz and Hundsnurscher (1994). The first complete formal systems of dialogue logic were constructed by Lorenzen (see Stegmüller, 1964 and Lorenzen, 1969). These systems were further developed and applied to the study of conversational argument exchanges by Barth and Krabbe (1982). The Lorenzen-type systems are species of what is called 'rigorous persuasion dialogue' (see chapter 2).

The purpose of the most detailed formal dialectical system presented by Hamblin was the 'exchange of information among the participants' (1971, p. 137). The Hamblin type of information-oriented dialogue was refined and developed by Mackenzie (1981). Hintikka (1981) constructed formal dialogue systems that are classified in our framework as information-seeking dialogues (see chapter 5).

In addition to the literature on formal systems of dialogue, there were also the developments from the pragmatic framework of conversational analysis proposed by Grice. Grice analysed inferences used in a conversational context governed by the cooperative principle (CP), which states that a participant in a conversation should make her contribution 'such as is required, at the stage at which it occurs, by the accepted purpose or direction of the talk exchange in which you are engaged' (1975, p. 67). Grice's rules for such an exchange include conversational maxims like 'avoid ambiguity' and 'be relevant.' The problem is that the exact purpose of such a conversation is not indicated, nor is any classification of different types of conversation given. What 'being relevant' means is not defined, and no exact or useful method for evaluating relevance is given.

Van Eemeren and Grootendorst have concentrated on one type of dialogue, but have not attempted to construct a formal theory (1984; 1992). Their framework is meant to be of a more practical kind that regulates argumentation in an everyday conversation of one particular type. They identified the traditional fallacies with violations of this type of dialogue they call the critical discussion (1984; 1987; 1992). This represents a highly conventionalized type of dialogue in which two parties agree to take part in an organized exchange of views on some particular issue where there is a conflict of opinions. But it also represents a fairly high standard of rational argumentation in which the parties agree to adhere to rules that define what sorts of moves they can make at each stage of the discussion. The purpose of a critical discussion is to resolve the conflict of opinions by rational means, where 'rational' means following the rules given for the critical discussion.

All these modern systems are dialectical in the sense defined by Hamblin (1970, p. 255): dialectic is the study of contexts of use in which arguments are put forward by one party in a rule-governed, orderly verbal exchange with another party. Hamblin put forward a number of formal dialectical systems, but did not try to classify everyday conversational exchanges into conventional types of dialogue in which two parties reason together for some purpose. Thus an important gap was left between formal dialectic and descriptive dialectic. The more practically oriented dialectical frameworks of Grice and van Eemeren and Grootendorst could not be connected to the formalistic dialectical structures of Lorenzen, Hamblin, Mackenzie, Hintikka, and Barth and Krabbe.

In this work I identify the main types of dialogue in which these arguments are typically used, and describe the structure of each type of dialogue so that they can be used as normative models in which the arguments can be evaluated as strong or weak, good or bad, correct or fallacious. The term 'dialogue' is used here as the generic term for a framework in which two (or more) parties reason together with each other by verbal exchanges in order to fulfil a conventionalized goal for such an exchange. The term 'conversation' is now also much in use, and is equally acceptable, but the term 'dialogue' is preferred for our purposes because it is a slightly more abstract and less misleading (in some ways) artificial term.

I have already given a classification of these types of dialogue in *Informal Logic* (1989a, pp. 9–19), in 'What is Reasoning?' 1990b, pp. 411–14), and with Krabbe, in *Commitment in Dialogue* (1995).[3] Also, chapter 4 of *A Pragmatic Theory of Fallacy* is dedicated to defining, in outline, the main characteristics of each of the six main types of dialogue of this sort. However, the job of giving a detailed and adequate analysis of these types of dialogue, one that would be broad and systematic enough to provide a solid basis for research to go forward in a theoretically well-developed and practically useful way in pragmatic logic has not been completed. That task is the primary focus of this work.

2. Informal Logic and Fallacies

Formal logic evaluates arguments as correct or incorrect insofar as a given argument is an instance of certain forms of argument that are recognized as valid. Thus formal logic has an objective standard against which the worth or adequacy of a given argument can be evaluated. These forms of argument are the familiar patterns of reasoning of propositional logic and quantifier logic. There is some dispute about exactly how the forms should be applied to actual cases of realistic arguments (Massey, 1975). But formal logic does at least have the decisive asset that the form functions as an objective standard for evaluating the worth of an argument in some clear respect.

Informal logic has long suffered from the lack of a clear standard as an objective basis for evaluating arguments. This lack of a relatively simple criterion may be partly a reflection of the fact that informal logic evaluates how an argument is used in a given context – a more practical and applied task that tries to judge real cases of arguments as they occur in a natural-language setting. Such an applied task of evaluation would understandably involve more interpretation of what the argument is supposed to be within a common framework of understanding common to the arguer and the audience or respondent. Even so, informal logic has failed to flourish as an academic discipline because it seems to have lacked even the basis for some kind of objective standard or framework for evaluating arguments.

The best that informal (applied) logic seems to have been able to do so far is to proceed by way of examples or individual cases. Certain well-known errors or very faulty arguments have been designated as fallacies, and the textbooks warn students to beware of these fallacies, or dangerous pitfalls in argument.

However, it is increasingly a problem endemic to the field of informal logic that, in some cases, arguments that seem to be of the same general type as the fallacies are (in some sense) reasonably good arguments that are, and ought to be, acceptable as legitimate ways of rationally persuading somebody to accept a conclusion.[4] Thus the field of informal logic is at a crisis point. How, generally, can we distinguish between the fallacious from the nonfallacious instances of these arguments?

The history of the subject of informal fallacies – well documented by Hamblin (1970) – shows two thousand years of benign neglect since Aristotle.[5] Most logic textbooks include a short section on informal fallacies; the Aristotelian influence is usually dominant, or so it appears on the surface, but the so-called standard treatment consists of a series of 'one-liner' examples with a brief, superficial commentary on the fallacy. Attempts are made to put Aristotle's classifications into a modern context, often with peculiar results. What we end up with is a superficial and often erroneous and incoherent treatment of the subject. The textbooks are now improving in this area, but their treatment remains inadequate because it has not been based on a serious enough research effort. In effect, too much research on the fallacies seems to be taking place within the textbooks themselves. This situation is not very good for research in the area, or for the textbooks as educational tools.

According to the new pragmatic theory I presented in an earlier work (1995), a sophistical tactics type of fallacy is the misuse of an argumentation technique as a tactic used by one participant to get the best of another participant in dialogue. The evaluation framework required to support this theory of fallacy is built on the presumption that arguments of the kind associated with the traditional fallacies take place in a context of dialogue with characteristic, conventional types. Each of these types of dialogue is a goal-directed structure of verbal exchange in which two or more arguers take part in reasoning together. In a given case, that is, a text of discourse containing argumentation, certain indications in the discourse will point to what type of dialogue exchange the participants are supposed to be engaging in. Evaluating the argument as having been used correctly or incorrectly, as being fallacious or not, requires judging how well the argument contributes to the goals of dialogue for the type of dialogue in that case. This pragmatic approach has significant implications for how we view fallacies.

For one thing, a technique or tactic of sophistical argumentation need not itself be an argument, even if it is a way of putting forward an argument, or a sequence of moves in dialogue associated with argumentation. Trying to diagnose the fault simply by finding a set of premises, a conclusion, and a gap or erroneous inference may miss the essential point. For another thing, sophistical argumentation is fallacious rather than genuine reasoning because it is used inappropriately in a context of dialogue with rules and conventions that exclude certain kinds of moves. What is a nonfallacious type of argument in one context of dialogue may be inappropriately and fallaciously used as argumentation in another context. Thus in order to understand that a move in argument is fallacious, we need to see that it is an overly aggressive manoeuvre which might be appropriate for a purely adversarial contest in one type of dialogue, but that it is out of place in the type of cooperative discussion needed in another type of dialogue which aims at trying to find the truth of a matter.

This pragmatic conception of fallacy has already been appealed to and presumed as a working hypothesis both tacitly and explicitly many times in my analyses of the informal fallacies in previous research. The practical handbook, *Informal Logic*, constantly relies on this conception of fallacy in working out and presenting analyses of virtually all the major informal fallacies. For example major fallacies are described as 'deceptive and powerful attack strategies in argumentative dialogue that can be used effectively to press forward against an opponent ... like the tricks and tactics used in wrestling to trip a stronger opponent and cause him to fall, or even to lose the match' (1989, p. 24). It is from this pragmatic conception that a systematic and general theory of fallacy will be developed in the following chapters.

It follows from this account that a valid argument is not necessarily a good argument, a reasonable argument, or even a persuasive argument, at least in the pragmatic sense of good, reasonable, or persuasive. A valid argument can be used badly, unreasonably, or unpersuasively in dialogue. For example, an argument designed to persuade a respondent could have premises that the respondent would never accept. Or a circular argument could be perfectly valid, yet be a bad or useless argument.[6] Whether an argument is practically good or not depends on how the argument has been used in a particular case to support the goals of dialogue that are appropriate in that case. The reasonableness or fallaciousness of the argument should be judged on the basis of an evaluation of how the argument was used by its proponent to contribute to the goal of the type of dialogue the participants in the verbal exchange were supposed to be taking part in.

In chapter 7 of *Fallacies* (1970), which focuses on the concept of argument, Hamblin explores several alternative conceptions of sets of conditions comprising a good argument, and finds all of them subject to difficulties, objections, and unclarities of formulation. This chapter, and subsequent work by Johnstone (1978), is highly revealing because it shows how little attention has been paid to examining the concept of argument, despite its central place in logic, philosophy, rhetoric, and related subjects. However, the incompatibility between these competing conceptions as sets of requirements for a good argument is less severe than Hamblin's discussion seems to suggest. For there can be many distinct and legitimate goals of argument in different contexts of dialogue. And each distinct goal can have different requirements that a good argument must meet in that context. Our orientation on this question needs to be readjusted towards asking what an argument is good for – that is, asking the pragmatic question of how the argument is being used to fulfil a goal of argumentative dialogue.

It is best to say that an argument is advanced within a framework or context of dialogue that defines the goal of argument for each of the participants in the dialogue. When an argument falls short of this goal, it is appropriate to speak of critical gaps, flaws, or fallacies. What we will do, in effect, is get back to the spirit of the Aristotelian origins of the study of the fallacies as sophistical refutations – arguments that can be used in dialogue as sophistical tactics, but that can also be used as reasonable arguments to further legitimate aims of dialogue when two persons reason together for some purpose in an orderly and recognizable framework of dialogue.

Aristotle, in *On Sophistical Refutations*, distinguished six fallacies dependent on language: equivocation, amphiboly, combination of words, division of words, accent, and form of expression (165b30–166b19). He also cited seven fallacies not dependent on language: accident, neglect of qualifications, ignoring the issue (irrelevance), arguing in a circle, consequent, mistaken cause, and multiple questions (166b28–168a17). Over the years, several new fallacies were added to this list, such as the contribution of Locke (outlined below), and the standard treatment of the fallacies evolved from this original list, with the various additions (Hamblin, 1970).

Before we briefly look at the main fallacies of this group, we need to go back to the ancient roots of applied logic, where certain types of arguments, or dialogue frameworks in which arguments are conventionally used, were recognized. The verb *dialegesthai* was used long before Plato and Aristotle to indicate the practice of maintaining a position in dispute with others (Smith 1993, p. 341). According to Kneale and Kneale (1962, p. 7), *dialegesthai* is the root of the word Aristotle used (*dialektikos*) to characterize a type of argument he called 'dialectical.'

3. Aristotle's Five Types of Arguments

In *On Sophistical Refutations*, Aristotle classified four kinds of arguments that are used in discussion. But in the course of his remarks, he also added a fifth kind called 'demonstrative argument' (165a38–165b12).

Of arguments used in discussion there are four kinds, Didactic, Dialectical, Examination-arguments and Contentious arguments. Didactic arguments are those which reason from the principles appropriate to each branch of learning and not from the opinions of the answerer (for he who is learning must take things on trust). Dialectical arguments are those which, starting from generally accepted opinions, reason to establish a contradiction. Examination-arguments are those which are based on opinions held by the answerer and necessarily known to one who claims knowledge of the subject involved (in what manner, has been described elsewhere). Contentious arguments are those which reason or seem to reason from opinion which appear to be, but are not really, generally accepted. Demonstrative arguments have been treated in the *Analytics*, and dialectical arguments and examinations have been dealt with elsewhere (in the *Topics*).

Didactic arguments are pedagogical arguments that someone teaching 'a branch of learning' would use. The other four kinds of argument are not as readily recognizable to the modern reader, and require careful explanation.

Both dialectical and demonstrative arguments use syllogistic reasoning, but differ in the kinds of premises they start from. Demonstrative arguments start from premises that are first principles (*archai*) of a science. Dialectical arguments start from premises that are generally accepted by the majority or by the wise (*sophoi*). At the beginning of the *Topics*, Aristotle distinguishes between these two types of arguments:

Reasoning is a discussion in which, certain things having been laid down, something other than these things necessarily results through them. Reasoning is *demonstration* when it proceeds from premises which are true and primary or of such a kind that we have derived our original knowledge of them through premises which are primary and true. Reasoning is *dialectical* which reasons from generally accepted opinions. Things are true and primary which command belief through themselves and not through anything else; for regarding the first principles of science it is unnecessary to ask any further question as to 'why,' but each principle should of itself command belief. Generally accepted opinions, on the other hand, are those which commend themselves to all or to the majority or to the wise – that is, to all of the wise or to the majority or to the most famous and distinguished of them. (100a25–100b23)

An Aristotelian demonstrative argument is relatively familiar to the modern reader. Euclidean geometry could serve as an example of orderly deductive reasoning that proceeds from an initial set of premises (axioms) which are supposed to be self-evidently true to conclusions derived only from the axioms, or prior conclusions drawn from the axioms by deductive reasoning. But dialectical reasoning is unfamiliar, even alien, to the modern reader. Dialectic seems to be a forgotten art. If 'dialectic' means anything to a modern reader, it is probably the Hegelian-Marxist notion of historical development, an idea that is not useful for logic, nor does it have any real bearing on the normative evaluation of arguments.

Kapp's account of Aristotelian dialectic describes it as 'a curious kind of mental gymnastic' that is 'scarcely to be expected by any modern reader':

It consists in either arguing about a proposed problem – any debatable problem – from probable premises, or, if one is attacked in argument, in avoiding self-contradiction. For this kind of philosophic exercise there are always two persons required, plus a problem; one person has the part of questioner, the other person the part of respondent and opponent. The questioner first proposes a problem, the respondent chooses his position, and then the questioner has to take as his view that side of the problem which was repudiated by the respondent. Now the questioner must continue questioning and try to draw a conclusion, or we may say, get a syllogism in favor of his view from such answers as he is able to elicit from the interlocutor. The part of the respondent is more passive; but he has to be on his guard against such concessions as will enable the questioner to get his conclusion. For if the questioner gets his conclusion, the respondent is obviously the loser, since he will be forced to deny what at the beginning he asserted, or vice versa. (1942, p. 12)

For the best example to illustrate dialectic, we can look at Plato's dialogues.[7] In fact, Aristotelian dialectic seems to be a development of what Plato called the 'dialectical method' or 'the art concerning discussions' (Robinson, 1953, p. 69).

But it is very difficult to pin down exactly what Plato meant by 'dialectic.' Robinson notes: 'The fact is that the word "dialectic" had a strong tendency in Plato to mean "the ideal method, *whatever that may be*"'

(1953, p. 70). Some say that the notion of dialectic was invented by Plato, but others have claimed that Zeno of Elea was the discoverer of dialectic (Robinson, 1953, p. 91). According to Kneale and Kneale, both Diogenes Laertius and Sextus Empiricus claim that Zeno was the inventor of dialectic (1962, p. 7). Such claims depend on what is meant by 'dialectic,' and it is clear that the meaning Aristotle gave this term was quite different from that of Plato, which in turn was likely different from what Zeno had in mind. Plato did see dialectic as being based on reality and as revealing the truth of a matter, whereas Aristotle reserved that role for scientific demonstration. Aristotle saw dialectic as being based on what seems to be so, or what is plausible (to the majority or the wise) (Evans, 1977, p. 84).

According to Aristotle in the *Topics*, dialectic has three (relatively modest) uses: (1) as a method of training (*gymnasia*) for teaching skills of arguing; (2) for arguing in casual conversational encounters; and (3) for questioning and discussing the first principles (*archai*) of a science, presupposed by demonstration (101a25–101b4).

What Aristotle meant by examination arguments (*perastikoi*) is also difficult for the modern reader to grasp. Guthrie writes that not all dialectic is competitive, and it can sometimes be used 'for testing and investigation' according to Aristotle. He calls peirastic 'testing or probing' arguments, and cites another type of argument he calls *exetastic*, for 'examining critically' (1981, vol. 6, p. 155). In the *On Sophistical Refutations* (172a30), Aristotle writes that everyone, not just those skilled in the use of dialectic, test by examination those who profess to know things. Thus he implies that examination arguments are used in ordinary conversational exchanges to critically probe or test what others say.

In the end, it is hard for a modern reader to grasp exactly what Aristotle meant by dialectical and examination arguments, and it seems that these terms have some meaning in the ancient Greek context that is no longer familiar. Also, as Hamblin notes, Aristotle is not quite sure himself whether dialectical and examination arguments are two kinds or one, and in different passages he 'makes each a subclass of the other' (1970, p. 59).

The fifth type of argument is contentious reasoning, which Aristotle describes in *On Sophistical Refutations* (171b24–171b30) as arguing to win a victory at any cost. Aristotle compares this quarrelsome type of argument as comparable to cheating in an athletic contest, an unfair kind of fighting where a person who is bent on victory will stop at nothing (171b26). Aristotle also describes another contentious kind of argumentation that is 'sophistical,' or used to make money or a reputation (171b28). In the *Topics* (100b23–101a4) Aristotle describes contentious reasoning as a spurious counterpart to dialectical reasoning based on 'opinions which appear to be generally accepted but are not really so' (100b25).

Plato described *eristic* or the art of quarreling as an opposite of dialectic, 'something superficially like dialectic, and yet as bad as dialectic is good, something against which the would-be dialectician must always be on guard' (Robinson, 1953, p. 85). According to Robinson, just as dialectic is taken by Plato to mean, at any stage of his thought, the best method of argument, so eristic tends to be whatever Plato thinks is a bad method at any given moment. At any rate, Plato thought that eristic was dangerous, and that care needs to be taken to prevent dialectic from degenerating into eristic.

4. The Waning of Dialectic

Aristotle's logic can be viewed as having two parts. One is the later syllogistic logic, developed in *Prior Analytics* and *Posterior Analytics* ('analytics' was Aristotle's term for what we call 'logic'). The other, developed earlier in the *Topics* and *Sophistical Refutations*, is the more practical and applied kind of logic which uses syllogistic in the five different kinds of argument cited above. This earlier logic tended to be more informal and contextual in nature, and dialectical argument was a central part of it.

Both kinds of logic continued through the Middle Ages.[8] The dialectical and topical framework of the applied logic was taught in various forms in medieval curriculum. The Obligation Game was a regulated type of argumentation exchange between two parties, with various rules and moves, where the proponent's goal was to trap the respondent in a contradiction (Hamblin, 1970, p. 126). Aristotle's account of the fallacies, and his theory of the topics, also continued to be taught in the universities and to appear in the logic textbooks.

However, Aristotle's applied logic seemed to atrophy, while his theory of the syllogism grew and flourished, which led to the development of formalizations that came to dominate the logic curriculum, and in the end, to be identified as logic itself, or the central and best developed part of it. The idea of dialectical argument was represented in a formalistic way by the Obligation Game and its variants, but eventually this idea disappeared as an important inclusion in the most widely used logic textbooks and in the university curricula. The idea of Aristotle's list of topics continued, but those teaching logic were less and less sure what to do with it, and eventually it came to be seen as a kind of formalistic and non-dialectical theory of conditional relations between pairs of propositions. The fallacies continued to be included in logic textbooks, in their Aristotelian form, with variations. But the practical and dialectical logic that had supplied the Aristotelian concept of a fallacy as a 'sophistical refutation' – a deceptive argument exchange of views between two parties reasoning together – fell into obscurity. The treatment of the fallacies was, for all intents and purposes, dormant for two thousand years. It remained in an undeveloped and neglected state (Hamblin, 1970).

Aristotle's concept of dialectical argument was based on the idea of reasoning from premises that are *endoxa*, propositions that seem to be true generally to the majority or the wise. What are *endoxa*? According to Barnes, they are reputable beliefs and opinions, including explicit opinions that people openly avow, and implicit beliefs entailed by these, ascribed to us by our actions or latent in our language (1980, p. 500). These kinds of propositions are *eikotic*, in Aristotle's sense, meaning that they are plausible but are not known or demonstrable as true. Although such propositions can be accepted as plausible, their acceptance should always be tentative in nature because there is the possibility that the opposite of a plausible proposition might be shown to be true (at some future point).

The term *eikos* is traditionally translated as 'probability,' but does not mean 'probable' in the modern sense of a proposition based on statistical evidence.[9] According to Kennedy, argument from *eikos* or plausibility, as the ancients saw it, would be excluded from being a scientific or exact notion (1963, p. 31). The classical example used to illustrate the idea of *eikos* came from a sophist called Antiphon (480 B.C.–411 B.C.) who cited the legal case of a man who had been killed in a lonely spot. One of the supplementary arguments used by Antiphon was that it was unlikely that muggers killed the man because his property was left at the scene (Kennedy, 1980, p. 27). Aristotle mentions a comparable case in the *Rhetoric* (1402a11) where a defendant argues that it is implausible that he assaulted a man who was bigger and stronger: 'How could a little fellow like me attack a big fellow like him?' In both of these cases, a hypothesis is shown to be implausible – not beyond the possibility of being true, but unlikely in relation to what one would normally expect in a certain kind of situation.

But dialectical argument, and with it the idea of plausible inference (so stressed by the sophists), seemed to fall into disfavour or even unintelligibility as a part of logic. These ideas have been discredited and pushed further aside in the modern period. Kennedy sees a strong comparison between the criticisms of the sophists in the ancient world and the shift away from dialectic (and also rhetoric) in the seventeenth century (1980, p. 222). As Jonsen and Toulmin (1988) have ably documented, Pascal discredited the so-called probable reasoning of the Jesuits and casuists (which really means plausible inference or reasoning based on *eikos*) as irrational, deceptive, self-serving, and even evil. In his *De L'Esprit Géométrique* ('Reflections on Geometry and the Art of Persuading'), Pascal proposes that all reasoning should be based on the Enlightenment paradigm of scientific geometric logic (deductive logic, based on self-evident axioms, used in a logical structure of argument comparable to Aristotelian demonstration) to give us 'unshakable proofs.' To supplement deductive reasoning, Pascal also introduces the scientific, statistical notion of probability, based on mathematical computation, to replace the old idea of casuistic plausible reasoning supposedly based on 'sophistry and ambiguity' (Pascal, 1966 [1659], p. 326).

With the advent of the Enlightenment model in which all reasoning was based on the scientific standards of deductive and inductive reasoning, the old idea of dialectical reasoning in Aristotle was cast aside as 'subjective.' In the twentieth century the transformation was complete – logic became a purely abstract mathematical calculus representing the kinds of propositional inferences studied by the Stoics and the syllogistic kind of logic developed by Aristotle. Dialectical argument based on plausible reasoning no longer made any sense to modern students and had no place in modern logical theory.

5. Locke's Four Kinds of Arguments

The Aristotelian idea of dialectical argument, representing a kind of rational thinking other than scientific reasoning in a domain of technical knowledge, was discredited with Pascal's new view of reasoning that took hold in the Enlightenment. Now science, and with it the new statistical analysis of probability, was held to be the only kind of rational thinking that was the route to the truth and that was based on reality. However, before this new Enlightenment outlook on logical reasoning took hold, one hold-out for the old Greek idea of 'probability' (or plausibility) as a basis for argument introduced some new fallacies to add to the longstanding group of fallacies in the Aristotelian list.

John Locke, in Book IV (chapter 17) of *Essay Concerning Human Understanding* (1690), observes that most of the things we do in everyday life are not decided or reasoned out on a demonstration based on knowledge that is not subject to doubt. Instead of being based on demonstration, Locke argues (chapter 15), such common reasoning that uses judgment on what to assent to in daily life is based on 'probability.' Locke did not mean mathematical probability of the kind invoked by Pascal, but plausibility of a kind comparable to the ancient idea of eikotic reasoning, or reasoning based on what seems to be so but which is subject to reasonable doubt, even when it is a rational basis for assent. At the beginning of chapter 15, Locke defines 'probability' as what 'appears for the most part to be so, and is enough to induce the mind to judge the proposition to be true or false, rather than the contrary' (Locke [1690] 1961, p. 363). He contrasts probable reasoning in this sense with what he calls 'demonstration,' of the kind used in mathematics (p. 364). In chapter 15, Locke cites the example of the Dutch ambassador who told the king of Siam that water in Holland sometimes gets so hard in cold weather that it could even bear the weight of an elephant walking on it. The king found such an assertion implausible (improbable), meaning that it did not appear to him to be true, based on what he thought to be so. On the basis of this idea of probability, Locke built a theory of reasoning and evidence to account for judging reasonable degrees of assent relative to evidence or grounds. Something could be probable for one person, as for the king of Siam, or it could be probable in the sense of being generally or commonly accepted as true (or false). According to Locke's theory, there is a small class of propositions that are based on knowledge, but the vast majority of reasoning is probable inference that leads to opinion rather than, strictly speaking, knowledge (Tully, 1988, p. 26).

In particular, Locke cites three kinds of arguments which he characterizes as opinion-based rather than knowledge-based. But he does not see these three types of arguments as inherently fallacious. Although he concedes that they do not 'advance us in our way to knowledge' in the way that empirical and scientific arguments based on 'light arising from the nature of things themselves' do, nevertheless they can prepare the way for truth by revealing errors in a person's thinking. These three techniques of arguments are ones that people use when reasoning with another party, according to Locke, and thus they could be described as dialectical arguments in the ancient sense of that word.

These three techniques appear to have been invented, or at least prominently named and identified, by Locke. In his *Essay*, there is a short passage near the end of the chapter called 'Of Reason' where Locke mentions all three of these kinds of argument. To the best of my knowledge, this passage is the first place in which the Latin names for our three fallacies are used in the modern sense they have in the logic textbooks (even if all three were clearly anticipated in passages in Aristotle). As Hamblin notes, this curious passage is self-contained, parenthetical to Locke's main discussion, and has usually been omitted in abridged editions. Hamblin quotes the passage in full to underline its importance in the history of the field of argumentation study. For Locke indicates in the passage that he has here invented the terms *argumentum ad verecundiam* and *argumentum ad ignorantiam*, and has given a succinct description of a kind of argument 'already known under the name of *argumentum ad hominem*' (Hamblin, 1970, pp. 159–60).[10]

It is especially notable that Locke does not condemn any of these three kinds of arguments as inherently fallacious or erroneous, although he does seem to indicate that they can be used to force assent in argument in a way that could be abusive. The passage begins: 'Before we quit this subject, it may be worth our while a little to reflect on *four sorts of arguments* that men, in their reasonings with others, do ordinarily make use of to prevail on their assent, or at least so to awe them as to silence their opposition.' Locke then goes on to individually describe the four kinds of arguments. The first, which he calls *argumentum ad verecundiam*, occurs when a man backs his arguments with the opinions of authorities who have gained a reputation of dignity, who require such 'respect and submission' that anyone who fails to concede the argument appears to be either impudent or insolent. The second, which he calls *argumentum ad ignorantiam*, drives one's opponent in argument to accept what one advances as a proof, 'or to assign a better.' The third type of argument, Locke writes, is already known as the *argumentum ad hominem*, and it is 'to press a man with consequences drawn from his own principles or concessions.' Where Locke got the expression *argumentum ad hominem* is unknown, but Hamblin (1970, p. 161) suggests that he probably picked it up from Aristotle's *De Sophisticis Elenchis*, from passages where Aristotle writes of 'these persons [who] direct their solutions against the man, not against his argument' (178b17; see also 183a21). This has been confirmed by Nuchelmans (1993, p. 43).

As well, Locke characterizes the three types of arguments by contrasting them all with a fourth kind of argument that he calls *argumentum ad judicium*.

The fourth is the using of proofs drawn from any of the foundations of knowledge or probability. This I call *argumentum ad judicium*. This alone of all the four brings true instruction with it and advances us in our way to knowledge. For: (1) It argues not another man's opinion to be right because I, out of respect or any other consideration but that of conviction, will not contradict him. (2) It proves not another man to be in the right way, nor that I ought to take the same with him, because I know not a better. (3) Nor does it follow that another man is in the right way because he has shown me that I am in the wrong. I may be modest and therefore not oppose another man's persuasion; I may be ignorant and not be able to produce a better; I may be in an error and another may show me that I am so. This may dispose me, perhaps, for the reception of truth but helps me not to it; that must come from proofs and arguments and light arising from the nature of things themselves, and not from my shamefacedness, ignorance, or error. (Hamblin, 1970, p. 160)

The more one reflects on this fascinating passage from Locke, the more it seems to yield fundamental insights into a distinctive kind of reasoning that has become murky, distorted, and neglected in recent times, namely, the ancient concept of dialectical reasoning.

Locke says that only the fourth kind of argument brings 'true instruction' or 'advances us in our way to knowledge.' But he does not write the other three types of argument off as totally worthless or fallacious. By suggesting that these other three kinds of argument have their legitimate uses (in addition to their abuses) in 'reasoning together,' he seems to indicate that these ways of producing assent can be legitimate ways of arriving at a reasoned conclusion when the 'light arising from the nature of things themselves' through the fourth way of knowledge is not conclusive, or even available, when for practical reasons a provisional conclusion must be drawn.

Locke claims that the kind of knowledge or guidance gained through the first three ways of reasoning is inferior to the 'true instruction' of the fourth way. This suggests that conclusions derived through the use of the first three ways of reasoning are less reliable and inherently more fallible than those derived by the fourth way. But room seems to be left for the possibility that the kind of plausible conclusions derived from the first three controversy-oriented kinds of reasoning can represent an instructional advance. Hitchcock appears to agree that the kinds of arguments cited by Locke do legitimately cause assent to a proposition in many instances, even though they 'generally do not bring knowledge' (1992, pp. 261–3). As Locke puts it, they may 'dispose me ... for the reception of truth,' although they do not 'help me ... to the reception of truth.' Although Locke is inclined to be generally wary and even somewhat disparaging about these three ways, he does seem to suggest that they can have a legitimate function of preparing the way for truth, if only by the negative route of clearing up confusion and errors. But it should be noted that, depending on how prevalent confusion and error are in human thinking, this function of clearing the way for the reception of truth may be of no small importance. It could correspond to what we now call 'critical thinking,' and to what the ancients thought of as dialectical argumentation.

Indeed, if we take the point of view that real discovery comes only through the exposure of error and ignorance (trial and error), the three ways of reasoning cited by Locke could be absolutely fundamental in understanding how human reasoning is used in everyday conversational arguments. Locke's balanced viewpoint, because it allows some legitimacy to dialectical argumentation in the ancient sense, is very enlightening to a modern reader. It shows not only how these three ways of producing assent can go wrong, or be systematically abused by an arguer, but also how they can be rightly used to prove a point in argument in a manner that fulfils legitimate goals of argumentation.

Personal attack, arguing from ignorance, and the appeal to expert opinion are three schemes of argumentation that can be used constructively to support legitimate goals of reasoned dialogue, or used destructively as weapons of deceit to attack an opponent and win over an audience persuasively by browbeating the opponent into submission. Indeed, these three techniques of argumentation are quite possibly the three most powerful methods of the critical thinker as well as the sophist. All three tactics are both very common and very effective (even when used fallaciously) in many familiar contexts of everyday argumentation. With the disappearance of dialectic, however, it came to be taken for granted that they could all be dismissed as inherently fallacious.

The goal of this book in setting out the various types of dialogue in which people reason together is not to concentrate on the negative aspect of fallacies and errors of reasoning, at least not exclusively. Rather, it is to provide a framework in which everyday arguments can be evaluated as correct as well as incorrect. However, the traditional fallacies are a primary area of application of the theory, and provide an important testing ground of its usefulness.

It is beyond the scope of this book to analyse all the fallacies, or even to analyse a few in any depth. But to illustrate how the theory works, and to indicate how it can be applied, I have selected a few of the major fallacies to comment on. For the reader who has not encountered these fallacies before, the ones we are mainly concerned with are described below. Many of the major fallacies are fallacies, at least to some significant extent, because they are failures of relevance. So we begin with these fallacies of relevance.

6. Fallacies of Relevance

Ignoratio elenchi (ignorance of refutation, or ignoring the issue) is the Aristotelian term for an argument that is irrelevant and therefore fails to prove what is supposed to be proved in a discussion. For example, suppose a lawyer in a criminal trial argues at length that murder is a horrible crime, and goes into grisly details which paint an emotional picture of the horror of murder and violent death. If this lengthy speech is not relevant to the question of whether the defendant in this case actually committed the crime of murder, the lawyer's speech could be irrelevant despite its persuasive effect. In the Aristotelian tradition, this type of failure would be called 'ignorance of refutation' because the lawyer's digression 'ignored' his real job in the case, which was to prove the defendant guilty – or, to put it another way, his job was to 'refute' the opposing claim that the defendant was not guilty of the alleged crime.

The *ignoratio elenchi* phrase can be thought of as an umbrella term for all kinds of fallacies or failures of relevance in argumentation. So many of the traditional fallacies can be portrayed as falling under this heading that relevance has been called a 'wastebasket category.' While it is true that relevance is often a problem with fallacies, and an important factor in its own right in critical argumentation, there are four fallacies especially where relevance is typically the major problem. These are the four emotional fallacies.

Argumentum ad populum (argument to the people) is the kind of argument that appeals to popular opinion or sentiment to support a conclusion. This argument has two forms (or schemes). One form is the following: everybody (or popular opinion) accepts proposition A as true, therefore A is true. Another form is the scheme: everybody (or some influential or popular group) is doing action x, therefore x must be the right thing to do (Walton, 1980). The second scheme is an action-oriented type of practical reasoning. This argument, in both forms, has tended to be portrayed as a fallacy by traditional accounts, under headings like 'appeal to the gallery,' 'appeal to popular pieties,' 'crowd appeal,' or even 'mob appeal.' But, for Aristotle, an argument based on what is generally accepted (*endoxon*) would not be inherently fallacious. Also, there is nothing wrong, in principle, with appealing to popular sentiments in argumentation. For example, in a democratic system, political arguments often try to appeal to popular opinion or sentiment through the use of opinion polls and the like (Walton, 1992c). Such a tactic can be fallacious in some cases, such as where it is used as an emotional appeal to cover up for failure to decide an issue by examining or bringing forward relevant evidence.

The problem with the emotional fallacies very often is that the appeal to emotion is used as a tactic to steer the argument away from the real issue of a dialogue. For when emotions are heightened, we easily lose track of the point, and an emotional appeal can be successfully used to cover up a weak case or a lack of evidence.

In this book, relevance will be defined dialectically – in relation to the goal of the type of dialogue the participants are supposed to be engaged in. In a critical discussion, for example, each participant has a thesis to be proved or defended, and this burden of proof basically defines what is relevant in the discussion, in chapter two, section four.

Argumentum ad misericordiam (argument to pity) is the kind of argument that uses an appeal to pity, compassion, or sympathy to support a conclusion. This argument takes the following general form or scheme: we should have sympathy for the wretched situation of this person *P*, therefore we ought to accept the conclusion of the argument that *P* maintains (Walton, 1996b). This argument tends to seem fallacious; we are more inclined to accept the textbook account of it as a fallacy if the word 'pity' is substituted for 'sympathy' in the argumentation scheme. But clearly, in some cases, such arguments are nonfallacious. For example, an appeal to solicit donations for medical research to cure a crippling disease that is devastating to many children may be quite justified in citing a case that arouses the pity of a potential donor (Walton, 1992c).

However, the traditional treatment of fallacies has stressed that such appeals often use the drama of an emotional appeal to cover up the lack of relevant considerations that should properly be addressed in making a case for a conclusion. Appeals to sympathy or pity can be used as a tactic to put emotional pressure on a respondent that is difficult to resist, but that covers up gaps in an argument. For example, a student may launch a dramatic appeal to pity in a plea for handing in an assignment late, even though he lacks legitimate substantiation of the kind required to qualify as a valid excuse. In such a case, the main job is to sort out what is relevant in relation to the burden of proof. What does the plea have to establish in order to be successful, and is the dramatic appeal relevant to this burden of proof? The problem is one of dialectical relevance in the given situation.

Argumentum ad baculum (argument to the stick or club) uses appeal to a threat to support a conclusion that is advocated (Woods and Walton, 1976). It has two distinctive schemes. The direct *ad baculum* type of argumentation occurs when one participant in a dialogue issues an overt (explicit) threat (or appeal to fear) to the other, saying 'Accept proposition *A* or I'll carry out this action *x* which will be harmful to you!' But the more common and subtle type is the indirect *ad baculum*, which occurs when the one participant expresses a speech act that is overtly a warning of the form 'If you don't do *x*, something bad (harmful) will (might) happen to you,' but that is covertly a threat (Walton, 1992c, chapter 5). Traditionally, the *ad baculum* has been regarded as a fallacy, and the textbooks often call this kind of argumentation 'scare tactics' or 'intimidation.' The indirect type of *ad baculum* argument takes the form of a covert threat which appears to the respondent, on the surface, to be a warning: 'If you don't vote for me as director of the firm, you might find yourself out of a job.' The implication made in this covert type of *ad baculum* argument is that the person making the 'prediction' of bad consequences is ready to carry them out, or to ensure that they happen, unless the other party accedes to his demand. Much depends here on how a text of discourse is interpreted – whether a threat has really been expressed and how it fits into the argument are important critical questions.

There is nothing inherently illogical or fallacious about making threats (Woods, 1988). In fact, practical arguments that are based on sanctions – like laws that impose harsh penalties for drunk driving – are *ad baculum* arguments that are not necessarily fallacious. Even so, the traditions of logic are right to warn of the dangers and tricks inherent in *ad baculum* arguments. They are very powerful arguments which are often used as successful and effective tactics to avoid a burden of proof in a critical discussion by shifting to considerations that are not relevant or legitimate as part of the discussion.

Evidently, much depends on the context of dialogue in evaluating such cases as fallacious or nonfallacious. In a critical discussion, threats are very much out of place (contrary to the goals of dialogue and to the openness required for good discussions), whereas in negotiation dialogue, threats (especially in the form of the indirect type of *ad baculum* argument) are commonly used argumentation tactics that are often tolerated as part of the cut and thrust of the bargaining process (see chapter 4, section 5 on the use of threats in negotiation dialogue).

Argumentum ad hominem ('argument against the man') is the use of personal attack against the proponent of an argument in order to refute or undermine his argument. Thus the *ad hominem* argument as characterized by the logic textbooks is different from the Lockean type of *ad hominem* cited above, which is really arguing from the other party's commitments or concessions in a dialectical framework. The *ad hominem* found in the textbook accounts is an essentially negative kind of argumentation which has several subvariants (Woods and Walton, 1977; Govier, 1983).

The first is the personal or 'abusive' variant in which the character or personal characteristics of the arguer are attacked, especially the arguer's rationality or veracity, as in 'I wouldn't believe Smith because he is a congenital liar, and has shown signs of mental instability in the past, therefore Smith's argument can be rejected.'

In the circumstantial variant, the attacker argues that the proponent's personal circumstances are in conflict with what he asserts or advocates in his argument – for example, 'Jones is a pacifist, but in his personal conduct, he is the most aggressive and combative person I have ever seen, therefore his position on war and peace is incoherent and/or insincere and ought to be rejected.' (This is the definition of the circumstantial *ad hominem* as a type of argument that I present in *Arguer's Position* [1985] where numerous cases are analysed.)

A third variant is the 'poisoning the well' type of *ad hominem* argument in which the proponent is said to have shown such a consistent and determined disregard for the truth that nothing he could possibly say could ever be taken at face value. This variant is a kind of extreme version or extension of the personal type of *ad hominem* argument.

A fourth variant is the bias type of *ad hominem* argument in which the attacker argues that the proponent has something to gain personally by supporting the conclusion he has advocated. The inference is that, because the proponent has an interest at stake, he cannot be impartial as an arguer for the conclusion he has put forward, and hence that conclusion can be rejected. (The classic case is presented in chapter 4, section 8). The 'poisoning the well' variant can also be an extension of the bias type of *ad hominem* argument.

The fifth variant is the *tu quoque* ('you too') type of *ad hominem* argument. In this type of argument, the attacker turns the proponent's condemnation of some practice around by saying, 'What about you? You do the same thing yourself – you're just as bad, therefore your argument is no good either.' This kind of 'you too' attack is common with many kinds of argumentation. But it is especially common and powerful when used as a reply to an *ad hominem* attack. Such back-and-forth *ad hominem* attacks are typically characteristic of a shift to a quarrelling type of dialogue.

It has been shown in Woods and Walton (1977), Barth and Martens (1977), Walton (1985; 1989) and Brinton (1985) that the *ad hominem* argument is not always fallacious. Johnstone (1959) even advocated the thesis that all philosophical argumentation is really of the Lockean *ad hominem* type. In cross-examinations in court (Graham, 1977) or in political debates in election campaigns, raising questions of character to attack a person's credibility is often a legitimate (presumptive and defeasible) kind of argumentation. Sometimes character is a relevant issue, and sometimes not. It depends on the context of dialogue, given the type of dialogue the participants are supposed to be engaged in. Very often, it is a question of relevance.

7. Other Important Fallacies

Argumentum ad ignorantiam (argument to ignorance) is the argument from lack of knowledge that a proposition is true (false) to the conclusion that the proposition is false (true). For example, 'We haven't heard from Robinson for ten years, and there has been no positive evidence, in all that time, that he is alive; therefore let us conclude that Robinson is dead.' This argument, if interpreted as concluding in a practical presumption such as for the purpose of settling Robinson's estate, could be a nonfallacious *argumentum ad ignorantiam*. However, if pressed too hard to support a highly dubious conclusion, the *argumentum ad ignorantiam* can be highly erroneous. A familiar example of its fallacious use is this example: 'Nobody has ever shown conclusively that ghosts do not exist; therefore we can conclude that ghosts exist.' Here we seem to have a fallacious, or at least highly dubious, argument (Woods and Walton, 1978). It seems then that the argument from ignorance can be a fallacy in some cases.

In *Arguments from Ignorance* (1996a), I present an in-depth study of the *argumentum ad ignorantiam* which shows that, far from being fallacious in every case, this type of argument is really an important underlying mechanism that is connected to the way presumptive reasoning works to shift a burden of proof in dialogue. It turns out that many presumptive arguments are really arguments from ignorance (lack-of-knowledge inferences to a defeasible but presumptive conclusion) that are not fallacious.

The fallacy of many questions, also often called the fallacy of complex question, is the tactic of packing presumptions into a question in such a manner that any direct answer will trap a respondent into damaging concessions. The classic case is the question, 'Have you stopped abusing your spouse?,' which traps a respondent into conceding the practice of spouse abuse no matter which direct answer she or he gives.

Whether or not the fallacy of many questions has been committed in a particular case depends on the prior context of dialogue in that case (Manor, 1981). For example, if a respondent has freely admitted her prior spouse-abuse activities in a discussion, then the asking of the spouse-beating question, for example, by an attorney in court, could be a legitimate, nonfallacious kind of questioning. However, in a different context, where the respondent does not admit to spouse abuse, or perhaps does not even have a spouse, the use of the same question in a dialogue could be fallacious. In this kind of case, it could be an overly aggressive tactic of questioning which (illicitly) mixes up the proper and logical order of questions in the sequence of dialogue. Thus, it turns out that the fallacy of many questions is really a sophistical tactics type of fallacy that requires a context of dialogue for evaluation (see Walton, 1989b).

Petitio principii is the fallacy of begging the question or illicitly arguing in a circle. For example, suppose Bob asks Helen to prove that this bicycle belongs to Roy, and Helen replies, 'All the bicycles in this area belong to Roy.' Should Bob take this argument as sufficient proof to justify handing over the bicycle to Helen, who claims to be Roy's representative? Probably not, unless there is some reason to accept Helen's general claim about all the bicycles in the area which is independent of the acceptability of her claim about this particular bicycle. Bob's suspicion is that Helen may be begging the question, trying to offer a 'proof' that this bicycle belongs to Roy by making a more general claim that rests on the presumption that this particular bicycle – the subject of the dispute – belongs to Roy.[11] The Latin phrase *petitio principii* means petitioning for (asking to be granted) the principle (or issue to be proved) in the discussion. Thus the fallacy of begging the question is a species of failure to fulfil proper requirements of a burden of proof by bringing forward as proof a presumption that has not really been proved. In my analysis of the fallacy of begging the question, this fallacy is shown to be a sophistical tactic of pressing a presumption ahead in a dialogue too aggressively without giving a respondent enough room to raise legitimate critical questions (see Walton, 1991).

An argument from authority appeals to expert opinion or to the pronouncement of someone with institutionalized office or power in order to settle an argument. These kinds of appeals can, in some cases, be a legitimate way of steering an argument in the direction of a conclusion (Younger, 1982). In other cases, however, they can be pressed too hard as illicit tactics to try to browbeat an opponent into giving up more easily than he should. The fallacious *argumentum ad verecundiam* (argument to reverence or respect) is the misuse of an appeal to authority in argument as a tactic to press for a conclusion more strongly than the evidence warrants. Appeals to authority are inherently presumptive in nature as arguments; they are fallible arguments that can easily go wrong, especially when misused by sophistical tacticians who know how to exploit respect for authority in persuading a respondent who can be impressed by such an appeal.

Chapter 10 gives a Lockean analysis of the *argumentum ad verecundiam* kind of argument that is not inherently unreasonable, but that can be used as a sophistical tactic in dialogue to browbeat an opponent in a critical discussion, for example, by appealing to her respect for authority. But it will also be shown in chapter 10 how the use of arguments that appeal to authority are very common in everyday argumentation, and that in many cases such arguments can be quite legitimate. In still other cases, they are poorly supported without being fallacious.

The straw man fallacy is the misrepresentation of an opponent's position in dialogue in order to make his position look bad in an attempt to refute his argument. In general, we do not know all the specifics of an opponent's position in argumentation in everyday dialogue, but typically in persuasion dialogue, in order to be effective one's arguments have to be based on premises that make presumptions about what that arguer's position can reasonably be inferred to be. Where such presumptions are not made in a fair or reasonable way, the fallacy of straw man comes into play. For example, it is a common tactic in argumentation to try to portray an opponent's position as being more extreme than it really is.

The concept of an arguer's position turns out to be all-important in the analysis and evaluation of the straw man fallacy (see Walton, 1985).

However, it will be shown below how position is to be defined using the device of an arguer's commitment set in a dialogue, after the fashion of Hamblin (1970).

In this book I will not attempt to give a full analysis of all of the fallacies that have now been introduced. The place for such a project is the continuing research on these individual fallacies, which investigates their underlying argumentation schemes and then shows how these schemes can be used in a deceptive manner in certain types of cases to unfairly get the best of a speech partner in dialogue. Here I attempt only the more narrow tasks of (a) showing how the arguments associated with these major fallacies are susceptible to different evaluation as fallacious or nonfallacious in different contexts of dialogue, and especially (b) defining the structures and main characteristics in sufficient detail so that they can be used as normative models in order to aid in the evaluation of the arguments in question.

Thus, my main task is to uncover the defining characteristics of each of these types of dialogue and put each bundle of characteristics into an organized, coherent structure so that it can function as a normative model which can be used to measure the worth or success of an argument. However, the reader needs to be convinced that going into such depth in investigating all the quirks and special characteristics of these types of dialogue is a worthwhile venture. And the best way to prove this to the reader is by showing how the types of arguments associated with the fallacies are highly sensitive to the context of dialogue in which the argument was put forward.

Hence, in the last chapter, after devoting a whole chapter to studying the properties of each of the six primary types of dialogue, I return to a consideration of the fallacies introduced in chapter 1. My goal is to show the reader how sensitive each of these types of arguments is to shifts or changes of context from one type of dialogue to another. At that point, the reader needs to be convinced that informal logic stands no hope of making further progress with its job of analysing and evaluating fallacies and with its more general objective of evaluating arguments as they occur in real cases of everyday verbal exchanges.

8. The New Approach to Dialectic

The problem that is currently posed for the advancement of informal logic is one of applying the concept of dialogue, as an organized structure, to cases of everyday argumentation, especially as typified by the sorts of problems posed by the major fallacies. The formal systems of dialogue that have proliferated in recent times appear potentially useful, but they are not sharply enough focused on the practical contexts of argument use that need to be studied in relation to the fallacies – they are too diffuse, too multiple, and too abstract. The model of the critical discussion is much more practical and applied. But, on the one hand, it appears too narrow to capture enough relevant aspects of the kinds of cases that need to be evaluated. On the other hand, it has not been developed at an adequate level of generality and abstractness to define itself as a characteristic type of dialogue that fits into the other types in an organized superstructure.

The key here is that the concept of dialogue has to be seen as a context or enveloping framework into which arguments are fitted so they can be judged as appropriate or not in that context. So the concept of dialogue needs to be normative: it needs to prescribe how an argument ought to be used in order to fit in as appropriate, and to be used rightly or correctly (as well as incorrectly, in some cases). But the concept of dialogue also needs to fit the typical conversational settings in which such arguments are conventionally used to make a point in everyday argumentative verbal exchanges.

The concept of a dialogue, in the sense developed in this book, is that of a conventionalized, purposive joint activity between two parties (in the simplest case), where the parties act as speech partners. It is meant by this that the two parties exchange verbal messages or so-called speech acts that take the form of moves in a game-like sequence of exchanges. It is presumed that both parties are aware of the significance of a particular type of move, in light of the purpose of the dialogue, and can respond with an appropriate countermove or reply. The pattern is that of 'turn-taking' in the sense of Sacks, Schegloff, and Jefferson (1974).

A typical example of a turn-taking sequence of moves is a question asked by one party and a reply given by the other party.

QUESTIONER: How can you prove that virtue can be taught?
RESPONDENT: Children learn codes of moral conduct every day, and they learn them from adults.

In this case, the moves are relatively simple. One is a question and the other is a complex (conjunctive) assertion, put forward as a reply to the question. In other cases, moves can be more complex.

One common form of a move in a dialogue is an *argument*, where one or more premises are put forward to support a conclusion or to bear on an unsettled issue that the conclusion is related to. Indeed, the concept of dialogue in this book is meant to be useful because it functions as a kind of framework or format in which arguments are used.

In this sense of dialogue, when an argument is used it is a good argument (or a successful or correct argument) to the extent that it contributes to the goal of the dialogue. But there can be different goals because there can be different types of dialogue in which the same argument can be used. Thus in the new dialectical method of evaluating arguments, an argument is correct or reasonable if it is used at some stage in a dialogue to contribute the overall goal of that type of dialogue by fulfilling the requirements for the kind of move an argument is supposed to be at that stage. The criterion of correctness or incorrectness of use of an argument is dialectical in the new sense, in Hamblin's sense, of making the evaluation of the argument a function of its occurrence at some point in a sequence of moves and countermoves where two parties are reasoning together in a purposeful verbal exchange.

Because it is a postmodern and relativistic standard of rationality, which allows for rational arguments both within and outside science, the new dialectic will inevitably appear objectionable and even frightening to many individuals. It is good to recognize that not everyone will like or welcome it.

9. Types of Dialogue

A *dialogue* is defined as a normative framework in which there is an exchange of arguments between two speech partners reasoning together in turn-taking sequence aimed at a collective goal. An argument, or other type of move in a dialogue, is relevant to the extent that it is an appropriate type of move at that stage of the dialogue, and to the extent that it is part of a connected sequence of argumentation in which the individual speech acts fit together to contribute to this goal. As well, each participant has an individual goal in the dialogue, and both participants have an obligation in the dialogue, defined by the nature of their collective and individual goals.

In some dialogues, the goal is to prove something, and in this type of dialogue, the primary obligation is the burden of proof. A burden of proof is a weight of presumption allocated (ideally) at the opening stage of the dialogue in order to facilitate the successful carrying out of the obligations of the participants during the course of the dialogue. The device of burden of proof is useful because it enables discussion to come to an end in a reasonable time.

One important type of dialogue is the critical discussion, which is well described by van Eemeren and Grootendorst (1984). It is a type of *persuasion dialogue*, meaning that the goal of each party is to persuade the other party to accept some designated proposition, using as premises only propositions that the other party has accepted as commitments.

The following classification of the six main types, and also various subtypes of dialogue studied in this book, may help to orient the reader.

1. persuasion dialogue
   1.1 critical discussion
2. information-seeking dialogue
   2.1 interview
   2.2 advice-solicitation dialogue
      2.2.1 expert-consultation dialogue
3. negotiation dialogue
4. inquiry dialogue
   4.1 scientific inquiry
   4.2 public inquiries (e.g., air disasters)
5. eristic dialogue
   5.1 quarrel
6. deliberation dialogue

(For comparable accounts of the different types of dialogue see Walton, 1989a, p. 10; 1990b, p. 413).

The concept of commitment is the basic idea behind all dialogue as a form of reasoned argumentation (see Hamblin, 1970; 1981; Walton, 1984; and Walton and Krabbe, 1995). In a dialogue, each participant has a set of propositions which is called that participant's *commitment set*. As the various speech acts of asserting, questioning, and so on are brought forward in turn by the participants, propositions are added to or deleted from the participants' commitment sets. One simple rule, for example, is that when a participant asserts a proposition it goes into her commitment set.

In *information-seeking dialogue*, the goal is for information to be transmitted from one party to the other. The *interview* is one type of information-seeking dialogue, for example. In Hamblin's formal game of dialogue (H), transfer of information is ostensibly the goal, but there do seem to be implicit aspects of the persuasion dialogue involved as well, even though Hamblin did not formulate explicit win-loss rules (see Hamblin, 1970, pp. 256–71).

Another type of information-seeking dialogue is the *advice-solicitation dialogue*, where the goal of the one party is to seek advice in order to carry out an action or solve a problem by consulting another party who is in a special position to offer such advice. This type of dialogue is not adversarial in the way that persuasion dialogue is.

An important type of advice-solicitation dialogue is the *expert-consultation dialogue*, where a non-expert in a domain of skill or specialized knowledge consults an expert in order to get expert opinion or advice in a form he can use for his purposes – to solve a problem or go ahead with a course of action in an informed and intelligent way. In this type of dialogue, the expert respondent has an obligation to offer her best advice in clear and accessible language while at the same time admitting her limitations and doubts. The obligation of the advice-seeker is to ask clear and specific questions that the expert can answer in relation to the problem at hand. A commonplace type of case is the physician-patient dialogue during medical treatments and consultations.

In *negotiation dialogue*, the aim for both parties is to 'make a deal' while bargaining over some goods or interests by conceding some things and insisting on others. Each side tries to figure out what the other side wants most, or feels is most important, of the goods at stake. Negotiations, like union-management bargaining, for example, are now often guided by professional mediators. Fisher and Ury (1991) describe methods of negotiation and mediation studied in the Harvard Project.

In *inquiry dialogue*, the goal is for the participants to collectively prove some particular proposition, according to a given standard of proof, or to show that the proposition cannot be proved at the present stage of knowledge. The intent of the inquiry is to be cumulative, to work only from established premises that will not require further discussion or retraction once set in place at the appropriate stage of the inquiry. The sequence of the inquiry is meant (ideally) to be linear or to branch in one direction so that circular argumentation can always be excluded.

The *scientific inquiry*, which Aristotle called the demonstration, requires that proof proceed only from premises that either are axiomatic or can be established by methods of inference accepted by standards in a particular branch of scientific knowledge. Other inquiries, like public inquiries into air disasters and the like, rely on expert testimony of scientific consultants. But the goal is the same. The purpose is to prove a conclusion by a high standard of proof that eliminates unverified presumptions from the line of advance.

Inquiries have three main stages. First, the data or findings are collected. Second, these findings are analysed, discussed, and interpreted in order to draw conclusions on what can be proved from them. Third, the results of the inquiry are presented to a wider audience or readership. It may be the third phase of presentation, where the order of proving is quite different from the order of finding, that corresponds most closely to what Aristotle called demonstration.

The *quarrel* is a type of dialogue where the goal of each participant is to verbally 'hit out' at the other and, if possible, defeat and humiliate the other party. The quarrel is typically precipitated by a trivial incident which sparks an escalation of emotions, and both parties adopt a stubborn or 'childish' attitude during the argumentation stage. The real purpose of the quarrel is a cathartic release of deeply held emotions so that previously unarticulated feelings can be brought to the surface – feelings that would not be appropriate to bring out for discussion in the course of a normal, polite, public conversation. The quarrel characteristically shows dialectical irrelevance because the participants jump from one issue to another.

In contrast to the critical discussion, neither participant in the quarrel is really open to changing his position, even when confronted by convincing evidence and reasonable arguments. The quarrel is not a good friend of logical reasoning; it is characterized by cavilling, by brushing logic aside, and by giving priority to the need to defeat the other party by any means, foul or fair, that comes to hand. The quarrel is typified by excesses and violent emotional outbursts.

The quarrel is a species of *eristic dialogue*, a type of dialogue which is almost purely adversarial, where finding the truth of a matter and paying attention to logical reasoning procedures are always subservient to winning out over the other party. Aristotle, in *De Sophisticis Elenchis* (171b22–25), compares contentious (eristic) argument to unfair fighting in an athletic contest where the participants are bent on winning at any cost and stop at nothing.

It is often presumed that the quarrel is a wholly bad type of dialogue, one that is best avoided altogether. But this point of view overlooks some valuable benefits of the quarrel (its structure is analysed in chapter 7). By allowing powerful feelings to be expressed through the articulation of deeply held grievances, the quarrel can have the valuable function of improving mutual understanding and cementing the bonds of a personal relationship. A quarrel can split two people apart, but if it has a good cathartic effect, it can function as a substitute for physical fighting, and draw people closer together in the course of a meaningful relationship.

As a normative model of how argumentation should be conducted, the quarrel is not too interesting or instructive in itself. However, in order to understand fallacies, it is necessary and vitally important that one sees how there has been a dialectical shift from some other type of dialogue (like a critical discussion) to a quarrel.

Finally, the *deliberation* type of dialogue involves an agent trying to decide what is the best or the most prudent course of action in a given situation, in relation to the agent's goals and the known or conjectured facts of the situation. Deliberation was very well described by Aristotle in the *Nicomachean Ethics*, but he did not think of it as a type of argument (it would have been sixth on his list), probably because, in his view, it did not use reasoning (*syllogysmos*), like the five types of argument cited above. Instead, practical wisdom (*phronesis*) is used in Aristotelian deliberation. However, in the new dialectic, reasoning can be practical (goal-directed, knowledge-based, situational). And so in the new dialectic, deliberation is presented as a type of dialogue in which arguments are used (see chapter 6).

10. Dialectical Relevance

A dialogue is a sequence of individual pairs of moves (speech acts), beginning with a first move. A sequence of argumentation is relevant to the extent that it is an orderly subpart of the longer sequence going from the first move to the goal of the dialogue. The goal of the dialogue is defined by its originating issue, which is the problem, question, or conflict the dialogue is supposed to solve, answer, or resolve.

A move in a dialogue is globally relevant if it makes a contribution to settling the issue of the dialogue, as part of the sequence of argumentation originating from the initial move. Thus global relevance pertains to the issue that the dialogue is all about, as a whole connected conversational exchange. By way of contrast, two moves in a dialogue are locally relevant to each other – this is a symmetrical relation – if they are related to each other at a single move or in the region of a particular move. For example, a reply may be locally relevant to a question that preceded it, at the just prior move by the other party, if it either answers the question or otherwise functions as an appropriate reply for that type of question, according to the rules of the dialogue. At the local level, criticisms of irrelevance often have to do with the nature of the question-reply relationship, as appropriately defined for a type of dialogue.

Care is needed in evaluating criticisms of irrelevance, however. Often one participant in a dialogue may accuse another of being evasive or irrelevant if the first participant feels that the other one has not answered his question. However, if the question itself is open to legitimate criticism in the first place, the respondent may be justified in not answering it (see examples in chapter 5). In such a case, the respondent may be justified in criticizing or even questioning the question. Such a reply may not be irrelevant at all, and the questioner should not be allowed to browbeat the respondent with aggressive charges that a fallacy of irrelevance has been committed.

At first, it was thought that relevance could be defined in a semantic way by adding various kinds of relations to propositional and quantifier logics. This approach was useful to some extent, but in *Topical Relevance in Argumentation* (1982) I showed that there are limits to the usefulness of it in defining a concept of relevance adequate to providing a basis for understanding the kinds of criticisms of irrelevance associated with traditional fallacies of relevance. This research indicated the need for a pragmatic concept of relevance in dialogue exchanges of argumentation, a species of conversational relevance in the sense offered by Dascal (1977). However, since relevance is a distinctively different concept in different types of dialogue, this pluralism has heretofore been the stumbling block in the analysis of relevance.

In chapters 2 to 7, I will define relevance separately for each of the six basic types of dialogue. In a given case of an argument used in conversation, relevance of the argument depends on the purpose of the type of dialogue in that case and how the argument was supposed to be used to fulfil some function in relation to that purpose. Thus the very same argument could be relevant in a negotiation dialogue, yet could be rightly judged to be not relevant as part of a persuasion dialogue. This postmodernistic pluralism yields an approach to dialectical relevance in this book that offers six distinctively different ways of explaining the nature of the relevance or irrelevance of an argument in a given case, depending on the type of dialogue exchange one was supposed to have been engaged in, relative to the given case.

In general, the perspective on evaluation of arguments put forward in this book is that an argument can be evaluated from a logical point of view in two different ways or respects. First, we can evaluate it as an inference, from premises to a conclusion, according to semantic standards (of deductive logic, in the most familiar kind of case, as valid or invalid). Second, we can evaluate how the reasoning, or chaining of inferences in the given case, was used in a context of dialogue for some purpose (as part of a conversational exchange). It is this second method of evaluation that is dialectical in the sense presented in this book.

This new dialectic clearly does go back to the old dialectic of the Greeks, as a general perspective and way of evaluating arguments in a context of dialogue. But 'dialectical argument,' as the phrase was used by Aristotle in particular, does not mean the same thing as it does in the new dialectic, where it refers not to just one especially important type of argument, but to the whole framework of the different types of dialogue that represents the different ways an argument can be used in the context of a conversational exchange. On many different points of interpretation, the exact relationships between aspects of the old and the new dialectic is a subject that is itself susceptible to dialectical questioning.

2

Persuasion Dialogue

Persuasion dialogue is the type of conversational exchange where one party – the proponent – is trying to persuade the other party – the respondent – that some particular proposition – the thesis – is true, using arguments that show or prove to the respondent that the thesis is true. The respondent is doubtful that this proposition can be proved or shown to be true,[1] and this doubt stems from the respondent's conviction that an opposed proposition – the negation or opposite of the thesis of the first party – is true. The respondent's job (role, obligation) is to bring forward arguments that show or prove that this opposed proposition is true. In either case, each party is trying to persuade the other to change her opinion, to accept the thesis of the other side. To accomplish this objective, each party tries to extract concessions or commitments from the other side, and then uses these propositions as premises for arguments to persuade the other side.

1. Main Characteristics

The goal of a persuasion dialogue is to test the comparative strength or plausibility of arguments on both sides of a controversial or contentious issue. The best example is the case study of the dialogue on tipping that I presented in *Plausible Argument in Everyday Conversation* (1992, pp. 7–11). In this dialogue, the two participants, Helen and Bob, have a difference of opinion on the subject of tipping. Helen thinks that tipping is a bad practice that should be eliminated. Bob disagrees with this point of view and feels that tipping is generally a good practice that ought to be retained. The dialogue arises when Helen and Bob are dinner guests of a man who has just returned from a business trip where he encountered problems about how much money he should tip waiters, bellhops, and cab drivers. Both Helen and Bob agree that tipping can often be a social problem that leads to many misunderstandings. But Bob feels that tipping has its good aspects as a way of rewarding a service that's performed courteously, efficiently, and with excellence. Helen disagrees with this view, arguing that the abuses that arise out of the practice of tipping outweigh the good effects, to the extent that we ought to conclude that tipping is generally a bad practice and ought to be discontinued.

In the dialogue that ensues, Bob and Helen interact with each other argumentatively, each giving reasons to support his or her views and arguments against the views expressed by the other. In this example of persuasion dialogue, the issue is whether or not the practice of tipping is a good thing. An *issue* in this type of case is defined as a pair of propositions where the one proposition is opposed to what, logically speaking, is the negation of the other proposition. This type of persuasion dialogue can be called a *dispute* in the sense that the one proposition is the opposite of the other proposition, and each party is trying to prove one of these propositions. In other words, what the one party is trying to prove is the direct opposite of what the other party is trying to prove. Hence, we can appropriately say that this type of persuasion dialogue is an instance of strong opposition or dispute. In this type of persuasion dialogue, both parties have a burden of proof. Here both parties have a positive burden of proof: each party has a proposition which he or she must prove.

In another, simpler kind of case, the burden of proof rests only with one party. In this kind of case, one party might take on a positive proposition – for example, that tipping is a good practice – and the other party might take the sceptical position of critically questioning that proposition without actually committing herself to the opposite proposition and thereby taking on a positive burden of proof as well. In this secondary or simpler type of case of a persuasion dialogue, the goal of the persuasion dialogue is to critically question the strongest arguments for a particular position on an issue.

It is important to distinguish between the collective goal of the persuasion dialogue as a purpose of a type of conversation and the goals of each of the participants. In a persuasion dialogue, each participant's goal is to persuade the other party that the proposition each has opted to argue for is true, or at least is plausible on a balance of considerations. The method for reaching this goal is for one party to use arguments that have as premises propositions that are commitments of the other party and then to use these premises in arguments that are appropriate or acceptable for this type of dialogue in order to prove the conclusion that the thesis (that is, the proposition one is supposed to prove) is true or is supported by these arguments.

What is distinctive about persuasion dialogue is that a participant's arguments are supposed to have as premises propositions that the other party is committed to. This means that the notion of commitment is central to persuasion dialogue as a type of organized conversation. It also means that the argumentation in a persuasion dialogue is interactive in the sense that one party's arguments are always directed towards the other party and are based on premises that are commitments of that other party. In a persuasion dialogue, the most important question is always whether a particular argument will reasonably persuade the other party.

Persuasion dialogue is also closely tied to, and begins with, presumptions for a commonly held opinion. In the case of the dialogue on tipping, popular opinion is pretty well split on this issue in any given audience. We would generally find quite a number of people who will support the idea that tipping is generally a bad practice which ought to be discontinued. But we are also likely to find a significant number of people who will oppose that view and support the idea that, even though tipping may lead to misunderstandings and bad consequences, it is generally a good practice and should be maintained if we deal with it in the proper way. Hence, the initial burden of proof in the dialogue on tipping is split roughly equally on both sides. Generally, in persuasion dialogue, if a proposition is widely or generally accepted at a particular time, then there would be a presumption in favour of it so that anyone who challenges or critically questions it will have to meet this presumption with appropriately strong arguments that will be acceptable to doubters.

In a persuasion dialogue, each party has a particular proposition designated as his or her thesis, and it is the main goal for a participant to persuade the other party that this particular thesis is true, or is supported by a preponderance of arguments. Hence, this particular proposition, the so-called *thesis* of the party, is very important in defining the arguer's commitment. It is the key to understanding the arguer's position and commitments as a whole. However, it is not exclusively this proposition that defines the whole commitment set of an arguer. As an arguer proceeds to engage in a persuasion dialogue, he or she will make certain moves – by asking questions, putting forward arguments, or agreeing to propositions which he or she finds acceptable – that will determine her commitments.

We use the concept of commitment here in the same sense used in Hamblin (1970; 1971). The idea is that there will be a repository, a kind of data bank called a *commitment store* which will keep track of all of the propositions that are commitments of a participant at any particular stage or point in the dialogue. Hamblin devised the concept of the commitment store or commitment set, which he thought of as a store of statements representing the totality of commitments of an arguer during the sequence of a dialogue (1970, p. 257). As the dialogue proceeds, propositions will be inserted into or deleted from this set. We could think of this set of propositions in physical terms as being a set of sentences chalked on a blackboard, written on a piece of paper, or recorded in a computer memory device or on a tape recorder.

In real life, we do not very often keep track of an arguer's commitments in a way that can be later verified by playing a tape recording of it, for example. But the persuasion dialogue in our sense is a normative model of dialogue, which means that it is a kind of ideal model of how an argument should be viewed and evaluated. So it does not necessarily correspond, in a one-to-one fashion, with arguments that take place in actual conversations. Since persuasion dialogue is a conventionally recognized type of conversational exchange, it is not a purely abstract model of argumentation. But it does have rules. The general idea is that there will be certain types of moves that would be permitted by the rules, and these moves will determine whether propositions are inserted into or deleted from the commitment stores of a player at that move.[2] For example, if a player makes the assertion, 'I now assert proposition A,' then A will go into his commitment store. When he makes the retraction or denial, 'I now deny or retract proposition A,' then, if proposition A was in his commitment store previously, it would be taken out or erased.

This structure is not a normative or ideal model of rational argument in the stronger sense that a participant must be consistent in his commitments, as Hamblin notes (1970, p. 257). Inconsistencies of certain kinds, particularly very visible ones, may be open to challenge or may even be required to be challenged by the other party. (These rules are listed in section 4 below, in conjunction with the description of one special type of persuasion dialogue called the critical discussion.)

2. Argument in Persuasion Dialogue

Certain common types of arguments or *argumentation schemes*, which represent kinds of argument normally used in a conversation, will be acceptable in a persuasion dialogue. Generally, the arguments used in a persuasion dialogue are not conclusive, for example, in the sense that they are deductively valid arguments with premises that are known to be true (or anything approaching this degree of conclusiveness). In order to be successful, arguments merely need to meet a burden of proof or a weight of presumption that is enough to reasonably persuade or convince the other party to modify her or his commitments.[3] These arguments in a persuasion dialogue will generally be of a presumptive sort based on defeasible and non-monotonic reasoning that is provisionally acceptable subject to exceptions or to later critical questioning. The idea is that such arguments are successful or acceptable if they respond appropriately to a certain type of question which matches the type of argument that is being used. So these arguments don't have to be conclusive to be satisfactory, but they are required to be tentatively or temporarily accepted by the other party, unless that party can find a sufficient reason to reject them or good grounds for criticizing them.

The purpose of using an argument in a persuasion dialogue is for one party to rationally persuade the other party to become committed to the proposition that is the original party's thesis. There are two ways to do this: one is to provide positive arguments to support the thesis; the other is the negative way of criticizing arguments that have been, or may be, put forward to support the opponent's thesis. Thus, persuasion dialogue is a normative model of argument in that the notion of rational persuasion does have some bite.

Argumentation that is put forward must serve a certain function – it must be useful for the purposes cited above. An argument is typically a sequence of reasoning based on premises that are the opponent's commitments, but in many cases it must also serve what I have called the *probative function* of argument (1991, pp. 293–7). The probative function means that the premises of an argument are supposed to have a greater proving value or plausibility value for the arguer to whom they are directed than the value of the conclusion that is supposed to be proved. The argument moves forward so that the plausibility of the premises as evidence can be transferred forward to the plausibility of the conclusion as a proposition that one should be committed to. It is

this forward movement of an argument that is identified with its probative function.

This notion of the probative function of an argument can be found in
Outlines of Pyrrhonism (Book 2, 143–4) where Sextus Empiricus describes
a proof as an argument that discovers a conclusion by means of pre-
evident premises. Sextus gives the following example of a probative
argument: 'If sweat pours through the surface, there are insensible
pores; but in fact sweat does pour through the surface: therefore there
are insensible pores' (1933, p. 241). This is said to be a probative argument in the sense Sextus refers to, which mean that the premises are pre-
evident and the argument deduces something non-evident by means of
these premises. The probative function is fulfilled in the sense that
someone who is not persuaded of the conclusion or who doubted it,
could be persuaded rationally by this argument, once the premises were
made evident to them and they accepted this form of an argument as
generally reasonable. In this case, the form of the argument is deductively valid, and presumably that would be an acceptable form of argument for this type of persuasion. It is clear that this important notion of
the probative function of argument was known to the ancient Greek philosophers whose arguments Sextus discussed.

The probative function is not the only possible function that an argument can have in a persuasion dialogue. It is also possible to have hypothetical arguments which are used in other ways. However, the
probative function of argument is highly characteristic of argumentation
in a persuasion dialogue, and the purpose of argumentation in a persuasion dialogue is to prove something to the other party, where to prove
means to support by premises that are commitments of the other party
in the form of an argument where the conclusion has some bearing on
the issue of the persuasion dialogue. This means that relevance is very
important in persuasion dialogue.

Generally, argumentation should be relevant to proving a thesis in
this type of dialogue. In any persuasion dialogue, there is an uncertainty
or unsettledness posed by the issue of the dialogue, and an argument is
relevant in a persuasion dialogue only if it is used somehow to bear on
supporting the arguments on one side or the other of the issue so that
this uncertainty or unsettledness can be resolved. It is not necessary that
a particular argument resolve the uncertainty or even that the conflict of
opinions in the persuasion dialogue be resolved. Nevertheless, for an
argument to be relevant, it should have some use for this purpose. Thus,
the general structure of a persuasion dialogue imposes constraints on

how argumentation is supposed to be used in that dialogue, and thus these constraints give the dialogue a normative structure that enables us to evaluate particular arguments as being weak or strong, appropriate or inappropriate, correct or fallacious in a given case.

The general structure of use of argumentation in a persuasion dialogue can be expressed by four constraints which, taken together, assure that the argumentation used will be relevant. Relevant argumentation in a persuasion dialogue is bound only by four requirements (rules):

R.1 The respondent accepts the premises as commitments.

R.2 Each inference in the chain of argument is structurally correct (according to an argumentation scheme).

R.3 The chain of argumentation must have the proponent's thesis as its (ultimate) conclusion.

R.4 Arguments meeting these three rules are the only means that count as fulfilling the proponent's goal in the dialogue.

Each single step of inference is chained to another step of inference, which results in a sequence of reasoning. If a sequence of reasoning used in argumentation in a persuasion dialogue meets all four requirements, it is judged to be a good (correct) argument as used in that type of dialogue. Here 'good' or 'correct' is used in the functional or pragmatic sense, and means that the argument is good or useful in contributing to the goal of the dialogue.

3. Commitment

Although Hamblin originated the notion of commitment in dialogue as being the central normative concept for models of dialogue in argumentation, the particular mathematical models of dialogue that he presented were not of the persuasion-dialogue type. Hamblin assumed that 'the purpose of the dialogue is the exchange of information among the participants' (1970, p. 137). Hamblin did not define exactly what constituted exchange of information, but he did take this notion to mean, for example, that there is no point in making any statement to someone who is not already committed to it. While his notion of exchange of information was not precisely defined, he did take it to have certain normative consequences. In *Logical Dialogue–Games and Fallacies*, I recommended a different approach, one in which the basic concept of persuasion dialogue is distinctively different from Hamblin's notion of the information-oriented type of dialogue: 'It seems to me much more likely that most of the traditional fallacies begin to appear as significant moves of argumentation in the context of disputation where the objective of one party is to prove something contestively to the other, utilizing or extracting commitments from the other. The objective is not to "inform" but rather to "persuade"' (Walton, 1984, p. 58). My notion of persuasion dialogue was qualified by showing how it works in several practical cases of structured dialogue exchanges (p. 110). In these cases, there are two parties and the goal of each party is to persuade the other to accept a certain proposition as true.

The basic problem in such a case is that it is clearly evident to both parties that the thesis of one is opposed to the thesis of the other. So the one party will be disinclined to accept, or become committed to, the thesis of the other party or to any proposition that seems directly or obviously to imply that proposition by means of the kinds of arguments acceptable to both parties. Hence there is in such a dialogue exchange what I have called a problem of strategy or persuasion. How does the proponent go about persuading the other party to accept some proposition given that this proposition is meant to be ultimately used to disprove the answerer's thesis? Several strategies are available (see the examples of dialogue cited in *Logical Dialogue*). One is the distancing strategy of picking a proposition that's not too closely related to the opponent's thesis so that he won't realize, or see directly, how this proposition is going to be used to refute his thesis or to prove his opponent's thesis. Another strategy is that of separating, where two or more propositions are proved separately and then eventually put together in an argument structure that is used to prove one's own thesis or to argue against an opponent's thesis. But, since the opponent may not perceive the intended use of these propositions when they are proved individually, it is much less likely that he will oppose them so vigorously.

It is evident, then, that strategy becomes very important in persuasion dialogue. Strategy involves connected sequences of arguments, called argumentation themes, that collect different individual arguments in some kind of global way to attack an opponent's thesis or to prove one's own thesis. Both the attacker and the defender will have strategies, and it is easy to see that the defender will be disinclined to take on commitments unless there is some good reason to do so. The more propositions one becomes committed to, the more 'ammunition' this gives an opponent to use as premises so that he can prove his own thesis or attack his opponent's.

One elementary strategic theme is the *loophole* or *way-out principle*

(Walton, 1984, p. 138). This advises a respondent to reject, or at least not become committed to, any statement that, together with other statements in the respondent's commitment store, directly or indirectly implies the opponent's thesis or casts doubt on the respondent's thesis. The advice given is the following instruction: if you see such a proposition that has such potential uses that go against your own interests, then reject it. This is the essence of the loophole strategy for the defending respondent.

In a persuasion dialogue, not only do the participants put forward arguments and assertions as speech acts that constitute their moves in the dialogue, but they also ask questions. The purpose of asking such a question is to try to get the opponent to accept propositions as commitments that can then later be used as premises. This is one very important type of question commonly used in a persuasion dialogue. The basic strategy for a proponent is to try and get enough of these commitments so that he can then prove his thesis or disprove his opponent's thesis using them as premises in arguments. But a respondent who has to answer such questions will, if he is rational, try to evade or avoid taking on any commitments, particularly ones that can be used against his side of the argument. Hence, it is important in persuasion dialogue that a respondent be given some kind of incentive to take on commitments.

Another aspect of commitment that is very fundamental in persuasion dialogue is the notion of retraction. Generally in a persuasion dialogue, participants are free to make retractions, but they cannot be altogether free to retract any proposition at any point in a dialogue. In other words, there must be some restraints on retraction, but these restraints must be fairly weak in the sense that participants should be allowed to change their minds or retract propositions if the argument reaches a point where they think such a retraction is needed to make their position defensible or comprehensible. This, then, is really the fundamental problem for persuasion dialogue. How do we deal with the problem of retraction? Under what circumstances do we allow retraction and under what circumstances should it be denied as a possible move? Hamblin suggests that commitment stores should not generally be required to be consistent. But if a participant takes up a position that is flagrantly or obviously inconsistent – if one of his commitments is clearly the negation of another of his important commitments, for example – then this sort of situation should not be allowed to pass unchallenged. The other participant may be forced to challenge his opponent's inconsistent position; if he does, then the opponent should be required to resolve the inconsistency or perhaps to remove one of the inconsistent pair of propositions. This is a kind of situation where some sort of possibility for retraction needs to be made; in general, it seems characteristic of persuasion dialogue that retractions should be fairly freely allowed.

However, there are some situations where retractions should not be too freely allowed, at least immediately. For example, suppose an arguer has committed himself to a proposition 'if A then B,' and later in the sequence of the dialogue, he also commits himself to the proposition A. Suppose further that *modus ponens* is an acceptable type of argument appropriate for this type of dialogue, and the respondent sees that proposition B could be used to raise critical questions or even refute his thesis, so he quickly retracts B. Here the respondent is in a kind of inconsistent situation because he has accepted the premises of an argument of which B is the conclusion, but once he sees that this argument implies B and what B can be used to do, he rejects B.

In this kind of case, there could be various solutions, but it seems like one good general solution is to allow him to retract B as long as he also retracts one of the premises that could be used to imply B. This kind of solution has been worked out in more specific detail in Walton and Krabbe (1995) for one particular subtype of persuasion dialogue. The general solution is that the respondent can't immediately retract B without penalty, but at some future point in the dialogue, he can retract B provided that he makes certain other moves that are also consistent with his other commitments and can be justified as legitimate moves in the sequence of dialogue at that point.

We will not try to give a solution to the problem of retraction here for all persuasion dialogue, but it needs to be noted that one of the central features of persuasion dialogue is that it should fairly freely permit retractions, and that the central problem of defining specific persuasion dialogues resides in defining precise rules for retraction. We will see later that there is a sharp contrast between persuasion dialogue and the type of dialogue which we will call the inquiry. In the inquiry, the dialogue is specifically designed to minimize or even eliminate the possibility of retraction of commitments.

4. Critical Discussion

One special type of persuasion dialogue is the critical discussion, which represents a higher standard of persuasion dialogue in certain respects.

According to van Eemeren and Grootendorst (1984), the purpose of a critical discussion is to resolve a conflict of opinions. The conflict is resolved, according to van Eemeren and Grootendorst, 'only if somebody retracts his doubt because he has been convinced by the other party's argumentation or if he withdraws his standpoint because he has realized that his argumentation cannot stand up to the other party's criticism' (1992, p. 34). Resolution of the conflict means showing that the point of view of the one side is no longer tenable as a commitment.

There can be two types of conflicts of opinion, according to van Eemeren and Grootendorst, and two subtypes of critical discussion corresponding to these. In the *simple critical discussion*, one participant defends a particular proposition known as her thesis and the other participant has the role of raising critical questions that cast doubt on that thesis (van Eemeren and Grootendorst, 1984, p. 85). In the *complex critical discussion*, each participant has a thesis, and the goal of each participant is to prove that her thesis is true (p. 90). Thus, the complex type of critical discussion would be classified as a subtype of persuasion dialogue, which we called a dispute in section 1.

A critical discussion, according to van Eemeren and Grootendorst, has four stages: a confrontation stage, an opening stage, an argumentation stage, and a concluding stage (1984, chapter 7). There are general rules for speech acts that are appropriate for each stage of the discussion. Ten of these dialectical rules are given in van Eemeren and Grootendorst (1987, pp. 284–6), and a reformulated and improved version of the same (or essentially the same) ten rules is given in van Eemeren and Grootendorst (1992, pp. 208–9), as quoted below.

Rule 1: Parties must not prevent each other from advancing standpoints or casting doubt on standpoints.

Rule 2: A party that advances a standpoint is obliged to defend it if the other party asks him to do so.

Rule 3: A party's attack on a standpoint must relate to the standpoint that has indeed been advanced by the other party.

Rule 4: A party may defend his standpoint only by advancing argumentation relating to that standpoint.

Rule 5: A party may not falsely present something as a premise that has been left unexpressed by the other party or deny a premise that he himself has left implicit.

Rule 6: A party may not falsely present a premise as an accepted starting point nor deny a premise representing an accepted starting point.

Rule 7:   A party may not regard a standpoint as conclusively defended if the defense does not take place by means of an appropriate argumentation scheme that is correctly applied.

Rule 8:   In his argumentation a party may only use arguments that are logically valid or capable of being validated by making explicit one or more unexpressed premises.

Rule 9:   A failed defense of a standpoint must result in the party that put forward the standpoint retracting it and a conclusive defense in the other party retracting his doubt about the standpoint.

Rule 10: A party must not use formulations that are insufficiently clear or confusingly ambiguous and he must interpret the other party's formulations as carefully and accurately as possible.

These ten rules define the critical discussion as a type of dialogue. As shown below, the critical discussion, so defined, is a subspecies of the more general persuasion dialogue. In the earlier literature, the terms 'critical discussion' and 'persuasion dialogue' were often used interchangeably or were considered to be equivalent terms. For example, in Walton and Krabbe, they are used as synonymous terms (1995, p. 68). But now the term 'persuasion dialogue' is to be defined as the more general category, and 'critical discussion' is defined as a subtype and especially idealized model of the persuasion dialogue. According to the new definition, persuasion dialogue is characterized by requirements R.1 through R.4, which correspond to rules 1, 3, 4, 7, and 9 of the critical discussion. Rules 2, 5, 6, 8, and 10 are external to (additional to) requirements R.1 through R.4. There is also one fundamental difference that is important to emphasize. A critical discussion, in order to be successful, must resolve the conflict of opinions at issue – one party must retract his thesis if he has failed to defend it by the closing stage of the dialogue. But in the persuasion dialogue, the dialogue can be successful if the maieutic function is achieved – that is, if light is thrown on the dark-side commitments of both sides, even if the conflict of opinions is not resolved by showing that one side has failed to defend his thesis against the conclusive argumentation of the other side.

An example of a persuasion dialogue that is not a critical discussion would be the tipping dialogue, in a case where neither side conclusively refutes the thesis of the other side, even though both sides bring forward strong arguments that reveal inadequacies in the arguments for the opposing thesis. According to the new definition, a critical discussion is a type of persuasion dialogue focusing exclusively on resolving a conflict of opinions.

Van Eemeren and Grootendorst use the terms 'point of view' or 'standpoint' as an arguer's expression of commitment in a critical discussion. According to their account, a language user can have three possible attitudes to an expressed opinion or proposition: a positive point of view, a negative point of view, or a zero point of view. Further, 'if a language user advances a positive point of view in respect of an expressed opinion, then he is further positively committed to that expressed opinion, and if he advances a negative point of view, he is committed negatively to that expressed opinion unless he revokes his positive or negative point of view' (1984, p. 79). For van Eemeren and Grootendorst, then, in a critical discussion the issue in the persuasion dialogue that defines the particular critical discussion is made up of two components: (1) a proposition or expressed opinion, and (2) a point of view or attitude towards that opinion which can be positive, negative, or neutral.

In general, for van Eemeren and Grootendorst, a participant in a critical discussion can have a pro or contra attitude with respect to a proposition depending on her expressed point of view (1984, p. 89). However, the attitude of critical doubt is not identical with a contra attitude, but represents a suspended point of view that does not involve a positive burden of proof or disproof of the proposition against which the critical doubt is expressed.

5. Nonexplicit Commitments

Another idea that is very important for van Eemeren and Grootendorst is that of unexpressed premises in argumentative discourse (1992, chapter 6). They point out that, in identifying and analysing argumentation as it occurs in natural-language discourse in a given case, an account must typically be given of premises that are not explicitly expressed as propositions but are implicitly or indirectly conveyed within the discourse. In such cases, in order to identify the premise, it is very important to make use of the context of the conversation in which the argument was put forward as evidence to indicate that a particular proposition was indeed meant to be a premise as part of a given argument. They rightly emphasize that the context of dialogue is essential to making such determinations and is therefore essential to evaluating typical argumentation in natural-language discourse.

However, the general problem here is that van Eemeren and Grooten-dorst, like Hamblin, regard the commitment stores as being in a commitment set – that is, a set of propositions that are known to the participants in the dialogue as argumentation takes place. However, this represents a kind of ideal of a rational exchange of views in argumentation where the participants clearly state or are aware of the propositions that constitute their commitments and those of the other party.

As noted in section 3, Hamblin requires that the propositions representing the commitments of the participants in a dialogue be represented as a set of public statements like a number of sentences written on a blackboard in public view of all the participants so that, if there were any doubt about whether either party was committed to a particular proposition, one could look at the blackboard to see whether this proposition was represented by one of the sentences written there. This represents a certain ideal model of reasoned dialogue. Ideally, it should be clear, in a logical conversation, what the commitments of a participant are, and there should be some way of determining at every move exactly what these commitments are. But this model of precision and rigour is, of course, usually not met in realistic argument in everyday conversation. Typically in argumentation, we have a pretty good idea of what an arguer is committing himself to when he makes a certain kind of move in the context of a discussion, but we are not exactly sure what this commitment amounts to as a specific proposition and whether, if we confront the arguer with this proposition, he will accept it as a commitment that he has incurred. In other words, in its representation of commitments, argumentation in everyday conversation is more sloppy or permissive in the sense that the commitments of the participants are represented only in a somewhat imprecise way which is subject to subsequent clarification and argumentation.

In *Logical Dialogue* (1984), I showed that, if we model dialogue on Hamblin's idea of the commitment store being a set of public statements, then the dialogue is not very interesting or realistic in certain respects in modelling the thrust and parry of everyday argumentation. The general problem is that, if both participants are very clear and precise about what their commitments are at any given move, then it will be very difficult for the one player to get concessions or to extract commitments from the other party, because it will be relatively clear to both parties that these commitments could then be used against that player in order to defeat his argumentation for his point of view. Accordingly, a somewhat more complex game was constructed in *Logical Dialogue* called CBV (pp. 252–5). CBV is an extension of the simpler game called CB which has the typical Hamblin feature that, once a move is made that requires a commitment according to the rules, then that commitment is immediately inserted into the commitment set of the arguer, and both he and his opponent are clearly aware from that point onwards that this proposition is definitely a commitment of that arguer. CBV introduces one additional complication. In addition to the Hamblin commitment set, which is on clear view to both players, each player has a second commitment set which is not on public view. This is called a veiled commitment set, hence the letter V for 'veiled' in the dialogue structure CBV. This second set of commitments is called a *dark-side commitment set*, in contrast with the other commitment set which is on public view and called a *light-side commitment set*. The dark-side set of propositions is a definite set which exists, but at any given point in the game, the players may not be able to clearly see which propositions are in that set. Typically, the arguers have a pretty good idea what is in that set and they can guess at it with some plausibility, but they're not absolutely sure whether a given proposition is really a commitment of the other arguer or even of themselves at any given point.

My intent in introducing this notion of the dark-side commitment set in *Logical Dialogue* was to make the concept of strategy in persuasion dialogue more interesting and more applicable to the kind of argumentation one commonly encounters in everyday conversation. As we've seen, the general problem with the Hamblin type of model of argumentation, once it is made precise in a logical dialogue game like CB, is that of extracting commitments from the other party. Once the other party clearly sees that such commitments can be used against him in subsequent argumentation, he will obviously refuse to commit to them, unless there is some mechanism in the game that forces him to make commitments of certain kinds. Then the notion of strategy will not be very interesting in the dialogue, and it will not very closely resemble the kinds of exchanges of argumentation that are typical of cases where informal fallacies and other interesting phenomena of the kind we wish to study occur.

In order to make the abstract model of persuasion dialogue more interesting, in *Logical Dialogue* I added a particular rule to CB called RDS (p. 251). The rule RDS states that, if a player says that he has no commitment to a proposition A, but A really is in the dark side of his commitment set, then A is immediately transferred to the light side of his commitment set. This rule means that if an arguer really is committed to a proposition A in virtue of the way he has put forth an argument at some particular point in a persuasion dialogue, but he tries to explicitly retract his commitment to A or otherwise deny that he is committed to A, then his commitment to A will in fact immediately be made apparent. What this means is that an arguer in CBV can never be in a position to deny or hide his being committed to a particular proposition if he really is committed to it in the sense that it is in his dark-side set of commitments.

This solution is one way of dealing with the problem of dark-side commitments in persuasion dialogue. Unfortunately, it too turned out to make for an abstract or idealized model of dialogue that was not all we could ask for in modelling the fallacies and other interesting aspects of argumentation. Although the game CBV was an advance in that it did model this interesting notion of the dark-side commitment set, this way of ruling on commitments still turned out to be too abstract and arbitrary in certain ways to model a more realistic kind of argumentation.

The games CAVE and CAVE+ which I presented in *Question-Reply Argumentation* (1989b) are based on the structure of the persuasion-dialogue model CBV. Like CBV, CAVE and CAVE+ have dark-side commitment sets, and they have the same kind of RDS rule which requires that a proposition be immediately transferred to the light-side of a participant's commitment set if he makes a move to retract that particular proposition but really is committed to it on his dark side. These two new abstract models of persuasion dialogue also had their interesting aspects in modelling certain phenomena of question-reply argumentation, but they too turned out to be arbitrary in certain respects in modelling all aspects of everyday conversational argumentation.

The basic type of persuasion dialogue defined only by requirements R.1 through R.4 is not only very simple, but could easily be modelled as a dialogue exchange between a computer and a human user. The software required is only an expert system shell programmed with a set of facts (simple propositions) and rules (conditional propositions). The facts represent the commitments of the computer and the rules represent its warrants for inferences. Using this simple framework, the computer can answer questions posed by the user, and respond to challenges or arguments put forward by the user, by posing arguments in reply that are made up of inferences based on the user's commitments. So the persuasion dialogue, of the type regulated only by the requirements R.1 through R.4, is very simple, and is easy to model as a formal dialectical system that could be programmed into a computer software package.

It is when we start adding all the other requirements of the critical discussion, besides the ones that can be represented by R.1 through R.4, that we run into all kinds of technical problems and philosophical difficulties about how to precisely state the exact requirements needed. Our general conclusion is that R.1 through R.4 represent the basic or minimal concept of the persuasion dialogue. Various enrichments of this basic model can be added on. When enough of them are added on, eventually what we get is the complex system of dialogue represented by van Eemeren and Grootendorst's ten rules – the critical discussion type of dialogue.

Our earlier look at Rule 5 of the critical discussion illustrates the situation very well. There are many technical methods of producing a system of persuasion dialogue that have a device for identifying something that is supposedly 'a premise that has been left unexpressed by the other party.' Not until it has been shown by future research which one of these systems works best will we be able to formalize the system of dialogue called the critical discussion.

But the simple model of persuasion dialogue represented by R.1 through R.4 is a precise system that can easily be implemented as a user-computer dialogue by existing technology. This simple model is the essence of the commitment-based persuasion dialogue, of a kind that is a precise formalizable system. The problem is how, and in what order, to add further rules and components to this basic system of persuasion dialogue so that the other features of the critical discussion can be represented.

The critical discussion is best seen as an ideal of conversational exchange that has elements that are not fully formalizable. But it represents an ideal goal that formal models of persuasion dialogue can be built up to approximate.

6. Rigorous and Permissive Persuasion Dialogue

The basic problem with the foregoing abstract models of dialogue is that most of them require a certain logical rigour in order for the rules to precisely regulate the moves that can be made at each point in the dialogue and to determine who has won and lost. On the other hand, a certain permissiveness of the type characteristic of Hamblin's dialogues, or of the type allowing for dark-side commitments, introduces flexibility, but could be criticized as being 'fuzzy' or 'loose.' The ultimate solution to this dilemma is to distinguish between two different types of persuasion dialogue, and then to construct a mechanism that allows for an embedding of the one type of dialogue in the other. In Walton and Krabbe (1995), the open Hamblin type of system is called *permissive persuasion dialogue* or PPD. It is characterized by reasonably permissive rules that allow the participants a good deal of latitude in what they assert, concede, retract, or ask during the course of a persuasion dialogue. The respondent to a question or argument, for example, is not generally forced to commit himself directly or definitely to a particular proposition at that point in the dialogue. Winning or losing a PPD is not the most important thing, although whether or not one is successful in argumentation is something that can be measured in a PPD and is of some importance. Nevertheless, what is more important in a PPD are the commitment sets that define the position of the arguer as the dialogue proceeds and what happens with these commitment sets over the course of the dialogue as it affects the evolution of the position of an arguer when refined through persuasion.

In a PPD, there are three types of commitments. First, there is the set of assertions to which an arguer is positively committed and has a burden of proof to argue for or support, if requested to do so by the other party. Second, there is the set of (mere) concessions in an arguer's commitment set. An arguer is committed to concessions only in a weaker sense. These are propositions he accepts 'for the sake of argument,' but does not have a positive burden of proof to support or defend as propositions. Thus concessions represent a weaker kind of commitment than do assertions. The third type of commitment is that of the dark-side commitment. These represent commitments that an arguer (or her opponent) may not be fully aware of at any given point in the persuasion dialogue, but that may come to be revealed during the argumentation in the further course of the dialogue exchanges.

So we could say that a participant in PPD is not fully aware of his own dark-side commitments, or those of the other party, and it is the job of the other party to try to refine or clarify these commitments – that is, to get them on the other party's light side, and have them formulated as precise propositions which everyone can see this person is definitely committed to.

It is a consequence of the way the critical discussion and the persuasion types of dialogue are defined in section 4 above that a *rigorous persuasion dialogue* (RPD) is a formal model of the critical discussion as a type of dialogue, whereas PPD is a formal model of persuasion dialogue. The reason is that an RPD type of dialogue is centred exclusively on the resolution of the conflict of opinions that is the issue of the dialogue. The party who fails to defend his thesis after the prescribed sequence of moves loses the dialogue, while the other party wins. In contrast, PPD is maieutic in nature with respect to its goal, and is not exclusively centred on the resolution of the conflict of opinions that is the issue of the dialogue.

In a PPD exchange, the rules permit fairly complex and permissive moves. A person can make assertions, ask questions, put forward arguments, and so forth all at the same move, although there is a limit on the number of speech acts of the kind that are allowed that can be put forward at a given move. By contrast, in a *rigorous persuasion dialogue* (or RPD) type of persuasion dialogue, each move is simple and is very definitely determined by the rules. Participants can ask a single question or put forward a single argument, but they must do so only by doing one kind of thing at a time at any given move, like asking a question or putting forward an argument. Then, for example, once an argument is put forward, the rules sharply delimit how the opponent must respond to that argument by making a matching type of response or move as required by the rules. In an RPD, there is just one proposition or initial thesis at issue and the one party, the proponent, defends or upholds this thesis while the other party has the job of challenging or questioning it. In an RPD, there are no dark-side commitment stores, but only light-side commitment stores. And the opponent only has a set of concessions, but no assertions, while the proponent only has a set of assertions, but no concessions. RPD is therefore asymmetrical. The role of the opponent is quite different from that of the proponent, and RPD dialogue is highly adversarial and only cooperative in a very minimal sense. This contrasts with PPD persuasion dialogue, where the rules of the two players are generally more similar and where the adversarial element is less dominant.

Each of these types of dialogue has its advantages and its weaknesses. The RPD type of dialogue is very precise, and it is very clear which sequence of moves constitutes a winning or a losing of the dialogue. PPD, on the other hand, is much more flexible, and winning or losing is much less important. In PPD, the rules and also the kinds of moves allowed are much more complex, and the tolerance of dark-side commitments in PPDs gives this type of dialogue a less sharp and rigorous formulation than that of the RPD.

The basic technical problem studied in depth in Walton and Krabbe (1995) is how to embed the one type of dialogue in the other. What is required is to allow the participants in a PPD the possibility of shifting to an RPD, where such a shift would represent an improvement in order to sharpen and clarify matters at a particular point so that the PPD could be expedited and helped to a successful conclusion. In other words, the problem is to define the right circumstances in which it should be the right of one party to demand an RPD from the other party in order, for example, to sharpen the commitments of the other party or make them more explicit so that the PPD could carry on in a more productive fashion. By means of such an embedding, the results of the clarification of commitment achieved by the RPD could be carried back into the PPD and utilized in the subsequent PPD. Such a shift from a PPD to a RPD represents the idea in conversational argumentation that sometimes it is useful and necessary to shift to a more rigorous and legalistic type of dialogue where, for example, the exact meanings of terms are clarified and very concerted attempts are made to specify in a rigorous way exactly what a party is saying and what his commitments are. Of course, this makes the dialogue slower and more laboured even while it also permits the dialogue to be more rigorous and precise. So there can be advantages as well as disadvantages to such a shift from the one type of dialogue to the other. But at certain junctures of a PPD type of dialogue, because of its permissive nature, it may be useful to slow things down a bit in order to achieve a greater degree of precision and to focus more explicitly on things that otherwise might be considered quibbling, like agreeing on the precise meaning of a word or determining exactly what a dark-side commitment precisely amounts to as a specific proposition that can be put into a light-side commitment store.

Ultimately, then, this dual view of persuasion dialogue is the solution advocated in Walton and Krabbe (1995) to the general problem of commitment originally posed by Hamblin's modelling of it in an abstract structure of dialogue. The solution is that there is no one simple abstract structure of dialogue that models the concept of persuasion dialogue in everyday conversation as fully and adequately as we would like for the purposes of argumentation theory. Instead, it is advocated that we should use two basically different types of abstract models of persuasion dialogue, each of which has its assets and liabilities. The rigorous type of persuasion dialogue is easily mathematically modelled, and it is very clear which party wins and which party loses a given sequence of the dialogue. The model is simple and rigorous. On the other hand, the advantage of the PPD is that, by modelling dark-side commitments and by being permissive in nature, it is a much more practically useful approximation of the kind of argumentation that we wish to study in connection with fallacies and other phenomena relating to the normative evaluation of argumentation in everyday conversation. Although the RPD has definite rules, and it is definitely clear what counts as a move by an arguer at any particular sequence of the dialogue, there is a certain open and permissive quality to such a dialogue, and it is cooperative in the sense that it operates on the assumption that the participants sincerely and honestly attempt to contribute to the goals of the dialogue and can be challenged where this is in doubt. This reflects the Gricean concept of argumentation as a cooperative process based on expectations of politeness in dialogue.

We could say, then, that the PPD and the RPD represent two end points in a continuum of types of persuasion dialogue. At the one end, the RPD is rigorous and precise in that there is a definite winning strategy and losing strategy. In each round of dialogue, there is a definite winner and loser which can be determined from the rules and the sequence of moves in a particular dialogue. At the other end is the permissive type of persuasion dialogue, where there are also definite rules and winning and losing strategies, but where winning and losing is less important. Here there can be important side benefits of the dialogue which can, to some extent, outweigh winning and losing as a kind of value that a particular case or instance of the dialogue might have. The value here is to be determined by the explicitization of commitments in the dialogue on the part of both participants and on any onlookers who may have listened to or read the dialogue and taken some value from it. In such a case, what may be important is not whether a participant was forced to change his commitments so much as what effect the dialogue had on his changing his way of expressing those commitments in a more carefully qualified way.

7. Maieutic Function

The goal of a critical discussion is the resolution of the conflict of opinions that initiated the dialogue. The critical discussion is successful where the goal is achieved to the extent that the thesis upheld by one party is shown to be true and the thesis defended by the other party is shown either to be open to critical questioning or not to have been proven as true by the argumentation in the dialogue. However, an interesting thing about many instances of persuasion dialogue in everyday conversation is that there can be benefits from the dialogue for both the participants and the onlookers even when the conflict of opinion is not definitively resolved one way or the other. For example, in the case of the dialogue on tipping cited earlier, both the participants and the onlookers gain quite a bit of understanding on the issue even though the dispute is not definitively resolved. Both Bob's and Helen's arguments turn out to be relatively defensible, and neither party is definitely victorious in the sense that one party has definitely showed that her thesis is true and also that the other party has failed to prove that his thesis is true. Despite this failure to achieve a definite outcome of winning and losing, both participants end up with a deeper realization of the implications of their own point of view as well as that of their opponent. Their more sophisticated positions on the issue of tipping follow from their giving reasons to defend their own views and also from the trenchant criticisms of the argumentation from the other side.

Though the goal of resolving the conflict of opinions was not met in this example – since neither side conceded defeat, and it was not clear that one side had triumphed over the other in the sense of one point of view being clearly better defended than the other – nevertheless, it could be said that the underlying position and evidential roots of the commitments on both sides have been more fully revealed through the course of their interactive argumentation and that this was a strong benefit of the persuasion dialogue. In terms of the PPD model of dialogue, we could say that the dark-side commitments on both sides of the issue of tipping have been more clearly revealed and articulated as light-side commitments as the discussion evolved. In Plausible Argument (1992), I called this aspect the maieutic function of persuasion dialogue, which means that the dialogue fulfilled a function of bringing dark-side commitments of the participants to light[4] – that is, the propositions were transferred from dark-side commitment sets to light-side commitment sets during the course of the persuasion dialogue.

Although neither Helen nor Bob gave up their original positions or resolved the conflict, the commitments of each side became more clearly articulated into a logically reasoned position as the argumentation moves on each side were advanced and articulated through the course of the persuasion dialogue. So we could say that, as a critical discussion, or by the even higher and more rigorous standards of RPD, the discussion between Bob and Helen was a failure. Even so, as a permissive kind of persuasion dialogue in which maieutic insight is held to be an important side benefit – and, in some respects, more important than who actually won or lost – the dialogue between Bob and Helen was successful. It was successful in that it deepened and sharpened the participants' insight into the issue of tipping and thereby refined the arguments as logical reasoning on both sides. In this sense, one could conclude that the persuasion dialogue on tipping was successful and did achieve its goal. Generally, the lesson is that persuasion dialogue in many instances can be judged successful as a type of dialogue if it achieves a certain level of maieutic insight for the participants and onlookers even though the conflict of opinions in the original controversial issue was not definitely resolved one way or the other. The gain comes here through the articulation and surfacing of the dark-side commitments of both participants during the sequence of the persuasion dialogue.

But another lesson here is that there are different subtypes of persuasion dialogue, and how one judges a given case of persuasion dialogue – as successful or unsuccessful – will depend on how one classifies it as a particular subtype. Any persuasion dialogue will begin with a conflict of opinions where there will be a certain weight of presumption in favour of one side or the other. But how strongly the argumentation in the critical discussion has to shift the weight of presumption in one direction or the other in order for the dialogue to be declared a success is a matter of how one classifies the type of subdialogue the participants are supposed to be engaged in.

The critical discussion, as a type of dialogue, demands a fairly high standard of rationality. As van Eemeren and Grootendorst describe it, entering into the critical discussion requires agreements by the participants that they both adhere to the rules of the critical discussion (1984; 1992). In particular, both must agree to rules that determine when such a discussion is terminated, the conditions under which one side is declared victorious, and so forth. It is clear that this is a relatively structured type of discussion which demands careful preliminary stages of confrontation and agreement by both sides prior to entering into the argumentation stage of any actual discussion.

However, in many cases of persuasion dialogue in everyday conversation, things are less clearly defined and less explicitly regulated than this framework requires, and the agreements to enter into a certain type of persuasion dialogue may be much more Gricean or presumptive in nature. In such cases of persuasion dialogue, the rules are permissive in the sense that there are general presumptions about politeness that are not explicitly stated or agreed to by any of the participants, but that are nevertheless simply presumptions that we make as part of the background context or setting of the argument situation. In such cases, the persuasion dialogue is highly permissive and open-ended, and the given rules – beyond the requirements R.1 through R.4 – do not sharply determine exactly which moves are permitted or which strategies win or close off the argument.

Even though such rules are implicit and permissive, they can be clear enough in some cases so that we can definitely say that a particular argument is a fallacy or is a kind of move that is an obstruction or should not be permitted in a persuasion dialogue at this particular juncture in the dialogue, in that it would be an obstruction to further constructive dialogue taking place unless the problem is clarified or ironed out between the two participants. So in cases like this, a PPD, despite its permissive aspect, does provide enough of a normative structure to give bite to a criticism that a participant has made a bad or wrong or inappropriate move which might be identified with one of the traditional fallacies, for example.

However, we can see that there are different subtypes of persuasion dialogue. Also, in some cases, there can be a shift or embedding from one type of dialogue to another. In particular, what we should be most aware of is that there is a possibility of shifting from a permissive type of persuasion dialogue to a more rigorous type of persuasion dialogue where the parties are forced to agree in a much more explicit and exact way on precisely what arguments they are putting forth, what questions they are asking, what their commitments are, and so forth. These complications are analysed in fuller detail in chapter 8.

8. The Problem of Enthymemes

One of the most basic problems of evaluating argumentation in everyday conversation is the problem of enthymemes. An *enthymeme*, as defined in the traditional logic manuals, is an argument that has a premise that is tacitly assumed, that is not explicitly stated in an argument. The traditional example is the argument, 'All men are mortal, therefore Socrates is mortal.' Here the implicit premise is that Socrates is a man, which is presumed to be part of the argument even though it is not explicitly stated as a proposition.

In this particular case, the argument as presented is deductively invalid; if we add the missing premise – Socrates is a man – it becomes deductively valid. Moreover, it is an item of general knowledge that Socrates is, in fact, a man, and so we would normally expect respondents or audiences of the argument to know and accept this and perhaps to plug it in as a premise that is also an assumption being made and advocated by the person who is advancing the argument.

In many cases, unlike in this one, it is relatively unclear whether a particular proposition is meant to definitely be a premise in the argument or not. Hence, this question of enthymemes is very much a practical problem for the analysis of argumentation in a text of discourse in the examples that are typically analysed and evaluated in logic classes. Van Eemeren and Grootendorst (1984) call this the problem of nonexplicit premises, a very good term for this type of phenomenon. Traditional logic textbooks have always found it difficult to deal with this problem because there appears to be no simple, straightforward, or successful way within deductive logic itself to solve the problem.

Some traditional textbooks recommend simply putting in any proposition that is needed to make the argument deductively valid. This is not a solution that works generally, for several reasons. First, many arguments are not meant to be deductively valid; they are inductive arguments, or perhaps presumptive kinds of arguments that were not originally meant to be deductively valid. In other cases, it may be unclear whether the person who advanced the argument really intended this particular premise to be part of his argument. In still other cases, there may be more than one proposition that could be plugged in to make the argument deductively valid. It may not be clear which proposition is the best candidate or which one matches the intentions of the arguer. The general danger here is the so-called enthymematic ploy of making every argument into a valid argument whether or not it was meant to be or should be.

In 'Enthymemes' (1983), I proposed that the problem of enthymemes could be solved by using the persuasion-dialogue structure CBV and the concept of dark-side commitment sets. This solution to the problem of nonexplicit premises involves modelling an argument in a text of discourse as an instance of permissive-persuasion dialogue where both parties have dark-side as well as light-side commitments which have emerged through the course of the persuasion dialogue. Judging whether a proposition is a nonexplicit premise of an argument is achieved by analysing the type of move the arguer has made, and then analysing, in light of the normative model of dialogue, just what propositions that argument has committed the arguer to at that move. In particular, such an evaluation of commitments as being appropriate as premises for a given argument will be determined by virtue of the rules for dark-side commitments in the persuasion dialogue. Here, a proposition could be inserted into an argument as an implicit premise if it is a dark-side commitment of the arguer, as judged by the argument he has put forward at that particular juncture of the persuasion dialogue, and in light of his previous commitments known to the other party. According to this solution to the problem of nonexplicit premises, a nonexplicit premise is judged and determined in a particular case not just by the abstract structure of the argument as deductively valid, or as corresponding to some other propositional structure of argument, but in terms of the arguer's commitment at that point in a context of persuasion dialogue with another party. According to this solution, then, the problem of determining what a participant's argument can correctly be said to be in a particular case in a text of discourse depends on the commitments of that arguer, as can be determined from both the given text of discourse and also its context, that is, in this case, reconstructing it using the normative model of persuasion dialogue.

To apply the concept of enthymeme to everyday cases of argumentation involves a number of subtleties. In understanding nonexplicit premises, it is in many instances necessary to understand that an arguer is directing his argument to a kind of standardized profile of the commitment set and the presumed level of knowledge of an audience or target group of respondents with shared knowledge, commitments, and expectations. To help explicate this aspect of enthymemes, Tindale introduces the concept of a *cognitive environment*, defined as 'a set of facts and assumptions which an individual, or in the case of shared cognitive environments, a number of individuals, is capable of mentally representing and accepting as true (although they may be mistaken in doing so)' (1992, p. 182). This refers to the tendency of a speaker to presume a certain cognitive level in an audience when addressing an argument designed to persuade or alter the commitments of that audience.

The solution for the problem of enthymemes in my earlier work ('Enthymemes,' 1983) now has to be modified in light of the new treatment of persuasion dialogue in Walton and Krabbe (1995). With the new treatment of enthymemes, one would have to consider not only the dark-side commitments of the arguer, but also how those commitments could be clarified in embedding the PPD into a more sharply formulated and rigorous type of RPD where the participant is forced to articulate the propositions that are his precise commitments in a more exact and rigorous manner. According to this solution, then, determining enthymemes in particular cases would be a kind of conditional judgment depending upon a subsequent embedding of a PPD into an RPD at some future point in a possible conversation between the two participants. This solution allows for the possibility that, in many cases, enthymemes are arguments where the missing premise cannot be definitely determined in a univocal way other than by making a conditional analysis dependent upon future sharpening of a participant's commitments in a subsequent sequence of dialogue. This solution has the disadvantage of a certain permissiveness, yet it does have the advantage of flexibility in fitting the kind of situation that is so common in everyday conversation, where the evidence for filling in enthymemes may be there but may not be totally conclusive. Even so, evidence of a contextual sort may be available in such cases and can be brought forward and evaluated by a critic of the argumentation.

9. Relevance in Persuasion Dialogue

One important factor in the picture of evidence for filling in an enthymeme is the relevance of the proposition being considered as a nonexplicit premise. To say that a premise is relevant in an argument for this purpose is to say that the premise could be used to fulfil a function of arguing for or proving the conclusion of the argument in the context of dialogue in which the argument is situated. The requirement that expresses this idea of probative relevance in persuasion dialogue is R.3, which requires that a chain of argumentation used in a persuasion dialogue must have the proponent's thesis as its ultimate conclusion. Thus any line of argument that veers away from this goal is a distraction or a red herring. And any argument that has an ultimate conclusion other than the one that is supposed to be proved (the proponent's thesis) commits the fallacy of irrelevant conclusion (*ignoratio elenchi*).

While all of R.1 through R.4 help to define the probative dialectical relevance of argumentation of the kind appropriate for arguments in a persuasion dialogue, R.3 is very central to expressing the core idea of dialectical relevance.

The conflict of opinions that poses the initial situation of a persuasion dialogue is the baseline for defining which moves in the dialogue are judged to be dialectically relevant or irrelevant. *Dialectical relevance*, according to the analysis given in chapter 1, means the relevance of an argument (or some component of an argument) in a context where the argument is being used to contribute to a goal of dialogue. According to the cooperative principle of Grice, participants in a conversation are asked: 'Make your conversational contribution such as is required, at the stage at which it occurs, by the accepted purpose or direction of the talk exchange in which you are engaged' (1975, p. 67). Thus, an argument used in a persuasion dialogue is dialectically relevant to the extent that it contributes, at the stage where it was used in the dialogue, to contribute to the goal of the dialogue.

Relevance in a persuasion dialogue is, for the most part, a contextual matter of how an argument is used in context to contribute to the goal of the persuasion dialogue. But it is also partly a local matter in a dialogue because it depends, first of all, on the type of move being made, such as a question, an assertion, an argument, or a request for clarification. It also depends on the previous move in the dialogue and its relationship to the move in question. But beyond this, the localized sequence of moves – represented by a profile of dialogue – derives its relevance from the purpose of the dialogue as a whole.

According to R.1, arguments used by a proponent in a persuasion dialogue to prove a particular proposition – the proponent's thesis – must be based on premises that are commitments of the respondent. Hence, this function of proving, the so-called probative function, represents a kind of relevance that is central to persuasion dialogue. A proposition is *probatively relevant* to another proposition only if it can be used to prove or cast doubt on this other proposition, according to the methods (argumentation schemes) of proving or casting doubt appropriate for a type of dialogue.

Propositions can also be topically relevant to each other without being probatively relevant. For example, the proposition, 'The book is red,' is topically relevant to the proposition, 'The sky was red at sunset on that terrible day,' even though the one proposition may not be probatively relevant to the other. To say that a proposition *A* is *topically relevant* to a proposition *B* in the sense of Epstein (1979; 1990) means that *A* and *B* share some common subject-matter overlap. In this case, both propositions contain the subject matter 'red.' (See also Walton, 1982). But as Berg has shown, topical relevance is a semantic matter that is not sufficiently sensitive to the objectives of speakers and hearers in a conversation to be able to encompass (by itself) the broad notion of relevance in a persuasion dialogue – the kind that is useful in evaluating fallacies of irrelevance (1991, 414–17). As Berg puts it, we need semantic relevance coupled with pragmatic relevance to achieve this goal of practical evaluation of arguments (p. 422).

Dascal (1977) agrees that a concept of conversational relevance is needed to account for the complex kinds of cases of judgments of irrelevance that Grice (1975) studied, where a speaker and a hearer collaborate in argument in a goal-directed conversation.

Dialectical probative relevance of an argument in a persuasion dialogue is determined by the probative function of that argument, as used at a particular move in a stage of the persuasion dialogue, in relation to the global burden of proof of the proponent of the argument.

There is another very important aspect of relevance in a persuasion dialogue. An argument is judged rightly to be relevant if it has a function in persuading the respondent – that is, in leading the respondent to alter his commitment by accepting a new commitment that he didn't accept before – by means of premises that are accepted as commitments by that respondent (in the prior dialogue). This aspect is comparable to what Blair (1992) calls *premissary relevance*, which is defined as the kind of case where a proponent presents a 'well-ordered argument' to a respondent for a proposition C, called the conclusion, and (1) C belongs to a constellation of propositions asserted by the proponent, which she (the proponent) accepts and believes to support C, and (2) which the proponent believes the respondent will accept and will believe to support C, and (3) the proponent 'does this as an attempt to convince' the respondent of the acceptability of C, and (4) the constellations of propositions asserted by the proponent do lend support to the acceptability of C (p. 205). In short, premissary relevance highlights the use of a premise that is a commitment of the respondent as part of the argument used to persuade the respondent, as required by R.1 through R.4.

Ralph Johnson expresses the concept of persuasion in terms of beliefs and changes of beliefs. This is quite different from the view of persuasion dialogue advocated above, where persuasion is defined in terms of commitment. Despite this difference, however, Blair's notion of premissary relevance does focus on what is primarily important about relevance in arguments in persuasion dialogue. A relevant argument is one that is probatively useful in persuading a respondent precisely because it is based on premises that are commitments of that respondent in a dialogue, as required by R.1.

10. Evaluating Criticisms of Irrelevance

Judging whether a question, proposition, argument, or other type of move is relevant in a persuasion dialogue depends on seven factors: (1) what type of dialogue the participants are supposed to be engaged in; (2) what the issue of the dialogue is in the given case; (3) what stage of the dialogue the move is in; (4) what the previous move was; (5) in the case of an argument or a reply to an argument, what the argumentation scheme is supposed to be; (6) what implicit premises are involved; and (7) what propositions the other party is committed to at that stage of the dialogue. People sometimes dispute whether an argument is relevant or not. In some cases, arguers even fallaciously or unjustifiably accuse opponents of committing fallacies of irrelevance. When such disputes arise in the context of a persuasion dialogue, the evidence to evaluate the claims on both sides is to be sought in the seven factors cited above, as revealed by the text and context of discourse in the given case.

To determine whether something is relevant in a given case, one first has to ask whether the dialogue is supposed to be of the persuasion-dialogue type and, if so, what the issue of the discussion is supposed to be. If the dialogue is supposed to be on the issue of tipping, then, generally speaking, whether something is relevant will depend on how it is linked up by an intervening chain of argumentation to one side or the other of this disputed issue.

Practically speaking, however, it may be a problem to determine whether a remark or argument is relevant if it was made at the early stages of a discussion, where the main arguments on both sides have not been brought forward yet. An argument may not appear to be relevant yet, at such an early stage, but later, when many more lines of argument have been explored, it may indeed link up with other matters that are relevant in the dispute. So at such an early stage, one party (the proponent) may say, 'I don't see how that remark is relevant to the issue,' and then the other (the respondent) may reply, 'If you give me a little time to develop my argument, I think I can show later how it will be relevant.' Here, the one party is asking the other to make a presumption of relevance as a collaborative move to contribute to the development of the discussion that will take place. How can the respondent (or anyone else) judge whether the proponent's argument is relevant? What the respondent must do is extrapolate the proponent's line of argument forward to see whether it is useful in contributing to the dialogue as it moves towards its goal.

If there is uncertainty, or a dispute about whether something is relevant at such an early stage of a dialogue, one side should not necessarily accuse the other side of committing a fallacy of irrelevance. Instead, a participant or critic should grant the other party some leeway, and ask that other party to give some indication of his future line of argument on the issue. Then everyone can get some idea how this present line of argument might fit into later developments that can be anticipated.

The general method for deciding relevance in such a case, then is one of extrapolating a line of argument forwards by conjecturing, or sketching out in general terms, the future line of argumentation that can be anticipated. Thus, raising the question of relevance in this kind of case is not so much an accusation of fallacy as it is a request for guidance on anticipated lines of argumentation.

The problem posed by so many cases of fallacies of irrelevance, of the kind cited in the textbooks (see chapter 1) is that there is a concealed, deceptive shift from a persuasion dialogue to some other type of dialogue. The problem is that a move or argument may be genuinely relevant in the context of this other type of dialogue. To all appearances, in the discourse in the given case, it may seem somehow to be relevant, even if it is irrelevant in the persuasion dialogue. This factor of shifting from one type of dialogue to another, which may give an argument a superficially persuasive but false and misleading impression of relevance, is taken up in chapter 8.

An important aspect of relevance highlighted by the kinds of cases studied by Grice (1975) is that one speaker must make presumptions about what the other speaker is likely to know or is likely to recognize as an *implicature* – a suggested conclusion that is drawn by inference by a hearer, based on the speaker's and hearer's common knowledge and expectations in familiar situations. For example, in a letter of reference on behalf of a candidate for a job, if the referee omits saying anything highly positive about important skills, but mentions only minor skills in a positive way, the hearer will take this as a condemnation of the job applicant. What is not said leads the hearer to draw a conclusion by implicature.

To account for evaluating relevance in this type of case, Dascal suggests using *heuristics* – a set of rules that would help a hearer to guess, rather than to deduce, implicatures (1977, p. 323). But Dascal stresses that he means 'guessing' in an 'educated' or 'systematic' way, rather than haphazardly (p. 323). Such rules, according to Dascal, should suggest to a hearer what kind of contextual features to focus on, instead of having to comb through the whole context of a dialogue exchange.

In our analysis, at least part of the function of such a set of heuristic indicators is filled by the dark-side commitment stores of the participants in a dialogue. The problem here is one of detecting subtle aspects of a conversation like irony or innuendo, where a reply appears to be irrelevant (at least on the surface), but has a deeper meaning or message by implicature. It is clear that, to cover such cases, the concept of relevance has to include the speakers' educated guesses about the commitments of the other, and must include normal expectations both of them share about 'common knowledge' as well as should social expectations. Also, relevance must encompass both speakers' presumptions that they understand the significance of each other's moves in the conversation and know how to reply appropriately. Given all these assumptions about what relevance includes, one speaker can then draw appropriate implicatures if the other replies in a way that appears to be irrelevant – the reply may not be irrelevant at all (under the surface), but may be an intentional signal to draw a particular conclusion by innuendo or implicature.

To capture these subtler aspects of conversational implicature, the concept of relevance in a persuasion dialogue must be pragmatically rich. It must be sensitive to a speaker's knowledge and commitments (both dark and light) at a given move and to that speaker's educated guesses about the knowledge and commitments of the respondent. To be truly conversational relevance, however, all of this information must be embedded in an understanding of how the move is situated in a global context of a persuasion dialogue.

There is an inferential element in judgments of relevance, the kind indicated in traditional formalistic relevance logics based on deductive models, like propositional calculus. But this inferential element is only one small part of the dialectical mechanism used to evaluate relevance of arguments or other moves made in a dialogue exchange. The steps of inference must be linked together in a dynamic forward chaining of argumentation towards a conversational goal.

3

The Inquiry

In a critical discussion, arguments go back and forth between the two sides. Since these are opposed arguments, the argumentation in a critical discussion is markedly adversarial in nature. The inquiry is a highly collaborative framework of argumentation, where a group of people get together to collect and organize all the relevant evidence on some particular proposition, both for and against. Then they assemble and organize this evidence, drawing out conclusions in an orderly fashion so that each conclusion can be definitely proved. The idea is to build a solid foundation as the inquiry proceeds so that in the end the proposition at issue can be definitely proved. Or if the evidence is insufficient to prove it, then that outcome can definitely be shown.

In this chapter we will see how the formal model of intuitionistic (constructive) logic developed by Kripke (1965) can be used to model the sequence of argumentation in an inquiry. Intuitionistic logic grew from a way of representing the kind of argumentation used in mathematical reasoning developed by L.J. Brouwer (1881–1966), which led to the construction of a logical calculus by A. Heyting in 1930 (the axioms of which are given in Kneale and Kneale [1962, p. 678]). A notable feature of intuitionistic logic is the absence of a principle that is true in classical logic, namely, the principle that either a proposition is true or its negation is true. Intuitionistic logic is concerned not with reasoning based on truth or falsity, but with reasoning based on warranted assertability (provability) of propositions. But according to the intuitionistic view, what is warranted as assertable at any given time depends on the information we have at that time. Because we sometimes lack enough information to know whether either a proposition or its negation is warranted as assertable, the principle of classical logic mentioned above fails in intuitionistic logic.

1. Main Characteristics

The goal of the inquiry is to prove that a particular proposition is true or false, or that there is insufficient evidence to prove that this proposition is either true or false. The method of the inquiry is to draw conclusions only from premises that can definitely be established as true or false so that there will be no need to go back and retract these premises and then establish a new line of reasoning based on different premises.

In this key respect concerning retraction of commitment, there is a very sharp and definite contrast between the inquiry and persuasion dialogue as normative models of argumentation. The persuasion dialogue has to be fairly liberal in allowing for retractions. It does not allow for retractions in all circumstances, but generally there is a presumption that retraction should be allowed except in certain situations. By contrast, in the inquiry, the whole intent is to minimize or even eliminate the possibility of retraction of commitments as the dialogue proceeds. The method of the inquiry is to only accept as conclusions propositions that are firmly established so that the inquiry can go ahead in one direction without continually having to loop back because the participants have changed their minds about some proposition that earlier was a part of the line of argumentation and advance in the inquiry. The key here is the idea that an inquiry is always supposed to be a kind of advancing process of argumentation where the beginnings are firmly established.

The most important defining characteristic of the inquiry as a type of dialogue is the property of cumulativeness. The inquiry is said to be cumulative in the sense that once a particular proposition is verified as true or inferred as true at any particular point in the inquiry, then that proposition must remain true at every succeeding point as the inquiry progresses. Cumulativeness in an inquiry means that the participants can't change their minds. Once they have derived a proposition as a conclusion of an argument, they can't retract it at some future point in the inquiry. Once established, it remains true or verified as a proposition that they are committed to in the inquiry.

It is important to emphasize that cumulativeness is a property of the goal of the inquiry as an ideal model of argumentation. This does not mean that retraction of commitments never happens in argumentation in an inquiry. It only means that the goal of the inquiry as a type of dialogue is to minimize or, if possible, eliminate retractions. What this means is that, in the context of an inquiry, retraction of commitment is regarded as a very serious step.

As clarified below, not all scientific argumentation is well modelled by the inquiry framework, and it is controversial whether scientific research conforms to the inquiry model of argumentation. However, in some cases, the kind of argumentation used in collaborative scientific research in a domain of expert knowledge – at the stages where results of a research investigation are gathered together and conclusions are drawn, and the findings are published by the researcher (or group of researchers) – does have the characteristics of argumentation used in an inquiry. When a researcher publishes her scientific findings in a field like physics, medicine, or astronomy, she is supposed to have proved the results very carefully, using the methods established in that field of science, to a high standard of burden of proof so that retraction of the propositions proved will not later be necessary. Of course, retraction will be necessary in some cases because scientific hypotheses are supposed to be falsifiable. But the assumption is that retraction will not be necessary.

A case in point is that of the astronomer, Andrew Lyne, who thought he had discovered a new planet. He observed a pattern of periodically blinking stars, and reached the conclusion that this observation could only be explained by the gravitational pull of a planet. After this claim had been accepted by the field of astronomy, Lyne re-examined the data and found that he had been fooled by two small measurement errors; he now had to retract his earlier conclusion that the pulsing he had observed was caused by a new planet.

Collins relates the impact of Lyne's retraction before an audience of astronomers:

In the *New Scientist*, fellow astronomer Ken Croswell describes the impact of the retraction before the packed audience as follows: 'There was a gasp from the audience. I was stunned, and saddened. My sympathy for him only increased as he explained how two minute errors had conspired to create the apparent periodicity ... I suspect every astronomer in the auditorium was thinking as I was: a similar mistake, equally trivial, could someday trip me up, and for a moment I felt the terror that must have gripped Lyne a week before the conference ... By the end of his talk, Lyne appeared shaken.' (1992, p. 16)

At the end of Lyne's talk, the audience burst into applause, presumably because his act of retraction before this audience 'required enormous grace and courage.'

Hence, even in the scientific presentation of results, where the context may be presumed to be that of an inquiry, retractions do happen. But where they do occur, they are regarded as very serious events, and are greeted with dismay and even trepidation by a scientist who has taken the step of publishing results of research.

2. Advancing States of Knowledge

The inquiry as a normative framework for argumentation can be thought of as a sequence of points where the points represent the advancing states of knowledge as more evidence is gained. We can construct an abstract theoretical model of the inquiry by thinking of the points as being joined by directed lines or arrows. Then the structure of the argumentation in the inquiry has the form of a tree or branching sequence of points going in one direction only.[1]

Kripke (1965) presented a semantic structure of intuitionistic logic that can be used to model the sequence of argumentation in an inquiry. The model is that of a tree structure, where the nodes of the tree H_i represent evidential situations at a given time, in which some facts are known but more facts may come to be known later. Propositions, A, B, C, ... , are said to be 'verified,' or known to be true, in a given evidential situation. If a proposition A is verified at a particular point of time H_1 in an inquiry, then A is written above the node H_1 in the tree diagram. Otherwise A is not written above H_1, which means that A has not yet been verified at the point represented by the evidential situation H_1.

The Kripke model of intuitionistic logic as representing the sequence of argumentation of the kind characteristically found in the inquiry can be represented by the example in Figure 3.1.

In the sequence of argumentation in an inquiry represented by Figure 3.1, the proposition A is verified, or proved to be true, at point G. However the proposition B is not verified at G. The inquiry could remain 'stuck' at G, without any new propositions being verified, or it could advance to the state H_1, where both A and C are verified. Or, alternatively, another possibility is that the inquiry could advance to point H_2, where B is verified as well as A. Then the inquiry could remain stuck at H_2, say, and no further progress might be made in verifying any new propositions. Or it could proceed to one of the new evidential situations H_3 or H_4. At H_4, C is verified, in addition to A and B. At H_3, no new propositions have been verified, but, still, H_3 is a different evidential situation from H_2. For at H_2, the possibility of verifying C remains open. But at H_3 enough knowledge has been acquired to exclude ever verifying C as true.

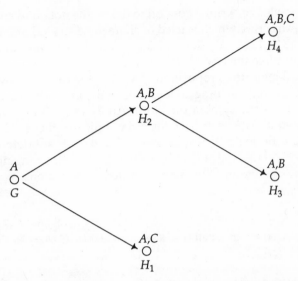

Figure 3.1 Example of Argumentation in a Kripke Model

Cumulativeness can be defined if we map the set of propositions in the argument onto the set of points or nodes in the tree that represents the sequence of the inquiry as it goes on. Then cumulativeness can be defined as a property in such a tree structure as follows: once a proposition is true and appears at a particular point in the tree, then that proposition will reappear and remain true at every succeeding point in the tree; that is, as we go from any particular node to the higher branches of the tree, once a particular proposition appears at that initial node, then it will appear at every succeeding node of the tree along the branches that are joined to that node as we go upwards from that node.[2]

The idea is that, once a proposition appears as true or verified at a particular node in the tree, then that proposition never disappears from, or is never erased, at any of the succeeding nodes in the tree: it always stays there and remains true as the inquiry goes on and on, branching through further moves. Woods and Walton (1978) give a logical definition of cumulativeness defined in terms of the Kripke model of intuitionistic logic. The model Kripke uses is that of a tree where a particular point G is always the origin or unique bottom node – the root of the tree – and there are a series of other nodes that are reached from the root by going along ascending branches of the tree, as illustrated by the example in Figure 3.1. Using this tree structure as a model of advancing states of knowledge, Kripke goes on to define the notion of an intuition-istic model structure which is used to characterize a kind of logic known as intuitionistic logic, a system of logic that lacks certain principles of classical logic, like the law of excluded middle.

In classical logic, the proposition 'A v $\rceil A$' is logically true (where 'v' is the symbol for 'or,' meaning 'at least one of the propositions joined by v is true,' and $\rceil$ is the symbol for 'not'). An example is the proposition, 'Socrates died in Athens or Socrates did not die in Athens.' However, in the intuitionistic logic of Kripke the 'or' and 'not' are defined by the following two clauses, using a binary function $\varnothing$ (P,H) ranging over the set of propositions and the set of evidential situations, respectively (1965, p. 94).

(*Def.* v): $\varnothing (A \text{ v } B, H) = T$ iff $\varnothing (A, H) = T$ or $\varnothing (B, H) = T$; otherwise $\varnothing (A \text{ v } B) = F.$
(*Def.*$\rceil$): $\varnothing (\rceil A, H) = T$ iff for all $H' \in K$ such that HRH', $\varnothing (A, H') = F$; otherwise $\varnothing (\rceil A, H) = T.$

The definition of 'or' given by (Def. v) is similar to that of classical logic, but the definition of 'not' is specially characteristic of intuitionistic logic. It says that $\rceil A$ is true at a point H_i if and only if A has the value T at no point accessible to H_i. In other words, $\rceil A$ is verified at a point H_i if and only if A fails to be verified at any point in the tree that can be reached from H_i (including H_i itself). So in intuitionistic logic, the expression '$\rceil A$' is read as meaning the stronger negation 'A is proved to be not true' as opposed to the weaker negation 'A is not proved to be true.' Hence, in the intuitionistic logic, the expression 'A v $\rceil A$' is read as 'A is verified or the opposite of A is verified,' which fails to be generally true. For exam-ple, if A is either verified or not verified, then the principle of excluded middle fails. It is characteristic of reasoning in this intuitionistic logic that it has the cumulative property as shown in Woods and Walton (1978, section 5). It is also shown here that Hamblin's basic type of dia-logue structure is not cumulative in this sense. It is easy to see that per-suasion dialogue as we have characterized it in chapter 2 is generally not cumulative in this sense.

One of the most interesting properties of the Kripke cumulative struc-ture of intuitionistic reasoning (see Woods and Walton, 1978, section 7) is that circular reasoning is banned – that is, the reasoning in the struc-ture of an inquiry always proceeds in a linear or branching fashion in one direction so that it is never allowed to circle back to the same point, so to speak. An example of this sort of sequence of argumentation is rep-

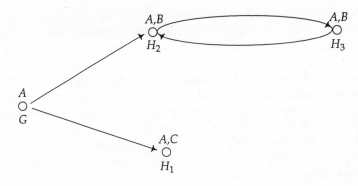

Figure 3.2 Circular Reasoning Excluded in an Inquiry

resented in Figure 3.2. Here the argument moves ahead from the evidential situation of H_2 to that of H_3. But then the sequence of argumentation
moves back from H_3 to H_2, closing a circle between these two points. It is
exactly this sort of circular argumentation pattern that is ruled out by
the tree structure of the reasoning used in a Kripke model.

We can never have circular reasoning, in the sense that an argument
proceeds from a set of premises to a conclusion and then loops back-
ward using that conclusion as a premise to argue back to one of the
initial premises again. This type of circular reasoning is always, by its
nature, inherently excluded from the inquiry. And, indeed, we could say
that circularity is the very thing that the inquiry is specifically designed
to try to exclude. The whole intent of the inquiry is to always move forward to minimize or eliminate the possibility of having to loop back to
the early points. The idea is that, once initial premises are established,
they can be left alone and we don't have to go back to retract them or
otherwise deal with them again as the inquiry progresses.

This is a somewhat oversimplified account of the technical question of
how circular reasoning is modelled in a Kripke intuitionistic structure;
in fact, there are different ways we could model circular reasoning in
such a structure (see Walton, 1991, pp. 315–24). Subsequent research by
Barth and Krabbe (1982) shows how the Kripke model of the intuitionistic logic could be expressed in a dialogue format. But the most general
point about the property of cumulative argumentation in the inquiry
has been made: the inquiry as a type of dialogue is very much against
the possibility of allowing any kind of circular reasoning that might

loop back from a conclusion to earlier premises once these premises have been established in a line of inquiry. The general intent of the argumentation used in an inquiry is to move forward in a linear or branching fashion so that knowledge can accumulate and move forward. In this context of dialogue, any kind of circular argumentation dramatically stands out as fallacious. It would be a kind of reasoning that would be inimical to this type of dialogue as a model of reasoned argumentation. The situation is quite different in persuasion dialogue, where circular reasoning is sometimes fallacious but is not generally so inconsistent with the aims of the dialogue as it is in the inquiry, and thus can be more easily tolerated or dealt with.

3. Aristotelian Demonstration

The reader will by now have noticed a basis for comparison between the inquiry as a framework of argumentation and one of the four types of argument classified by Aristotle in *On Sophistical Refutations* (see chapter 1). The inquiry is very similar to what Aristotle defined as 'the demonstration' (*apodeixos*) in the first book of *Posterior Analytics*. According to Aristotle, in a demonstration the premises must be primary and indemonstrable so that these premises themselves do not require demonstration in order to be known (71b26). He went on to add that the premises must be the causes, that is, the grounds or reasons of the conclusion and better known than the conclusion and prior to it (71b29). He even explicitly noted that circular argumentation is excluded from a demonstration: 'Now demonstration must be based on premises prior to and better known than the conclusion; and the same things cannot simultaneously be both prior and posterior to one another: so circular demonstration is clearly not possible in the unqualified sense of "demonstration" (72b25). Aristotle further added some qualifications of this technical point, but generally it is clear from what he wrote that there is a strong antipathy between the concept of a demonstration as a type of argumentation and the possibility of circular reasoning in that type of argumentation. In this sense, Aristotle's demonstration is very similar to the notion of an inquiry and could be seen as a species of inquiry.

In *Posterior Analytics*, Aristotle wrote: 'By demonstration I mean a syllogism which produces scientific knowledge' as a conclusion, based on premises that are 'true, primary, immediate, better known than, prior to, and causative of the conclusion' (71b18–71b22). Syllogistic reasoning is possible without these requirements (71b24), as in dialectical reasoning, but such syllogistic reasoning would not be a demonstration, because 'the result will not be knowledge' (71b25). As Irwin explains, Aristotelian demonstration is ultimately based on first principles (axioms) that cannot themselves be proven by demonstration, and then the sequence of demonstrative argument proceeds from these naturally prior propositions to prove posterior propositions based on them (1988, p. 123). According to Aristotle in *Posterior Analytics*, trying to prove first principles by demonstrating them would be a kind of circular reasoning (72b26–72b35). And since circular reasoning is not, for Aristotle, a proper kind of demonstration of a conclusion, it follows that the first principles cannot be proved by demonstration.

According to Irwin, there are two kinds of priority in an Aristotelian demonstration: natural priority and epistemic priority (1988, p. 124). Aristotle is a realist in that he thinks that first principles are prior and better known by nature 'in so far as they mention the things that are prior and better known' (Irwin, 1988, p. 123). But they are also epistemically prior in the following sense defined by Irwin (1988, p. 124), who cites *Posterior Analytics* (71b31–71b33): to say that A is epistemically prior to B means that we can know A without knowing B, but that we cannot know B without knowing A. This idea of an argument having a forward direction based on the premises being prior to the conclusion is also characteristic of the inquiry.

In the demonstration as a type of inquiry, the argumentation always moves forward from premises that are better established than the conclusion.[3] The idea is that, in such a sequence of argumentation, one never has to loop back to the prior points so that the line of argumentation is progressive, and that subsequent conclusions can be established on the basis of premises that are verified in a solid way so that they don't need to be subsequently questioned or doubted within the inquiry or demonstration itself.

Another very important property of the inquiry as a type of argumentation, which also applies to the comparable notion of the Aristotelian demonstration, is that of *evidential priority*, which means that the premises are better established as evidence than the conclusion they are being used to prove. In any step of argument in an inquiry, the premises are supposed to be evidentially prior to the conclusion because the intent is to base the conclusion on the premises, to boost the verifiability of the conclusion. The idea is that, if something is a conclusion, it is supposed to be doubtful or problematic – lacking in support from a point of view internal to the inquiry – so that the premises, once established, can be used to remove this doubt or to build up the grounding or evidence behind the conclusion to give it greater support.

In section 2 of this chapter, we saw how the Kripke model of intuitionistic logic excludes circular argumentation from the sequence of argumentation. It is (by this means) provable that the inquiry context of argument characterized by evidential priority is a normative model of dialogue where circular argumentation is excluded from counting as an appropriate way to prove a conclusion. Defined in a Kripke tree structure of advancing evidential situations, the notion of evidential priority as a requirement for argumentation in the inquiry context of dialogue gives the argument a particular direction going from premises to conclusions that excludes circular argumentation, that is, arguments going from a conclusion back to a premise.

4. Is Scientific Argumentation an Inquiry?

It is an interesting and much disputed question in the philosophy of science whether the inquiry is an appropriate model for scientific reasoning. Aristotle makes it clear in the first few pages of *Posterior Analytics* that, for him, the demonstration was the best model for scientific reasoning.[4] Another well-known exponent of the inquiry as the best model for scientific and also philosophical reasoning was Descartes.[5] In recent times, philosophers of science have intensely debated whether the so-called foundationalist view of science, representing the inquiry as the best model of scientific reasoning, does give a good account of how scientists actually arrive at conclusions and settle disputes among themselves.

The current view in this debate seems to favour the notion that the inquiry is not a good model of scientific reasoning, or at least not one that is very realistic in approximating how scientists actually reason in the various stages of scientific argumentation on hypotheses. In sociological studies of how scientists conduct argumentation and resolve their disputes, the type of dialogue they use seems much more like a persuasion dialogue than an inquiry. Recent sociological studies of science have pointed out how often scientific results have to be withdrawn or corrected and, in some cases even retracted, because of fraud and deception (Broad and Wade, 1982). Thus the more popular view now seems to be that scientific argumentation is more like a persuasion dialogue in which there are conflicts of opinion and different points of view among the scientists, who try to promote their arguments and refute those of their opponents.

Early on, Collingwood expressed just such a view about the progress of science:

My first lesson in what I now regard as my own subject, the history of thought, was the discovery, in a friend's house a few miles away, of a battered seventeenth-century book, wanting cover and title-page, and full of strange doctrines about meteorology and geology and planetary motions. It must have been a compendium of Descartes' *Principia*, to judge by what I recall of its statements about vortices; I was about nine when I found it, and already knew enough about the corresponding modern theories to appreciate the contrast which it offered. It let me into the secret which modern books had been keeping from me, that the natural sciences have a history of their own, and that the doctrines they teach on any given subject, at any given time, have been reached not by some discoverer penetrating to the truth after ages of error, but by the gradual modification of doctrines previously held; and will at some future date, unless thinking stops, be themselves no less modified. I will not say that all this became clear to me at that childish age; but at least I became aware from reading this old book that science is less like a hoard of truths, ascertained piecemeal, than an organism which in the course of its history undergoes more or less continuous alteration in every part. (1939, pp. 1–2)

It is easy to be sympathetic to Collingwood's view that the progress of science is not like that of an inquiry, but more like a sequence of questioning, rejecting, and refining prior views and theories. However, my purpose here is not to advocate that the progress of science is (empirically) or ought to be (normatively) that of the inquiry. In fact, I doubt this. Rather, my contention is only that the inquiry is an important type of dialectical framework of human argumentation in everyday conversation and other places where reasoning is used (including science), and that to evaluate arguments, the normative framework of the inquiry is essential. The inquiry is embedded in commonplace human thinking as a context of the use of everyday argumentation. Therefore, in order to evaluate such arguments, it is important to see them, in some cases, as being embedded in the normative conversational framework of the inquiry as a type of dialogue. Thus foundationalism is an important part of the rhetoric of scientific discourse.

Although it is easy to superficially identify the inquiry with scientific reasoning, several questions need to be separated here. The inquiry is a normative model of dialogue and is not meant to be an empirical description of how any group of persons, such as scientists, actually conduct argumentation in real cases. The empirical question of how scientists argue and settle their claims in the professional marketplace of scientific argumentation is a question for sociology, whereas the normative question of what form good or correct or nonfallacious scientific argument should take is a question of logic, a normative question of argumentation, of how argumentation should be evaluated as correct or incorrect by means of general standards of what constitutes a correct or incorrect argument.

Scientists, in their rhetoric, often attempt to convey an ideal model of scientific argumentation as a species of inquiry. In these rhetorical moments – for example, when scientists are exhorting their students to use scientific methods for presenting their results to other scientists or to the public – they stress the need for careful use of experimental methods and for mathematical models to verify the conclusions drawn from their premises. They stress the use of careful logical reasoning – often emphasizing deductive logic, in moving from these established and verified premises to conclusions that are put forward as scientific findings. Scientists of a foundationalist persuasion frequently suggest or imply that the inquiry is the model of scientific argumentation that they prefer as their normative ideal. And, indeed, some (but not all) case studies of how argumentation is used in scientific research reveal characteristics of the inquiry model of dialogue.

In mathematics, Euclidian geometry provides a good example of the kind of cumulative model of argument characteristic of reasoning in the inquiry. All the axioms and theorems are numbered so that, when one derives a theorem, it is only permitted to derive it from theorems or axioms that have a prior or earlier number in the system. This is a clear indicator of the property of evidential priority in this type of argumentation, and it indicates that circular reasoning is clearly meant to be unacceptable as a proof in this type of argumentation. Mackenzie (1980) showed in detail how circular reasoning is excluded from Euclidian geometry as a model of argumentation that has this requirement of evidential priority.

Another factor that should be taken into account is that the argumentation used in scientific research characteristically goes through several stages of development. At an early stage of devising an experiment or posing a problem, rough conjectures are advanced in the form of hypotheses suitable for future testing and exploration. The argumentation at this early stage takes the form Collingwood indicates: there is a competition between untested rival theories and much use of abductive reasoning–guesswork based on alternative explanations of puzzles and unsolved problems. But then at a much later stage, when the results of an investigation are published, the argumentation is much more orderly and structured by an organized development of reasoning based on evidential priority and cumulative argumentation, using the language of 'proof' and 'verification.' We might contrast these two stages by characterizing the sequence of argumentation in them as, respectively, the order of discovery and the order of presentation. It is this latter presentation of results where the argumentation is best modelled by the inquiry.

5. Other Subtypes of Inquiry

Another type of inquiry is the *empirical inquiry* which is typified, for example, by a public inquiry into an airline crash. If the cause of the crash is not immediately evident, it may be very important for reasons of safety and to settle lawsuits to try to determine as exactly as possible what happened. In some cases, an official inquiry may be activated to answer this question.

Once this type of inquiry has been launched, it typically goes through several stages. During the first stage, there is collecting of evidence. For example, experts may go to the site of the crash to collect physical evidence and also the black box or flight recorder. These experts will pool the relevant data, and then consult other experts who have also examined the data. Next is a kind of discussion stage where all the parties attempt to interpret these findings and discuss what conclusions can be reached or what they indicate. During this discussion stage, the parties try to reach some sort of agreement on what conclusions can be drawn or at least locate their points of disagreement. At the end of this discussion stage, the parties either individually or collectively write some kind of report on the conclusions of the inquiry. Finally, there is a presentation stage where the document or report is communicated to the public or made available to a wider readership. It is this last, presentation stage that is often identified with the inquiry itself. However, the reasoning in this presentation stage is quite a distinctive type of argumentation in itself and does not necessarily represent the kinds of reasoning appropriate at the prior stages. Aspects of clarity, pedagogy, and the organization of the argument are very important, since this presentation is the official statement of the results which is directed to outsiders, as well as to colleagues in the field. The presentation needs to be put in an orderly way so that everyone can appreciate the sequence of reasoning in the inquiry and also see how the inquiry was exhaustive in laying out all the available evidence and in making carefully reasoned conclusions drawn from this initial evidence.

One factor that distinguishes different subtypes of inquiry is whether or not the inquiry takes place exclusively within a particular discipline or domain of knowledge and admits expert testimony in domains that come into the inquiry. For example, an article or book that reports results of some scientific research can be viewed as a presentation based on the type of dialogue called the inquiry. In this type of case, the inquiry itself will occur exclusively within some closed academic discipline or domain of knowledge. The inquiry will use the methods appropriate for this discipline and be restricted to insiders or to those who are qualified to take part in such a discussion. On the other hand, public inquiries into air disasters, for example, are typically much more open-ended in that many of the propositions used as premises in the argumentation in the inquiry are based on testimony given by experts, often scientific experts in particular fields, whose opinions are solicited.

The type of inquiry that presents the results of an investigation in a particular discipline – for example, a scientific discipline – is much more likely to appear to exhibit an impersonal kind of reasoning in which there is really no dialogue. This is something of a calculated impression. In presentation of the inquiry, the personal element is suppressed. In writing a report of an inquiry, all the activities are attributed to an impersonal process. Instead of showing people asking questions or finding answers, the conclusions and determination are portrayed impersonally as a cumulation of propositions in an advancing set of states of knowledge. This calculated appearance of objectivity is very much in accord with the cumulative method of the inquiry. All the evidence has purportedly been collected and conclusions carefully inferred from this body of evidence so that, supposedly, the final report of the inquiry represents a solid account of the 'objective facts.'

Although this impersonal aspect is often associated with the inquiry itself, as a whole process, such a portrayal of it is misleading. The appearance of being impersonal is really characteristic only of the presentation or concluding stage of the inquiry. It represents the preference for agreement and unanimity that is characteristic of the inquiry as a collaborative frame-work of argumentation. In many cases, the text of discourse for the inquiry represents the presentation of the outcome. But in the case of a public or legal inquiry – for example, the royal commission that is so popular in Canada – the dialectical aspect of it is much more evident, and it is very clear that this type of inquiry involves quite an extensive process of discussion and dialogue.

The Kripke model of the argumentation of an inquiry, as a set of advancing evidential situations where propositions are verified, represents the inquiry as an impersonal sequence of reasoning. In this model, the inquiry seems to be not like a dialogue at all, but like an objective process of the cumulative collection of knowledge where propositions impersonally come to be verified in a set of advancing states of knowledge. The dynamic is that of movement towards a greater increment of knowledge, rather than that of a dialogue exchange of questioning and replying between two parties or a group of investigators. The first to explicitly model the inquiry as a dialogue process where some participants or companies interact by reasoning with each other was the analysis of Barth and Krabbe (1982). However, this analysis was based on the earlier mathematical analysis of the structure of intuitionistic logic formulated as a type of rule-governed, orderly dialogue exchange between two parties that was given by Kamlah and Lorenzen (1967) in the logical propaedeutic of the Erlangen school. An excellent summary (in English) of the logical system used by Kamlah and Lorenzen – the so-called logical propaedeutic – is presented by Krabbe (1996, pp. 253–63). Kamlah and Lorenzen, who were leading members of the Erlangen school, show how intuitionistic logic can be formally modelled as a dialogue exchange, defined by rules of attack and defense, between a proponent and an opponent in a game-like exchange with rules for winning and losing. Here, for the first time, was a formalized model of the argumentation in the inquiry as a context of dialogue.

How the formalization of intuitionistic (constructive) logic by the Erlangen school works is illustrated by the definitions of 'or' and 'not' given for constructive logic (see section 2 above). Disjunction (or) and negation (not) are defined by the Erlangen formalization using the following rules, as outlined by Krabbe:

(*Def.* v *Er.*): Suppose a speaker acts as the proponent of the thesis A v B, that is, he asserts the disjunction A v B. The opponent of this thesis is then entitled to attack the complex statement by casting doubt on all of it at once. The proponent may now choose one of the two component statements and attempt to defend it. If he succeeds, he wins, and in this case he at once wins definitively. If his defense fails, he loses, but at this stage he does not lose definitively, since he can still substantiate his statement in a second round of defense, if he produces a successful defense of the other component statement. If this second defense is undertaken and succeeds, the proponent wins after all, and then the outcome is definitive; if the second defense fails as well, the proponent loses definitively.

(*Def.* ⅂*Er.*):   Suppose a speaker acts as the proponent of the thesis ⅂*A*, that is, he asserts the negation ⅂*A*. To attack the assertion ⅂*A*, the opponent is to contradict the proponent and assert *A*. If the opponent subsequently proceeds to defend *A* successfully, then he obtains a definitive victory. If, on the other hand, the opponent is unable to defend *A* successfully, then he loses and the proponent of the thesis ⅂*A* wins definitively. (1996, p. 258)

These rules give the reader an idea of how Kamlah and Lorenzen construct a dialogue logic of argumentation for the inquiry comparable to the formalization of Kripke.

A normative model of the inquiry as a cumulative type of dialogue, built on the logical foundations of the work of the Erlangen school, was given by Barth and Krabbe (1982, pp. 243–57). The basic principle behind Barth and Krabbe's model of the inquiry type of dialogue is what they call the principle of preservation or cumulation of agreement (p. 243). This principle is the assumption that the body of positively agreed-upon sentences in an inquiry never decreases, but always either remains constant or grows. According to Barth and Krabbe, this process of preservation or cumulation of agreement in a dialogue is a realistic assumption in the sense that it can be said to hold with respect to some companies or participants in a dialogue for a limited period of time (p. 244).

In other words, in any real type of argumentative discussion that is like an inquiry, there will be retraction of commitments, and, in general, new information will lead to new agreements and the disappearance of old agreements. As Barth and Krabbe put it, this kind of process of renewal of agreement happens all the time 'in science, in religion, in practical life' (p. 244). Thus the abstract model of the inquiry as a type of dialogue that is cumulative is not one that will be met with at all points in all cases of every given text of discourse that represents an inquiry proceeding as a sequence of argumentation in a real case. In scientific discourse and in argumentation in public inquiries, conflicts of opinion arise within the argumentation in the inquiry, which leads to commitments being retracted at some point along the sequence of reasoning. Thus this cumulative property characteristic of the normative model of inquiry as a type of argumentation represents an ideal of rational argument where the participants get together and collect all the relevant information; at an early stage, they eliminate the inconsistencies and conflicts of opinion so that enough of a basis for agreement is present for them to consolidate these results together. At a later stage of the inquiry, these results are presented in an orderly fashion which stresses the cumulative aspects and the growth of agreement in the sequence of reasoning that took place in the prior dialogue. This stress on agreement, in some cases, makes the inquiry appear to be a kind of impersonal sequence of reasoning where there is simply a growth of facts through the collection of information, where these verified data establish particular hypotheses, and that step, in turn, leads to an orderly sequence of premises and conclusions that exhibit the results of the reasoning in the inquiry.

As well as the more elaborate types of inquiry conducted within a scientific discipline or in a public inquiry, there can also be relatively simple cases of common-sense inquiries. We can at least use the adjective 'common sense' here to indicate that this subtype of inquiry is a very plain and ordinary sort in everyday argumentation and features a simple kind of problem of everyday life. For example, suppose my bicycle has a flat tire and I look into the situation to try to find out what is wrong. This too represents a kind of inquiry, or it can, but it lacks the more elaborate features of the other types of inquiry, such as the group collecting data and arriving at agreement, or presentation of the official results of the inquiry at the concluding stage. Before studying some cases of this common-sense subtype of inquiry,[6] it is useful to separate the function of argument from that of explanation in such cases.

6. Argument and Explanation

Although the focus here is on the inquiry as a framework of dialogue for argumentation, it is important to realize that the inquiry is also often a framework for explanation. Both explanation and argumentation use reasoning, but the purpose of these two uses of reasoning are generally quite different. The purpose of an argument is to settle some issue that is open where there are two possible points of view or sides to the issue. Explanations start from a very different presumption. The presumption that makes an explanation appropriate is that a particular proposition is true or can be taken for granted as representing some factual occurrence, and the purpose of the explanation is to give some account of why it happened.

An inquiry, in a broader sense of the word, can be undertaken to explain why or how something happened. The problem is to explain why it took place or to find the cause. This preliminary type of inquiry (in the broad sense) leads to various competing hypotheses about the cause, but the existing evidence may not be conclusive one way or the other. This is the kind of situation that typically leads to an inquiry in our more narrow sense of the word. In such a case, the inquiry becomes a framework of argument. And the purpose of the inquiry is to prove that a particular proposition is true, or to prove that it is true or false, or if this cannot be proven, at least to prove that, on the basis of the evidence, the issue cannot be resolved one way or the other.

In reality, these two functions of argument and explanation may be mixed, and a particular example of an inquiry may often seem to shift back and forth from explanation to argumentation. In the case of an air disaster, for example, the inquiry is launched because certain aspects of the disaster are not understood. The initial purpose of the inquiry is to explain the disaster as an occurrence that took place. But mixed in with this explanatory function is a function of argumentation because there will be various plausible hypotheses concerning the cause, such as pilot error or technical failure. Argumentation is put forward during the course of the inquiry which attempts to support and verify some of these hypotheses (subsets of them), and to refute, or find evidence against, the other competing hypotheses.

At some point, the inquiry selects one hypothesis that exhibits growth of agreement. Since one proposition is supported by the explanatory evidence collected, the argumentation then provides a cumulative network of evidence which moves forward to support (or refute) that particular hypothesis as the proposition that is proven true (or not) by the results of the inquiry.

Thus the inquiry begins by examining different possible explanations for the crash, but its ultimate purpose is to conclusively prove or disprove these initial hypotheses, and to provide, as a result, a build-up of evidence that will prove or disprove a particular proposition as a hypothesis. In the course of the inquiry, much of the argumentation takes the form of arguments to the best explanation, where various competing explanations of the evidence are evaluated. But, ultimately, the purpose of the inquiry, in the normative sense of this term used in the new dialectic, is to provide a methodical, comprehensive, and conclusive proof or disproof of a particular proposition, based on the cumulative build-up of evidence as knowledge of the facts is collected, assessed, and verified.

Both explanation and argumentation use reasoning, and the kind of reasoning used in an inquiry for these two ends is often compatible, and of the same sort, so that it is normal to find argumentation and explanation mixed in an inquiry. Here we view argumentation in an inquiry as being directed towards the goal of proving that a particular proposition is true or is not true. But we must be careful to note that this frequently involves the allied purpose of providing an explanation, and that in particular cases explanation and argumentation need to be carefully distinguished as distinct and different uses of reasoning. During the initial stages of an inquiry, data are collected and explanatory hypotheses are put forward and discussed. During the argumentation stage, one hypothesis is selected as the target and is evaluated as being either supported or not by the dynamic sequence of reasoning emerging through the course of the inquiry. At these initial stages, certain hypotheses are selected as vehicles or objects for verification or falsification as the inquiry proceeds.

7. Black and Beardsley on the Inquiry

In their early textbooks on informal logic, Max Black (1946) and Monroe Beardsley (1950) identify the inquiry as a normative framework in which arguments can be evaluated as correct or lacking in justification; as well, they provide helpful descriptions of the many leading characteristics of the inquiry. Black identifies the inquiry as a method of answering a question or solving a problem where no existing procedure is known to guarantee an answer directed towards answering the specific question or solving the specific problem (1946, p. 247). According to Black, such a problem can be one of two types: it can be a technical problem defined as 'one whose formulation calls for the understanding of complex notions and the possession of special information which are not generally available to an average person' (p. 248), or it can be a common-sense problem whose resolution calls for no special background knowledge or specialized training.

As a case of an inquiry of a common-sense problem, Black gives the example of a student who confronts the problem of finding a book that he lost on the way home from the library. The last time the student remembers having the book was in a drugstore, but he can't remember its name or location. He sits down and tries to recall any relevant information that might help him solve this problem, and remembers that the drugstore was beside a jewellery store. On looking up drugstores and jewellery stores in the yellow pages, he finds a long list of drugstores but only a short list of jewellery stores. To solve the problem, he scans down both lists and soon finds a drugstore and a jewellery store located on the same street with practically the same number. He concludes that this drugstore was probably the place where he left the book. To confirm his hypothesis, he phones this drugstore and finds that his book has been kept there for him. That process characterizes the inquiry in this case as proceeding by the adoption of a tentative hypothesis and the confirmation of this hypothesis by evidence. As Black reconstructs the case, deductive inference as well as the recollection of facts play an important part in the inquiry (1946, pp. 248–50).

According to Black, it is not characteristic of the inquiry to explore every possibility that might be relevant to solving the problem (p. 250). Instead, the procedure of the inquiry is to begin by taking several assumptions or hypotheses for granted and then to focus attention on the testing of these hypotheses. Moreover, Black thinks that the process of narrowing down to these so-called main hypotheses is a procedure of reasoning that calls for creative insight and cannot be reduced to a rule that can be codified or simply quantified (p. 251).

Black's example of an inquiry represents a simple and basic type of case that is quite different from the much more elaborate and organized public or scientific inquiry. In Black's case, the framework of argumentation seems as if it were information-seeking, or perhaps a kind of deliberation on how to solve a practical problem. However, the framework of argument in Black's case is that of the inquiry: the student is engaged in a process of verifying a hypothesis constructed on the basis of intelligent guesswork (by comparing the two lists in the yellow pages). To the extent that the student is definitely verifying a hypothesis, the reasoning he uses in his argumentation can be viewed as being part of a kind of common- sense inquiry meant to find out the facts of a matter.

Beardsley's early textbook also outlines many important characteristics of the inquiry as a type of context of argumentation (1950, pp. 517–47). Beardsley sees the inquiry as a process of thought in which hypotheses are considered dynamically and evaluated in relation to collected facts. He gives the example of someone who arrives home at night and turns on the light switch but finds the light doesn't go on. This person then investigates several hypotheses or avenues of inquiry. He tries the switch a few times, looks to see if the bulb is burned out, and then perhaps checks the fuse box, and so forth. If he finds, for example, that there is evidence that the bulb is burned out and then replaces that bulb with a new one and the new bulb works, then the inquiry has been successful and may be concluded.

Beardsley's description of the inquiry as a framework of reasoning is fairly similar in general outline to Black's description. According to Beardsley, the inquiry begins with a feeling of perplexity, or the presenting of a problem in the form of an unanswered question. The source of the difficulty is then located, and based upon the individual's previous knowledge of how electrical circuits work and so forth, he advances several working hypotheses which are then tested.

One potential problem with Beardsley's example is that, in certain respects, what is involved seems more like an explanation than an argument. When the person arrives home and sees that the light does not work, we presume that he is seeking an explanation for this fact. Although it is perhaps true to say that he is seeking more than this, he is first seeking some kind of explanation, then testing out this explanation and other possible competing explanations, and finally taking steps to correct the problem – to make the light work again. In this particular example, the goal is practical action as much as it is proving the truth of a proposition, even though argumentation is certainly involved. In the case of both Black and Beardsley, the example could be interpreted different ways. Even so, the description Beardsley gives of the various stages of an inquiry provide an excellent account of the distinct phases of this type of dialogue as a framework of argumentation.

Beardsley distinguishes four distinct stages. The first consists in 'putting the question, after a careful examination of the problematic situation,' which involves both a description of the problematic situation and then a question that expresses the problem in context. In the second stage, a hypothesis is devised to answer the question. In the third stage, consequences are deduced from the hypothesis. In the fourth stage, those consequences are tested (1950, pp. 519–21).

It is interesting that Beardsley sees the sequence of reasoning used in testing the consequences in an inquiry as taking the form of a conditional argument that affirms the consequent, a form of argument that is not deductively valid. As Beardsley puts it, 'The conclusion does not follow necessarily.' Nevertheless, the fact expressed in the consequent confirms the hypothesis of the antecedent as a piece of evidence, making it plausible or probable relative to other competing hypotheses. Thus, this part of the reasoning, according to Beardsley, considers numerous plausible and relevant hypotheses which are tried out and then rejected if not confirmed by the evidence collected.

Although it is natural to focus on this stage of evaluating hypotheses as being characteristic of the argumentation in an inquiry, Beardsley shows how the inquiry can often go wrong at the beginning stages. As he puts it, a hypothesis is an answer to a question, and 'the answer will not be of much use unless we have asked the right question' in the first place (p. 522). If the question is confused or badly stated, then the inquiry will go wrong from the very beginning because those involved lack a clear understanding of the problem. Beardsley writes that sometimes people speak as though we engage in an inquiry when talking about 'the problem of unemployment' or 'the problem of security,' for example. But here we can have a problem with the formulating of problems because the concepts of unemployment and security are so complex and, at the same time, vague and problematic that they tend to mix up many problems together. These questions lack sufficient clarity or specificity to be good problems to begin within a well-directed inquiry that is likely to be successful. Thus, Beardsley has rightly emphasized here that inquiry must be considered as a dynamic framework of argumentation in which different deficiencies or obstructive failures can occur at various stages and even during the very beginning phases of asking the question or formulating the problem.

In a remark that is reminiscent of Collingwood's insight (quoted in section 4), Beardsley states that 'Effective thinking is guided by questions,' and one of the fallacies Beardsley identifies as corresponding to an important kind of failure in this initial stage of the inquiry is the traditional fallacy of the complex question (or fallacy of many questions) (p. 525). The problem is the asking of two questions at once. One question is presumed or presupposed by another, so that when we go forward in an inquiry on the presumption that we are asking a single question, confusion and logical problems are inevitable. Thus, as Beardsley sees it, there are three stages in the answering of the question as the inquiry moves forward. In the first stage, we formulate a question worth answering or try to get that question clear enough so that a successful inquiry is possible. In the second stage, we formulate various hypotheses that propose tentative answers to the question, and then in the third stage, we attempt to verify or falsify these hypotheses using logical reasoning based on the evidence that has been collected as part of the inquiry (pp. 526–7). As well as a reasoning component to the inquiry, there is an empirical component that involves the collecting of evidence – both empirical evidence and evidence extracted from the reasoner's own thinking through his knowledge of common situations. The example given by Beardsley illustrates these three stages very well.

Beardsley identifies another kind of fallacy or logical problem in the argumentation characteristic of the process of inquiry: proposed hypotheses that are too vague or that, for various reasons, are impossible to verify. The general requirement is that formulated hypotheses need to be sufficiently clear and well expressed so that they are, in principle, testable. Accordingly to Beardsley, the hypothesis must be such that consequences can be deduced from it that refer to some possible experience that can be verified or falsified by the collection of data. In other words, such a testable hypothesis must have a predictable power, and this is what gives it its function in answering the kind of question posed by the problem in an inquiry.[7] This requirement of argumentation in an inquiry is crucial to understanding many of the fallacies that occur in this context. So it is interesting to see that not only did Beardsley clearly describe the inquiry as a normative framework in which argumentation can be evaluated as successful or not, but he also pinpointed specific failings of the kind of logical reasoning used in an inquiry that can be identified with some of the traditional informal fallacies.

Beardsley's textbook shows insight into the usefulness and properties of the inquiry as a distinctive conversational context of argumentation that needs to be considered when evaluating critical thinking. These textbook insights count against Hamblin's general conclusion, in his survey of the textbook treatment of fallacies, that the standard treatment was stale and worn out to the point where very little can be learned from it that is original or deeply useful for argumentation theory (Hamblin, 1971). What Black and Beardsley say about the inquiry has not been very well appreciated by other textbook writers or by scholars in argumentation theory. Although their accounts of the inquiry are not expressed in the very structured way of scholarly contributions, they do express a deep insight and feeling for what is important in grasping the pragmatic evaluation of the uses of arguments in everyday reasoning.

8. Cases of Public Inquiries

In 1993 the Canadian government set up a public inquiry to investigate the country's blood supply system after learning that over 1,000 hemophiliacs and blood transfusion patients had contracted the AIDS virus from contaminated blood they received between 1980 and 1985. It was hoped that the inquiry would provide a basis for overhauling the $220 million blood system in order to ensure that this kind of tragedy did not happen again. The inquiry had an initial budget of $2.5 million, and a deadline for the final report was set for September 1994. Justice Horace Krever was named to head the inquiry. Two lawyers served as co-counsels to ask questions at the inquiry, and because many of the aspects of the inquiry were technical and scientific in nature, a scientific adviser was appointed to assist the investigators. The commission's two full-time investigators were former members of the RCMP. It was their job to locate witnesses, conduct preliminary questioning, and collect documentary evidence (Picard, 1993, p. A2).

Most of the work in the initial stages of any inquiry involves collecting information based on the testimony of witnesses. Much of this testimony in the Krever inquiry involved stories of anguish and anger from people who had been infected by the AIDS virus through the country's blood supply; in some cases, testimony came from the next of kin of victims who had died. Another source of testimony was an international panel of medical and business experts appointed by Krever to assess Canadian standards for blood safety in light of those in other countries.

The inquiry is an abstract normative model of reasonable argument; as such, no real case of any dialogue exchange in an actual text of discourse will exactly represent all the features of the inquiry, as we are using the term here. In any real public inquiry of this sort, at many junctures the inquiry will shift into a kind of conversational exchange which is, or appears to be, much more like a persuasion dialogue, quarrel, deliberation, or information-seeking type of dialogue. Nevertheless, in broad outline, such an example of a public inquiry will instantiate the key characteristic features of the inquiry as a type of structured framework of argumentation.

The key aspects of a public inquiry that identify it as a subspecies of the inquiry type of dialogue include the attempt to pose a clear question or problem and, in the initial stages, the collecting of data that are relevant to the problem. Then comes the argumentation stage of putting forward hypotheses that will be the main candidates for being verified by this data and the testing of these hypotheses on the basis of the evidence collected. The intent is to collect as much information as possible, to substantiate it as solidly as possible, and then to collect together and state the hypotheses in such a perspicuous way that the inquiry can move forward to the next stage of testing those hypotheses. In all these stages all through the sequence, the general purpose is to make the inquiry as cumulative as possible so that it does not become bogged down in endless questioning or persuasion dialogue at any particular point and does not have to reroute back to the initial stages. The goal is for the inquiry to keep continually moving forward in one direction with an incremental build-up of knowledge so that conclusions can be drawn from premises that are well established as commitments and will not need to be retracted. Through this cumulative process of argumentation, the inquiry moves forward to conclusions that can withstand subsequent questioning or criticism. The final stage of the public inquiry focuses on a report of the outcome. The report needs to clearly demonstrate that evidence was collected carefully and scientifically and that the conclusions were derived in an orderly and logical way. Such conclusions are based on the orderly and cumulative structure of argumentation that characterizes the sequence of reasoning throughout the inquiry.

Real public inquiries sometimes fall short of this abstract model of argumentation. Certainly there are cases of inquiries that have failed. One example is a Canadian royal commission inquiry that was formed in 1989 to investigate new reproductive technologies and recommend policies on their use. The sequence of the inquiry was characterized by bitter infighting among the chief participants; at one point, dissident members of the commission resigned and then criticized the inquiry. This example indicates that argumentation in the inquiry may be as often characterized in real cases by its failures as much as by its successes. The examination of actual cases of argumentation in the context of inquiry may often rightly focus on fallacies and other errors of reasoning that affect this type of argumentation.

In the case of the Canadian blood system inquiry, problems arose early in the proceedings. More than forty individuals and groups who were given the opportunity to respond to potential charges of wrongdoing filed lawsuits in federal court to prevent Justice Krever from making any findings of misconduct that could be used as a basis for future criminal or civil court actions against them. Lawyers for the Canadian Red Cross Society argued that the publishing of such allegations would turn the inquiry into 'a criminal trial masquerading as a public inquiry' (Picard, 1996, p. A4). This argument suggests that the inquiry has shifted to a different type of dialogue, a criminal trial. The argument is very interesting because it suggests that one type of dialogue can shift illicitly to another type that is not appropriate in light of the assumption that the dialogue was supposed to be of a particular type. (Such dialectical shifts, from one type of dialogue to another, are studied in chapter 8.)

The blood inquiry case illustrates some of the problems that can beset a public inquiry, preventing it from proceeding towards its goal by delaying its progress, by turning the line of argument in a different direction, or even by shifting the inquiry to a different type of dialogue altogether. Bryan Schwartz, a law professor at the University of Manitoba, has criticized the public inquiry as an institution that has been too popular in Canada, particularly in controversial cases where individuals can be cross-examined in public without the safeguards against hearsay, innuendo, and personal charges that they would have in a trial (Saunders, 1996, p. A6). He maintains that public inquiries tend to be on some broad problem or area of public concern that is not defined specifically enough to allow the inquiry to really prove anything. According to Schwartz, a typical public inquiry tends to make up the rules as it goes along, whereas in a court case 'evidence and testimony are tightly restrained by rules that ensure that statements are relevant to the specific charges and are backed up with concrete proof' (CBC interview, 28 June 1996). The problem is that, if the inquiry shifts towards a format for laying blame for allegations of wrongdoing by individuals, the rules of relevance, evidence, and examination of witnesses are not well designed for fairly conducting such a trial-like dialogue.

These criticisms of the public inquiries in Canada suggest that there is a tendency for actual cases of public inquiries to deviate or drift away from the abstract model of the inquiry as a type of dialogue, where a specifically designated proposition is to be proved or disproved on a basis of a cumulative build-up of well-established premises. A public inquiry into a controversial problem or broad area of public concern may require such a wide-ranging and unconstrained kind of dialogue framework of argumentation that it fails to meet standards of relevance and evidence appropriate for an inquiry in the new dialectical sense.

9. Profiles of Dialogue in the Inquiry

The way that Barth and Krabbe interpret the kind of cumulative argumentation modelled by intuitionistic logic is distinctively different from the way that Kripke interprets it. The Kripke model, as typified by the example represented in Figure 3.1, portrays the sequence of argument in an inquiry as an impersonal process. Propositions are 'verified' in 'evidential situations,' and then the inquiry advances to new stages where more propositions take on the property of being verified at that stage. But verified by whom, or against whose objections? We are not told. The notions of proponent and respondent are not used or defined in the Kripke model. In contrast, in the Barth and Krabbe formalization, a *dialectical subject* is defined as 'any company of users of language that are or that have been or that may become engaged in critical discussions, with themselves or with one another' (1982, p. 243). The Barth and Krabbe view of intuitionistic (constructive) logic represents a sequence of argumentation in which there is a growing body of sentences on which positive agreement has been reached by a dialectical subject (to paraphrase their characterization). Thus, from Barth and Krabbe's viewpoint, the inquiry is not an impersonal process in the way it is seen by Kripke. Instead, it is seen as a process of growth of agreement in a set of dialectical subjects.[8]

Barth and Krabbe model the argumentation in an inquiry using three structures (pp. 245–7). This is very similar to Kripke's use of the tree model, illustrated in Figure 3.1. Both formalizations appear to be similar, but there is a key difference. In chapter 10 of *From Axiom to Dialogue*, Barth and Krabbe also model particular kinds of argumentative exchanges between a proponent and a respondent (opponent) using so-called tableaux, represented by strips, or sequences of attacks and replies to the attacks by the two parties (the proponent and the respondent). To be 'correct,' the moves in each sequence must conform to the dialogue rules, which are based on the way the logical connectives are defined – as indicated briefly in Krabbe's two definitions of 'or' and 'not' in his article 'Dialogue Logic and Formal Dialectics' (see section 5, above.

Numerous examples of sequences of argument exchanges in dialogue (strips) regulated by intuitionistic logic are also presented by Felscher (1986, pp. 345–9). These examples of dialogue strips cited by Felscher are very similar to the Lorenzen-style strips used by Barth and Krabbe. It seems likely that these strips could be helpfully used to model profiles of dialogue in an inquiry.

In a Barth and Krabbe strip, the proponent begins by making an assertion, and then the opponent 'attacks' that assertion by questioning it according to the rules (indicated, for example by the definitions of 'or' and 'not' described by Krabbe). For example, suppose the proponent makes an assertion of the form '*A* or *B*'. The opponent can reply by 'attacking' this statement by questioning whether it is agreed upon by the company. The proponent, at the next move, must defend either *A* or

B, but he can choose which one to defend. If he chooses *A* and succeeds in defending *A*, then he wins the dialogue. But if he fails to defend *A* successfully, then he must go back and try to defend *B*. If he succeeds, he wins the whole dialogue exchange, but if he fails, the opponent wins.

The strip representing the sequence of argumentation in this case is given below. To extend the case a little further, let's assume that *D* is one of the propositions that both parties have already agreed to, but *C* is not one of those propositions.

Proponent	Opponent
A or *B*	Why '*A* or *B*'
Because *A*	Why *A*?
Because *C*	No commitment *C*
Because *B*	Why *B*?
Because *D*	You win!

In this example of a strip, the proponent cannot use *C* to justify *A*, because *C* has not been agreed to as verified in the inquiry. So he has to defend *B*, and does so successfully by using *D* as his basis of justification. The example of a strip given above is not expressed in the precise form and notion of either Barth and Krabbe or Felscher. But it gives the reader an idea of what a strip looks like. Generally, if the proponent successfully defends his initial assertion in a dialogue exchange against all the attacks made by the opponent (as allowed by the rules), then the proponent wins. If the opponent successfully attacks any statement of the ones that he is allowed to attack – that is, if the proponent does not successfully defend that statement – then the opponent wins the dialogue exchange. The strip, or tableau, represents the sequence of attacks and defences in a given dialogue exchange of moves. The tableau lists all the proponent's moves in a column on one side and all the respondent's moves, matching those of the proponent at each exchange, on the other side.

Such a tableau can function as a profile of dialogue. Given any actual sequence of exchanges between a proponent and a respondent in the form of a strip, we can check this strip to see whether each move was played according to the rules. If one or more moves violated a rule of the cumulative dialectical structure defined by the formal model, then we can say that the actual sequence of dialogue fell short of, or deviated from, a proper profile of dialogue as determined by the rules for this type of dialogue. So the strip can function as a normative tool for evaluating argumentation in a given case, according to the standards of correct or appropriate argumentation required in this particular type of dialogue. If Barth and Krabbe's formal model represents the inquiry type of dialogue, then the strips in their tableau sequences can be used to evaluate argumentation as being correctly used or not, as applied to an inquiry on a particular subject.

Such a formal modelling of profiles of dialogue in the inquiry is also extremely helpful because it is a useful tool that enables an evaluator to judge whether a given argument or move in an inquiry should properly be said to be dialectically relevant. A move in argumentation is dialectically relevant in an inquiry if it fits into a strip representing a sequence of dialogue exchanges that traces back (by a correct sequence of pairs or moves by the proponent and opponent) to an initial assertion by the proponent, which itself can be traced back by a connected series of strips to the original proposition at issue in the inquiry (the proposition to be proved or disproved). In short, the strip can function as a profile that enables an argument evaluator to determine dialectical relevance in an inquiry in much the same way that the profile of dialogue is used as a tool to evaluate claims of relevance in other types of dialogue.

However, there are some open questions about using Barth and Krabbe's formal model when evaluating argumentation for relevance in the inquiry.

10. Relevance in the Inquiry

Relevance of argumentation in the inquiry is determined, first, by the stage of the inquiry. During the initial stages, there is the definition of the problem to be solved or the proposition to be investigated. Next comes the collection of relevant data, which need to be verified and established. Then, as Beardsley notes, clear and specific questions need to be asked as the inquiry proceeds to formulate tentative hypotheses. During this discovery stage, guesswork or conjecture – in the form of abductive reasoning, using inference to the best explanation – is a characteristic type of argument used. A question can be called relevant if it formulates a hypothesis that can be verified or refuted by the collected data, in such a way that the inquiry is moved forward to its ultimate goal of proving the global proposition to be investigated.

Once a hypothesis has been formulated, relevant evidence is selected from the data pool of verified propositions and brought to bear on the hypothesis. This leads to the establishment of results in the form of further propositions that are verified or falsified, thus moving the inquiry along. Once premises are firmly established, with the company of investigators all agreeing that these propositions have been verified or are known to be true, then conclusions can be drawn representing the results (outcome) of the inquiry. This stage of drawing conclusions from the (now) established premises is the argumentation stage, where the participants agree among themselves on what the inquiry has established and proved. Following this stage is a closing stage, where the official results of the inquiry are recorded in a document by the participants or designated representatives. Then this officially recorded result of the inquiry is published or presented in some form to the public.

Thus relevance in the inquiry is a sequential notion. Any argument, or type of move in the inquiry, is relevant to the extent that it builds on the previous sequence of propositions that have been verified in the earlier stages of the inquiry. Each move must have a function in the question-reply sequence of argumentation that drives the inquiry forward in a build-up of cumulative evidence directed towards proving the ultimate proposition that represents the goal of the inquiry. Any deviation from this carefully structured, interlocking network of cumulative aggregation of verified results can normatively be judged to be dialectically irrelevant.

Some questions remain concerning the modelling of relevance in the inquiry by the Barth and Krabbe (or Kripke) formalizations of intuitionistic logic. Does relevance, as determined by the strips profile of dialogue method in these formal systems, model dialectical relevance over the whole sequence of cumulative argumentation throughout all the stages of an inquiry? Or does it do a better job of modelling relevance during the sequence of argumentation in a particular stage? And what about the Kripke tree models representing the cumulative build-up of prepositions agreed upon by a company of investigators, as presented by Barth and Krabbe? What part of the inquiry does this model of argumentation represent? And does it represent something different from the dialogue represented by the strips?

These questions about formalization of argumentation in the inquiry need to be investigated more carefully, both by those who have developed these formal systems of intuitionistic logic and by those who need to apply them – for example, by researchers in artificial intelligence who need to use formal models of dialogue to do such things as develop more user-friendly computers that can engage in natural dialogues with a human being. Some closing conjectures are ventured here, even though more study is needed. Certainly these conjectures do not represent the last word on the subject.

It seems that the strips best model the kind of argumentation that would normally occur at the argumentation stage of an inquiry, at the point where the party of discussants are coming to agreement on what the findings of the investigation imply, or prove as conclusions, now that these findings have been collected. Moreover, it seems that the Kripke tree structure, representing the cumulative build-up of agreed-upon propositions, best represents the presentation stage of the inquiry, the closing stage where the results of the inquiry are presented to a wider audience.

Whatever the answer to these questions of how to best use formal models to represent different stages of the inquiry, it is clear that intuitionistic logic as a normative model does not represent the argumentation in the earlier, discovery stage of the inquiry as well as it represents the argumentation in the later stages.

4

Negotiation Dialogue

It might be tempting to identify argument with persuasion. But thinking that persuasion is the sole purpose of argument and, therefore, identifying argumentation exclusively with the persuasion type of dialogue,[1] is too narrow a view to represent the way argument is typically used in everyday conversations. For argument is also frequently used in negotiation. The goal of negotiation dialogue is distinctively different from the goal of persuasion dialogue and the inquiry. In both the persuasion dialogue and the inquiry, the goal of a participant is generally to prove that some proposition is true or false, or at least to argue that it is true or false by giving evidence to support it. In negotiation dialogue, however, matters of the truth and falsity of propositions are secondary. They are relevant to some extent, and in certain situations they can be important, but the main goal in putting forward an argument is to try to get a good deal. In other words, the issue in a negotiation dialogue is not truth or falsity, but rather money or some kind of goods, economic resources, or other items of value that are at issue. What the other participant is committed to, in the sense of accepting as true propositions, is the central factor in persuasion dialogue, and it is also a central factor in the inquiry. But in negotiation dialogue, this kind of commitment to the truth or falsity of propositions is much more tangential.

1. Main Characteristics

In negotiation dialogue, when one participant puts forward an argument, it is to make offers and to try to get concessions in order to make a deal. When the other party makes such a concession, it is not in the form of something he believes or accepts as being true or based on good evidence.[2] It is simply a material concession that he is willing to make – a kind of bargaining chip that he will concede to the other party as part of a deal, so that the other party will give him some comparable kind of bargaining chip back. It is this kind of back-and-forth exchange of concessions that is the heart of negotiation dialogue.

In the initial situation or issue of a negotiation dialogue, there is a set of goods or services or tradable supplies which includes something both parties want, and each participant has some items that can be traded with the other. The goal of a participant in a negotiation dialogue is to get as much of these goods or services as she needs or wants by trading those that she has with the other party. The method of argument is one of bargaining, in which the arguer tries to find compromises or trade-offs that are acceptable to the other party and that also fulfil her own goals or expectations. Making a deal or reaching an agreement involves some gains and some losses with the initial set of goods or services being divided up in a way that both parties can accept or at least agree to. The goal is not for one party to totally defeat the other by taking all the goods or services.

The key thing is that each party approaches these initial goods or services with a different set of priorities or values. Both sides try to get what matters most in their set of priorities or values by trading items that are less important. In a negotiation, it is unlikely that both parties will get everything they want, and there is an expectation of some losses or concessions in the trade-off between parties. The outcome is generally less than what each side would consider ideal. In the process of a successful negotiation, the positions of both sides start out from extremes or opposites, and then converge towards a middle position that is acceptable to both. Both sides incur losses or concede some things that are important to them in the interest of getting other things they value more.

Fisher and Ury give quite a different picture of the goal of negotiation dialogue. According to their account, the normative goal of negotiation is to produce a wise agreement, if agreement is possible. A *wise agreement* is defined as 'one that meets the legitimate interests of each side to the extent possible, resolves conflicting interests fairly, is durable, and takes community interests into account' (1991, p. 4). This is a fairly idealistic account of the goal of negotiation dialogue; indeed, it seems to be an inappropriately high normative standard because it brings in other factors that are external to negotiation dialogue. Nevertheless, to meet this goal, Fisher and Ury recommend following the method of principled negotiation: when there is a conflict that blocks bargaining between the two parties, they should move to deciding the issue on its merits, which means they 'should insist that the result be based on some fair standards independent of the will of either side' (p. xviii). This is good practical advice in many cases, but it takes us outside the normative model of the negotiation dialogue.

According to Fisher and Ury, this method of principled negotiation can be boiled down to four maxims. (1991, pp. 10–11). First, separate the people from the problem. Second, focus on interests, not positions. Third, generate a variety of possibilities before deciding what to do. Fourth, insist that the result be based on some objective standard.

With the first maxim, Fisher and Ury are addressing the issue of emotions becoming tangled up with negotiation and erecting an obstacle to successful bargaining. Separating the people from the problem means that a participant should try to attain a certain objectivity and refrain from attacking the other side personally. The general nature of this problem has to do with *ad hominem* arguments that focus on personal attack.[3]

What Fisher and Ury mean by the second point depends on the distinction between interests and positions. An interest represents the underlying objective of a participant in a negotiation dialogue. In other words, the whole dialogue is based on an initial conflict of interest. According to Fisher and Ury, 'The purpose of negotiating is to serve your interests' (1991, p. 50). Positions, on the other hand, represent the explicit concessions or demands that a participant makes in the course of a negotiation. A position is a kind of commitment that one party explicitly makes and that binds both parties in the subsequent negotiations.

The third maxim recommends searching for a wide range of possible solutions that might reconcile the interests of both parties, instead of focusing too narrowly on one particular position. The fourth maxim recommends negotiating on a basis that is independent of the will of either side and turning to some objective standard that both participants can agree on or that at least does not just represent the position of one side. (We return to a discussion of this fourth maxim, in connection with the cement case in section 7.)

These four maxims all represent argumentation tactics that are useful in negotiation dialogue. It should also be added that empathy is a very important quality for an effective negotiator. In this context, without empathy it is impossible for one party to understand what the other party really wants and what her priorities are within her list of wants.[4]

Gaining an insight into the commitments of the other party during a negotiation dialogue is a very important skill.

2. Subtypes

The classification of subtypes presented by R.E. Walton and P.B. McKersie (1965) seems to be generally accepted in the field of negotiation studies. By and large, it is acceptable for our purposes, with a few reservations noted below. According to their analysis, there are four subtypes of negotiation dialogue (pp. 4–6). In the first type called *distributive bargaining*, the goal of one party conflicts with the goal of the other, which mean that the dialogue is a zero-sum game between the participants in the sense that one person's gain is the other's loss. The second type is called *integrative bargaining*, and instead of there being a basic conflict between the goals of the participants, the interests of both parties can be integrated to some extent. The third type of negotiation dialogue is called *attitudinal structuring*. Here the issue is not purely economic, but concerns relationships between the participants and attitudes like friendliness, trust, or respect. In this type of dialogue, the issue is not, at least directly, goods or services or other overt economic considerations, but personalities and motivations. The fourth type of negotiation dialogue is called *intra-organizational bargaining* where the goal is to bring the expectations of one side into alignment with those of the other. For example, at a certain stage of developments in a labour negotiation, the local union and the international union have to get together in order to agree on their objectives before they negotiate with management. This type of negotiation is distinctive in that it involves broad agreement at the outset, in a kind of case where both parties belong to the same group or are on the same side but nevertheless still have some differences to iron out.

The distributive type of bargaining is an abstract model of negotiation dialogue that has the advantage of theoretical simplicity, but it is not generally applicable (without abstraction) to many realistic cases. The reason is that the interests of both parties can usually be integrated with each other's to some extent. For example, suppose that I am having an argument with the chairman of my department about whether I should teach the Argumentation Course in a particular year. My position is that I should teach the course that year, and his position is that I should not. The conflict appears to be a zero-sum game because his position is the direct opposite (negation) of mine. But during the argumentation that takes place between the two of us, I discover that his real goal is not to block the Argumentation Course from being offered that year, but to keep enrolment high in our department. It emerges from our conversation that his objection to my teaching the course that year is that philosophy enrolments will be lowered because the Argumentation Course is a small class, while the other course I would teach in its place, Introduction to Logical Reasoning, is a large class. Thus in typical everyday negotiation dialogue, the conversation between the two parties often reveals that what initially appeared to be a zero-sum game really turns out to be an instance of the integrative bargaining type. Once the chairman's goal, his real interest or position, is revealed in the course of our conversation, the possibility opens up that he would not object to my teaching the Argumentation Course that year if it could be plausibly argued that enrolment would be high enough.

3. The Game-Theory Model of Negotiation

One model of the argumentation in a negotiation involves seeing the dialogue as a series of offers and counter-offers, as in the following case where two parties are negotiating the sale of a piece of farm equipment used for planting.

Case 4.1
PROPONENT: I'll let you have it for $100,000.
RESPONDENT: I'll give you $85,000 for it, and pay cash immediately.

Here negotiation dialogue is like a game that has pay-offs. The two parties are competing to divide up this pay-off, a kind of outcome that can be expressed in dollars or in some other numerical way of quantifying the values of the pay-offs. This view of negotiation has led to economic models of bargaining that use game theory as their model of the argumentation between two parties in negotiation dialogue. Game theory explains strategic behaviour by assuming that the participants in a game have the goal of maximizing their wins (positive pay-offs) and minimizing their losses in an exchange of moves (Schelling, 1960, p. 4). Game theory seems to be an attractive way of modelling the argumentation in negotiation dialogue, provided that the pay-offs are emphasized as the goal of each participant and that the moves in the dialogue are primarily seen as offers and counter-offers that have the aim of fulfilling this goal.

Putnam and Jones have criticized this economic-oriented games-theory model of negotiation on two grounds. First, games of economic exchange limit negotiation to zero-sum conflicts, where one party gains a fixed outcome that the other loses (1982, p. 264). But they note that a typical case of negotiation frequently involves the kind of integrative bargaining identified by Walton and McKersie (1965), where solutions can be expanded and altered in a non-quantitative way, and can benefit both parties. Second, economic models ignore 'social interaction' in negotiation, 'the factor that leads bargainers to understand one another's expectations, to submit to each other's influences, and to collaborate on joint settlements' (p. 264). Although the shortcomings of economic models have led researchers to adopt various social interaction and behavioural models of bargaining, these adaptions modify assumptions in the classic game-theory model. But Putnam and Jones still criticize the dominance of the game-theory models of negotiation on the grounds that even the newer theories fail to do justice to the central place of communication and information exchange between participants in negotiation dialogue.

The problem with the game-theory, economic-oriented model of argumentation in negotiation is that it overlooks both the very important role of commitment-based argumentation and the equally important role of practical reasoning (the kind used in deliberation dialogue, as shown in chapter 6). Negotiation, as a normative model of argumentation, needs to focus not just on fixed, economic outcomes that a participant wants to gain as a pay-off, but also on what the participant is more deeply committed to as a policy or goal, and on the means he thinks is required to bring about this goal. Thus negotiation should focus not just on the wins of one player as opposed to the contrary losses of the player, but also on how the goals of the participants in a negotiation dialogue can be defined and articulated by communication in the verbal interactions between the players in the dialogue. And it needs to focus on how needs are related to ends in the practical reasoning that is involved in bringing about these goals in relation to the given resources available in a case where goods and services may be in short supply. Where limited resources are available, negotiation needs to focus not just on a fixed outcome, but on the practical realities (as perceived by the participants) of whether, or how, that outcome can really be achieved by the collaboration of both parties in the bargaining.

Therefore, in the new dialectic, the game-theory model of negotiation is not wholly wrong, but it is oversimplified insofar as it concentrates exclusively on one particular aspect of the sequence of argumentation in negotiation dialogue and pays less attention to other central aspects. Consequently, in order to achieve a more adequate and useful model of negotiation dialogue for the new dialectic as a normative framework of reasoned argumentation, the model not only should include sequences of offers and counter-offers, as illustrated in case 4.1, but should also include the kinds of moves and counter-moves illustrated in the following case 4.2.

Case 4.2

PROPONENT: You are being quite reasonable to not want to pay $100,000 for a machine that does not plant soy beans, if planting soy beans is a main goal for you. But according to our reports, the market for soy beans has poor prospects for the future. And the soil in your area is not right for soy beans because of its high acidity.

RESPONDENT: Well, perhaps you are right. But can this machine be modified so that it can be used to plant soy beans, in case I should move to a different farm?

In this case, one of the farmer's goals is to plant soy beans. But the farm machinery salesman questions whether this plan is realistic, given the farmer's soil conditions. The farmer concedes the point, but in turn asks a practical question about how or whether the machine can be modified for this purpose.

To model this kind of argumentation, the theory of negotiation dialogue in the new dialectic must go beyond the game-theory model not just by taking into account the pay-offs in bargaining argumentation, but by seeing the use of practical reasoning by one party to alter the commitments of the other party as a central profile of argumentative exchanges that makes up the fabric of argumentation of this type of dialogue. Hence, in the new dialectical theory of negotiation dialogue, commitment of the participant, as modified during subsequent moves of the exchange, is a central concept in the profile of dialogue.

4. Commitment in Negotiation Dialogue

Commitment in negotiation dialogue is defined by what Fisher and Ury call 'the interest,' or what could be called the underlying objective of a participant in the negotiation. Each participant has an interest, and in distributive bargaining, the interest of one participant conflicts with that of the other. But as the dialogue proceeds, this interest is clarified and sharpened, so that what is really important to the arguer becomes more explicitly defined. Thus new possibilities for satisfying trade-offs and concessions arise. This process of clarification contributes to the efficiency and also to the quality of the negotiation dialogue as a whole.

When we compare Fisher and Ury's notion of negotiation dialogue with our previous analysis of persuasion dialogue as a model of normative dialogue, there is an interesting similarity between what they call interests and what we call the dark-side commitment set of a participant. There is also an interesting similarity between what they call the positions of the participants and what we call the explicit or light-side commitments. One of the main problems in negotiation, according to Fisher and Ury, is that each side tends to have multiple interests in a negotiation, and it may be difficult to define these interests exactly or for each party to identify them. As an aid in 'wise negotiation,' Fisher and Ury recommend looking behind positions for interests: 'A position is likely to be concrete and explicit: the interests underlying it may well be unexpressed, intangible and perhaps inconsistent' (1991, p. 44). Among the methods Fisher and Ury recommend to help identify a participant's interest in negotiation are the asking of 'why' questions and the use of empathy – that is, the technique as they call it, of 'putting yourself in the shoes of the other person' (p. 44). This process of clarifying interests appears to be very similar in general outline and in the methods used to the process of clarifying dark-side commitments in persuasion dialogue. And, indeed, many of the problems of retracting commitment and trying to extract commitments from a respondent that we studied in persuasion dialogue (see chapter 2) seem to be comparable to the kinds of tactics advocated by Fisher and Ury in negotiation dialogue (pp. 172–7). For example, they recommend moving towards commitment gradually, which is very similar to some of the strategies of persuasion dialogue, such as trying to split up commitments, and so forth, so that a gradual sequence of argumentation is used to move towards proving one side's thesis from the commitments of the other side.

Walton and McKersie focus on a different aspect of commitment in negotiation dialogue. They view the concept of commitment as central to negotiation dialogue, but see it as being different from the kind of commitment that is characteristic of persuasion dialogue and the inquiry. They define commitment as 'the act of pledging oneself to a course of action' (1965, p. 50). By allowing for implicit commitments, Walton and McKersie invite a certain comparison with the type of commitment characteristic of persuasion dialogue. But by bringing in the notion of action, their account also suggests that goal-directed practical reasoning could have an important role in argumentation in negotiation.[5]

Commitment in negotiation dialogue has a practical quality that is comparable to commitment in the deliberation type of dialogue. In both of the types of dialogue, commitment is towards a course of action.[6] In negotiation dialogue, commitment implies a readiness or willingness to undertake a course of action of a certain type in certain circumstances. This contrasts with persuasion dialogue, where commitment represents an opinion, an acceptance of a proposition as true.

In negotiation dialogue, the communication of commitments is associated with the making of offers, threats, and promises. What is especially important in evaluating such moves is the aspect of how firm or how flexible a commitment is. Putnam and Jones summarize four important dimensions of this aspect of commitment.

Research on the way commitments were communicated revealed four dimensions: flexibility, finality, specificity, and consequence (Walton & McKersie, 1965). Flexible commitments relied upon ambiguous messages while firm ones were characterized by clear communication. Flexible commitments frequently led to the use of accommodations and reciprocal concessions whereas firm ones entailed the risk of escalating the conflict. Bargainers conveyed firmness through language patterns of finality, specificity, and explicit consequences; e.g., 'We must have a 10% raise or we will go on strike.' In contrast, bargainers communicated flexibility through the use of tentative language and indirect requests; e.g., 'We must have the kind of package we've proposed or we will have difficulty selling it to the membership.' Most statements of commitment ranged from maximum firmness to maximum flexibility. (1982, p. 272)

There is some comparability with persuasion dialogue here, where ambiguity, tentative language, indirect speech acts, and argument from consequences are also used. But in negotiation dialogue, these arguments are used in a different way. And the concept of commitment is itself different in negotiation dialogue, in that it is commitment to an interest, as opposed to commitment to the truth or falsity of a proposition that may bear no relation to any interest the arguer has at stake.

In other respects, however, commitment is comparable in persuasion dialogue and negotiation dialogue. In both types of dialogue, the incurring of a commitment is done by making a certain type of move, by conceding a proposition or making an assertion. And once the commitment is made, a proposition is inserted into the speaker's commitment store. Henceforth, this speaker is held to this proposition which indicates his position on the issue.

In negotiation dialogue, the incurring and retraction of commitments by an arguer is a function of the kind of move made at a particular stage of the dialogue in relation to the rules for that type of move. Thus, just as in persuasion dialogue, the turn-taking and commitment rules function together.

At the argumentation stage of the negotiation, the rules are similar in certain respects to those of the critical discussion. In other respects, they are different because they reflect the difference in the goals and methods of the two types of dialogue. Donohue gives a set of fourteen rules for the type of negotiation dialogue called *distributive bargaining* (1981a, pp. 111–13). One rule says that attacking an opponent's position obligates the opponent to respond or to defend himself; if he does not, he risks conceding the point that is under attack. This rule is a kind of structural dialogue rule; at the same time, it pertains to commitment. What it means is that, if a participant doesn't respond to a critical argument or attack by the other side, then, by presumption, it is taken that the respondent concedes that the criticism is valid and he gives up this particular commitment at that point in the negotiation. This is a kind of dialogue or turn-taking rule in the sense that it specifies an obligatory kind of response by one party to a certain type of move by another party. But it is also partly a commitment rule because it indicates that a no-response move amounts to, and will be taken as, a retraction of commitment.

Another of Donohue's rules says that, when one party proposes an offer to a respondent, the respondent is obliged at least to consider the offer, not ignore it. This is a kind of presumptive rule; if the offer is ignored, the party who made the offer will interpret this lack of response as a rejection of the offer. This interpretation of rejection, then, has implications for the commitment set of the party to whom the offer was made. Hence, this rule is also a kind of dialogue rule that has to do with turn-taking, but it is also a commitment rule that relates to the development of the commitment sets as the dialogue proceeds.

5. Relevance and Irrelevance

Whether an argument is relevant in a negotiation dialogue is determined by the original agenda in which the interests of both parties are stated. But it also depends on the stage of the negotiation where the argument (or question, concession, or other type of move) is used, as well as on the rules for the moves at that stage.

The general outline of the structure of the negotiation as a type of dialogue is similar to that of the critical discussion in that, ideally, an agenda is set during the confrontation stage which states the issue or issues to be resolved by the dialogue. Again, as in the critical discussion, in negotiation, problems can occur where the agenda is not stated in a clear or well-formulated enough way to guide the discussion towards a successful conclusion. This means that the concept of dialectical relevance is very important to the normative structure of the negotiation as a type of dialogue, as it is in the critical discussion. In both types of dialogue, fallacies of relevance occur when one party tries to distract the other, or inadvertently gets off the track of the discussion, by raising questions or putting forward arguments that don't really bear on the central issue.

However, relevance is intrinsically different in the two types of dialogue. In a critical discussion, an argument is relevant to the extent that it bears on proving that one of the original propositions is true or that it subjects the proposition to critical questioning. In negotiation dialogue, an argument or other kind of speech act is relevant if it is the right kind of move – like a concession or an offer – that is, a step that contributes to the resolution of the original conflict of interest by agreement of both parties. In the critical discussion and the persuasion dialogue generally, and in the inquiry as well, relevance means contributing to the function of proving that a particular proposition is true or should be accepted as true by one of the parties in the dialogue. Relevance in a negotiation, on the other hand, refers to the kind of move that has a function in contributing to an ultimate resolution of the conflict of interest which is set as the agenda of the negotiation.

Relevance in negotiation dialogue is determined by linking together the sequence of interactive moves in a given case and then using a profile of negotiation dialogue to compare the existing case to what such a sequence of moves looks like in a normative model of appropriate negotiation dialogue. The profile of dialogue not only needs to take into account the original conflict of interests (the issue or ultimate pay-offs that are the goals of both parties). It also needs to take into account how the argumentation has evolved towards, or away from, this original issue in the connected sequence of argumentation as compared to the normative profile that can be reconstructed from the case. Such a normative profile should be built up on the moves of each party, as they interact with the moves of the other party, with each argument by each party at each point in the dialogue supposedly being based on the commitments of the other party. The logical inferences in such argument moves in a negotiation are typically not represented by deductive and inductive models of logical reasoning alone. In many instances, arguments in negotiation dialogue are based on practical reasoning that is goal-directed, knowledge-based, and action-guiding (see Walton, 1990a). In the use of this type of reasoning in a negotiation, one party tries to determine what the other party's goals really are (based on his commitments, as evidenced by his prior moves in the dialogue) and to raise questions about the means to carry out these goals.

Thus a move in a negotiation dialogue is relevant if it fits into the profile of dialogue that is appropriately matched to the actual sequence of practical reasoning used by the participants in the given case. For example, if a husband and wife are negotiating about who should carry out some household task, the argumentation may turn on many practical sub-issues, such as how the task should be carried out, when it should be carried out, who can do it most efficiently, what kinds of skills and equipment are needed, and so forth. All of these arguments involve sequences of practical reasoning concerning the means of carrying out the task and the importance of the task as a goal (or as practically related to a goal) which may be more important as a commitment to the one party than to the other.

On the other hand, an argument or move in a negotiation dialogue is dialectically irrelevant if it is out of place in the profile of dialogue that ties the argumentation together. The nature of the problem of irrelevance in a negotiation is clearly indicated by Gulliver (1979). At the beginning stage of negotiation, an original disagreement is fairly clear, such as a rejected demand for repayment of debt or for a wage increase. But as the discussion evolves between the parties, new details appear and dormant issues come to be part of the ongoing discussion. As Gulliver puts it, 'Seeming irrelevancies may get caught up, both material and affective' (p. 126). As the dialogue proceeds, new issues are introduced, and if the original agenda was vague, new complaints and demands swell the agenda as the discussion proceeds. Once the negotiation spreads to these other matters, discussion of these new concerns actually have the effect of blocking discussion of the original issue.

Irrelevant arguments can be fallacious in negotiation dialogue where they block successful progress of the discussion. One way to prevent this kind of problem is to try to get clear agreement on the issues at the outset. Thus, an important factor in the confrontation stage of a negotiation is the process of formulating the agenda. In some cases, this issue is itself highly negotiable, and participants may have intense disputes about which issues should be on the agenda and in what order they should be discussed. Just as in the critical discussion, agreement on the issue and clarification of the issue are important first steps in successful resolution of the dispute. But in negotiation dialogue, the agenda itself is very much subject to negotiation, even though it is strongly influenced by the underlying interests of the participants.

But what sort of fallacy is irrelevance in a negotiation? Is it a sophistical tactic that can be used by one party to delay or confuse the efforts at negotiation of the other party? Or is it a kind of blunder – more the error of reasoning type of fallacy – like shooting oneself in the foot?

In formulating rules for distributive bargaining, Donohue makes it clear how irrelevant moves in a negotiation can sometimes be instances of the second type of fallacy (1981a; 1981b). In one of his rules, he shows how irrelevance is a problem that tends to weaken the bargaining of the party who makes the irrelevant move in a negotiation. According to this rule, making utterances that are 'unclear or unrelated to the negotiation are generally viewed as demonstrating lack of confidence' (1981a, p. 111). Furthermore, he notes that such a move does not constrain the next utterance in the dialogue and, therefore, 'may result in relinquishing control of the interaction.' Thus, irrelevant moves in a negotiation carry a severe penalty for an arguer not only by making him appear weak or lacking in confidence. Since an obviously irrelevant move does not constrain the other party to making a particular type of next move in response, in effect, the original speaker has relinquished control of the dialogue and leaves an opening for attack by the other side. It seems, then, that irrelevance in a negotiation dialogue can be a dangerous tactic that may severely weaken an arguer's line of bargaining.

In another rule, Donohue says that, when a participant relinquishes control of the negotiation dialogue, the other party has the right to change the topic or control the direction of the subsequent dialogue. This rule indicates clearly how irrelevance not only is a general normative failure in a negotiation dialogue, but also constitutes a very important type of strategic failure which the other party can take advantage of. Distributive bargaining is a highly competitive type of dialogue, and as noted by Walton and McKersie (1965), it can be defined generally as far as its strategies are concerned as a zero-sum game. However, there are also important aspects of agreement in that the participants should begin the dialogue with a clear agenda and, in order to successfully resolve the dispute, should only make responses that are appropriate and relevant at any given stage or particular focal point in the evolution of the dialogue.

Jacobs and Jackson show how child-custody disputes can lead to 'digressions' when the participants 'seem to lose track of the point of finding mutually agreeable custody/visitation arrangements.' Instead of sticking to the negotiations over custody, the participants exhibit a tendency to use *ad hominem* attacks against each other: 'The digressions seem to reflect disputants' preoccupation with censuring and blaming the other party and with defending themselves against attributions of moral failure that might be formed from the arguments' (1992, p. 163). The resulting series of insults, threats, and attacks is an obstacle to the progress of the negotiations because it functions as an irrelevant line of argumentation, a digression from the central dispute.

It is our conjecture, however, that fallacies of irrelevance are the most acute problems, and are used most successfully as sophistical tactics, in cases where there has been a shift from one type of dialogue to another, or in cases where there is confusion about what type of dialogue the participants are really supposed to be engaged in. The importance of this factor can best be appreciated when we reflect on the problems posed by the use of threats as arguments. Threats are generally perceived as irrelevant moves in persuasion dialogue. But they can be relevant, in many cases, in negotiation dialogue. *Ad hominem* arguments are readily perceived as irrelevant, or as a digression, in a persuasion dialogue or a negotiation, but they can be relevant if the whole point of the discussion is to blame the other party for some culpable action. When a shift from one type of dialogue to another occurs during a sequence of argumentation, an argument that appears to be relevant may not be. This deceptive appearance of relevance is a characteristic indicator of a fallacy of irrelevance.

6. Threats as Arguments

Threats are a normal part of negotiation dialogue, and should not be considered inappropriate or fallacious (at least in all cases) in this context of conversation. For example, in a strike negotiation, the union representative says, 'If you don't meet our conditions, the members will go out on the picket line tomorrow morning.' This type of threat is a nor-

mal part of negotiating, and not necessarily an illicit type of argument
move that is contrary to the goal of negotiation as a type of dialogue. As
an appropriate part of a profile of dialogue in argumentation in a negotiation, such a threat could be a relevant argument.

It is important to distinguish between two kinds of threats that are
typically used in argumentation (see Walton, 1992c, pp. 170–4). A *direct
threat* is a species of argument from consequences where the proponent
tells the respondent that he (the proponent) intends to carry out some
action that will have bad consequences from the respondent's point of
view unless she (the respondent) carries out some other action. An *indirect threat* is an indirect speech act that functions at the surface level as a
warning from the proponent to the respondent – 'I wouldn't do that if I
were you because bad consequences could happen' – yet both parties
realize that the proponent is stating that he intends to bring about these
bad consequences. The purpose of using the indirect type of threat is to
leave room for the proponent to claim plausible deniability. If accused of
having made a threat, he could reply, 'I never made a threat – it was just
a warning.' Direct threats are much harsher, and generally regarded as
inappropriate even in negotiation dialogue. Indirect threats are much
more common and more acceptable as a normal part of negotiation dialogue.

Threats are so integral to negotiation dialogue that many of the rules
for negotiation formulated by Donohue involve making threats and
responding appropriately to them. One rule says that threatening an
opponent obligates the opponent to respond to the threat; otherwise, he
risks antagonizing the user of the threat (1981, p. 111). The presumption
here is that the threat will be viewed as serious once it is stated, and if
the respondent does not reply appropriately, he faces a penalty. The penalty arises when the party who made the threat becomes antagonized by
this refusal to respond seriously, making it more difficult for the respondent to carry on with successful bargaining to support his side of the
negotiations.

Penalties or sanctions can be very important in conversational
exchanges of argumentation where the dialogue has a practical aspect,
that is, where the goal is to solve a practical problem, or get some sort of
action (see Walton and Krabbe, 1995). In such cases, the use of sanctions
can be closely tied with the rules for gaining commitment.

Walton and McKersie even go so far as to define commitment in negotiation dialogue primarily in terms of threats. As they see it, commitment in negotiation dialogue 'can be either primarily demands or

threats but always involves some element of both' (1965, p. 82). Commitment in negotiation dialogue is distinctively different from that of persuasion dialogue. Commitment in a negotiation dialogue generally, and appropriately, involves an element of either demanding or threatening, and also of making monetary offers, whereas this kind of argumentation in a persuasion dialogue would be a highly inappropriate way of trying to get the other party to make commitments. It would be regarded as not only dramatically inappropriate, but also highly aggressive, and as indicating the kind of attitude that characterizes the committing of fallacies.

The key fallacy here is the *ad baculum* fallacy, which should perhaps be redefined contextually as the use of an argument to make a threat in a persuasion dialogue in order to try to get the other party to accept a conclusion or to incur a commitment to a proposition as true or acceptable. There is a sharp contrast here. Although the use of threats as tactics to make arguments in persuasion dialogue is readily and rightly regarded as fallacious, the same kind of speech act, or the making of a similar kind of threat, might not be fallacious in a negotiation dialogue where threats are generally not regarded as inappropriate. Of course, some threats can be highly inappropriate in a negotiation dialogue, but, generally speaking, arguments that try to extract commitments, or that make commitments through demands or threats, not only are commonplace in negotiation dialogue, but are legitimate tactics and may be regarded as generally legitimate kinds of arguments to carry out the goals of negotiation dialogue. This means that, in an *ad baculum* argument, what might be fallacious in the context of persuasion dialogue or critical discussion might not be fallacious if the context were different, that is, if the context were that of a negotiation dialogue.

The central account of argument methodology for negotiation dialogue given by Walton and McKersie is concerned with the identification of what they call *commitment tactics*. Some of these tactics feature techniques for making a threat appear credible and effective to an opponent in negotiation, such as conveying the idea that the arguer has a taste for a fight and is willing to fulfil the threat (1965, p. 103). Another tactic is for the arguer to be seen making overt preparations to fulfil an expressed threat. According to Walton and McKersie, using this tactic will convince the opponent of the willingness and capacity of the arguer to bring about the consequences expressed in a threat or to accept these consequences. These tactics make it very clear just how intimately threats are tied to the notion of commitment in negotiation dialogue. In negotiations, arguments that make a threat, directly or indirectly, are generally regarded as moves that contribute to the goals of successful bargaining.

Thus the use of a threat as an argument can be relevant in a negotiation dialogue. Such cases of relevant threats typically involve indirect threats that are used to bargain with the other party and that cite negative consequences of some goal or action that the other party is committed to. Such an argument expressing a threat is a subtype of argumentation from negative consequences, a form of argument used in practical reasoning with another party to try to get that party to steer clear of a projected course of action that (it is alleged by the arguer) will have negative consequences on the goals of that other party. (The precise form of argumentation from negative consequences will be explained in chapter 6.) Of course, an argument from negative consequences is not necessarily an argument that poses a threat, but threat-posing arguments are a subspecies of arguments from consequences of a kind that can be relevant in negotiation dialogue.

In short, arguments expressing a threat should not be regarded as fallacious *ad baculum* arguments within the context of a negotiation dialogue. To pin down the fallaciousness of *ad baculum* arguments, we need to understand the nature of the dialectical shift from a persuasion dialogue to a negotiation dialogue.

7. Dialectical Shifts from Negotiation

As noted earlier, Fisher and Ury recommend moving to a fair standard that is independent of either side when a conflict blocks a negotiation. They offer the following example, which we will call the cement case.

Case 4.3
Suppose you have entered into a fixed-price construction contract for your house that calls for reinforced concrete foundations but fails to specify how deep they should be. The contractor suggests two feet. You think five feet is closer to the usual depth for your type of house.

Now suppose the contractor says: 'I went along with you on steel girders for the roof. It's your turn to go along with me on shallower foundations.' No owner in his right mind would yield. Rather than horse-trade, you would insist on deciding the issue in terms of objective safety standards. 'Look, maybe I'm wrong. Maybe two feet is enough. What I want are foundations strong and deep enough to hold up the building safely. Does the government have standard specifications for these soil conditions? How deep are the foundations of other buildings in this area? What is the earthquake risk here? Where do you suggest we look for standards to resolve this question?' (1991, p. 82)

According to Fisher and Ury, horse-trading, or continuing the bargaining by haggling, would not lead to a wise agreement in this kind of case. A better alternative, in their view, is to ask the kinds of questions they cite in the cement case, which seek some standard that is independent of the will of either side.

What Fisher and Ury recommend here is a shift, at least temporarily, to an information-seeking type of dialogue in order to answer relevant questions about the government's standard specifications, earthquake risks, and depth of foundations of other buildings in the area. (At least this is how what they recommend is best seen in our theory of the different types of dialogue.) These kinds of questions can only be usefully answered by shifting to some other type of dialogue, generally an information-seeking type of dialogue or an inquiry type of dialogue. Once this information-seeking dialogue is successfully completed and the answers are made available to both sides, we can shift back to the negotiation, and the information garnered through the information-seeking dialogue can then be used in the subsequent negotiations to arrive at a wiser agreement.

The word 'wiser' here even suggests a well-informed agreement based on relevant information that can help both parties see what is useful and necessary in the given situation, so that neither party will have problems in the future because of the cement foundation's being put in improperly. Fisher and Ury see this principled aspect of the dialogue as part of the negotiation. They define it as a principled negotiation, but in our terms, it is a kind of change from one type of dialogue to another – what could be called a 'dialectical shift,' so what is a negotiation dialogue temporarily shifts to another type of dialogue.[7] In the kind of recommendation Fisher and Ury have in mind, once the information-seeking dialogue is successfully completed, the participants then shift back to the negotiation dialogue. According to that interpretation, the information-seeking dialogue becomes a part of – is subjoined to – negotiation dialogue. It forms an interlude, so to speak, in the negotiation dialogue, where the conversation shifts to a framework of a different type. The negotiation can benefit from this interlude or build on it by utilizing the results of the information-seeking dialogue as premises or conclusions to make the negotiation better informed and, hence, more successful in reaching a good agreement.

In our terms, then, the cement case can be interpreted in the following way. The goal of the negotiation is to reach a good agreement – an agreement that both parties can accept and live with, that is not too heavily weighted towards the interests of one side, and that will not lead to forseeable bad consequences for either side. To reach a good agreement in a negotiation dialogue, it is sometimes useful at a certain juncture to shift to a different type of dialogue, like an information-seeking dialogue, which can actually improve the quality of the original dialogue and give it better prospects of a successful conclusion.

In short, Fisher and Ury's analysis of negotiation dialogue as a normative structure is somewhat narrow in that it fails to recognize how other types of dialogue function around the periphery of negotiation dialogue, where negotiation shifts into another distinctively different type of dialogue. It is understandable why they focus exclusively on the negotiation as opposed to these other types of dialogue. But this fragmented view of negotiation dialogue can be improved by adopting a wider and more pluralistic viewpoint on the subject of argumentation generally.

In light of our analysis of the quarrel as a distinctive type of dialogue in chapter 7, it is interesting to note that Fisher and Ury suggest that one important goal in negotiation is to avoid useless quarrels. Because participants tend not only to focus too rigidly on their own positions, but also to get emotionally involved and attack the other party personally, there is a strong tendency for negotiation dialogue to degenerate into a quarrel. Jacobs and Jackson (1992), for example, have documented the tendency for negotiations over child custody in a divorce mediation session to degenerate into personal attacks, insults, and blaming of the other party.

Fisher and Ury suggest various practical methods for avoiding this dangerous but common development. Once again, however, it would be more useful if they recognized that the shift from negotiation to quarrel is a shift to a distinctively different type of dialogue and that this kind of shift has important characteristics that are useful in helping us improve the quality of negotiation by dealing with this tendency for quarrels to interfere with successful negotiation. The problem here is that the quarrel itself has a distinctive normative structure as a type of dialogue; if we learn to recognize it, then it helps us identify when the danger of a shift from another type of dialogue to a quarrel is likely to occur, or when it has occurred in a given case.[8] This takes us to the concern of chapter 7 – the quarrel as a type of dialogue.

8. Solutions for Deadlock

The main line of argumentation in a negotiation dialogue takes the form of a sequence of offers and concessions that ideally converge towards a middle position where both interests can be satisfied. But what happens if the argumentation ends in a *deadlock*, a pair of positions that cannot be matched or fitted together so that the interests of both parties are satisfied? As the advice of Fisher and Ury indicate, sometimes the best way to proceed is to break off negotiations, temporarily at least, and proceed to some other type of dialogue, like an information-seeking dialogue.

Sometimes such a shift is neither necessary nor desirable, and the negotiation can serve as a means for clarifying and prioritizing our underlying commitments. Negotiation, in such a case, serves as a process of testing our commitments and making them more precise, as the following example illustrates.

Case 4.4
I am negotiating with a salesman on a new car I have made an offer on. After a process of continued negotiation, the two of us have come to a deadlock. The problem is that I have certain requirements in a car – it must have certain features, like air-conditioning, antilock brakes, and so forth. But the type of car I want, with all these features, costs more than I am prepared to pay. My family and I have set an upper limit, and the salesman calculates that he simply cannot, at this time, sell me a car of the kind we want with all these features at this price.

The negotiation is deadlocked. What can we do? Perhaps it is best to just wait, if possible, or to seek out more information by going to other dealers, looking at used cars, and so forth.

Another possibility is that I can look inward to clarify my own position and decide what is most important. For example, my family might discuss what features are most important to them, and whether there is room to go a little higher in our price limit to get these features or whether some of them can be given up. This process is one of internal compromises within our own position. It might turn out that some of our requirements are less important than others, or that some of them can be waived or reduced in order to get others. Once the whole package is weighed, perhaps a standby or modified position can be arrived at, one that is not ideal but that can be held in reserve as a possible solution to the deadlock if nothing better is forthcoming through other avenues of proceeding.

One solution to deadlock is Fisher and Ury's method of going to a third, neutral party, who decides the outcome on the basis of 'objective principles.' This dialectical shift may be a reasonable shift if both parties agree to it and see no better alternative. But the problem is that this way of deciding the issue may not lead to a good agreement, in our sense of being an outcome that both parties can live with and that satisfies their underlying commitments. It may satisfy the deeper commitments of one party but not the other, and thus lead to a feeling of dissatisfaction. Or, even worse, it may not satisfy the dark-side commitments of either party.

Another solution that we advocate here is for both parties to look inward, make some compromises in defining their own commitments and priorities in a more finely qualified way, while at the same time basing their moves on an estimate of the commitments of the other party. This less confrontational approach may involve some losses. But it will allow one party to preserve what is most important to him in the sense of defining his dark-side commitments in terms of clearly defined but flexible values, specific actions, or commodities. And at the same time, it will enable a participant to base his moves on judgments of what is most important to the other. This solution may be hard to accept because openness to compromise suggests that one party is a 'loser,' that he has not been aggressive enough to get the best of the other party. Unfortunately, this kind of attitude can be carried too far in confrontational negotiations, and often indicates a shift to the quarrel.

Beacon Expert Systems has developed a software program, called 'Negotiator Pro,' that offers advice on what sort of questions participants should ask when bargaining in a negotiation. This system is based on the principle, 'Those who negotiate the best agreements know not only which questions to ask their adversaries, but which questions to ask themselves' (Unger, 1992, p. 455). In 'Negotiator Pro,' an important part of the system is the building of a 'negotiation personality profile' both of the other party and of yourself. To build the profile of the other side, you must work 'on a best-guess basis' (Unger, 1992, p. 455). This way of giving advice on how to carry out productive negotiations rightly emphasizes the importance of the personal element, the element of building negotiation on a careful construct of both your own underlying commitments and those of the other side.

Curiously, this approach suggests that the *ad hominem* type of argument, of using the commitment of the other party as a basis for trying to get him to accept a proposition, is central to negotiation dialogue. Moreover, it appears that it is nonfallacious (at least generally) and is a reasonable kind of argument to recommend as an important tool in productive negotiation. This may be puzzling to readers who are familiar with the *ad hominem* argument as a fallacy in informal logic.[9] We return to this puzzle in the last chapter where some of the traditional fallacies are reconsidered.

9. Bias and Advocacy

There is an inherent difference between negotiation dialogue and persuasion dialogue; the former is interest-based, while the orientation of the latter towards discovering the truth of a matter. This difference is important in issues related to bias and advocacy.

Following is a classic case of the bias type of *ad hominem* argument (from Walton, 1989a, p. 149). Let us call it the acid rain case.

Case 4.5
Bob and Wilma are discussing the problem of acid rain. Wilma argues that reports on the extent of the problem are greatly exaggerated and that the costs of action are prohibitive. Bob points out that Wilma is on the board of directors of a U.S. coal company and that therefore her argument should not be taken at face value.

Bob's argument is classified as a bias type of *ad hominem* argument. He uses this allegation of bias to attack Wilma's argument, suggesting that we ought to give less credibility to her argument because she has an interest in advocating one side of the issue. Bob argues, in effect, that Wilma is basing her argument on concealed self-interest instead of looking at the evidence on both sides of the issue in a balanced way, which is characteristic of a critical discussion. Bob's *ad hominem* argument is based on an allegation that there has been a dialectical shift. Instead of engaging in a fair-minded critical discussion of the acid rain issue, as the participants are supposed to be doing, Wilma is covertly bargaining – that is, advocating the corporate point of view that she is paid to promote. What gives Bob's bias *ad hominem* argument its special sting is that Wilma did not announce her corporate ties at the beginning of the discussion and appears to have attempted to conceal her bias.

This case is a fundamental one because it raises a lot of questions about how to define and understand bias and advocacy as general concepts. There is advocacy in persuasion dialogue: each party argues for and supports his own point of view as strongly as possible (within the limits allowed by the dialogue). We could say that each side has a bias. But this type of bias is normal, and does not necessarily indicate that a fallacy has been committed or that there has been some defect or error in the argument. However, if a bias is pushed too hard – so that it interferes with the empathy, openness, and balance necessary for the conduct of a critical discussion – an acceptable or 'good' bias can become a 'bad' or interfering bias, the kind that ought to be subject to critical censure.

The problem in this acid rain case is not that Wilma's argument that the extent of acid rain has been exaggerated is, in itself, a bad or inappropriate kind of advocacy. Her advocacy of this point of view in a persuasion dialogue is normal, reasonable, and appropriate. However, as soon as we are told she is on the board of directors of a coal company, we suspect that a different type of advocacy may be involved. Advocacy, in this context, means interest-based bargaining, and Wilma has a 'vested interest' because she stands to gain by promoting the one point of view. We end up wondering if this is really the basis of her argument, rather than the kind of open-minded looking at the evidence on both sides that is characteristic of the critical discussion.

Bias and advocacy are two important concepts that remain to be investigated on the basis of the different types of dialogue as a general framework. However, we already need to note that the bias type of *ad hominem* argument can be understood as a kind of allegation of a shift to negotiation dialogue from another type of dialogue.

10. Advocacy Advertising

What type of dialogue is the kind of argument presented in an advertising message supposed to be part of ? Another perplexing question: what is the purpose of a 'commercial' (or other form of advertising message)? Although we are very familiar with commercial ads, we have not in the past had occasion to reflect on the classification of argumentation in this format under the category of a normative model of dialogue.

This issue has practical implications for the analysis and evaluation of fallacies in the area of informal logic. The fallacies outlined in chapter 1 are frequently condemned by logic textbooks because they are 'daydreams and delusions' perpetrated on us by those 'hucksters' and 'ballyhoo artists' of our time, the advertising agencies. From Copi and Cohen's widely used logic textbook (1990), the famous passage on the *ad populum* fallacy springs to mind.

Those who rely most heavily upon arguments *ad populum* are now to be found in advertising agencies, where the use of that fallacy has been elevated almost to the status of a fine art. Every attempt is made to associate some product being advertised with things of which we can be expected to approve strongly, or which excite us favorably. The breakfast cereal is associated with trim youthfulness, athletic prowess, and vibrant good health; whisky is associated with luxury and achievement, and beer with high adventure; the automobile to be sold is associated with romance, riches and sex. Every device, appealing to sight and sound and smell, is brought to bear: the men who use the advertised product are clear-eyed, broad-shouldered and distinguished; the women are slim, lovely, very well-dressed – or hardly dressed at all. Advertisers, as we know well, often sell us daydreams and delusions of grandeur. So clever and persistent are the ballyhoo artists of our time that all of us are influenced in spite of our resolution to resist. In one way or another the hucksters penetrate our consciousness, even our subconscious thoughts, manipulating us to their purposes with relentless appeals to emotions of every kind. (pp. 103–4)

If an advertising message is supposed to be a critical discussion where the argument presents evidence to back up its claim, or if it is supposed to be an information-giving type of dialogue that informs us about products, then the condemnation of these 'relentless appeals' by Copi and Cohen is fully justified. For psychological appeals used to 'penetrate our consciousness' are not arguments that contribute to the goals of either of these two types of dialogue. Indeed, they are impediments to the goals of dialogue, and are rightly condemned by Copi and Cohen for committing fallacies of relevance.

But is a commercial ad supposed to be a critical discussion or an information-seeking type of dialogue? Either of these hypotheses seems implausible. They both seem to hold advertisements to a much higher standard of logical reasoning than really seems fair or appropriate.

But it is hard to classify exactly what type of dialogue the argument in a commercial advertisement should fall under. We know that the purpose of the ad is to sell a product, and that the goal therefore is to promote sales and the interests of the sponsor of the ad. We expect the commercial to have a bias of this sort; we don't expect it to be the kind of balanced presentation that we see in a news report. As a type of argument, the discourse in the commercial seems closer to the negotiation dialogue than it does to persuasion dialogue. It is partly an attempt to persuade, but not necessarily by logical reasoning. It is really more of an attempt to get us to buy a particular product. It offers us a deal, so to speak. And in this respect, it seems to be more closely related to bargaining, to making an offer, than it does to reasonably persuading us to accept a particular proposition as true or false. However, there are some ads that are more of the 'advocacy' variety, that try to persuade us to adopt a particular point of view on some issue.

Classifying advocacy advertisements has become a legal problem. If an ad is classified as a political speech, it is exempt from the Federal Trade Commission's regulation covering deception and falsehood. The U.S. Supreme Court has ruled that commercial speech is subject to such a regulation to ensure that it is accurate and not deceptive.

But in the case of an advocacy ad, how do we tell which of these two categories it falls into? In 1983 the U.S. Supreme Court, in the case of Bolger v Youngs Drug Products Corp., ruled that ads containing both political and commercial speech are classified as commercial speech if three criteria are present: the ad is paid for; the ad refers to a specific product; and the ad is economically motivated. This case has been summarized by Middleton (1991).

Case 4.6
In *Bolger*, the Court ruled that some pamphlets distributed by a condom manufacturer were commercial speech even though the pamphlets discussed venereal disease, a political and social issue. One of the informational pamphlets deemed commercial described the advantages of a number of Trojan-brand contraceptives. Another pamphlet discussed condoms without reference to Youngs' products, although the company was identified at the end of the pamphlet. The Court said that Youngs' 'direct comments' on public issues such as venereal disease would merit full constitutional protection, but not statements 'made in the context of commercial transactions.' The pamphlets were commercial speech, the Court said, because they were purchased by Youngs, referred to Youngs' condoms and were economically motivated. (p. 79)

According to Middleton, the most important factor in determining whether an advocacy ad is an instance of commercial speech is whether it makes a commercial offer.

We can see the similarity between the type of dialogue that includes advertisements and the negotiation dialogue. For one of the most important aspects of commitment in negotiation dialogue is the specification and formulation of the commitment by making an offer, a pledge that could result in a deal if the other party takes it. A commercial ad is like one part or phase of a sequence of argumentation in a negotiation dialogue, whereas an advocacy ad is much better viewed as an argument in a persuasion dialogue.

These problems of classifying argumentation in advertisements, and in sales dialogue generally, remain puzzling, open questions. We return to them in chapter 9.

5

Information-Seeking Dialogue

In information-seeking dialogue, the respondent appears to the proponent to be a repository of information that the proponent cannot get access to other than by questioning the respondent. The role of the respondent is to transmit this information by giving answers or replies that are as clear and as helpful as possible. Hence, this type of dialogue is asymmetrical in nature, yet highly collaborative and non-adversarial.

1. Main Characteristics

The information-seeking dialogue starts with an initial situation in which one participant has, or appears to have, some information that the other party wants. Unlike the previous three types of dialogue, in the information type the goal is not to find out or to prove whether a particular proposition is true. This can sometimes be the case, but usually the questioner wants, or needs to find, information on a particular subject, information he needs in order to solve a problem or to carry on some task. The role of the other party is to give the relevant information to the questioner.

In Grice's theory, the concept of informativeness is conveyed by the first maxim of quantity: 'Make your contribution [to a conversation] as informative as is required' (1975, p. 67). This suggests that a reply to a question should give not just information, but information that is helpful, that is a contribution to the goals of dialogue.

In the opening stages of an information-seeking dialogue, there is a presumption that the answerer is willing to give the information sought by the questioner to the extent that he can. And there is a presumption that the questioner wants this information badly enough so that he is willing to make persistent attempts to extract it from the respondent. Here the information-seeking type of dialogue shows itself to be highly asymmetrical, unlike the three previous types of dialogue that are symmetrical in the sense that both participants have comparable or roughly equal roles. In the information-seeking type of dialogue, the roles of the questioner and the answerer are different in nature (Hintikka, 1981; Hintikka and Saarinen, 1979). During the argumentation stage, the method of the questioner is to ask questions, whereas the type of move made by the respondent is generally to give as direct answers as possible to these questions.

We see information-seeking dialogue as a verbal exchange between two parties, one of whom has specific information that the other party wants or needs. Some writers see the information-seeking dialogue in a different way; Hintikka (1981) and Hintikka and Saarinen (1979), for example, see information-seeking dialogue as an exchange between a reasoner who is collecting information and a second party, called Nature, who supplies information.

Sperber and Wilson (1986) define relevance in a context that appears comparable to what we are calling information-seeking dialogue. They treat relevance as a relation between a proposition and a context (p. 107), and the relevance of a proposition is defined as the extent to which its contextual effects are large and easy to infer (p. 125). They give the following example.

Mary and Peter are sitting on a park bench. He leans back, which alters her view. By leaning back, he modifies her cognitive environment; he reveals to her certain phenomena, which she may look at or not, and describe to herself in different ways. Why should she pay attention to one phenomenon rather than another, or describe it to herself in one way rather than another? In other words, why should she mentally process any of the assumptions which have become manifest or more manifest to her as a result of the change in her environment? Our answer is that she should process those assumptions that are most relevant to her at the time.

Imagine, for instance, that as a result of Peter's leaning back she can see, among other things, three people: an ice-cream vendor whom she had noticed before when she sat down on the bench, an ordinary stroller whom she has never seen before, and her acquaintance William, who is coming towards them and is a dreadful bore. Many assumptions about each of these characters are more or less manifest to her. She may already have considered the implications of the presence of the ice-cream vendor when she first noticed him; if so, it would be a waste of processing resources to pay further attention to him now. The presence of the unknown stroller is new information to her, but little or nothing follows from it; so there again, what she can perceive and infer about him is not likely to be of much relevance to her. By contrast, from the fact that William is coming her way, she can draw many conclusions from which many more conclusions will follow. This, then, is the one truly relevant change in her cognitive environment; this is the particular phenomenon she should pay attention to. She should do so, that is, if she is aiming at cognitive efficiency. (pp. 48–9)

Mary sees three things in her perceptual field, but William's coming towards her and Peter is the most relevant piece of information because its 'contextual effects' are large. Mary immediately starts drawing inferences about this piece of information and ignores the other 'less relevant' things that she also observes. But what does 'relevant' mean for Sperber and Wilson, if Mary is presumed to be engaged in some goal-directed type of dialogue?

If we view Sperber and Wilson's theory of relevance as an account of conversational relevance, it is best seen as a theory of informativeness. According to Berg, 'It is as if our one and only goal in life were to amass mounds of information, as economically as possible' (1991, p. 419). Sperber and Wilson also stress the importance of collecting information in human cognition: 'It seems that human cognition is aimed at improving the individual's knowledge of the world. This means adding more information, information that is more accurate, more easily retrievable, and more developed in areas of greater concern to the individual. Information processing is a permanent life-long task' (1986, p. 47). They define the chief goal of human cognition in terms of collection and use of information:

Our claim is that all human beings automatically aim at the most efficient information processing possible. This is so whether they are conscious of it or not; in fact, the very diverse and shifting conscious interests of individuals result from the pursuit of this permanent aim in changing conditions. In other words, an individual's particular cognitive goal at a given moment is always an instance of a more general goal: maximizing the relevance of the information processed. We will show that this is a crucial factor in human interaction. (p. 48)

Berg sees the goal of a conversation's participants in Sperber and Wilson primarily as one of collecting information. Commenting on these passages cited from Sperber and Wilson, he writes:

In my mind this conjures up images of the legions of professional information gatherers employed by national intelligence organizations, who spend all their time poring over the world's verbal output, culling and filing whatever might increase the nation's storehouse of information. Their single goal (professionally) is to accumulate information, which they do blindly and relentlessly, as best they can on their (possibly) limited resources. (1991, p. 419)

Whether or not this is a fair or complete view of Sperber and Wilson's account, Berg is right to point out that they postulate a framework of cognition that could be called a sort of information-seeking or information-collecting dialogue.

However, it seems that what Sperber and Wilson have in mind is a kind of collection of information by an agent engaged in goal-directed reasoning prior to some sort of action or a deliberated response to new information from the agent's perceived situation. We would classify this as practical reasoning in deliberation dialogue. (Further comments on Sperber and Wilson's example appear in chapter 6.)

In our own approach to information-seeking dialogue, we see the paradigm as a dialogue exchange between two parties. This type of exchange is comparable to persuasion dialogue in that both participants have commitment stores. But in the case of information-seeking dialogue, this set of propositions represents a pool of information, a set of propositions that is known to, or contained in, the one participant and that is lacking in the other participant. Our concept of the information-seeking dialogue could be extended, in the way Hintikka proposes, to a framework of reasoning in which information is collected from Nature or from a reasoner's external situation.

In both our account and that of Hintikka, the classification of the different types of questions that can be asked is integral to our understanding of information-seeking dialogue. One type of question asked is the so-called yes-no question, which gives the respondent only two options. As is well-known to anyone who has studied traditional fallacies, however, this form of questioning has its limitations, and it is frequently more useful for the questioner to ask what are called open-ended kinds of questions which give a respondent more freedom to make careful distinctions and give a reasoned answer in more depth.

Another type of question is the why question. In information-seeking dialogue, a why question is generally a request for the respondent to explain or clarify something. In contrast, in persuasion dialogue, a why question is typically a request for the respondent to prove a proposition or to support one of his commitments by putting forward an argument.[1] Such proving types of responses to why questions do sometimes come into information-seeking dialogues. But, generally, a why question tends to be a request for an explanation in this type of dialogue.

2. The Interview

An information-seeking dialogue is concluded when the original question posed in the dialogue has been answered, or when the sequence of questions and replies indicates that the information possessed by the respondent is insufficient to answer the question.

There are many different subtypes of information-seeking dialogue. One type is the kind of dialogue that takes place during a recruiting interview by a representative of a company looking to hire new employees. The goal of the questioner in such a case is to ask the right kind of questions that would enable the company to judge the candidate's abilities and suitability for this particular opening. A good question in this type of dialogue, then, is one that seeks out information relevant to this question of ability and suitability. A bad question is one that blocks or interferes with this goal in the dialogue.

According to the account of the employment interview given by Kaiser, the interviewer and the candidate are 'on differing wavelengths' (1979, p. 48). The goal of the interviewer is to find the best person for the job, while the goal of the candidate is to give a good impression in order to get the job. Kaiser advises the interviewer to keep to an exact plan of the conversation, instead of following his mood, and to focus on specific topics, like the applicant's adjustment within a group of colleagues, his or her ambitions, and so forth (p. 49).

In order to test an applicant's honesty, 'negative-suggestive' questions may be used. According to Kaiser, 'Generally employment interviews are a form of competition between the applicant and the interviewer from the company. For this reason there are built-in lie-detector questions like: "Do you sometimes read the magazine *Economic Planning*?" when such a magazine doesn't exist. These question traps are called negative-suggestive questions (1979, p. 49). It is an interesting issue whether such questions used in the context of an employment interview ought to be called fallacious, in a way comparable to other kinds of question traps recognized in logic (see sections 6 and 7 below). It can be argued that it is legitimate to use tricky, deceptive, or tactical moves, such as negative-suggestive questions, in an employment interview.

Such an interview is inherently competitive, to a large extent, so that the use of tactical manoeuvres by both sides is, at least to some degree, a natural and expected part of the argumentation. However, it is possible to distinguish a number of different types of bad interview questions: questions that are too personal; questions that require only a yes or no answer; and generic questions like 'What are your career aspirations?' which are too general and not tied closely to the candidate's job or experience (Gay, 1992, S22). These types of questions are not fallacious, but are 'bad' questions in the sense that they do not contribute to the goal of the interview and may impede it.

Another subtype of information-seeking dialogue is the kind of media interview where a correspondent interviews a celebrity so that the program can be edited and then played to a wider audience. The goal of this type of interview is normally to find out some interesting facts or revealing things about the celebrity's personal character and commitments that would be of interest to a wider audience.

According to Kaiser's analysis of the talk show as a species of journalistic interview, the purpose of this type of dialogue can take two forms, depending on the intention. One intention is to 'extract the innermost thoughts, opinions and plans from the individual questioned, to show surprising aspects of a personality who is always seen exclusively in the role of politician, movie-star or scientist. Alternatively, the intention may be to report objectively, without personal bias, particular circumstances and events' (1979, p. 101). The primary, or at least the general, goal is to reveal 'surprising' things about the interviewee's personality. However, in special cases, as Kaiser notes, the objective is to focus on a more specific topic with the aim of eliciting and reporting information.

As with a lot of these interview dialogues, the skill involved in making a successful exchange comes at the early stages where the interviewer makes the respondent feel relaxed enough to give honest answers that represent his real views and not defensive answers that try to hide something. The skill of an interviewer in this type of case lies in making the exchange seem similar to a friendly, personal conversation, and not in putting pressure on the respondent in an attempt to extract commitments.

According to Kaiser, research indicates that certain types of questions characterize the interviewing skills used in the celebrity interview or talk show. One characteristic is that the questions tend to be sharply provocative. Another is that 'as much as possible, all interesting aspects corresponding with the desires of the public are discussed' (1979, p. 102). A third is that the choice of words is often colourful, dramatic, and direct. Thus the general mechanism underlying the technique of questioning can be described as 'provocation, then follow up at weak points' (p. 102). The interviewee is challenged to give his opinion on some controversial issue, and the interviewer finds that some of his answers can be used as premises to construct arguments that reveal aspects of the issue that are of interest to the public.

The technique of using provocation in the interview involves injecting the semblance of a persuasion dialogue into the sequence of argumentation in the information-seeking dialogue. For example, if the interviewee is an actor in violent thriller movies, the interviewer can pose the general question, 'Do you think that violence in the media causes children to presume that criminal behaviour is acceptable?' On such a controversial issue, the interviewee will be forced to defend whatever viewpoint he accepts when he gives any direct answer to the question. Thus the interviewee has to think about the issue and engage in a brief persuasion type of dialogue that presents argumentation for one side of the issue. During the course of this subdialogue, the interviewee asserts some particular proposition, such as, 'Well, violence can be portrayed sensitively, if the actor can show deep emotion.' The interviewer seizes on this assertion and then develops a new question that reveals matters of interest to the public, such as, 'Does the deep emotion you show on the screen reflect your own personal experiences in life?' In such a case, a miniature persuasion dialogue is encapsulated within the sequence of argumentation in the information-seeking dialogue.

Use of these techniques of questioning in celebrity interviews and talk shows is very familiar because this ritualized type of interview dialogue has become so popular in television programming.

3. Searching a Database

Another simple and familiar type of case of information-seeking dialogue involves the process of searching through a computerized database to collect information on a subject. One familiar kind of database is the collection of titles and abstracts of books and articles in an academic field.

The questioner might be looking for some specific item of information, but typically he is looking for information on a specific topic or for a particular author. In such a case the computer program begins by setting out a list of options on the screen. For example, one option is to search under the author heading, another is to search under subject headings, and a third is to search under title headings. Let's say the researcher chooses to search under the topic heading and keys in two topics, personal attack and fallacy, which are joined by the conjunction sign. The computer program is instructed to search for all of the articles and books on the topic of personal attack and all of the articles in books on the topic of fallacy, and then to search through these two lists and find a list of articles and books that is common to both, that contains both topics. The computer program informs the user how long this list is and asks whether he wants a print-out. If the list is not too long, the user might ask for a listing of all these titles and then the computer program provides that information on the screen.

The general principle in searching for this kind of information is that the researcher can reduce the length of the list by asking questions that are more specific in subject matter. This is an important practical limitation because generally a researcher wants a list that is manageable, that is neither too long nor too short. (For further examples and characteristics of electronic information-seeking, see Marchionini, 1995.)

This kind of searching through a computerized database for information is a fairly simple case of information-seeking dialogue in which a number of parameters characteristic of more complex types of exchanges, like the celebrity interview, are not present. It is presumed to be clear to the user at the beginning what type of information the computer has in its database, and the user's goal is to extract some subset of this information that is of particular interest. The main problem here is devising key words that accurately reflect this interest in a way that is conducive to a useful search. The computer program is set up so that in the initial stages it asks the user questions, but in the main stage of the dialogue, it is the user who poses the key questions to the computer program. The computer program then follows these instructions by picking out the designated subset of its database.

This type of case seems to be such a straightforward one of searching for information that we might wonder how argumentation is involved. Is the researcher arguing with the computer database, or is the computer database somehow arguing with the researcher? Here the structure of information-seeking seems to have been pared down to such a simple series of exchanges that it does not appear to involve argument in any obvious sense. Argument is always directed towards resolving an unsettled issue that is open to contention or doubt. Information-seeking dialogue is always directed towards answering an open or unanswered question, and in this sense, it is directed towards resolving something that is unsettled. But information dialogue, especially in the computerized database case, seems less oriented towards contentiousness and proving propositions that the other party doubts or opposes. Therefore, it seems less argumentative in nature than the other types of dialogue. However, as we will see below, the asking of a question often contains an implicit argument.

It is true generally that the information-seeking dialogue is used as a preparatory method of collecting data on which to base premises that can be used in argumentation in other types of dialogue. For example, information-seeking is obviously an important part of the early stages of the inquiry. However, the information-seeking dialogue does contain argumentation. Frequently, as in the case of the media interview type of information-seeking dialogue, the argumentation will be readily evident when the respondent tries to defend his point of view or justify his personal position.

In the computer database type of case, however, the element of argumentation is much less evident. Here argumentation comes primarily in two ways. One is in the choice of key words and the presumptions about their usefulness in searching for the desired information. Another lies in the use of the data collected from the list of items supplied by the computer program. The user typically sorts through the list and cancels the ones that turn out not to be useful, thus paring the list down to a subset of items that meets his needs. Throughout the sequence of argumentation in this type of dialogue exchange between a user and a computer database, the goal is to collect not just any information, but a particular set of titles or references that will enable the user to answer or collect information on some initial question. And we can analyse this sequence as argumentative, because certain premises are selected and inferences are made, so that conclusions can be drawn from those premises on whether an initial question can adequately be answered by supplying information relevant to it.

4. Position to Know

Another common subtype of the information-seeking dialogue is illustrated by the type of case in which one party is in a position to know the location of something and the other party proceeds to ask a number of questions in order to find it. For example, a passerby approaches me at the entrance to the University of Winnipeg and asks where Bryce Hall is. The presumption behind the asking of this question is that my being in this location gives some evidence that I may be familiar with the university. There is a presumption that I am probably in a position to know the location of Bryce Hall. It's not that this person thinks that I am some sort of expert on the University of Winnipeg, but he presumably thinks that I look like the kind of person who is probably familiar enough with the location of the various buildings and halls in the university that I could supply this information. In answer, I point to a nearby building and say, 'In order to get to Bryce Hall, you go through that doorway and then up to the next level.' My answer, in effect, gives him a series of instructions that will lead him to the location. The questioner has presumed rightly that I am willing to take enough time to give him this information, and once he gets it, he presumes that it is likely that I am telling the truth. I could be lying or giving him false instructions but, should that be the case, the cost to him is relatively small, for once he gets to the designated point he could always ask somebody else how to get to Bryce Hall.

In this type of case of information-seeking dialogue, since the cost to both parties is small, there is a presumption by the questioner that the respondent is willing to supply this information if he can. And there is a presumption on the part of the respondent that he is obliged to be as helpful as possible either in giving the information if he knows it or in directing the questioner to another plausible source of information. These are normal presumptions of politeness that are defeasible, but they set in place reasonable expectations at the opening stages of a sequence of information-seeking dialogue of this type.

Woods criticizes Sperber and Wilson's account of relevance because it fails in the following case: Harry stops Peter in the hallway of a building and asks, 'Where is the office of the Rector, please?' and Peter replies, 'You're standing in front of it' (1992, p. 197). According to Woods, Peter's response does not qualify as relevant in Sperber and Wilson's account (1986). This shows that their analysis of the concept of relevance does not fit the concept of relevance needed for information-seeking dialogue. (For an analysis of relevance in information-seeking dialogue, see section 9, below. For our own account of the type of relevance Sperber and Wilson's analysis does fit, see chapter 6.)

In some cases of this type of information-seeking dialogue, the goal is not to just find out whether a particular proposition is true or false or to find information about some selected topic; rather, the question is a practical one of how to do something, how to carry out some particular task. For example, in the Bryce Hall case cited above, the questioner seems to primarily want to know the location of the hall, but clearly it is also implied that he is going there, that he wants to get to Bryce Hall. He also wants or needs to know the best way to get to Bryce Hall, since there may be more than one route or some obstacles in getting there easily. In other words, the questioner is saying to the respondent that he has a certain goal in mind and is seeking advice on how he can best or most easily achieve that goal in his present circumstances. In a case like this, then, goal-directed practical reasoning is involved, and the information-seeking type of dialogue may be mixed in with, or joined to, a kind of deliberation dialogue. The questioner is asking the respondent to join with him in deliberations on how to carry out some task on which the two are, in effect, collaborating. The primary function of the respondent is not to act with the questioner in carrying out the goal, but simply to provide information that the respondent needs to carry out the goal himself.

This subjoining of information-seeking dialogue to other types of dialogue is typical of argumentation in everyday conversation, and it is this factor too that often gives the information-seeking dialogue its argumentative force. The information is needed to verify or collect premises that will subsequently be used in a deliberation or inquiry in order to reason forward towards conclusions as a basis for action or to prove that some alternate conclusion is either true or false. In these cases, the argumentation in the information-seeking dialogue is not always obvious on the surface, but it is present, and premises are being used as a basis for inferring conclusions that are ultimately directed towards resolving doubt or some unsettled issue.

5. Classification of Questions

A useful list of the types of questions characteristically used in the information-seeking dialogue is given by Harrah (1984, p. 716). While not complete, this list gives the reader an idea of the characteristic types of the most common questions. They include whether, yes-no, which, what, who, and why questions, as well as deliberative questions, disjunctive questions, hypothetical questions, conditional questions, and given-that questions. Deliberative questions ask 'What shall I do now?' A hypothetical question is, 'If you had a proof of such-and-such a theorem, how long would it be?' A conditional question is, 'If you now have a proof, how long is it?' An example of a given-that question is, 'Given that this one proposition is provable, is it the case that this other proposition is also provable?'

With all of these types of questions in the information-seeking dialogue, it is useful to distinguish between an answer and a reply. An answer supplies the requested information or makes the commitment requested by the question. A reply can be an answer or any other move at that stage of the dialogue that is allowed by the rules appropriate for the particular case. For example, a reasonable reply that is not an answer includes 'I don't know.' or 'I don't know the answer, but Bob can tell you the answer to that' or 'That question isn't very clear. Could you tell me what you mean by such and such?' All these responses may be legitimate replies, but they are not answers.

In information dialogue, and in other types of dialogue as well, the argumentative aspect of a question may be hidden by its surface form. For example, a question may have the surface form of a yes-no question, while under the surface it may contain important presuppositions or presumptions that, in effect, make the question into a very aggressive argument.

The informal logic textbooks are very familiar with this problem, and there are a number of traditional classifications of fallacies of question-asking that come under this heading. One is the famous fallacy illustrated by the question 'Have you stopped cheating on your income tax returns?' On the surface, this question has the form of a yes-no question, but if the respondent gives a yes or no answer he will be trapped into conceding a commitment that will be significant in its impact on the subsequent sequence of argumentation. If he answers yes, this implies that he has cheated on his income tax and is therefore guilty of breaking the law. If he answers no, this seems to superficially indicate denial of the charge. But, literally speaking, replying 'No, I have not stopped' implies that he is continuing to cheat on his income tax. Either way, the respondent is trapped. He becomes committed to a proposition that would, or at least could, be used by the questioner to attack and defeat his side of the case in subsequent argumentation. For once he has conceded that he is guilty of cheating on his income tax, either in the past or in continuing to do so, the other party can use an *ad hominem* argument, citing his culpability and therefore his untrustworthiness as a source of information or as a sincere contributor to argumentation in dialogue. At this point, the respondent's credibility may easily be destroyed, and his ability to continue with the dialogue in an effective or credible manner would be ended. Hence, this type of complex question is labelled a fallacy in the sense that it's a powerful tactic of deception. It appears on the surface to be an innocent yes-no question that has no substantive or significant presumption built into it, but as soon as the respondent answers either yes or no, he becomes committed to a proposition that could be the instrument of his subsequent defeat in the argument.[2]

The question in this kind of case exploits the limited options of the format of the yes-no question to launch an attack against the respondent. Here the analysis of the fallacy has to do with the sequence of questions and reply in the *profile of dialogue* – a connected, but relatively short and localized (in relation to whole dialogue) sequence of questions and replies, where each move is based on the previous moves in the exchange (Krabbe, 1992). Such profiles of dialogue have already been illustrated in the inquiry type of dialogue (see chapter 3), but the particular features of a profile of dialogue in the information-seeking type of dialogue are somewhat different.

Figure 5.1 is an example of a profile of dialogue for the asking of the question 'Have you stopped cheating on your income tax returns?' in an information-seeking dialogue, where 'you' represents the respondent. The profile represented in Figure 5.1 shows that this question is only appropriately askable in the sequence of dialogue if the answer has been 'yes' at both nodes in the tree diagram where the prior two questions were asked (in the order pictured in the diagram). If in a given actual case the respondent's commitment was to the 'no' answer at either one of these two nodes in the diagram representing the dialogue, then the normative profile of dialogue would not match up with the sequence of argumentation in the real case.

The problem in such a case is revealed by the profile of dialogue in Figure 5.1. 'Have you stopped cheating on your income tax returns?' is a yes-no type of question, meaning that only one of two direct answers by the respondent is allowed as an appropriate response in the dialogue. But no matter which answer is selected, as the profile shows, the presumption is that the respondent has answered 'yes' to the two prior questions in the dialogue.

Thus whether or not a fallacy has been committed depends on how or whether the actual case matches up with the profile of dialogue. If the respondent has already admitted cheating on his income taxes in the previous exchanges in this profile, then the question 'Have you stopped cheating on your income tax returns?' could be legitimate and nonfallacious. But in another case, where the respondent is not committed to

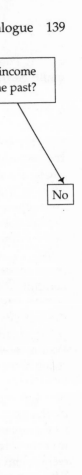

Figure 5.1   Profile of Dialogue for the Income Tax Question

having cheated on his tax returns at all, asking the very same question could be rightly evaluated as fallacious.

6. Presuppositions of Questions

This brings us to the subject of the presumptions and presuppositions that are built into the questions. In general, every question has a set of presuppositions; that is, a set of propositions such that, if the respondent gives a direct answer to the question, he will become automatically committed to those propositions in the strong sense of being obliged to defend them in subsequent argumentation. This is the strong, pragmatic sense of the term 'presupposition' as defined in Walton: 'A presupposition of a question is a proposition that is presumed to be acceptable to the respondent when the question is asked so that the respondent becomes committed to the proposition when he gives any direct answer' (1989a, p. 28). This definition is quite different from the many semantic accounts of the concept of presupposition that have been given over the years.

The distinction between an answer and a direct answer is made in Walton (1989b, p. 7). A *direct answer* supplies the exact information requested by the question, whereas an *indirect answer* supplies some of, but not all or exactly, that information. Pragmatically speaking, then, a direct answer is one that supplies exactly those commitments solicited by the respondent's asking of the question. The key thing about the fallacy of many questions, as shown in the profile of the income tax question considered above, is that any direct answer automatically traps the respondent into conceding damaging admissions so that the only option left open to the respondent is to challenge the question itself – to point out that it has presuppositions, and to deny or question his own commitment to those presuppositions in the given case.

Consideration of the logical problems posed by several different types of these tricky questions suggests that sequences of questions and replies in information-seeking dialogue appear to be relatively innocent; that is, they appear not to contain significant argumentation that bears on an arguer's commitments very directly one way or the other. But under the surface such a sequence may be highly argumentative because it contains presuppositions that function as arguments. In effect, the question itself is better analysed as an argument rather than simply as an ordinary yes-no question, or why question, or one of the other types of questions listed above.

The use of questions based on argumentative presuppositions can be deceptive because the focus of the dialogue is on the choice required by the direct answer to the question. Hence, the focus is shifted away from the argumentation inherent in the presumptions in the questions. This psychological aspect of attention shifting in complex questions containing presuppositions has been noted by Andreas:

People typically focus on what they can agree or disagree about, while ignoring what is presupposed. When listeners do not notice presuppositions, the ideas unconsciously sink in and the listeners accept them as if they are true, without being consciously aware of the shift that has taken place. If we turn the statement 'It's good that you are willing to express yourself' into a question – 'Do you think it's good or bad that you're willing to express yourself?' – we focus the listener's attention more strongly on the choice offered rather than the presupposition behind the choice. (1992, p. 60)

The use of the method of profiles of dialogue, as applied to a given case, reconstructs the implicit sequence of argumentation and makes the normative structure of the dialogue explicit. What was concealed by the shift of attention is now revealed.

The key is that analysis and evaluation of whether such questions are fallacious in a given case require not only an examination of the question itself, but also an examination of the profile of dialogue in which the question is embedded, the commitments of the respondent in the dialogue, and the context of dialogue in which the question was asked.

7. How Can a Question Be a Fallacy?

How can a question be a fallacy? Questions are often more like arguments than they appear to be because they typically contain presuppositions or presumptions that indirectly, and in a subtle manner, implicate conclusions. Such questions function like arguments precisely because any direct answer, or attempt to give a direct answer, results in significant commitments for the respondent, commitments that are potentially or actually damaging to the respondent's side of the case. What makes such questions tricky and deceptive argumentative moves is that the questioner is then likely to use them as part of a strategy of argumentation in subsequent questioning or answering sequences which will trip up the respondent and cause him to admit guilt or to make concessions that will be used to defeat his side of the argument. (See Walton, 1989b, pp. 71–4; Hintikka, 1987.)

As noted, the respondent's attention is shifted away from the argumentative presumptions contained in the question, and so he (or the audience) may take any direct answer to the question as an affirmation of the respondent's commitment to these presumptions, even though the respondent may not be committed to them at all. Thus the fallacious aspect relates to the deception involved in the shifting of attention away from important arguments implicitly conveyed in the dialogue, and also to the entrapment of the respondent by requiring a direct answer that suggests commitment to the implicit presumptions. But some might say that a fallacy is a fallacious argument. So how can asking a question be fallacious?

While generally there is a presumption in informal logic that a fallacy is a fallacious argument, in the case of questioning there appears to be a need to rethink this presumption because a question is not an argument. But a partial solution to this problem resides in the observation that, in the traditional fallacies and the kinds of cases we are concerned with here where tricky and deceitful argumentation occurs, a question functions like an argument, or on deeper analysis, it really is an argument at a pragmatic level, as revealed by the profile of dialogue.

It follows, then, that the information-seeking dialogue often does contain argumentation, but that this argumentation is subtly concealed by the syntactical form of the speech acts which appear to be only questions. However, to the extent that these questions contain presumptions and presuppositions that have argumentation force, in effect they function like arguments and ought to be treated as arguments in a dialogue exchange.

A study of parliamentary debates clearly indicates how widespread these practices are in everyday conversation and particularly in political debate (see Walton, 1989b). Questions asked in parliamentary debates frequently function as arguments that are not only very complex, but also clearly intended to be damaging attacks implying that the respondent and probably his whole party are guilty of engaging in disgraceful conduct of some sort. Also, the aggressive use of loaded terms in such questions indicates that they have a very definite and strong argumentative component. In general, giving a direct answer to such a question is very dangerous in an argument; it may be far better for the respondent to react to the question by replying to it in another way – for example, by questioning the questioner, or by pointing out the presuppositions of the question, and then asking whether loading the question with such presuppositions is appropriate. The more usual response, however, is an emotional attack on the questioner that implies that he is equally guilty of the same kind of conduct that he has accused the respondent of engaging in.[3] The frequent result of such an emotional reply is for the information-seeking dialogue to disintegrate into a quarrel.

8. Expert Consultation Dialogue

Another subtype of the information-seeking dialogue is the expert consultation dialogue where one party, a questioner, seeks information or advice from another party who is an expert in a particular domain of knowledge or in some practical or technical skill. An expert is a source of information, and, as a specialist, he or she has privileged access to a domain of knowledge or skill. The questioner, as a layperson in that field, is not in a position to directly or completely verify whether the propositions vouched for by the expert really are true or not, based on internal evidence in the field. So the layperson accepts what the expert says is true, based on a presumption that the expert is honest and knows what he is talking about.

Experts have extensive experience and skills in a domain of knowledge or a craft. However, a questioner may be a user of this expertise even though, as a layperson, he does not have direct access to this knowledge or craft. The questioner must try to extract information by a process of intelligent questioning in a dialectical exchange where the questioner has to draw presumptive conclusions based on what the expert says.

According to Johnson, an expert can be defined as an individual who exhibits five defining characteristics (1983, pp. 78–9). First, the expert can do things and answer questions that the layperson cannot because of his special training and experience or knowledge in his field of expertise. Second, experts exhibit a high degree of knowledge or are proficient in their actions. Third, experts have certain clever tricks or subtle methods for applying what they know to problems. Fourth, experts are good at sorting through irrelevant information to get at a basic issue or to information which is useful for a task. Fifth, experts are good at recognizing problems as special cases of kinds of problems they have encountered before.

Thus we can define an expert in contrast to a layperson. A layperson may not be totally ignorant of some field of expertise, but we expect him to have only an average level of knowledge of that field. An expert is an individual who has knowledge in a given field and generally has enough advanced knowledge and experience that he has attained a certain level of proficiency. However, there can be degrees of expertise. Dreyfus and Dreyfus distinguish various stages in the skill-acquisition process: the novice stage, the beginner stage, the stage of competence, the stage of proficiency, and finally the stage of expertise (1986, p. 31).

According to Dreyfus and Dreyfus, expertise is a kind of holistic situational understanding – at least at the higher levels – that cannot be expressed as any calculative sequence of reasoning that proceeds by a simple method of applying clearly stated rules to given facts (p. 36). Although they concede that analytical procedures of inference may be more characteristic of expertise at the beginning level, at the higher levels expertise is a more intuitive notion. This same idea is also advanced by Woods and Walton who argue that expert judgment is in many cases based on intuition, a kind of reasoning derived from familiarity with the subject matter of expertise which cannot be spelled out in so many steps of logical reasoning easily accessible to a non-expert. Woods and Walton put forth the hypothesis that an expert's say-so may be based on inarticulable background elements and special skills that may not be completely amenable to representation as some explicit sequence of propositions which can be explained or reproduced so that a layperson can completely understand why and how the expert arrived at this particular conclusion (1974, p. 136). If this is so, then the layperson who draws conclusions from what the expert says may do so on a dialectical basis of presumption, rather than by some process of duplicating, step by step, the reasoning that went into the basis of the expert's conclusion.[4]

Because the layperson is not himself an expert, however, this lack of direct accessibility to the expert's knowledge and reasoning is not necessarily an obstacle to his becoming skilled at questioning experts. People in certain professions, like lawyers, often learn to do this very well for a living. Anyone who has had the experience of going to a physician for advice on some medical problem and then trying to explain to some third party exactly what the doctor said will realize that there are many intrinsic difficulties in obtaining and processing good advice from an expert and drawing the right conclusions from it.

An example of an expert consultation dialogue is the kind of case where you hire a financial adviser to help organize your financial affairs. You need information on what investments are possible, what plans you should make for your pension, and so forth. The adviser sits down with you and provides the relevant information you need to arrive at a decision. In this kind of dialogue exchange, it is important that both parties have an awareness of limitations. The expert must be able to know when he does not know something, or when he can't solve a particular problem or answer a question, and respond by indicating his ignorance. The questioner must realize that he is not an expert in the field and proceed cautiously, avoiding the pitfalls of misunderstanding technical terminology and misinterpreting what the expert is trying to say.

It is important for the layperson to ask the right questions in such a dialogue, and it is critically important for the expert to answer questions in a way that the layperson can clearly understand without being inaccurate. Studies in expert knowledge representation show that, as an expert becomes more advanced in a field, he tends to lose awareness of the specific methods that he uses because he relies more on skills of practice which have become intuitive over the years.[5] Therefore, it may be especially difficult for an expert who has a high level of expertise to communicate the knowledge that he has in some sort of explicit form, or to justify it in a way that the user can understand the conclusions that he has arrived at. This has been called the *paradox of expertise*: as an individual becomes more of an expert in a field and is able to do more tasks more efficiently and accurately, he also tends to lose awareness of what he knows. This kind of problem makes it inherently difficult for good communication to exist between an expert and a layperson/questioner in a specific case. There are many characteristic types of communication failures in such cases which are well known to those who have studied informal fallacies. The traditional fallacy of the *argumentum ad verecundiam* or 'fallacy of improper appeal to authority' is the general term traditionally used to cover these breakdowns of communication and failures of argumentation in expert consultation dialogue.

9. Peirastic and Exetastic Dialogues

When consulting an expert for information or advice on how to proceed with a course of action, more than merely the passive acceptance of what the expert says is commonly part of the argumentation (and should be). For what the information or advice of the expert is may not be clear to the layperson, and clarification may be necessary. Probing what the expert really means is often an important part of what makes this kind of information-seeking dialogue successful. Moreover, better understanding of what the expert means can frequently best be achieved by critically challenging what the expert has said. This kind of argumentation involves testing the expert's advice by comparing it with what is known by 'common sense' outside of the field of expertise, or by asking the expert to give reasons why a particular proposition is accepted in her field of expertise. The 'testing or probing arguments,' which Aristotle called peirastic, and the 'examining critically' arguments, which Aristotle called exetastic, are important parts of, or adjuncts to, information-seeking dialogue.

Strictly speaking, in information-seeking dialogue, the goal is for information to be transferred from the one participant to the other. But in order to facilitate this flow of information, in many cases various kinds of testing, probing, and critical examination arguments – which in the new dialectic seem to involve persuasion dialogue more than information-seeking dialogue – are both useful and necessary.

It is hard to know exactly what Aristotle had in mind when he referred to peirastic, or examination arguments, and exetastic arguments. But the account of these kinds of arguments given in chapter 1 suggests that, since they involve the testing of opinions by critical probing of the reasons to support them, these arguments fit better into the critical discussion framework than into the information-seeking framework of dialogue. Whatever Aristotle really meant by these categories of argument, the study of expert consultation dialogue suggests that arguments used to probe, test, and critically examine expert opinions are important tools to enhance the quality of this type of information-seeking exchange.

The hypothesis put forward here is that the probing and testing and the critically examining types of arguments, which could be called peirastic and exetastic, respectively, are subspecies of critical discussion arguments. And so, in turn, in the new dialectic the peirastic and exetastic categories of argumentative conversational exchanges can be classified as mixed types of dialogue that are partly information-seeking in nature and partly persuasion dialogue. More specifically, both these types of arguments may be classified as instances of persuasion dialogue that are used for a particular purpose within the general framework of information-seeking dialogue.

The peirastic type of dialogue may be said to occur in two subtypes of cases. First, an information-seeker in an expert consultation dialogue, for example, may need to probe the reasons why the expert accepts a particular proposition. This need arises for several reasons. In one type of case, what the expert says is unclear or appears to be implausible. Second, an information-seeker may need to test an expert's opinion critically. Here we may have a case, for example, where what this expert says conflicts with what another expert says. A familiar type of case is the critical examination of an expert's opinion when the expert is cross-examined in court by the opposing attorney. The testing type of peirastic argumentation arises in similar cases. In some cases, it even involves the joining of an inquiry to the information-seeking type of dialogue.

The unresolved historical question is whether the examination types of argument (including peirastic and exetastic arguments as subtypes) are, for Aristotle, subspecies of dialectical arguments, or whether they represent a different type of argument. The more general questions involve exactly what Aristotle meant by dialectical argument and whether dialectical argument for Aristotle would be the same as persuasion dialogue or a subcategory of persuasion dialogue. These are difficult questions of interpreting Aristotle's philosophy, and will be considered further in chapter 9. However, it may be recalled from chapter 1 that *endoxa* for Aristotle also includes 'things accepted by the wise' – (see also Bolton [1990, p. 209]). Hence, it could well be that, for Aristotle, dialectic has a role to play in expert consultation dialogue with an individual who has specialized scientific or technical knowledge.

10. Relevance in Information-Seeking Dialogue

In information-seeking dialogue, failures of relevance are often most noticeable at a local level. For example, in an interview the reply given by the interviewee may not answer the question at all. Once we start to look for such failures of relevance in interviews, we notice how common they are – for example, in televised news interviews and on talk show interviews. This is called local-level irrelevance because the reply either fails to answer or is not relevant to the specific question asked at that point in the interview. Thus, to start to define relevance in information-seeking dialogue, it is necessary to examine the different types of questions asked and to determine the range of relevant replies for each of these types of questions.

The most obvious kind of relevant reply to a question in an information-seeking dialogue is a direct answer. However, simply because the respondent lacks the required information, it may be legitimate for him to give an indirect answer, or even to reply, 'I don't know.' There can also be a range of relevant replies that are not answers at all, either direct or indirect.

As noted in sections 6 and 7, if the question itself contains questionable presuppositions, it may be permissible, and even obligatory, for the respondent to reply by questioning the question. The extent to which this sort of flexibility in replying is to be allowed is very much a function of the type of dialogue and the speech event of the particular situation. The revealing and modelling of the more global kind of failure of relevance implicit in cases of the fallacy of many questions require the use of the profile of dialogue technique to reconstruct the proper sequence of questions and replies in the dialogue structure of a case. In cases like the 'Have you stopped cheating on your income tax returns?' question, the problem is that the respondent is pressured into giving a direct answer that may (depending on the particulars of the given case) be based on prior commitments that were not previously secured as answers by the questioner, as would be required by the correct sequence of prior argumentation indicated by the profile of dialogue for the case. The fallacy, then, is a tactic of not allowing the right sort of flexibility that a respondent should properly have by trying to force questionable presumptions into place as commitments of the respondent.

In expert consultation dialogue, the expert respondent needs to be active in helping the questioner to ask the right questions, to express the questions in a favourable way to elicit information, and to question or suggest improvements in the phrasing of questions, particularly those with significant presuppositions. However, in many instances the questioner also needs to be active as well. The questioner not only must ask for clarification of assertions that he does not understand, but must also be ready to challenge assertions he does not accept by asking the expert, 'What is your evidence for that opinion?' The questioner should not be unduly submissive to the opinion of the expert, and must be ready to ask the expert to back up what appears to be a questionable opinion. The expert should be willing to respond to such requests for proof.

Although primarily a subtype of information-seeking dialogue, expert consultation dialogue also involves occasionally shifting to examination argumentation that is really a persuasion type of dialogue. However, the argumentation in this peirastic or exetastic interlude can be relevant to the global sequence of argumentation in the information-seeking dialogue it is contained within. It can be relevant because the examination argumentation can be useful in helping the respondent use the expert advice more effectively by coming to understand the reasons behind the expert's assertions. By coming to understand why the expert has the opinion that she has, the user can better see how to apply that opinion to the use he has for it. Thus, the critical discussion contained in the examination argument interlude can enhance the value of the expert consultation dialogue. The general study of such dialectical shifts from one type of dialogue to another will be taken up in chapter 8.

Local relevance is very important in determining whether a reply should be judged relevant. The biggest, or at least the basic, factor is the type of question. For example, there are only two direct answers to a yes-no question, so the range of relevant replies to this type of question is much more restricted than it is for some other kind of questions.

In many cases, implicit steps in the sequence of argumentation linking the question and reply may need to be filled in. For example, Manor cites the following sequence of dialogue: 'Who ate the cake? Go ask mommy' (1982, p. 72). Here the reply is not a direct answer, nor does it seem to be even an indirect answer. But it does have a function as part of an information-seeking dialogue. It says, in effect, 'I don't know, or I can't say.' But it also directs the questions to a source where she can presumably find the requested information. Thus the reply is relevant if there is a reasonable presumption that 'mommy' is a good source of information for getting an answer to the question.

Many case studies of question-reply sequences taken from Hansard, which records the debates of the House of Commons in Canada, reveal that the questions asked by opposition ministers are highly aggressive and complex. They contain presuppositions that attack the respondent, and the government ministers generally, for all kinds of bad practices. The questions are, in fact, highly loaded, aggressive attacks on the respondent and her associates. Although the parliamentary rules for debate forbid such abuses, the Speaker of the House is generally quite permissive in allowing them to take place routinely. It is well to remember in such cases, as we are reminded by Hitchcock (1992, p. 259), that questions as well as replies can be evaluated as irrelevant.

In such cases, if the respondent were to give a direct answer to the question, he would be conceding that he is guilty, which would provide the questioner with an effective platform for further attacks. Hence, the respondent frequently gives a reply that may seem fallacious because it attacks the questioner, or criticizes or questions the question itself. When this occurs, the questioner may retort, 'That's irrelevant! You are simply avoiding the question.' Here the charge of irrelevance can be specious, because, by challenging the question, the respondent may be giving the best possible reply in the circumstances.

Relevance should be judged globally, in light of the purpose of the dialogue, as well as in relation to the specific requirements of the types of questions that occur at the local level. The local requirements cannot always be taken literally, at face value, because there may be global factors at work that make a broader, contextual judgment necessary.

The purpose of asking a question during Question Period in the House of Commons is to press for information or action (*Beauchesne*, 1978). This would make such a debate an instance of information-seeking dialogue or the deliberation type of dialogue (see chapter 6). However, as we will see in chapter 9, political debate is a mixed type of discourse that poses special problems for evaluating fallacies and question-reply argumentation sequences.

6

Deliberation

Deliberation as a type of dialogue is typified by the argumentation in a town hall meeting, where a group of concerned citizens get together to discuss and attempt to solve a practical problem. They discuss different ways of proceeding or propose solutions, and they divide into factions or points of view, each arguing that one of these proposed lines of action is the prudent course to pursue. In the end, however, the aim is for them to come to agreement on a line of action or policy they can implement together.

1. Main Characteristics

The initial situation of deliberation dialogue is the need to take action to solve a problem or generally move ahead in some practical sphere. Joint deliberation is a type of dialogue in which two parties reason together on how to proceed when they are confronted by a practical problem or conflict, or more generally, any need to consider taking a course of action. The most important kind of question posed in a deliberation is the 'how' question that seeks out a way of doing something, that asks, for example, 'How can we do this?' or 'How should we proceed in this situation?'

In many, but not all, cases of deliberation, there is a conflict between two possible courses of action, and a choice needs to be made between them. Where such a conflict exists, the kind of reasoning may be called decision-making. Deliberation is not always confined to decision-making, but generally involves discourse with another party in deciding how to proceed in particular circumstances in relation to the goals of the two parties.

In our normative model of deliberation, we think of the basic case of two parties deliberating together. Deliberation is a symmetrical type of dialogue: the two parties perform the same roles in putting forward suggestions and making recommendations on how to proceed in trying to fulfil their goals by taking some form of action in a given situation.

Deliberation is sometimes thought of as a solitary process of practical reasoning, and in such a case our model of deliberation as a type of dialogue is not directly applicable to this kind of reasoning. However, even in the solitary case, we can often think of deliberation as a kind of dialogue that takes place between a person and some sort of hypothetical other party to the discussion. This is the kind of case where we speak of a person playing the role of devil's advocate. In working out a course of action, he tries to discover some of the potentially bad consequences of this course of action by putting himself into the position of someone who might be opposed to it and asking what sort of objections or counter-arguments he or she might have to the proposal he is considering. Then by weighing the pros and cons in a solitary fashion, perhaps by drawing up a list of the arguments for and against a particular proposed course of action, a deliberator can arrive at a more balanced and prudent view of the factors that should affect his deliberation.

Wright shows how ordinary deliberations are guided by a particular question that has been tacitly posed. He calls this an *implicit question* (1995, p. 572). In some cases – such as 'What route should we take?' – the question is obvious; in other cases, it is implicit, even though we feel no need to mention it. Wright sees the line of reasoning used in a deliberation as having a dialogue structure of argument set into motion by the asking of an implicit question, a question that is replied to in a sequence of dialogue exchanges.

Thus deliberation, for the purpose of evaluating arguments, can generally be thought of as a normative framework of dialogue in which argumentation occurs, and the arguments in a deliberation dialogue articulate the reasons for and against committing to a particular proposal for a line of conduct that is being entertained. The agent who is deliberating will have a goal or typically a set of goals which will play an important role in the argumentation in the deliberation. Generally speaking, in the kind of deliberation we have in mind, there will be two parties who share common goals and also some information on their particular situation and are trying to find a means to carry out these goals by discoursing together. They are looking for a prudent course of action or a course of action that, as they see it, is the most practical way of carrying out their joint goals.

The two parties who deliberate together are called agents. An agent is

an intelligent entity who is aware of the external situation, and by acting, the agent can bring about changes in that situation, be aware of the
resulting changes, and modify his or her future actions accordingly.
Wooldridge and Jennings claim there is a weaker notion of agency,
according to which an agent has the following four characteristics: (1)
autonomy, or control over actions; (2) social ability, or capacity to interact with other agents in dialogue; (3) reactivity, or ability to respond to
changes in an environment; and (4) pro-activeness, or the ability to take
the initiative instead of just reacting to something (1995, p. 116).

It may also be possible to have a deliberation in which the two participants have different goals, or perhaps even conflicting goals, but this is
not the primary model we have in mind.[1] In the basic case, the two participants share common goals and a common pool of information which
represents how they understand their circumstances. Deliberation, in
this sense as a type of dialogue, is highly cooperative and has only a
small adversarial component. It is a kind of joint effort to collaborate in
working together towards implementing goals that two parties have in
common, where they share a set of circumstances or where these circumstances are relatively similar for the two parties. In other words,
both of the parties have some common interests or goals in a deliberation, and they are attempting to work together to carry out these goals in
a way that is satisfactory for both of them.

Deliberation, as noted above, arises from a problem that requires
thinking through a sequence of practical reasoning to arrive at the best
or most practical solution. The problem can be an ethical one, or a technical problem requiring expert skills or knowledge, or a scientific problem, or any kind of practical problem we encounter in our normal
activities. Often the problem is posed in the form of a dilemma – that is,
a situation where two alternative solutions are possible, but each of
them has seriously negative consequences. So the problem faced in a
dilemma is to find some way of slipping between the two horns, to find
some way to justify choosing the least worst course of action. But the
dilemma is just one form of the various practical kinds of arguments
used in deliberation.

2. Practical Reasoning

Deliberation has to do with actions and intentions, as well as the framework of practical reasoning in which an agent tries to carry out a set of
goals based on knowledge of a particular situation.

Practical reasoning is a type of goal-directed reasoning that concludes in an imperative to action (Walton, 1990a). In the simplest type of case, practical reasoning is based on a practical inference that has two types of premises. The major premise is a *goal premise* in which the agent states that he has a particular goal to carry out. The second premise, called the *means premise*, states that, according to the agent's estimate of his circumstances, such and such is a particular means of carrying out this goal in that situation. The conclusion states that the agent ought to select the particular course of action designated in the means premise as a way of proceeding. The word 'ought' here can be described as a practical 'ought,' that is, it cites a prudent or practical course of action that is based on assumptions made in the premises, assumptions that this agent has particular goals and also some knowledge of his given situation. The goal of deliberation generally can be identified with the ultimate conclusion of such a sequence of practical inferences. The ultimate goal is to reach a conclusion on how to act prudently in a given situation in order to realize specific goals.

THE BASIC INFERENCE SCHEMATA

Necessary-Condition Schema

N.1 My goal is to bring about A (Goal Premise).
N.2 I reasonably consider on the given information that bringing about at least one of $[B_0, B_1, ... B_n]$ is necessary to bring about A (Alternatives Premise).
N.3 I have selected one member B_i as an acceptable, or as the most acceptable, necessary condition for A (Selection Premise).
N.4 Nothing unchangeable prevents me from bringing about B_i as far as I know (Practicality Premise).
N.5 Bringing about A is more acceptable to me than not bringing about B_i (Side-Effects Premise).

Therefore, it is required that I bring about B_i (Conclusion).

Sufficient-Condition Schema

S.1 My goal is to bring about A (Goal Premise).
S.2 I reasonably consider on the given information that each one of $[B_0, B_1, ... B_n]$ is sufficient to bring about A (Alternatives Premise).
S.3 I have selected one member B_i as an acceptable, or as the most acceptable, sufficient condition for A (Selection Premise).

S.4 Nothing unchangeable prevents me from bringing about B_i as far as I know (Practicality Premise).

S.5 Bringing about A is more acceptable to me than not bringing about B_i (Side-Effects Premise).

Therefore, it is required that I bring about B_i (Conclusion).

As outlined above, the basic schema of a practical inference has five premises. The Side-Effects Premise is concerned with the known or projected consequences of the course of action being considered. If the course of action has known or projected negative consequences, then that factor will go against bringing about the goal. Is bringing about the goal of such a strong positive value that it is worth doing even in the face of the negative consequences that are likely to go along with it? A judgment of relative value or worth has to be made. As shown below, this judgment represents an important kind of argumentation that is very common in deliberations.

Practical reasoning in a deliberation dialogue is used in a dialectical way, where the proponent of a line of practical reasoning is opposed by a respondent who questions this line of reasoning or proposes an alternative course of action. The proponent puts forward the argumentation scheme for practical reasoning (SP):

(SP) A is the goal.
       B is necessary to bring about A.
       Therefore, it is required to bring about B.

The respondent criticizes or questions the proponent's argument using the set of critical questions (CQ) that match (SP):

(CQ)   Are there alternatives to B?
       Is B an acceptable (or the best) alternative?
       Is it possible to bring about B?
       Does B have bad side-effects?

The dialectical sequence of argumentation in a deliberation can be normatively represented as the opposition between these two sides on how to solve the problem that is the issue of the deliberation.

The concept of practical reasoning is attributed to Aristotle, whose doctrines are somewhat fragmentary but give a clear idea of the notion.

For example, in his book *On the Movements of Animals* (701a18), are two examples that clearly indicate the sort of inference he had in mind. One is the following inference with two premises:

Case 6.1
First premise: I should make something good.
Second premise: A house is something good.
Conclusion: At once I make a house.

In this example, the agent seems to somewhat hastily rush forward to set into action the proposition in the conclusion. Another example given by Aristotle is a little more complex, and suggests chaining together several practical inferences in order to make up a longer sequence of practical reasoning:

Case 6.2
Premise 1:   I need covering.
Premise 2:   A cloak is a covering.
Conclusion 1: Therefore, I need a cloak.
Premise 3:   What I need, I have to make.
Premise 4:   I need a cloak.
Conclusion 2: Therefore, I have to make a cloak.

The second example from Aristotle indicates how such a sequence of practical reasoning could be quite complicated since it includes several sub-arguments with different goals and possible actions that might be considered. These variants and complexities in the structure of practical reasoning as distinctive forms of argumentation are more fully explored in Walton (1990a, chapter 2). In some cases, there can be different means to carry out the same goal.

Neither of these examples from Aristotle appears to be a deductively valid inference, and this has often puzzled philosophers.[2] What type of inference, then, could they be? The answer is that they represent a distinctive type of reasoning called *practical reasoning*, which is different from deductive and inductive reasoning, and which is inherently defeasible in nature, being based on generalizations that describe what is normally the case subject to exceptions in particular kinds of situations. This type of reasoning is a distinctive kind of knowledge-based reasoning that guides argumentation characteristically used in the context of deliberation dialogue.

The first premise of a practical inference states a goal, and the second premise states a means to obtain the goal, as far as the agent sees the situation. But this qualification, 'as far as the agent sees the situation,' is very important to our understanding of practical reasoning as a distinctive type of reasoning. The basic idea is that the so-called agent carries out actions that have consequences or effects in the situation, or circumstances external to the agent, and that the agent is (or can be) aware of these consequences. Thus the agent is not only a thinker, but also an observer and an actor, who can see the external situation (collecting information or input from it) and reacting to new information by carrying out actions and revising commitments (Wooldridge and Jennings, 1995).

This framework of basing practical reasoning on modification of an agent's commitments suggests that, to some extent, deliberation can be based on the information-seeking dialogue. Deliberation can be wiser or more informed, to the extent that it is based on better or more complete information on a relevant issue. In section 10 below, this common relationship between information-seeking dialogue and deliberation dialogue is analysed in more depth. This relationship represents a kind of case where one type of dialogue is joined to another during a sequence of argumentation.

3. Argument from Consequences

Deliberation is such a common framework for the most familiar kind of reasoning in everyday argument that it is easy to overlook it as an important normative model of dialogue. If we consider an ordinary, homely example of such an exchange in daily conversation, it is apparent how the various characteristics are exemplified. A good example of this kind of everyday deliberation is the following case.

Case 6.3
A professor normally rides his bicycle to work every day and starts his working day by giving a lecture in the morning to one of his classes at the university. But on this particular day, as the professor and his wife wake up, the weather report is predicting a severe thunderstorm. They decide it would be unwise for the professor to ride his bike, and so they proceed to discuss how he might get to school that morning. He says, 'Well, I think the best thing would be to take the bus, because there is a bus that goes near the university and, if I hurry, I can catch one that will get me there in time to meet my class.' She

replies, 'Well, you might miss the bus and, if you miss it, for sure you'll be late for your lecture. And, anyway, you'll have to walk a fair distance from the bus stop to the university, and it could be raining by then. No, I had better give you a lift in the car.' He replies, 'If you drive me in the car, then you'll be late for work today.' She replies, 'No, I don't have an early appointment today and, anyway, it doesn't take me very long to detour a little bit out of my way and drop you off. I won't be late.' He replies, 'Well, if you're sure that it's not going to be a problem for you.' She replies, 'No problem. I'll drop you off.'

This example illustrates two people deliberating together to solve a problem. The problem is that there is an obstacle to their normal way of doing things, and they need to consider alternative ways of accomplishing their goal. In this simple case, they consider two alternatives and then decide on a preponderance of considerations for the one. She commits herself to the course of action she has proposed, and since she is the primary agent of this course of action, he agrees to her proposed solution. Here the two parties are deliberating on the possible or plausible consequences of the two lines of action they are considering – the action of taking the bus versus the action of taking the car. They are engaging in a kind of argumentation that is called argument from consequences.

Argument from consequences is a reasonable and commonly used type of argument that has the following two forms. The variables A, B, C, ... represent states of affairs that can be brought about, or prevented from coming about, by an agent.

(AC+) If A is brought about, then, as a consequence, B will come about.
       B is a good (positive) state of affairs.
       Therefore, A should be brought about.

(AC–) If A is brought about, then, as a consequence, B will come about.
       B is a bad (negative) state of affairs.
       Therefore, A should not be brought about.

B can, in some instances, also be a compound state of affairs or a conjunction of states of affairs, $B_1 \wedge B_2 \wedge ... \wedge B_n$ where the B_i in all cases is said to be good (in AC+) or bad (in AC–). The strength of an instance of argumentation from consequences depends on how serious (good or bad) the cited consequences are; how many consequences are cited; and how likely the cited consequences are, given the action being considered. But these are not the only relevant factors in evaluating argumentation from consequences. As a species of practical reasoning used in deliberation, argument from consequences needs to be evaluated by asking various critical questions appropriate for this type of reasoning (see section 2 above), such as whether there are alternative courses of action to the one being considered.

The following argument is an instance of argument from positive consequences (*AC+*) in a deliberation.

Case 6.4
If the cigarette tax is reduced, cigarette smuggling will be eradicated.

The eradication of cigarette smuggling is a good thing.

Therefore, the cigarette tax should be reduced.

The following argument is an instance of argument from negative consequences (*AC–*) in a deliberation.

Case 6.5
If the cigarette tax is reduced, smoking-related illnesses, like lung cancer, with the pain and suffering of victims, will increase.

Increased incidence of smoking-related illnesses, like lung cancer, with the pain and suffering of victims, are bad things.

Therefore, the cigarette tax should not be reduced.

In this case, it is evident that the argument from positive consequences and the argument from negative consequences come to opposite conclusions. Clearly one important factor in evaluating the two arguments together is a comparative weighing of the worth or seriousness of the value of the positive consequences against the worth or seriousness of the negative consequences. If the probability of the outcomes is factored in, the evaluation takes the form of the familiar kind of cost-benefit calculation used in modern decision theory.

Clearly, then, argument from positive consequences and argument from negative consequences are commonly used kinds of arguments. And in many (but not all) instances, they can be reasonable arguments to use.

(*AC+*) and (*AC–*) are closely related to another type of argument that is very familiar in logic. If we put the two instances of arguments from consequences together, the combined argument has the form of a dilemma.

4. The Dilemma

Negative argumentation from consequences is very closely related to a form of argument well known in traditional logic – the dilemma. The idea of a dilemma in ordinary speech involves a choice between two courses of action, neither of which is good, but where one or the other must be chosen. Hurley defines *constructive dilemma* as 'a valid argument form that consists of ... two conditional statements, a disjunctive premise that asserts the antecedents [of the two conditional statements] ..., and a disjunctive conclusion that asserts the consequents' (1994, p. 339). The following example, given by Hurley (p. 339), shows how constructive dilemma does represent the idea of a dilemma in ordinary speech:

> Case 6.6
> If we choose nuclear power, then we increase the risk of nuclear accident.
>
> If we choose conventional power, then we add to the greenhouse effect.
>
> We must either choose nuclear power or conventional power.
>
> Therefore, we either increase the risk of nuclear accident or add to the greenhouse effect.

The constructive dilemma has the following form:

> (*CD*) If *A* then *B*
>   If *C* then *D*
>   Either *A* or *C*
>   Therefore, either *B* or *D*.

This form of argument is deductively valid in the propositional calculus in classical logic.

One way of attacking a dilemma is to slip between the horns by trying to find a third course of action as an alternative to the two courses of action posed by the disjunctive premise. For example, in the case cited above, we might look for some third source of power, other than conventional power or nuclear power (unless conventional power is, by definition, non-nuclear power which leaves no third alternative possible). Or we might try to decrease our use of power, so that we do not need to choose either nuclear or conventional power. This alternative might not be realistic, however.

This dilemma seems to leave some (perhaps limited) room to slip between the horns. But some dilemmas do not leave any room at all for this form of attack because the disjunctive premise is a tautology. Hurley gives the following example of such a dilemma (p. 341):

Case 6.7

If we encourage competition, we will have no peace.

If we do not encourage competition, we will make no progress.

We must either encourage competition or not encourage it.

Therefore, we will either have no peace or make no progress.

In this case, the disjunctive premise is a tautology. It cannot be proven that it is false, and hence there is no possibility of refuting the dilemma by using the attack of slipping between the horns. Here the dilemma can be attacked by grasping one of the horns – that is, by showing that one of the conditional premises is questionable.[3]

In deductive logic, the constructive and destructive dilemmas are modelled as deductively valid forms of argument. But evaluating a dilemma as an instance of practical reasoning used in a deliberation dialogue involves weighing the value of the goals against the assessed values of the possible or plausible consequences of carrying out the means for achieving these goals. Thus the kind of dilemma found so often in deliberation dialogue is best evaluated using the argumentation scheme and the critical questions for practical reasoning.

Another kind of argument that is less common but is nevertheless used in deliberation is the slippery slope argument. It is a special subtype of argument from consequences involving a graduated sequence of negative consequences (see Walton, 1992a).

5. Stages and Dynamic Aspects of Deliberation

The initial situation of a deliberation is characteristically a practical problem which impedes carrying out one's goals in a particular situation where this blockage needs to be overcome by undertaking some course of action. Or, in some cases, it could be that an omission, or a failure to act, is the prudent course designated. In some cases, the problem is a dilemma.

Every such case of deliberation can be reduced to two sides – a pro and a contra – with respect to some proposed course of action.[4] At the opening stage, the participants agree to deliberate together to work towards finding a solution to this problem. When we come to the argumentation stage, one party takes up the pro position and the other party takes up the contra position. Then, during the argumentation stage, each brings forward the strongest reasons for his recommendations, and critically questions the arguments put forward by the other side. The closing stage of deliberation is typically dictated by practical constraints of time and capabilities in a given situation.

Deliberation is argued out on a basis of burden of proof because there may not be enough time to do enough research to acquire enough knowledge to resolve the issue definitively one way or the other – for example, by undertaking an inquiry. Burden of proof is set differently in deliberation than it is in scientific research. There is a certain conservatism in scientific research that is consistent with the demand for established and verified proof in the inquiry. In a scientific study of a disease or health hazard, the burden of proof rests with the side that must prove that some suspected agent really is the cause of the phenomenon in question by supplying evidence based on controlled studies and other kinds of replicated data. Proctor calls this assumption of statistical reasoning in scientific research a counterpart of the legal presumption that a person is held to be innocent until proven guilty: 'Evidence is adduced to refute the "null hypothesis" (the presumption of no effect), and only if a sufficiently strong case can be made is the null hypothesis rejected' (1995, p. 261). But according to Proctor, in medicine or public health 'the logic is different' and the burden of proof is reversed. A chemical that is being considered for regulation may be considered dangerous in public health deliberations on the grounds that a potential hazard should not be overlooked, even if secure scientific research has not proved that it is dangerous.

This difference in the way of laying burden of proof is based on two different 'logics' or uses of reasoning in scientific research versus public health deliberations:

The contrast between scientific and public health conservatism usually translates into different perceptions of what is most in need of protection. Most scientists adhere to an implicit empiricism, requiring that they be cautious about making statements of fact. Risks are often expressed as minimal and, for that reason, scientific conservatism is sometimes regarded as (and sometimes used as) a ploy to stonewall efforts to limit risks. Scientists who worry first and foremost about the integrity of science are, in fact, more likely to underestimate than to overestimate the hazards of a particular substance or situation. By contrast, administrative agencies such as the EPA are entrusted with protection of public health and safety, and 'conservatism' for them generally means erring on the side of caution. Public health conservatism of the kind reflected in the EPA's preference for 'worse-case' scenarios is designed to minimize public harm. (Proctor, 1995, p. 262)

In scientific research, it is best to wait until results have been confirmed, to err on the side of caution instead of announcing a result prematurely. In deliberation, *tutiorism*, or being on the safe side in taking care to avoid action that is potentially dangerous (even if the danger of consequences is not known for sure), is a basic principle.

In deliberation, even doing nothing at all is a form of action that may have definite consequences, and deliberating about at least a tentative way of proceeding may be necessary. Hence, deliberation typically involves presumptive reasoning based on what is known, or is thought to be the case in a particular situation, even though this incoming information may be highly subject to change. So closure of the argumentation stage is based on a balance of considerations that defines the weight of presumption needed in order to call an argument successful in carrying forward a proposed line of action that is thought to be the most prudent. Thus, closure of deliberation is typically of a tentative nature, and it may often be necessary to reopen deliberations at a later stage if the situation changes and relevant new information appears.

Goals may also be subject to change in many cases. Like the other types of dialogue we have examined, one of the most difficult problems with deliberation is articulating goals clearly enough in the first place to give the argumentation a clear direction.

Like negotiation, deliberation is frequently subjoined to information-seeking dialogue. The second premise of the practical inference is based on what the agent knows or thinks to be the case in a particular situation. This means that this type of premise is based on factual information, or information that the arguer has good reason to think is factual. Here deliberation can exhibit a dialectical shift to information-seeking dialogue, where more information is collected to enable the agent to deliberate more intelligently about what to do in that situation. We could say that good or successful deliberation is informed, to the extent that it is based on the collection of a good body of intelligence or information about the situation the deliberators find themselves in. This functional joining of information-seeking to deliberation is considered further in section 10.

There are eleven dynamic aspects of the argumentation used in the normative structure of deliberation as a type of dialogue that contains intelligent practical reasoning by an agent (see Walton, 1990a, pp. 142–3). The first aspect is the setting of goals. Goals are defined as designated propositions that describe possible courses of actions that can be carried out by the agent. Once designated by the agent, a goal tends to remain fixed or stable. However, the goal can be further specified by an agent in relation to particular circumstances. The primary means of accomplishing this process of specification in deliberation is the putting forward and retracting of commitments in the sequence of dialogue.

The second aspect is the set of actions produced by the agent. These actions are regarded as events that are partly external to the agent but that affect the agent's situation and that have consequences. The capability of producing actions makes arguments from consequences relevant. The third aspect is knowledge, which can be defined as opinion or reasoned opinion which represents information or presumed information that is external to the agent but that comes into his commitment store. The agent then uses this knowledge or evolving commitment set as the basis for his decision on courses of action. In general, there is a presumption that the agent can observe the external world, or has some way of collecting information relevant to his particular situation. This knowledge can also include conditional propositions that express generalizations about normal expectations based on the agent's experience, skills, or information he receives from others.

The fourth aspect of dynamic argumentation in deliberation is called feedback, which is defined as error correction that occurs when the agent monitors the consequences of his outgoing actions and takes this information into account in processing his subsequent actions. For example, if the agent observes a line of consequences that go contrary to the goals he is committed to, then he may be able to change his line of action to prevent these consequences from occurring. This element of feedback indicates that there is very often a circular quality to the kind of reasoning that takes place in deliberation.

The fifth aspect is the complexity of the act sequence. As we observed in Aristotle's simple case of the cloak, sub-actions can often be joined together with goals in an extended sequence of reasoning. Characteristic here is the organization of such a sequence of actions into an ordering or hierarchy, based on levels of abstraction; that is, more general propositions about goals, or about what can normally be expected to take place in a situation, are linked with more specific propositions about what is actually happening or what is being done in this particular situation.[5]

A seventh aspect of the dynamic use of arguments in deliberation is the capability of the agent to formulate hypothetical questions in order to project possible lines of consequences of his actions. All deliberation is future-oriented and has to do with possible outcomes of courses of actions that could potentially be adopted. This feature is another reason why the conclusions of practical reasoning in deliberation tend to be tentative and defeasible, for we can never predict the future with certainty and typically deliberation is based on hunches and guesswork.

An eighth important aspect of dynamic argumentation in deliberation is plasticity. This property is characteristic of flexible decision-making and retraction of commitments when a given line of action seems to be having bad consequences or is running into obstacles. A choice may have to be made in midstream to try an alternative possible line of action. Plasticity, then, is characterized by both multiplicity of means available to carry out a goal and a certain flexibility or openness in the selection of these means, so that there may be a certain jumping back and forth or deciding in midstream to retract commitments and try an alternative way of proceeding. This means that, in deliberation, commitment is not regarded as too strongly fixed and, as in persuasion dialogue, there should be quite good possibilities for retraction of commitments.

A ninth aspect of dynamic use of argumentation in deliberation is often called knowledge or memory, which essentially amounts to the commitment set of the participant. According to this characteristic, an intelligent deliberator should keep track of both his goals and the actions or steps already undertaken in order to make subsequent moves coherent with this given set of commitments. The agent should then have a memory or knowledge base in which this set of commitments is recorded. Thus, at some junctures of deliberation, the line of argumentation involves retraction or erasure of previous goals or designated actions and replacing them with alternative propositions. In the simplest kind of case, we can think of the goals of deliberation as being fixed, but in any more realistic case, we may have to model the normative structure by allowing goals to be modified or changed as the deliberation proceeds.

The eleventh aspect of dynamic argumentation is called criticism, which refers to the ability of the agent to criticize or evaluate actions, goals, and plans as the dialogue proceeds. An important task of such criticism is to uncover practical inconsistencies in a deliberator's commitment set which function as significant obstacles standing in the way of the agent achieving his goal.

6. Aristotle's Account of Deliberation

For Aristotle, deliberation primarily involves a solitary individual, but his definition of the main characteristics of deliberation is highly consistent with our account of deliberation as a normative structure of dialogue. He even defined excellence in deliberation in the *Nicomachean Ethics* (1142b15) as a kind of correctness of thinking. In other words, deliberation for Aristotle is something that involves reasoning, which makes his account of deliberation compatible with our view of it as a normative framework of reasoned argument.

However, in his works on logic, like *On Sophistical Refutations* and the *Topics*, Aristotle does not seem to be concerned with deliberation as a kind of logical reasoning, or as a context of dialogue in which argumentation should be evaluated on the basis of correct or incorrect reasoning or logical failures and fallacies. Aristotle did not list deliberation as one of his five types of argument, probably because *syllogismos* was not the kind of reasoning he saw as characteristically being used in deliberation. Deliberation is not primarily discussed in his logical works, but he does give an account of it in his ethics. Thus, there appears to be an important difference between our analysis here of deliberation as a normative model of dialogue, in which argumentation should be evaluated, and Aristotle's account of it, which seems to be primarily ethical in nature. Even so, the leading characteristics of deliberation as a process that are given by Aristotle appear to be highly consistent with our account of deliberation as a type of dialogue framework for reasoned argument.

Aristotle gives a clear and self-contained account of deliberation in the *Nicomachean Ethics* (1112a20–1113b25), but it is a preliminary analysis that leads to a discussion of the ethics of voluntariness, choice, and responsibility. Deliberation does indeed have this ethical aspect, but in our somewhat different point of view, we have studied it as a structure of conversation in which certain characteristic kinds of argumentation are used.

Aristotle writes in the *Nicomachean Ethics* (1112a30–1112b1) that we deliberate about things that are in our power. In other words, a sensible person only deliberates about things that he can change, not about something eternal or fixed. Aristotle also observes that 'We deliberate about things that are in our control and are attainable by action' (1112b7), and that 'Any particular set of men deliberates about the things attainable by their own actions' (1112b8). Thus, according to Aristotle's concept of deliberation, a sensible person does not deliberate about 'matters fully ascertained and completely formulated as sciences' (1112b8).

Here is a characteristic difference between the inquiry and the deliberation. In fact, Aristotle notes that we deliberate more about the arts than about the sciences (1112b9), because there is more uncertainty in arts or practical skills, and uncertainty is characteristic of Aristotle's notion of deliberation. For Aristotle, we deliberate about things that are inherently subject to change but, according to his notion of the inquiry or scientific demonstration, argumentation there needs to be based on first principles that can be firmly fixed.[6] And the laws or general rules of the reasoning in demonstration are based on universal generalizations that 'generally hold good,' and are not subject to exceptions in the same way that generalizations in a deliberation tend to be. As Aristotle puts it in the *Nicomachean Ethics*, 'Deliberation then is employed in matters which, though subject to rules that generally hold good, are uncertain in their issue: or where the issue is indeterminate, and where, when the matter is important, we take others into our deliberations, distrusting our own capacity to decide' (1112b10). This is an excellent characterization of the deliberation as a type of dialogue because it stresses the defeasible nature of the argumentation in a deliberation, which is generally based on presumptions that hold only tentatively and are subject to exceptions. His account also stresses the indeterminacy of the information that finds its way into the premises of a deliberation because, in deliberation, the agent's knowledge of his circumstances is so typically subject to change and retraction.

Moreover, it is interesting to observe here that Aristotle also cites the case of taking others into our deliberation, and seeing deliberation as a type of dialogue exchange where a person can interact argumentatively with the opinions of another person in order to get a better basis for making a decision. This characteristic is highly indicative of the normative model of deliberation that we sketched above because, in this kind of deliberation, the particular circumstances of an agent's given situation tend to be constantly changing and, hence, deliberation by its nature is subject to careful and intelligent revision and retraction of commitments as new information comes in. Consequently, a certain flexibility is a good quality in deliberation, and it is generally important to be open to new information, not be too dogmatic or fixed in one's commitments. There is a contrast again here with the inquiry because the inquiry involves higher standards of burden of proof and a systematic attempt to avoid any retraction of commitments.

Aristotle also makes it clear in his discussion of deliberation in the *Nicomachean Ethics* (1113a15) that deliberation involves practical reasoning as the principal method of argumentation, and that what we deliberate about is how to achieve goals by means of actions that are possible in an agent's given situation. As Aristotle puts it, 'The province of deliberation is to discover actions within one's own power to perform.' According to Aristotle, then, we do deliberate not principally about the facts, but about the means to carry out ends or goals.[7]

It is worthwhile repeating that, in his work on logic, Aristotle does not explicitly view deliberation as a normative model of dialogue for evaluating arguments in exactly the way we have modelled deliberation dialogue here. Further discussion of the questions of what Aristotle means by dialectical argument, and how this fits in with our analysis of persuasion dialogue and other types of dialogue, is taken up in chapter 9. Despite all these qualifications, however, the account Aristotle does give of deliberation, as a distinctive framework of reasoning, is highly compatible with our analysis of deliberation as a type of dialogue.

It is interesting to note in passing that Aristotle clearly recognizes argument from consequences as a distinctive type of argument. In the *Topics*, he writes: 'When two things are very similar to one another and we cannot detect any superiority in the one over the other, we must judge from their consequences; for that of which the consequence is a greater good is more worthy of choice, and, if the consequences are evil, that is more worthy of choice which is followed by the lesser evil' (117a7–117a10). He recognizes the same mode of argument again in the *Rhetoric*: 'since in most human affairs the same thing is accompanied by some bad or good result, another topic consists in employing the consequence to exhort or dissuade, accuse or defend, praise or blame' (1399a14–1399a15). Following this explanation of argument from consequences, he links it to the dilemma form of argument (1399a16). But while Aristotle recognizes argument from consequences, and also describes deliberation as a process (very well, from the point of view of the new dialectic), he does not see these concepts as normative models or structures of argument in the way that the new dialectic does. These differences may stem from Aristotle's seeing *phronesis* in a somewhat different way than practical reasoning is seen in the new dialectic.

7. The Town Hall Meeting

In some cases, deliberation dialogue occurs in a more complex and structured format than the relatively simple kind of instance represented by case 6.3. A good example is the kind of political deliberation that takes place in a parliament, congress, or legislature where some solution to a problem is proposed in the form of a bill or piece of legislation, and the two sides who represent two different points of view on the bill deliberate on it. This type of case admits of complications because it occurs within an elaborate institutional framework.

Deliberation can also occur in a fairly complex but simpler setting where a precise bill or legislative solution has not yet been proposed, but the problem has been aired and the assembly is looking around for possible solutions and discussing some solutions that have been put forward as proposals. Lascher gives a nice example of this type of case of deliberation, called the town hall meeting. The Rhode Island case, as Lascher calls it, concerned the debate in the Rhode Island Assembly on whether or not to bring in no-fault insurance. Reformers advocated bringing in a no-fault system similar to that in other states. According to Lascher, the problem to be addressed was the perception that insurance rates were too high and 'had become increasingly burdensome for average Rhode Island citizens' (1994, p. 37). This view was accepted by the legislators interviewed by Lascher, and the general perception in the legislative assembly was that a problem needed to be solved by changing to a different system of auto insurance.

The no-fault advocates argued that the change to a new system would lower the costs of insurance. The argument of the opponents of the no-fault insurance was put in the form of a *modus ponens* argument by Lascher: 'Opponents argued that, because a no-fault system would fail to lower premiums, industry reform would succeed in lowering insurance rates, industry reform would leave intact insurance claimants' ability to sue for pain and suffering compensation, and no-fault unfairly makes good drivers pay for bad drivers, no-fault should be rejected and an industry reform measure should be enacted' (p. 43). As Lascher shows, this sequence of argument can be put into a *modus ponens* form and reconstructed as a deductively valid sequence of argumentation. The first four propositions cited in the quotation are premises, and it is asserted by the no-fault opponents that all four premises are true. By *modus ponens*, it is then asserted (by inference) that the conclusion (the last proposition in the quote) is true.

It is also important to realize that this argument is an instance of argumentation from consequences. The opponents of the no-fault system are arguing that, not only would the no-fault system fail to offset what are cited as the bad consequences of the existing system, but the new no-fault system would itself have bad consequences that might even outweigh the bad consequences of the old system. This type of argumentation from consequences that weighs the good outcomes against the bad is very typical of argumentation in political deliberation of the town meeting type. As Lascher puts it, this argument 'revolved around the advantages and disadvantages of different systems for consumers.' More particularly, the argument revolves around what are cited as the good or bad consequences of the proposals advocated by either side. Each side adopts an argument from good consequences to support its own proposal by arguing, in effect, that its proposal generally has good consequences or a favourable balance of good over bad consequences and, therefore, ought to be accepted. At the same time, each side uses negative argumentation from consequences (or argumentation from bad consequences) to criticize or refute the arguments of the other side. This argument runs as follows: 'Your proposal has bad consequences or an unfavourable balance such that the bad consequences can only outweigh the good consequences and, as a result, we ought to reject it as a prudent course of action or a good solution to the problem of our deliberations.'

One of the no-fault opponents' representatives, Steven Smith, cited the encouraging of competition as an important goal for industry reform in the insurance industry. The implicit argument here, as shown by Lascher, was the claim that the no-fault proposal would fail to lower insurance rates because it would not encourage competition; that is, it would lead to bad consequences, to a situation of non-competitiveness, which would create a chain of bad economic consequences that, over a period of time, would result in escalating costs for insurance. The general line of argument was that the new proposal for no-fault insurance would fail to lower insurance rates and, of course, the main argument in favour of the no-fault proposal was that it would result in a lowering of insurance rates. So here, once again, a species of argumentation from consequences was being used by the one side against the other.

This type of case is a good example of deliberation dialogue, both because it is common to many political debates and public policy discussions and also because it features some of the leading characteristics of reasoning in deliberation, such as argumentation from consequences. However, there is a subtle difficulty with cases of political dialogue of any kind because, generally, this kind of discourse tends to mix together several of the types of dialogue we have already identified.

8. Public and Political Deliberation

The town hall meeting is an example of public deliberation on a small scale, but political decision-making in democratic countries is based on public deliberation on a much larger scale.

According to Yankelovich, public opinion polls are frequently misleading because they take only a single snapshot of an evolving public judgment on an issue as the public goes through various stages of a process of deliberation (1991; 1992). Yankelovich gives the example of a public opinion poll on protectionism that seems to indicate that 70 per cent of those polled accept the idea of protectionism (1992, p. 22). But as soon as the people polled are informed of some of the plausible consequences of protectionism – for example, that they might have to pay more for certain products or that they might have less choice in products – the approval rating may drop to 26 or 28 per cent. This radical drop illustrates that the results in a public opinion poll depends very much on whether or how the public has deliberated on an issue.

Yankelovich summarizes a seven-step sequence of deliberation that the public characteristically goes through in thinking about an issue. First, people become aware of a problem. Second, they develop a sense of urgency to solve it. Third, policy-makers offer proposals to solve the problem. Fourth, people confront obstacles and trade-offs involving conflicting goals. Fifth, people begin to 'work through' the trade-offs entailed in the different proposals. Sixth is the stage of 'intellectual resolution,' where people resolve to take action. Seventh is the stage of public judgment, where people make up their minds about what to do. This process of public deliberation is very similar to the sequence of stages of argumentation in a deliberation dialogue, except that in public deliberation a large group of people are involved in the process and input comes from legislators and the media.

It might be tempting at this point to leap to the conclusion that all argumentation in political discourse could be modelled as a deliberation, where various alternative solutions to a problem are considered and the consequences evaluated. This hypothesis would be premature, however, because political discourse is very complex as a type of dialogue. If we look at a legislative debate on an issue like capital punishment or abortion, for example, it seems more like a persuasion dialogue, although it might have some elements of a deliberation as well.

In some cases, political debates in legislatures or congresses are instances of persuasion dialogue more than of deliberation. As an example, let us consider the early stages of a legislative debate, where a very controversial topic like abortion or euthanasia is being discussed, but no specific proposal has been made, no solutions advocated, nor is a bill or proposal being voted on. Here, the conversation is more of a preliminary general discussion of the issue as a topic of political and public controversy. In a case like this, the discourse may take the form of a persuasion dialogue rather than a deliberation because the participants are not deliberating on how to take action to implement particular goals, but are discussing the pros and cons of the issue in a much more general way and perhaps debating whether abortion, for example, is a good practice or a bad practice. Since at this stage they are not debating specific courses of action, such as a legislative bill or proposal, the debate can be more usefully modelled as a persuasion dialogue.

Another complication here is that very often in the early stages of political debates there is an information-collecting phase where experts are brought in to give testimony or information. In another type of case cited by Lascher, deliberative decision-making debates begin with public hearings and members of the public who have information to contribute are brought in before the debating begins (1994, p. 17). This means that, in many cases of discourse that we might initially classify as having the form of deliberation dialogue, there is a phase that could be better modelled as a kind of information-seeking dialogue where the goal is not deliberating – at least yet – on proposals for outcomes, but rather collecting information that might be useful in improving such deliberations.

Another complicating aspect of modelling political dialogue is that any kind of political debate is generally based on, or incorporates, negotiation. In nearly all political debate, there are interests at stake and the principal speakers are advocates of these interests. For example, members of congress or parliament represent constituencies, voters, parties, and other alliances that all have specific interests at stake, often financial ones. Part of the political process involves representing these interests, and this is a legitimate part of the political process in western democratic systems. Hence, it can't be ruled out that political debate contains negotiation.

All in all, then, we see that political discourse generally is a mixed type of dialogue which contains elements of several of the different types of dialogue we have examined. So looking at arguments critically, or evaluating for fallacies in a particular case of political debate, tends to include an element of arbitrariness. Treating the argument as part of a critical discussion, for example, or as a straightforward case of deliberation, poses a considerable danger of oversimplification.

Nevertheless, this does not mean that we cannot look at a particular case of a political debate, like the Rhode Island case cited by Lascher, as an instance of one particular normative model of dialogue, like the deliberation. But we must be clear on exactly what it is we are doing. Even though a text of discourse of a political debate may contain elements of negotiation, persuasion dialogue, and so forth, we can still look at it from the point of view of a deliberation and use the normative structure of deliberation as a model for evaluating the argumentation in the debate. Nevertheless, we must always be alert to the possibility that there can be dialectical shifts to other types of dialogue within the discourse. Because of its tendency in practice to mix together several of the different normative types of dialogue, political discourse is a unique case. We return to a further detailed consideration of it as a mixed type of discourse in chapter 9.

9. Relevance in Deliberation

Relevance in deliberation is determined by the sequence of practical reasoning that connects the given argument to the original issue of the dialogue. Practical reasoning connects goals to actions that are presumed to be means for realizing these goals. So it is the fitting together of goals and actions that is the connection that defines relevance in a deliberation dialogue.

In the Rhode Island case, the issue (to a significant extent) revolves around the use of argumentation from consequences by the opposed sides. Thus, to be relevant, an argument needs to fit in somewhere in a projected sequence of possible consequences of the adoption or non-adoption of a policy of no-fault insurance in Rhode Island, and other places where the situation can be compared to that of Rhode Island. Also relevant is the connection of these lines of action and consequences to goals that are important to the citizens of Rhode Island, such as saving costs and improving services.

What is distinctive about relevance in deliberation generally is that it is defined by a sequence of practical reasoning that links goals and actions and that it is directed towards the solution of a practical problem of action in a particular situation.

As we noted in connection with Aristotle's cloak example, practical reason is a sequential joining together of a series of practical inferences. The conclusion of one sub-inference plays the role of a premise in the next sub-inference. This lengthy sequence of practical reasoning connects up a set of sub-goals and actions (means) to the big issue, which is the main question to be settled by the global deliberation as a framework of the argumentation in the case. Relevance of an argument or a question in deliberation dialogue is determined by how it fits into this global network of practical reasoning in the given case.

Relevance, in a deliberation dialogue, has to do with ways and means of solving the problem posed as the main issue of the deliberation. Argument from consequences is frequently used here, because deliberators are often concerned about the possible side effects of their actions. Thus, the initial problem that the deliberation was set into motion to resolve is what determines whether something is globally relevant or not in the deliberation. But as different solutions to the problem are posed, and different consequences of these proposed solutions are considered, more and more detailed factors will be shown to be locally relevant in one way or another.

As well, whether or not there is relevance in a deliberation depends on the stage of the deliberation. Something that is relevant at one stage may be irrelevant at another stage of a deliberation. At the early stages of a deliberation, it may be hard to tell whether something will turn out to be relevant at some later stage of the argumentation. Judging whether something might become relevant later, even though it is not relevant at an early stage of the dialogue, involves trying to project the argument forward to see if a sequence of connections is plausible. Thus, as with other types of dialogue, we may have to make a 'best guess' at whether something is likely to become relevant later, based on what we know now about the likely lines of controversy and argumentation as the dialogue evolves.

10. Relevance across Joined Dialogues

Another complication in determining relevance or irrelevance of arguments in deliberation is that, in some cases, another type of dialogue will be joined to a deliberation dialogue, where the sequence of argumentation runs over the juncture. A common example already noted is where a deliberation dialogue is preceded by an information-seeking dialogue, and the information collected in the information-seeking is used as an important part of the basis for making the deliberations. This kind of joining of these two types of dialogue is common because practical reasoning is based on a 'knowledge' premise.

The kind of information-seeking dialogue that is involved here is reminiscent of the case of Mary, Peter, and William in chapter 5. Mary saw the approach of William as 'the one truly relevant change in her cognitive environment,' according to Sperber and Wilson (1986, p. 49). Why was this so? According to Sperber and Wilson's account, it was because Mary drew many more conclusions from this piece of information than from the other new information she perceived. According to our analysis of this case, Mary picked out this particular new, incoming information as relevant and important because she would soon have to react to it. Should she try to 'brush off' William politely so she could continue her much more interesting conversation with Peter? And if so, how could she do this? In other words, the imminent arrival of William on the scene posed a practical problem for Mary and so she needed to begin deliberating immediately on how to proceed.

In what sense, then, was William's perceived imminent arrival relevant? Here we could define 'relevance' in all kinds of different ways. But in what framework of dialogue for argument should this proposition be seen as a relevant argument? The answer is that we see Mary observing her external circumstances while sitting on the park bench with Peter. New information comes in to Mary, the 'agent,' in the form of three events she perceives – the ice-cream vendor, the ordinary stroller, and her acquaintance, William. The first two pieces of information are of little practical import from Mary's point of view, at least, there is no evidence they will affect her situation. However, the arrival of William, the 'dreadful bore,' is replete with all kinds of significant consequences. From a practical point of view, it is highly relevant information. It poses a problem, and immediately prompts deliberation on how best to proceed.

What is shown here is that deliberation is connected to information-seeking dialogue (and in some cases, to expert consultation dialogue) through practical reasoning. What will turn out to define relevance in deliberation is the sequence of connected inferences that constitutes the practical reasoning in a case. But what is also shown is that the item of information in the one dialogue is relevant to the argumentation in the other dialogue as well, because the one dialogue is functionally related to the other. The information is useful in the deliberation dialogue because it is needed as a basis to make the deliberation a better informed one. Although there has been a shift from one type of dialogue to another, it is a 'licit' shift (in the language of chapter 8), which means that the one dialogue helps and does not interfere with the other. We now turn to a different type of case where the shift is more dubious and involves a failure of relevance.

Argumentum ad consequentiam has been featured under the heading of informal fallacies in some logic textbooks. For example, in a section entitled 'Informal Fallacies,' Rescher defines this type of argument as follows: 'In an *argumentum ad consequentiam* ('appeal to consequences') the premises deal only with the consequences that are likely to ensue from accepting the conclusion, and not with its truth. Logically speaking, it is entirely irrelevant that certain undesirable consequences might derive from the rejection of a thesis, or certain benefits accrue from its acceptance' (1964, p. 82). Rescher cites the following example as an instance of this fallacy (p. 82).

Case 6.8
The United States had justice on its side in waging the Mexican War of 1848. To question this is unpatriotic, and would give comfort to our enemies by promoting the cause of defeatism.

But what exactly is fallacious in this argument? Rescher makes no further comment, but van Eemeren and Kruiger offer a clue in their description of the *argumentum ad consequentiam:* 'The *argumentum ad consequentiam* ... is a fallacy in which unfavourable light is cast on a thesis by pointing out its possible consequences, without the rightness of the thesis itself being disputed' (1987, p. 90). The fallacy occurs because, in a case like 6.8, there is a thesis being disputed in a critical discussion, and the argument from consequences used in the case does not bear on (is not relevant to or useful for) the resolution of the dispute about this thesis. In case 6.8, the thesis being disputed is that the U.S. had justice on its side in waging the Mexican War in 1848. The consequences of questioning this thesis – namely, giving comfort to our enemies – does not provide evidence that bears on the rightness or wrongness (truth or falsity) of this thesis. However, because it seems somehow to discourage the questioning of this thesis, or to make it appear that arguing against it is wrong, the *ad consequentiam* appeal is fallacious.

In case 6.8, the failure of relevance can be explained by the illicit shift from the critical discussion about which country had justice on its side in the 1848 war to practical deliberations about whether taking a stand on this issue might have certain bad consequences. From the practical point of view of winning the war, the argument from consequences might make good sense. If it would give comfort to our enemies, or give them something to use in their propaganda, that would be a good reason to avoid taking the stand that Mexico had justice on its side in the 1848 war. In the deliberation context of dialogue, such an argument from consequences provides a good reason, and is a good argument. But if we shift back to the original context of dialogue – the critical discussion of which country had justice on its side in the 1848 war – the argument from consequences is not relevant in that dialogue. It is not a good reason for accepting the conclusion that one country or the other was justified in waging war.

In this case, a deliberation dialogue was preceded by a critical discussion such that the sequence of argumentation ran through the one context of dialogue and into the other. But the argument from consequences, although relevant in the deliberation dialogue, is not relevant when used in the persuasion dialogue on the issue of justice in the 1848 war. In a case like this, relevance needs to be evaluated not just in a deliberation, but with respect to how the deliberation is joined to another type of dialogue.

7

Eristic Dialogue

The word 'argument,' as it is used in everyday conversations, includes the idea of a quarrel, a kind of angry or adversarial verbal exchange based on a conflict between two parties (perceived or real). Logicians have traditionally suppressed this meaning and have defined 'argument' in terms of reasoning, a kind of orderly sequence of steps of inferences from premises to a conclusion. But the logician's definition of 'argument' is artificial, and certainly at odds with the ordinary, more robust, and inclusive conversational meaning of the term.

If we are to have a pragmatic conception broad enough to deal with the sophistical tactics type of fallacies, the quarrel needs to be studied both in its own right as a type of dialogue and also as a subtype of the eristic dialogue, where the goal is to win a verbal victory by any means. Indeed, many of the sophistical tactics type of fallacies are fallacies precisely because there has been a dialectical shift from a critical discussion to a quarrelling type of dialogue, where one participant uses aggressive tactics to get the best of the other, with 'no holds barred.' This quarrelling type of dialogue has its own distinctive characteristics as a framework of argument.

With the exception of the ancients (notably Plato and Aristotle) logicians of the past have pretty well expunged eristic dialogue from their concept of argument. It's not hard to see why. Too often, the quarrel is no friend of logic.

1. The Quarrel as Paradigm

In a quarrel, the paradigm of eristic dialogue most familiar in everyday conversation, the individual goal of each participant is to 'hit out' verbally at the other party. This suggests that the quarrel is a purely antagonistic exchange, and has no real value or worth as an argument. Although this may be true of many trivial quarrels, a serious quarrel can arise from deep grievances or pent-up emotions that need to be expressed verbally in argumentation. Here the quarrel has a collective benefit (a cathartic function), allowing powerful feelings to be vented as a verbal alternative to physical fighting. By allowing both sides to express grievances or feelings that are not normally subjects for polite conversation, the quarrel gives each side a deeper insight into the feelings of the other party – an insight that can facilitate a smoother relationship in the future.

In a quarrel, the aim of each party is to defeat the other in an adversarial contest. But a serious quarrel also involves some collaboration. A participant casts off normal constraints against mentioning delicate subjects, and expresses his feelings, even at the cost of offending or deeply disturbing the other party. For example, one person may have an annoying mannerism that the other person does not dare to mention for fear of giving offence. But during a quarrel, it is acceptable, given the heightened emotions, to attack the other person by citing how 'detestable' this habit is to others. This sort of personal attack is out of place in polite conversation, but in the context of the quarrel, such an offence may be more tolerable because both sides are personally attacking each other.[1]

Often quarrels seem silly and pointless to onlookers. But emotional involvement in a quarrel puts a different perspective on a disagreement. What appears trivial on the surface can be a symptom of underlying grievances that are very important to two persons involved in a day-to-day relationship. Quarrels do have a serious side because they can reveal serious suppressed grievances and feelings.

In some cases, a quarrel breaks out in a natural but unpredictable way, when one party cannot contain an unexpressed grievance any longer. But in other cases, argumentation in eristic dialogue is put on purposefully to impress others. For example, academics may use combative argumentation to 'cut an opponent to shreds' in order to show other academics how clever they are.

In other cases, a quarrelsome mode of argument may be adopted as an attempt to entertain an audience. Tannen cites the following example of 'the culture of critique' (1994, p. A17).

Case 7.1
Several years ago I was on a television talk show with a representative

of the men's movement. I didn't foresee any problem, since there is nothing in my work that is anti-male. But in the room where guests gather before the show I found a man wearing a shirt and tie and a floor-length skirt, with waist-length red hair. He politely introduced himself and told me he liked my book. Then he added: 'When I get out there, I'm going to attack you. But don't take it personally. That's why they invite me on, so that's what I'm going to do.'

When the show began, I spoke only a sentence or two before this man nearly jumped out of his chair, threw his arms before him in gestures of anger and began shrieking – first attacking me, but soon moving on to rail against women. The most disturbing thing about his hysterical ranting was what it sparked in the studio audience. They too became vicious, attacking not me (I hadn't had a chance to say anything) and not him (who wants to tangle with someone who will scream at you?) but the other guests: unsuspecting women who had agreed to come on the show to talk about their problems communicating with their spouses.

In this case, the oddly dressed man announced in advance that his arguments would be eristic in nature. His quarrelsome attack was a calculated strategy of argument.

In other cases, it may be less clear that someone who is engaging in a quarrel has adopted the eristic framework of argument for some definite purpose. For example, a radical feminist who argues that men are bad, irrational, and cannot be trusted, who exhorts her colleagues to take action in the fight for women's issues, may not realize or admit that she is engaging in eristic dialogue, even though she uses words like 'fight' and 'struggle' to describe what she is doing.

The quarrel is mainly of interest to psychiatrists and social scientists who study the psychological and sociological dynamics of human relationships. Does it have any normative value for logic as a model of argument? At first glance, the answer seems to be no, for the critical discussion is the most important model of argumentation, according to recent advances in pragmatics, and quarrelling is a very inefficient way of conducting a critical discussion. From this perspective, it seems that the quarrel is not worth mentioning at all, that it is not a significant form of argument from a logical point of view. But when we study fallacies, the quarrel turns out to be very important because what makes a fallacious argument seem valid (or plausible) is a dialectical shift from one context of dialogue where an argument tactic is properly and appropriately used to another context where its use goes against the goal of the first dialogue. (See chapter 9 for a deeper analysis of how the understanding of such dialectical shifts is crucial to the analysis and evaluation of fallacies.)

2. Eristic Dialogue

The quarrel, a subtype of the eristic dialogue, was well known to the ancients.[2] According to Kerferd, Plato often uses the term 'eristic' (*eristikos*) to refer to the use of techniques of argument to win victory in a verbal exchange: '[Eristic] derives from the noun *eris* meaning strife, quarrel or contention, and, as Plato uses the term, eristic means 'seeking victory in argument,' and the art which cultivates and provides appropriate means and devices for so doing. Concern for the truth is not a necessary part of the art – victory in argument can be secured without it, sometimes more easily so. It follows that eristic as such is not strictly speaking a *technique* of argument' (1981, p. 62). For Plato, the goal of eristic dialogue is to succeed – or appear to succeed – in an argumentative exchange by gaining victory over an opponent. Hence, eristic dialogue is not a technique of argumentation, but a kind of forum or goal-directed setting in which techniques of argumentation, including fallacies and ambiguities, can be used to get the best of an opponent. Such skills are illustrated in Plato's dialogue *Euthydemus*, which shows professional sophists attacking each other's arguments with all sorts of clever sophistical tactics and subterfuges designed to cleverly trip up an opponent.

Eristic dialogue is a combative kind of verbal exchange in which two parties are allowed to bring out their strongest arguments to attack the opponent by any means, and have a kind of protracted verbal battle to see which side can triumph and defeat or even humiliate the other side. This type of dialogue is characterized by its very dominantly adversarial nature. You could say it is a kind of no-holds-barred combat where powerful verbal arguments of any sort are allowed, even where they would not be regarded as appropriate in a more polite type of dialogue like a persuasion dialogue or a deliberation.

Although the word 'eristic' derives from the Greek word meaning strife, eristic dialogue is not purely adversarial or free of rules. The participants must necessarily take turns to sustain this type of dialogue. And in other respects, eristic dialogue requires minimal elements of cooperation. But, in general, this type of dialogue is characterized by its dominantly adversarial nature. The rules are very minimal, and the focus of argumentation tends to be on directly attacking the other party even in a personal manner. In fact, *ad hominem* argumentation or personal attack in argument is a major characteristic of eristic dialogue as a type of conversational exchange.

A leading indicator of the eristic dialogue is the apparently irrelevant *ad hominem* attack which seems to appear out of nowhere, especially a personal attack that is persistently reiterated by an arguer. A good example is the case of the long parliamentary debate in the Canadian House of Commons on Bill C-110, the Northumberland Strait Crossing Act, as recorded in Hansard (14 June 1993). In the debate on this proproposed legislation, several members of Parliament begin discussing the costs and benefits and other particulars to establish a fixed link between Prince Edward Island and mainland Canada. (These speeches continue for some seven pages of recorded debate.) Suddenly, in the middle of the debate, Jim Fulton, the member for Skeena, interjects that both of the leading parties, the Liberals and the Tories (Conservatives), 'often operate sleazily.' This remark is followed by a lengthy attack on the 'sleasiness' of the Conservatives and Liberals; the centrepiece of it all is an *ad hominem* attack on Prime Minister Kim Campbell, who once admitted that she had smoked marijuana.

Case 7.2
The Liberals want to squeeze and sleaze their way and get a few extra votes out of a few seats in the Maritimes. The Tories want to use the fixed link as a banner to wave around the Maritimes saying they are going to do something big for all the voters out there. They are going to spend $1.47 billion building a bridge that has never been assessed.

They do not want to talk about that. They want to pretend that everything is above board. It is not. This Chamber is well on the road to acting in contempt of court. It bothers me and I think it should bother the Canadian public that this place has become so entirely out of touch that the law does not seem to matter.

It is like the person who has just become Canada's Prime Minister, the hon. member for Vancouver Centre. She said before her campaign began that she had smoked marijuana. When asked during the leadership campaign she said she had smoked marijuana but she did not break any law by doing it. Every dean of law in the country said that was not true. If one smoked marijuana, one broke the law.

Five hundred and thirty thousand Canadians have a criminal

record for smoking marijuana. They are all supposed to keep their criminal records. They cannot get bonded jobs. They cannot do anything but it is okay. A person can be the Prime Minister of Canada and break the law ...

Canadians are getting really sick of this stuff. I am getting really sick of it. There is one law for the grand elevated elite who sit on the government side as Prime Minister or whatever. The law applies only to the great unwashed. It applies to those Canadians who have to pay the taxes and the piper.

Here is a chance for Parliament itself to do it right. This project from New Brunswick to Prince Edward Island has never been assessed. It is the law in Canada. The Liberals say they will attach some conditions. This is the same bunch of environmental thugs, SCI, who were involved from start to finish in the Oldman River dam in Alberta.

The last part of Fulton's interjection attempts to establish a link of relevance between his personal attack on Campbell and the general issue of government-funded infrastructure projects by accusing the Liberals of being 'environmental thugs' in another project, a dam construction project in Alberta. But is this suggestion of a relevant connection convincing? Not really. It seems that Fulton is really out to launch a personal attack on Kim Campbell, and to use that to question the ethics and the credibility of the Liberal and Conservative parties This attack is a quarrelsome interjection that is not dialectically relevant to the persuasion dialogue (or deliberation) on the Northumberland Strait Crossing Act.

3. Stages of the Quarrel

As a highly emotional type of dialogue, the quarrel tends to erupt or to break out suddenly rather than arising through some explicit agreements by the participants.[3] The quarrel is characterized by personal attack, and is thus not generally regarded as a friend of logic. As the old saying goes, 'The quarrel generates more heat than light.' The conventional opinion seems to be that the quarrel really has nothing to do with logic or reasoned argumentation at all. This perception is based on some wisdom because, as we will see, the quarrel is inimical to logic in an important way. Nevertheless, going against the conventional opinion here, we will argue that is it important to understand the quarrel as a normative model of dialogue in order to properly investigate fallacies and other failures and breakdowns of reasoned argumentation because other types of dialogue, like persuasion dialogue and deliberation, have a tendency to break down or to shift into a quarrel. In fact, this shifting during the sequence of an argument from another type of dialogue into a quarrel is often one of the most important indicators that a fallacy has been committed.

The initial situation of the quarrel is the existence of unspoken disagreements, grudges, or differences that exist between two parties. In any lasting relationship between two parties, there will generally be build-up of perceived slights or offences on both sides which may not be noticed by the one party. In everyday conversation, such complaints tend to be suppressed because they represent small perceptions of insensitivity or differences of point of view that would not be appropriate to bring up as part of polite conversation. For example, in business negotiations, one party may have to ignore the other party's cultural or personal differences that are a small source of some offence. If one party were to dwell on these small differences too much, or continually bring them to the surface, they would function as a continual interruption to the conversation and thus an obstruction to the goals of the dialogue. The goal of the quarrel is to allow these hidden grievances or differences to come to the surface and to be expressed explicitly and dealt with in an appropriate framework.[4]

There is a tendency to think of quarrels as a hindrance to communication. And sometimes they are. However, bringing underlying differences out in the open in a quarrel can cement a communicative relationship instead of destroying it. The quarrel does this by casting off restraints and moving to a less polite and less regulated type of dialogue where both parties are allowed to attack the person of the opponent in an emotional way. Thus, the quarrel, like an athletic contest, allows an outlet for a certain kind of controlled aggression. The goal of each party in a quarrel could be described as attacking the other party verbally, using arguments that centre on the other party's personal characteristics and behaviour.

Typically, the argumentation in a quarrel is of the so-called counter-blaming type. Each party uses arguments that focus on blaming the other party for some culpable act. The quarrel arises when one party feels resentment over some hidden injury caused by the other side. The first stage of the quarrel is the announcement of this hidden grievance or injury, which may then lead the other party to express similar feelings about some injury for which the other party is held responsible. This typically takes the form of the *tu quoque* type of *ad hominem* argument, where each party engages in a personal attack on the other party.

The emotional expression of antagonism at the opening stage of the quarrel functions as a kind of announcement that this will not be a polite type of dialogue like a deliberation or a critical discussion. Usually, the quarrel begins accidentally, as an interruption in some other type of conversational exchange. What prompts the quarrel is likely some trivial incident which has very little to do with the kind of argumentation that surfaces as the dispute of the quarrel. This trivial incident functions as a kind of gateway allowing hurt feelings to pour out. Once the argumentation stage begins, the quarrel may exhibit this same disjointedness or irrelevance, skipping around from one topic to another or one grievance to another in a seemingly random manner.

The quarrel has been studied empirically by Infante and Wigley; they use a verbal aggressiveness scale to identify a quarrel in a particular text of discourse. Their indicators of a quarrel include character attacks, attacks on the competence of the other party, insults, ridicule, blaming the other party, and profanity (1986, p. 61). Several of these types of indicators are associated with what is called the *argumentum ad hominem* in informal logic. As mentioned in chapter 1, this kind of argument which is used to attack the other party by raising questions about his or her character – and in particular, character for veracity – is a leading characteristic of the quarrel. Indeed, the quarrel is associated in many cases with several of the traditional informal fallacies recognized by the logic textbooks, as well as with the *argumentum ad hominem*.[5]

This association of the quarrel with fallacies indicates that usually a shift from another type of dialogue, like a persuasion dialogue, to a quarrel is a serious indication of some critical shortcoming, like a fallacy. However, the quarrel should not be wholly condemned from the point of view of argumentation as an altogether worthless or corrupting type of dialogue. As noted above, the quarrel can have the good function of providing a vehicle for the expression of hidden grievances, allowing them to surface in conversation so that they can be recognized and by both parties in a personal relationship.

This beneficial aspect of the quarrel works through a cathartic effect, whereby the hidden, underlying antagonisms are brought out into the open and acknowledged by both parties. When a quarrel is successful through its argumentation stages, both parties not only become aware of these hidden grievances, but can learn to become more sensitive to them by realizing how important they are to the other party.

At the closing stage of a successful quarrel, both participants 'make up,' which means they adopt a continuing basis for the relationship, having acknowledged and made allowances for the expressed grievances of the other party. At the closing stage of a successful quarrel, then, one party declares to the other: 'I didn't realize before that these underlying antagonisms were so important to you, but I now recognize the significance of them, and I think enough about the value of continuing our relationship that I will make an effort to be more sensitive on these questions in future relationships with you.' Thus the quarrel can have two possible outcomes. It can break the relationship of the two parties apart and destroy it, or it can strengthen the relationship by building in tolerances for differences that exist between them.

4. Closed Attitude of Eristic Dialogue

The key characteristic of eristic dialogue is its adversarial nature, as expressed in the old adage that says: 'If you are not for us, you are against us.' This closed attitude is characteristic of another subspecies of the quarrel called the *group quarrel*, which is an institutionalized type of eristic dialogue involving groups of individuals or parties where the one party opposes the other in an eristic confrontation (see Walton, 1992b, chapter 3).

A good example of the group quarrel is wartime propaganda which describes the enemy in highly pejorative terms that would be regarded as impolite and insensitive during peacetime. The enemy is always portrayed in a negative light, and everything the enemy does is cited as evidence of evil intentions. When any of the enemy's actions or any event in the wartime context are described, they are portrayed as some sort of bad outcome that the enemy is responsible for. So the whole discourse, in its argumentation and also in its language, is heavily biased towards blaming the other side for all the bad things that are happening. A kind of closed attitude is characteristic of this type of discourse; there is no willingness to concede that the other party could be right or could have the stronger argument. Therefore, under no conditions, should we give in and concede that the other party's argument may be correct or reasonable.

In the quarrel, there is no openness to defeat of this kind. In this respect, a very strong contrast exists between the quarrel and the persuasion dialogue as normative models of argumentation. We saw in our analysis of persuasion dialogue that one of its central characteristics is the necessity for each party to be open to conceding defeat by the argumentation of the other side, if that argumentation is found to be based on good evidence and is a strong and reasonable justification of the proposition advocated. In the quarrel, there is no openness to the argumentation of the other side and no willingness to admit defeat. In the quarrel, the argumentation is always focused on personally attacking the other side and defeating the other side at any cost or by any means.

In a group quarrel, it is impossible for anyone involved to be neutral. Any attempt to be neutral or to take an open stance, as in a persuasion dialogue, or to concede that the other party may have a good argument, will be interpreted as 'defeatism,' or as having, in effect, joined the enemy. This closed attitude is very distinctive of eristic dialogue, a characteristic that clearly marks it off from all the other types of dialogue we have examined above.

5. Plato on Eristic Argument

The ancient Greeks were familiar with eristic argument as a distinctive method of relating to another person in a conversational exchange. Plato points out many of the characteristics of eristic argument in various places in his writings, and contrasts eristic argumentation with what he called dialectic or dialectical argument. According to Robinson, Plato uses the term 'eristic' to mean the opposite of dialectic: 'something superficially like dialectic and yet as bad as dialectic is good, something against which the would-be dialectician must always be on guard' (1953, p. 84).

For Plato, dialectic is a conversational art that proceeds by question and answer and is directed towards the search for 'what each thing is' – its essence or essential meaning – (see the *Republic*, 533b). But dialectic requires cooperativeness and honesty on the part of the participants. In the *Meno* (75cd), we are told that dialecticians are gentle and friendly with each other, that they try to speak the truth, and that they answer questions 'by means of things of which the questioner admits a knowledge' (Robinson, 1953, p. 85). Thus the metaphor to describe dialectic is the 'road' or the 'search,' according to Robinson. These remarks suggest that Platonic dialectic is similar to an expert consultation dialogue in certain respects, and perhaps also to the inquiry. In the main, however, it seems to be most like the kind of dialogue we have defined as the critical discussion.

It is not easy to define exactly what Plato meant by 'dialectic.' Robinson adopts the hypothesis that 'dialectic' is just the word Plato uses at different stages of his thought to refer to the best method of argumentation, whereas eristic 'tends to be whatever Plato happens to think of as bad method at that moment' (p. 85). According to Robinson, Plato tends to change the meaning of 'dialectic' during different periods, and the best general account of what he means by this term is 'the ideal method, *whatever that may be*' (p. 70). Similarly, Plato's use of the abusive term 'eristic' is applied differently, at different stages of his thought. But it always means the opposite of 'dialectic,' and refers to the bad or degenerative type of dialogue that dialectic can deteriorate into, a danger to be avoided in dialectic.

Part of Plato's definition of 'eristic' involves a shift (or the possibility of one) from dialectical argument to eristic. Eristic, for Plato, is a dangerous counterpart to dialectic. The metaphor for eristic, according to Robinson, is the 'fight,' where the cooperative principles of dialectic cease to apply (p. 85). Eristic dialogue is not concerned with truth but, according to the *Euthydemus*, with a childish contentiousness that uses all kinds of clever and deceptive tricks to trap an opponent and win a victory in the discussion in an aggressive, unfriendly way.

Sometimes Plato uses the word 'antilogic' in place of 'eristic' to refer to the art of quarrelling, which suggests that, in this type of argumentation, a participant tends to take a posture of maintaining the opposite of whatever the other party is arguing (Robinson, 1953, p. 85). One aspect of dialectical argumentation that frequently worried Plato was its tendency to degenerate or shift into a disorderly and destructive antilogic that is used to attack everything at random. For example, in the *Republic* (537e–539a), Plato remarks that, when young boys get a first taste of argumentation, they use it like a kind of a game, 'like puppies to worry and tear with their argument, whoever is at hand.' This represents a worrisome kind of danger about dialectic in that it can be misused to frivolously attack people in a kind of eristic game of quarrelsome argumentation. In the *Sophist* (255), Plato defines eristic as 'skilled dispute for the sake of victory by question and answer.' We can easily understand Plato's worry about eristic dialogue if we look at the Socratic method of dialectic. Socrates uses a question-and-answer technique which often has the outcome of refuting the respondent or trapping the respondent in contradiction, and to a superficial observer, this appears quite similar to quarrelling. Robinson notes that part of Plato's antagonism towards eristic dialogue can be appreciated once we see that he needs to be vigilant about the possibility that even Socrates could be perceived as falling into this degeneration of reasoned dialogue by using a kind of quarrelsome attack on his respondent's arguments.

Both Plato and Aristotle advocate reasoned argumentation in dialogue as their primary philosophical method. However, both also worry about the possibility of the shifting of dialectic, as they call it, into eristic dialogue. They both very strongly advocate reasoned dialogue (which each calls 'dialectic') of a kind that is similar to persuasion dialogue (or perhaps a subtype of it) as a method of philosophical argumentation.[6] They are also aware of the possibilities of the negative side of dialectic, the possibility that it could deteriorate into a kind of quarrelsome or eristic dialogue which is identified with fallacies and other abuses of reasoned argumentation. It is not easy to see exactly what Plato meant by the term 'dialectical,' and there have been many attempts to interpret the meaning of this term by Plato scholars. Aristotle gives a more specific definition of 'dialectic' (as explained in chapter 1), but even here there is considerable room to question whether he sees it as a type of persuasion dialogue or some other type of dialogue that only shares some characteristics with persuasion dialogue. We return to a fuller consideration of some interesting aspects of this controversial question in chapter 9.

6. Aristotle on Contentious Argument

Especially in *On Sophistical Refutations* (171b5–172b8), Aristotle takes some systematic pains to draw a careful distinction between what he calls contentious or quarrelsome argumentation and dialectical argumentation. The defining characteristic of contentious argument, according to Aristotle, is that it uses 'merely apparent reasoning' – that is, reasoning which appears to be genuine and may even have a true conclusion (171b12). Both types of argument, according to Aristotle, use the technique of a question-and-answer exchange between two parties, but Aristotle sees dialectical argumentation as using genuine reasoning only. According to Aristotle, 'Any merely apparent reasoning on these topics is a contentious argument, and any reasoning which merely appears to accord with the subject-matter, even though it be genuine reasoning, is contentious argument' (171b17). As well, he contrasts quarrelsome argument with sophistical argument (171b32).

It is clear that Aristotle specifically recognizes one important subtype of eristic dialogue, which had also been recognized by earlier philosophers, including Plato, as a distinctive type of verbal exchange in which argumentation occurs. This can be called *sophistical dialogue*, and it consists of a kind of staged intellectual quarrel where the two parties use clever and subtle arguments not only to defeat the opponent by exhibiting a more powerful and clever argument, but also to show how clever they are to a wider audience. The best example of this is the case of the two clever Sophists who attack each other with all kinds of clever verbal tricks in Plato's dialogue *Euthydemus*.

Aristotle, following Plato, categorizes the Sophists as a professional class of debaters who use their skills of eristic dialogue to make money. By pointing out that the Sophists were engaged in eristic dialogue, Plato and Aristotle were highly successful in discrediting them down through the generations. It has been a matter of considerable controversy whether this denunciation is wholly deserved. But, since very few of the writings of the Sophists have survived, the weight of presumption has been against them. Subsequent generations have taken the term 'sophist' to mean someone who is dishonest and deceitful, who engages in clever quarrelsome arguments to take unfair advantage of a partner in conversation.

According to Aristotle, the Sophists use contentious reasoning so that their eristic arguments will appear to be dialectical and they will appear to be wise. As he puts it, 'If the semblance of victory is the motive, the argument is contentious; if the semblance of wisdom is, it is sophistical' (171b35). So contentious or quarrelsome arguments are used to achieve the semblance of victory. The goal is to appear to win by using reasoning that appears to be genuine when it is really not. Sophistry uses the same kind of eristic argumentation but the goal is slightly different. The goal is to appear to be wise.

The eristic type of dialectic in the new dialectic does not mean the same thing as what the ancients called eristic argument in the old dialectic. For both Plato and Aristotle, eristic is the opposite of dialectic. But how Plato defined 'dialectic' tended to shift over the course of his writings, and was not at any point exactly what Aristotle meant by 'dialectic,' namely, a type of argument defined as syllogistic reasoning from endoxic premises. It does not seem possible to fit these ancient categories into those of the new dialectic because, first, dialectical argument in the ancient sense does not necessarily correspond to persuasion dialogue in the new sense and, second, eristic dialogue in the new dialectic is not the polar opposite of persuasion dialogue.

However, in *On Sophistical Refutations*, Aristotle describes contentious argument as 'an unfair kind of fighting in argument' that can be used by

Sophists in a deceptive way 'to get a semblance of victory' (171b24–171b25; 171b34). Here he is giving a clear and graphic description of the main features of eristic dialogue. In linking sophistical argumentation and the committing of fallacies (sophistical refutations) to eristic argument, Aristotle is also making an extremely important statement about the analysis of fallacies that is preserved in the new dialectic. Fallacies are associated with deceptive shifts from one type of dialogue to another in the new dialectic, especially shifts to the eristic type of dialogue.

Clearly Aristotle was well aware of eristic dialogue as a method of argumentation, and he took pains to give us this rather careful and elaborate way of distinguishing between eristic and dialectical argumentation in a particular case. What is most characteristic of Aristotle's way of distinguishing between the two is his use of the notion of the semblance of genuine reasoning or good argument in his definition of eristic argumentation.

7. Modern Revival of Eristic Argument

After the Greek period, very little sustained attention was paid to the idea of eristic dialogue as a distinctive type of framework of argumentation. The whole dialectical idea of argumentation as an interpersonal sequence of reasoning exchanges between two parties was definitely not part of the mainstream of Western thinking.[7] The idea that a quarrel represents a kind of argumentation suitable for logical investigation seems to be far beyond the scope of the dominant idea in logic that argument is a kind of abstract relation on a set of premises and a conclusion, and has nothing at all to do with two parties quarrelling with each other in an eristic verbal exchange.

Recently, however, a few commentators have attempted to revive the ancient idea of eristic argument. Kotarbinski compares eristic argument to the exchange between opponents in a battle (*la lutte*), in the kind of military combat studied by war theorists like Clausewitz. According to Kotarbinski, the elements common to military combat and eristic argument (as a type of verbal exchange) include surprise, menace or threat, burden of proof, and finally, the idea that understanding the commitments of the other party is very important in this type of exchange (1963, pp. 20–1). The reasoning in both types of events is characterized by what Kotarbinski calls 'praxiology,' or the science of efficient, goal-directed practical reasoning.[8] By making this comparison, he shows an awareness that eristic argumentation is a distinctive type of verbal exchange, with many properties that are similar to the kind of antagonistic exchange that is characteristic of a military battle.

Flowers, McGuire, and Birnbaum define what they call 'adversary arguments' in terms of personal attacks, or what we call *ad hominem* arguments (1982, p. 276). They give the example of two disputants arguing about the Arab-Israeli war, and begin by asking the question, 'Who started the war?' Then each side attacks the other for causing the war. Finally, the dialogue focuses on *ad hominem* attacks where one side uses arguments that attempt to cast total blame for the event on the other side. Flowers, McGuire, and Birnbaum call this 'responsibility attribution,' which means that, if a participant performs an action that leads to some bad consequences or outcome, then it is presumed that the person was responsible for that event unless the action can be justified (p. 277). They develop a logic of personal attacks that represent certain characteristic sequences of argumentation, which they say represents the thread of argument characteristic of adversary argumentation. What they call 'adversary argument' is very similar to, or has many of the leading characteristics of, what we call eristic argumentation, and especially the quarrel (pp. 283–5).

Bronniman distinguishes several characteristics that he calls 'agonistic' elements in dialogical exchange. He characterizes these agonistic elements as violations of the Gricean maxims of politeness for dialogue.[9] Among the important agonistic elements he cites are insults, threats, especially threats to end a conversation, and apparent cooperativeness that is not genuine (pp. 88–91). Another important characteristic is a high degree of obedience to the maxim of relevance on the part of one party, but the very reverse of this on the part of the other. The kind of case Bronniman describes appears to be describable in our terms as a shift towards a quarrel from a more cooperative type of dialogue instigated by the one party to the dialogue in a unilateral way. As the one party begins to quarrel or engage in eristic dialogue, it may be difficult for the other party to resist the direction the conversation is taking. (This is a kind of gradual shift to the quarrel which we will examine in chapter 8.)

Another characteristic of the quarrel as a type of argumentation is noted by Tannen (1994). Because it is an adversarial type of dialogue, participants concentrate on looking for weaknesses in the arguments of the other side that they can attack. This naturally leads to a common tendency to distort the position of the other side in order to make it appear weaker and more susceptible to counter-arguments. According to

Tannen, participants in a quarrel are 'listening for weakness in logic to leap on, points they can distort to make the other look bad.'

Characteristic of this type of technique of arguing is the straw man argument, the type of argument that proceeds by portraying the other party's position in a way that does not represent their real commitment, but makes it look worse, and then uses this simulated, attributed position as a target for attack.[10] The technique is to take this simulated position and use it as a premise base to draw out absurd or untenable conclusions, as a source for counter-arguments to attack the other side. As noted in our analysis of persuasion dialogue, unfortunately this type of quarrelsome counter-attack is very much at odds with the goals and methods of persuasion dialogue, for persuasion dialogue depends on empathy and on representing the opponent's point of view accurately and sympathetically as a basis for one's own arguments. In this important respect, then, the quarrel and the persuasion dialogue as distinctive types of goal-directed conversational frameworks for argumentation are sharply at odds.

8. Relevance in Eristic Dialogue

It is characteristic of the quarrel that it skips around from one issue to another, thereby exhibiting a general failure of relevance of the kind associated with the other types of dialogue. In other words, the quarrel is characterized as a sequence of argumentation by its lack of connected structure. It seems to be a kind of anarchy of argument – of argument running wild. If so, what kind of profile of dialogue can be used to identify an argument in a given case as an instance of eristic dialogue? The answer is that there is really no profile of dialogue characteristically found in quarrels, except that a quarrel is typically composed of alternating *ad hominem* arguments, where each side keeps personally attacking the other side.

However, there is another way of recognizing some subtypes of eristic dialogues where a kind of deceptive pretence is involved. In this kind of case, it is clear that the *ad hominem* attacks used in the eristic argumentation are not really relevant to the issue that is supposedly being discussed, but the attacker finds some sort of adventitious and weak connection in an attempt to make a show of relevance. Thus, at least there is a kind of pretence, even if it is not very convincing, that the arguer is engaging in a non-purely quarrelsome type of dialogue, like a deliberation or a critical discussion.

A nice illustration of this kind of case is the interjection by Sheila Copps in a long debate on the Family Allowances Act (Bill C-70) in the Canadian House of Commons (see Walton, 1995, pp. 164–70). Copps interjects by attacking the prime minister on a current allegation that the government failed to inspect cans of tuna properly. She argues that this tuna fish scandal shows that the government lacks competence and concern for the people. In her argument, the scandal is used as a springboard for an *ad hominem* attack which is not really relevant to the debate on the Family Allowances Act. However, when the Speaker of the House challenges her argument for its lack of relevance, she retorts that 'a great many women who are housebound' are being attacked by 'the big tuna industry' and by government officials who 'apparently could not care less about the health of thousands of Canadian men and women.' In other words, she argues that the tuna fish issue is relevant because there is a sort of connection between the marketing of tuna fish and family allowances. Copps argues, not very convincingly, that her attack on the government over the issue of the tuna fish scandal is relevant to the discussion of the Family Allowances Act.

But is it really relevant, in the sense of its being an important or useful argument in the deliberations on this bill? Not really. Copps introduces the scandal as a way of making the opposition – in this case, the government – look bad. She is attacking their credibility. Of course, an *ad hominem* attack of this sort can be relevant in a political debate. But in this case, the failure of relevance, and the unconvincing attempt to establish it, is a good indicator of a shift to eristic dialogue.

The quarrel is characterized by its very failure of relevance, which puts it in direct contrast to the other types of dialogue in the new dialectic, each of which has a distinctive profile of kinds of moves in its sequence of argumentation that is the test for dialectical relevance of arguments used in that type of dialogue. The quarrel skips around from one issue to another in an apparently unconnected pattern of argumentation. And, typically, the quarrel is an irrelevant intrusion in the argumentation sequence of another type of dialogue. However, as noted in case 7.2, if the quarrel has a positive characteristic as a type of orderly dialogue, it is the repeated pattern of *ad hominem* attacks.

9. Subtypes of Eristic Dialogue

Another characteristic of eristic dialogue is that argumentation in a quarrel frequently involves duplicity or pretence. A participant in a

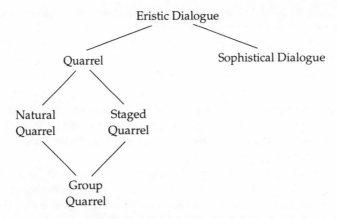

Figure 7.1 Subtypes of Eristic Dialogue

quarrel often tries to take the high ground by implying or stating that the other party is quarrelling while he himself is engaging in a cool-headed and rational critical discussion. The implication is that the speaker himself is being very reasonable and logical and the other party is being emotional, irrational, and quarrelsome. This move itself represents a kind of quarrelling technique of argumentation because it is a way of blaming the other party for some culpable behaviour, for violating the rules of the critical discussion by continually quarrelling and committing logical fallacies. But, in a quarrel, this tactic can be a kind of pretence or deception that is used to make false allegations in an attempt to make the other party look bad. This characteristic is not essential to eristic dialogue as a type of conversation exchange (see Walton, 1992c, p. 136). But it is a common occurrence in quarrelling, and it is often a good indicator that a quarrel is taking place, or at least that one party in the dialogue is shifting towards a quarrel or adopting a quarrelsome attitude.

Frequently, both parties in a quarrel will use this tactic of argumentation: 'Each party exhibits a righteous indignation that the other party is being so unreasonable, so selfish, so emotional, when her own arguments are so eminently rational and logical' (Walton, *Emotion*, 1992c, p. 136). Thus, Aristotle was right to focus on the appearance of good reasoning as a key characteristic of contentious argumentation, even though the kind of duplicity cited here is probably not exactly what he had in mind.

In the new dialectic, several subtypes of eristic dialogue can be classified, as in Figure 7.1.

The basic, as well as the most familiar and simple, type of quarrel is the natural quarrel, which arises spontaneously from the need to bring hidden feelings to the surface. This type of eristic dialogue tends to burst on the scene suddenly, and is a surprise to both the participants in the dialogue. In contrast, the staged quarrel (illustrated by case 7.1) is a calculated tactic by one side and generally a surprise for the other side. The group quarrel may be partly staged or natural. But it is not an explicitly calculated type of argumentation for all parties in a dialogue, and the participants in the group may not even really be aware, or want to admit, that they are quarrelling.

The sophistical type of eristic dialogue is a calculated tactic used to impress onlookers with how clever an arguer can be in disputation, and it is also designed to show up the opponent as a less clever and able reasoner. The idea is to discredit the credibility of the opponent by making him appear inept or unskilled in rational argumentation.

10. Identifying Characteristics of Eristic Dialogue

To sum up: there are five identifying characteristics to help identify and classify cases of eristic dialogue, even though relevance is a problem to identify. First, an indicative characteristic of the quarrel involves a truculent, personal attack, with one side trying to blame the other for some culpable behaviour which allegedly occurred in the past and which led to bad consequences. This characteristic involves the repeated, sudden, or irrelevant use of *ad hominem* arguments. Second, eristic dialogue generally is characterized by the kind of closed attitude that refuses to admit defeat and seeks victory at all costs. Third, eristic dialogue uses the straw man tactic of unfairly attempting to make the position of the other side look bad. Fourth, it is further characterized by a high degree of irrelevance that skips around randomly from topic to topic in an apparently disorganized sequence of argumentation. However, quarrels are not completely chaotic or disorganized sequences of argumentation in dialogue. The participants do take turns, and the responses of one to the arguments of the other are connected over short sequences, even if occasionally they tend to skip widely from one topic to another. Fifth, some subtypes of the quarrel exhibit a kind of duplicity or deception which is associated with a dialectical shift or a pretence of not quarrelling.

The organized group quarrel can be a highly ritualized type of argumentation that exhibits a degree of organization. Each side develops a rigidly fixed position which the adherents learn to copy, both in particular arguments and style of presentation, and each side develops routine patterns of using stereotyped arguments to accuse the other side of wrongdoing. In a routine and stereotyped way, the other side is portrayed as a group that can never be trusted, and that is always using deceptive tricks to take unfair advantage of its opponents. Thus the arguments of the other side are always portrayed to be lies or propaganda that are used to deceive opponents. The imputation is that the other side is always engaged in eristic dialogue; it can never be presumed that the group is engaged in a persuasion dialogue based on Gricean maxims of sinceriety and politeness. This is a way of sealing off the group, of ensuring that the group does not take the arguments of the other side seriously, for fear that group integrity and loyalty might be damaged by any openness to arguments from the other side.

Plato's approach of defining eristic as the opposite of dialectic may have something to be said for it. Many of these identifying characteristics of eristic dialogue stand in contrast in the new dialectic to properties of the other five types of dialogue (and especially persuasion dialogue). For example, whereas an important characteristic of persuasion dialogue is its openness to opposed argumentation, eristic dialogue is characterized by a closed attitude that refuses to admit defeat. While the other types of dialogue require relevance of argumentation in order to be successful, eristic dialogue is characterized by a general failure of relevance as it skips around from one issue to another. In keeping with its negative (contrastive) characteristics, eristic dialogue also is primarily of negative import in logic. As an argument deteriorates from some other type of dialogue exchange into a quarrel, the argument becomes problematic and a focus of interest for logical evaluation.

Thus, eristic dialogue does have a characteristic structure, which is useful to know about when studying fallacies, as well as other faults and failures of argumentation that can be used to get the best of an opponent in verbal exchanges of reasoning. Contrary to conventional wisdom and initial appearances, then, the quarrel is worth studying as a normative structure of dialogue that can give us insight into the evaluation of argumentation as correct or incorrect in a particular case. Although there is truth in saying that the quarrel is no friend of logic, nevertheless, in studying fallacies it is often very valuable to understand how a fallacy is based on a dialectical shift from a quarrel to another type of dialogue during the sequence of argumentation. And it is exactly this kind of shift, as we will see, that characterizes the committing of fallacies.

8

Dialectical Shifts

The importance of the shifts from one type of dialogue to another during the course of an argument exchange has been examined in a number of cases thus far. In some cases, a discourse is mixed, in the sense that the sequence of argumentation in the text of discourse contains elements of two or more types of dialogue. But, in other cases, the argument exhibits a distinct shift, in the sense that one type of dialogue ceases and another type of dialogue begins.

1. Types of Shifts[1]

During the course of a conversation between two or more parties there can be a change in the context of argumentation, or a dialectical shift, from one type of dialogue to another, even if there has been no explicit announcement of the closing or beginning of a dialogue. Empirical studies by Gumperz show, for example, that students knew from a change of 'register' when a conversation shifted from an academic discussion to personal chat. What made the shift detectable was a change of pace and attitude in the speech exchanges.

Here is another example of a dialectical shift: a union-management negotiation group finishes its bargaining session and adjourns to the bar where members of the group start arguing about which soccer team is the best that year. All the same participants take part in both sessions, but the context of the argument changes, as well as the topic. One dialogue is a negotiation, and the second is a kind of persuasion dialogue about which soccer team arguably has the best prospects.

In this case, the first dialogue is properly closed off, presumably by the chairperson or mediator in charge of the meeting. Then there is a clear break, and even a change of venue, that marks the transition to the opening of the second dialogue. In some cases, the transition is not so clearly marked. The one dialogue can be 'sandwiched in' between the prior and subsequent parts of an enveloping sequence of dialogue of another type. Practical reasons sometimes cause an interruption, but then the dialogue quickly shifts back to the original type.

Another example from an everyday conversation shows how common dialectical shifts are. In the following case, there is a sudden dialectical shift from a critical discussion to a kind of information-seeking, action-directed dialogue.

Case 8.1 The Bicycle Path Case
While Karen and Doug cycle down the bicycle path, they are deep in conversation. As they cycle along, they discuss the pros and cons of living in a house versus living in a condominium. Doug says, 'Sometimes the walls in those condominiums are pretty thin, and you can hear the neighbours.' Karen replies, 'Yes, but with a condominium it is easier to travel. You don't have to worry about cutting the grass or having the walk shovelled while you are away.' Doug agrees, 'Yes, that can be expensive.' Just then they come to a junction in the road and pass a sign that gives the directions to the next villages. Karen immediately says, 'I think if we turn to the right, the path goes to Nordwijk. Do you want to go to Nordwijk?'

Karen's last speech introduces a quick shift in the conversation, necessitated by their practical need to pay attention to directions. After they return to the junction and start along the path to Nordwijk, the critical discussion of house versus condominium resumes. But with Karen's last comment comes a shift from the critical discussion to another type of dialogue that is concerned with a practical decision.

In our previous cases of argumentation, many examples of dialectical shifts have been cited (see, especially, chapter 5). One is the use of the technique of provocation in the interview, where there is a shift from information-seeking dialogue to persuasion dialogue. Another is the argument on the income tax question, represented in the profile of dialogue in Figure 5.1. Another is the shift from information-seeking dialogue to a peirastic type of dialogue that, in the new dialectic, is analysed as a type of persuasion dialogue. In this kind of argument, peirastic and exetastic arguments are used to probe, test, or critically examine an expert opinion in an advice consultation dialogue.

As well as the shift from one type of dialogue to another – external shifts – as illustrated by the cases cited above, there is another type of dialectical shift called the internal shift which is a shift within the same type of dialogue. Among the various types of internal shifts classified in Walton and Krabbe (1995, p. 108), one type is especially worth remarking upon here. A shift of issue occurs in a dialogue when an argument, or move in the dialogue, changes the original issue of the dialogue. It is this kind of shift that is frequently involved in failures of dialectical relevance in argumentation. In other cases, fallacies and other problems of dialectical irrelevance can be associated with external dialectical shifts. Not all dialectical shifts are associated with fallacies of relevance. In some cases, like the ones cited above, there can be a dialectical shift but the relevance of the argument is preserved.

2. Licit and Illicit Shifts

In the bicycle path case, the shift from the critical discussion to the action-directed dialogue is very rapid. Here the shift is a dialectically legitimate (licit) one, because there is the recognition of an immediate practical need to talk about directions. Once this question is settled, the conversation shifts back to the critical discussion. Even though there is no formal closing of the first dialogue, there is a good reason to close it, and since it can be resumed with no real loss, there is nothing illegitimate or suspicious about the shift.

In the bicycle path case, the argumentation in the deliberation dialogue, on whether to go to Nordwijk and so forth, is not relevant to the argumentation in the persuasion dialogue on the issue of condominiums versus houses. In contrast, in the cement case in chapter 4, the argumentation on foundation depths, after the shift is highly relevant to the argumentation taking place in the negotiation dialogue before the shift.

These cases bring out the important principle that dialectical relevance in argumentation sometimes transfers over shifts, and sometimes does not. This principle is very significant, because it shows that relevance is not always internal to one context of dialogue only. Sometimes arguments in one context of dialogue can be relevant to arguments in another context of dialogue. This transfer of dialectical relevance takes place where there has been a dialectical shift.

But why does the argumentation continue to be relevant after the shift in the one case but not in the other? In the cement case, the one dialogue is functionally joined to the other; that is, the second dialogue contributes to an improvement in the quality of dialogue in the first. By contrast, the shift in the bicycle path case is an interruption; the two dialogues are not functionally connected – one is simply a temporary break in the other.

Some dialectical shifts are definite and sharp, where there is a *déplacement* of the one type of dialogue by the other. In other cases, there is a gradual shifting or *glissement* from the one type of dialogue to the other. In some cases, the two types of dialogue overlap, and we have a mixed dialogue. A mixed dialogue can enhance the quality of the original dialogue because the second dialogue is functionally related to the argumentation in the first dialogue. An example is an appeal to expert opinion during the course of a critical discussion. A panel is having a discussion on whether to build a new nuclear reactor, for instance, and experts are consulted on the issue of safety. Here an intelligent solicitation and use of the expert opinions can greatly improve the quality of the critical discussion.

Some dialectical shifts, however, are illicit, and these illicit shifts are often associated with informal fallacies. Jacobs and Jackson studied several transcripts of dialogue recorded during divorce-mediation custody disputes, and found that gradually the dialogue moved away from the issue of custody towards 'petty squabbling' (1992, pp. 163–9). The dialogue appeared at such sequences to become 'chaotic,' and 'any relevance of what is said to the purpose of arriving at a custody arrangement that is in the best interest of the child seems purely coincidental.' The dialogue degenerated into *tu quoque ad hominem* exchanges, which Jacobs and Jackson characterize as 'censure, blame,' and 'shift' of 'moral responsibility.' Instead of ignoring these character attacks, the two parties could not resist continuing to reply in kind. This is a gradual illicit shift to the quarrel, because the *ad hominem* attacks are not really relevant to the central purpose of the initial dialogue.

To judge whether a shift is licit or illicit in a particular case of argumentation, we first have to pin down the original context of dialogue. Then we have to identify the new context, and decide whether the shift is licit or illicit by looking backwards and judging by the goals and standards of the original context. Is the new dialogue supporting those old goals, or at least allowing forward movement on their fulfillment, or is it blocking them? Was the shift agreed to by the original speech partners, or was the shift unilateral, or even forced by one party?

Shifts from negotiation dialogue to critical discussion are common in divorce dispute mediation, and mediators often try to encourage this kind of shift, because it can be a positive direction that fosters constructive agreement. For example, a divorcing couple's arguments about child custody can be very positive if the dialogue shifts to a critical discussion on how well each party is equipped to look after the child. If both parties are working, who is free to look after the child? Who is best at providing a structured life for the child? Who has shown the most interest and support in looking after and spending time with the child in the past? A good deal of research on this type of shift in divorce mediation cases has been done by Jacobs and Jackson.

This type of case can be compared to the cement case in chapter 7, which Fisher and Ury classify as a case of principled negotiation (1991). Instead of trying to 'score points' in hard-nosed bargaining, after the shift the participants pose questions that can be answered more objectively by looking at evidence. By engaging in a critical discussion, they come around to a more dispassionate, less personal type of exchange, one that is not so close to quarrelling. In this type of case, the quarrel is always lurking under the surface of the discussion, and it is all too easy for the dialogue to degenerate into a sequence of 'counter-blaming' and personal attack.

Shifts that go from another type of dialogue to a quarrel are always dangerous and often illicit. This type of shift is closely associated with the *argumentum ad hominem*. For example, the negotiation between the union and management of Eastern Airlines during the strike in 1989 shifted gradually from a negotiation dialogue to a quarrelling type of dialogue. The unions turned Frank Lorenzo, the chief executive officer of Eastern, into a symbol of greed and ruthlessness after he tried to cut costs by cutting back on wages. The union adopted the tactic of making Lorenzo the issue of the dispute by portraying him as a 'brutal, unscrupulous autocrat.' This approach was enthusiastically adopted by the employees of Eastern who booed and shouted, 'There's the slimeball!' when shown a picture of Lorenzo. According to a report in *Newsweek*, Lorenzo was not the bad person portrayed in these attacks.[2] But as this *ad hominem* attack escalated, the workers became 'obsessed' with it, and the 'fight became so personal that any possibility for compromise was lost,' according to *Newsweek*. In this case, the gradual shift to the quarrel, forced into place by one side, eventually destroyed the possibilities for constructive negotiation in time to address the problem. The outcome was a prolonged deadlock, and the company went into bankruptcy.

3. Licit Shifts to and from Expert Consultation Dialogue

It needs to be emphasized that not all dialectical shifts are the illicit kind that has a negative impact on the quality of argumentation in a discussion. For example, during the course of a critical discussion, we may need to collect more information, and so we shift temporarily to an information-seeking type of dialogue to improve the quality of the discussion. In other instances, it may be useful to shift to an expert consultation type of dialogue to enhance the quality of the original critical discussion.

Case 8.2
You and I are having a critical discussion about whether a program of voluntary euthanasia would be a good policy. Using argumentation from consequences, you argue that such a policy would lead to all kinds of abuses, that all kinds of people would be killed against their wishes, for financial or political reasons. To counter this, I argue that a policy of voluntary euthanasia exists in the Netherlands. In an additional argument, I state that this policy is working fairly well, and does not exhibit the kinds of abuses cited. At this point, there is a disagreement between us on exactly what is happening in the Netherlands. If the dispute begins to turn on this point, it may be an obstacle to the resolution of the critical discussion, if we do not have enough information to throw light on the question of whether the euthanasia policy in the Netherlands is working very well or not. To help with this obstruction to the dialogue and to make the critical discussion better informed, it would be useful to bring into the dialogue information on how the Dutch medical system is coping with euthanasia, such as reports written by experts who have some direct knowledge of this situation. In the critical discussion, we could use this information, and also subject it to questioning and evaluation, during the subsequent course of the critical discussion.

How this incorporation of the one dialogue into the other should be carried out, to be fair to both sides in the critical discussion, is a moot point. But, in principle, it should be possible for such a shift to take place as an interval in the critical discussion, during which there is a temporary change-over to an information-seeking type of dialogue. Van Eemeren and Grootendorst implicitly recognize the value of this kind of shift when they recommend the use of an 'intersubjective testing procedure'

(ITP) in critical discussion – a procedure by which language users agree at the opening stages of a discussion how they will determine whether a proposition ought to be accepted or not during the course of that discussion. They recommend that such a testing procedure might consist of 'consulting oral or written sources (encyclopedias, dictionaries and other works of reference) or it might include the joint conduct of observations or experiments' (1984, p. 167). Van Eemeren and Grootendorst recommend that the shift to such a procedure should have certain requirements, including the consent of the participants in the original critical discussion on which sources of information are acceptable and how these sources are to be evaluated. In some cases, both parties might agree to accept what the source says, at least tentatively, as a basis of presumption for continuing a dialogue. In other cases, parties might accept such source-based information but subject it to questioning.

In other kinds of cases, one participant in the critical discussion might bring in his own source of expert opinion, who might disagree with another source of expert opinion brought in by the other side. Even when the expert opinions contradict each other, bringing in expert advice might enhance the quality of the original critical discussion.

In other kinds of cases, such as those studied in chapter 5, there is a shift from an expert consultation dialogue to a dialectical interlude, where the respondent engages the expert in a kind of persuasion dialogue that critically examines the reasons behind the expert's opinion. This dialectical shift from expert consultation dialogue to persuasion dialogue was evaluated in chapter 5 as being not only licit, but highly constructive in enhancing the value of the expert consultation as a source of good argument and advice for the user. The judgment of the new dialectical theory is that this type of shift in a sequence of argumentation preserves relevance, because the persuasion dialogue is useful in fitting in with the goals and profile of the advice consultation dialogue.

How can two dialogues be functionally joined in this manner, so that the argumentation in one actually contributes to the argumentation in the other? The formal structure that models such a joining of two dialogues has been called an 'embedding' (Walton and Krabbe, 1995, pp. 163–6). An example of an embedding involves a 'tightening up' from a permissive persuasion dialogue to a rigorous persuasion dialogue; the two sides of the dialogue enter a phase where they become more 'hard-nosed' and legalistic by defining their terms more carefully and insisting on clarification of tight standards of reasoning. But the same formal structure of an embedding underlies other kinds of dialectical shifts, like those from an information-seeking dialogue to a persuasion dialogue, or vice versa.

4. Illicit Shifts and Fallacious Arguments

Dialectical shifts tend to become a problem, from a point of view of the critical analysis of argumentation, when there is an illicit shift, especially one that involves a deception or misunderstanding, during an argument that goes from one type of dialogue to another. This type of problem tends to occur in the kind of case where one party is unaware of the shift, or is trying to deceive the other party by concealing the shift, or in some cases, where both parties are unaware of the shift. It is in these kinds of cases that failures of dialectical relevance are associated with fallacies.

Irrelevant arguments based on illicit and deceptive dialectical shifts are a severe and fundamental problem in argumentation in all the types of dialogue we have studied, for it is a basic assumption of a dialogue that a respondent understands the previous move of the other party and interprets it correctly. Otherwise, the chain of relevant argumentation in a dialogue sequence is broken. A response that would be relevant in one type of dialogue can be disruptive and problematic in another, even if the argument used is essentially the same.

But where an arguer exploits such a shift to try to deceive the other party, how do we find the evidence to evaluate the argument and find the fallacy? What kind of evidence should we look for? The key factor in making normative judgments about argumentation in such a case is the need to look backwards and to determine, on the basis of the textual and contextual evidence, what type of dialogue the arguers were supposed to have been engaged in at the outset of their verbal exchange. Let us call this type of backwards-looking judgment the retrospective evaluation of an argument.

Some cases of retrospective evaluation are based on an explicit agreement by the two parties to take part in a certain type of dialogue. In other cases, conventions and institutions enable us to clearly make this determination. But in many cases of argumentation in everyday conversation, such agreements are implicit and can be determined only by making a contextual judgment of the expectations of the participants, by looking at the evidence given through their verbal exchanges, as the sequence of arguments proceed.

In some cases, it is not clear to the participants themselves, or to anyone else, exactly what type of dialogue they were supposed to be engaging in when they had an argumentative exchange, and it is precisely this indeterminacy that is often exploited by deceitful and fallacious arguments. In evaluating such arguments, the best we can do is make a conditional judgment that such and such an argument would be fallacious if evaluated from the point of view and standards of argumentation appropriate for a particular type of dialogue.

For example, consider case 7.2. In the midst of a lengthy debate on the Northumberland Strait Crossing Act, a participant launches into an *ad hominem* attack on Conservative leader Kim Campbell, who had admitted to smoking marijuana. This sudden interjection in the debate can be viewed, according to the new dialectical theory, as a shift from the debate – supposedly containing a deliberation on whether to vote for a particular bill – to an eristic type of dialogue. The use of the *ad hominem* argument in this case is a good indicator of a shift to the quarrel. The tuna scandal case (chapter 7, section 8) also can be said to contain a shift to the quarrel, as the argument moves from a debate on the Family Allowances Act to an attack on the government, which was accused of wrongdoing in the tuna fish scandal.

But in these cases, can we rightly judge, according to the standards of the new dialectical theory, that the *ad hominem* argument was dialectically irrelevant to the debate? Both cases are complicated by the fact that political debate is a mixed type of dialogue that may contain legitimate elements of eristic dialogue (the 'bear pit' aspect of partisan politics in a democratic system), as well as elements of deliberation and persuasion dialogue. Political debate is very much a type of mixed discourse, and so it is problematic to declare that the *ad hominem* arguments used in these two cases of parliamentary debate are fallacious on the grounds that the shift to the quarrel is a basis for evaluating the *ad hominem* argument as irrelevant.

There is another important factor to be considered in both cases: the internal dialectical shift to a different topic. In the midst of a lengthy debate on a specific bill, in both cases there is a sudden shift to an entirely different topic – in the one case, it is the smoking of marijuana by Kim Campbell, and in the other case, it is the topic of tuna fish. Such a radical internal shift is also evidence of dialectical irrelevance.

5. The Infomercial

A particularly interesting type of case where argumentation of a questionable sort is based on exploiting a dialectical shift is the 'infomercial.'

Initially, an infomercial has the format and appearance of a news report, supposedly a type of information-seeking dialogue, or of an informed talk show, which appears to have the framework of a critical discussion. But as the argumentation proceeds, the infomercial gradually turns into a sequence of commercial advertising to promote a particular product. By the end of the infomercial, the host is frankly plugging a particular product. Usually a toll-free number appears on the screen so that viewers can phone in and buy the product immediately. The argumentation in this type of program exploits *glissement*; there is a gradual dialectical shift from a kind of dialogue that purports to be presenting information to a commercial sales pitch.

Before 1984, the U.S. government set time limits on commercials, and banned commercial messages that ran longer than a few minutes on television. When these limits were removed, it became profitable to fill late-night slots with lengthy commercials. However, since no one – even a late-night viewer – was likely to sit and watch a half-hour commercial, the infomercial format was invented.

The technique behind an infomercial is to gradually lull the viewer into watching the commercial sales pitch by exploiting an initial expectation that he is watching a news or talk show. This initial expectation is built up by the format of the infomercial. For example, the presenter usually looks like a typical news anchor who is sitting at a desk and reporting ostensibly factual events, something that appears to be a news story. So the whole format, with its gradual shift to a different type of dialogue, is based on a kind of deception that appeals to expectations viewers have from watching news programs and talk shows.

A '20/20' news report described a number of these infomercials.[3] According to this report, they have all the trappings of a talk show or news program, such as expert panellists, breaks for commercials, and closing credits. But beneath these appearances, they can more accurately be described as 'half-hour commercials.'

One infomercial, which has grossed $150 million, tells viewers how to get rich by dealing in real estate. Another one is a self-improvement tape, telling viewers how they can 'condition [their] mind and emotions.' This tape grossed so much money – $40 million – that the producer called it his 'Batman.' Other successful infomercials described in the '20/20' report include a cooking stone that supposedly seals in juices; a 'miracle protector' car wax that protects the paint on a car even when hamburgers are fried on it; and a Magic Wand hand mixer. Another infomercial, introduced by a man who announced that he was 'your inside information investigator,' claimed to have rediscovered 'nature's formula for youth,' which turned out to be bee pollen. This infomercial sold $3.5 million worth of bee pollen before the Federal Trade Commission put a stop to it.

Infomercials are probably relatively harmless because viewers are tuning in to what is going on. As the institution of the infomercial itself becomes more highly publicized, fewer viewers will really be deceived into thinking that what they are seeing is a genuine news report. Even so, the mixing of the two formats is inherently deceptive, because it confers an aura of legitimacy on sales argumentation that might not be nearly so plausible without the trappings of the infomercial.

The infomercial is of special interest from the point of view of the new dialectic because it illustrates the normative aspect of evaluating argumentation in relation to a context of dialogue which raises conventional expectations that the dialogue is supposed to be of a particular type. If an argument is supposed to be part of a news report – a species of information-seeking dialogue – then it should be judged by the standards of argument appropriate for that type of dialogue. If there is an illicit or concealed dialectical shift, and the argumentation launches into a sales pitch, then that argumentation should be judged by the original standards and issues that the dialogue was supposed to be about. Viewers may not be aware of the transition from this original format of dialogue to the sales pitch, and they may not even remember what the dialogue was supposed to be about in the first place. But from a normative point of view of the new dialectic, the argumentation in the later sales pitch segment of the infomercial should be judged by the standards of the initial format. The sales pitch should be evaluated as dialectically irrelevant.

6. Deceptive Format

The correspondent in the '20/20' program, John Stossel, cited two forms of deceit involved in infomercials. First, 'Some infomercials push products that don't do what they say they'll do.' And, second, 'The format itself can be deceptive.' This deceptiveness of format can be explained as follows. What is really a commercial is made to look like a talk show, and the presentation is designed to make it appear that the endorsements given by the speakers are spontaneous. For example, Stossel cites the case of the hand-mixer infomercial, where the man who presents the material appears to be a talk show host, but is actually the president of the company that manufactures the product.

There is a dialectical shift involved in this deceptive format. The info-mercial is really a form of commercial argumentation designed to sell a specific product, but it appears in the guise of an information-presenting type of dialogue, presumably based on the kind of investigation and balanced reporting appropriate for a news format. In other cases, the infomercial purports to be the kind of critical discussion or debate that is characteristic of a talk show discussion of a controversial topic. The problem is that both these types of dialogue, which appear to be pre-sented by the infomercial, require a balanced presentation and an exam-ination of viewpoints on both sides, neither of which is a characteristic requirement in the presentation of commercial advertising. Hence, this deceptiveness of format cited by Stossel is based on a dialectical shift in the argumentation presented in the infomercial.

Although the Federal Communication Commission rules in the U.S. require that infomercials be identified as such at either the beginning or the end of the presentation, it is questionable whether this is sufficient to make many viewers remember that the presentation is an advertise-ment, and not a presentation of information.

The following case is based on a report published in *Broadcasting* (16 April 1990).

Case 8.3
One infomercial for sunglasses monitored by the Federal Trade Com-mission 'falsely claimed that a 30-minute ad called *Consumer Challenge* was an independent consumer program such as *60 Minutes* or *20/20.*' Moreover, according to a FTC report, the ad falsely claimed that the infomercial producers had conducted an independent and objective investigation of the sunglasses. The FTC brought charges against the producers, and the case was eventually settled 'without any admis-sion of liability by the respondents.'

The FTC is involved in ongoing litigation against other producers whose infomercials allegedly made false and deceptive claims.

The argumentation in these infomercials should be evaluated by embedding the sales arguments into the longer sequence of argumenta-tion that began with a news format. The news-presentation format requires the reporting of unbiased factual information and a balanced presentation of relevant arguments on both sides of an issue where per-suasion arguments are being considered. But then what happens when a sales pitch – a one-sided advocacy argument whose purpose is to convince viewers to buy the product by presenting overwhelming arguments – is embedded in the information-seeking format? The sales pitch ends up not only being an extremely poor and inefficient way of fulfilling the goals of the information dialogue, but also interferring with the goals of the prior type of dialogue, or even preventing them from being realized. On this basis, the argumentation in an infomercial should be evaluated as disruptive and negative from the normative standpoint of the new dialectic.

An FTC action against a major producer of infomercials charged that three infomercials misrepresented the effectiveness of a weight-loss device, a baldness cure, and a remedy for impotence (Lambert, 1990). These infomercials allegedly defrauded consumers. The FTC action also claimed that the infomercials presented misleading formats by masquerading as talk shows or investigative news reports, and that more disclosures should be required so viewers know that what they are watching is a paid advertisement.

7. Success and Evolution of Infomercials

Despite lawsuits and criticisms that they are misleading, infomercials have turned out to be financially successful. According to Grover, in 1989 infomercials sold about $450 million worth of goods. The FTC has forced some infomercials off the air and required them to refund money, as well as making others insert disclaimers, but the leading infomercials are financially successful enough to absorb these losses and carry on. So profitable has this business been that larger companies are now turning to infomercials.

According to a report by Colford, Bell Atlantic is testing out a situation comedy called 'The Ringers' in which the plot line incorporates different uses of the telephone (1992, p. 8). This thirty-minute commercial, complete with laugh track, has a format that combines a situation comedy with the presentation of information on phone services, and moves towards a commercial presentation which advertises services provided by Bell Atlantic. According to Garfield, the program does have a 'paid advertising message' disclaimer which flashes at least three times during the program (1992, p. 52). Even so, it is likely that unsuspecting viewers will think that they are looking at a real situation comedy. Garfield describes 'The Ringers' as 'advertising camouflaged as programming,' and calls it a kind of deception because viewers are gradually lured into the commercial message under false pretenses.

The increasing respectability of infomercials is indicated by a report in *Automotive News* (1993, p. 26), which shows that this form of advertising has gained acceptance among leading auto-makers. In September 1991, Volvo produced a thirty-minute infomercial on car safety which included statistics about accidents and footage showing the crash testing of Volvo automobiles. The infomercial also included footage of owners giving testimonials about accident survival. According to a report by Levine in *Forbes*, infomercials are evolving from an older type that was less sophisticated to a newer type that tries to avoid outright deception by walking a finer line 'between entertainment and deception' (1993, p. 102).

The example of the older type of infomercial cited by Levine is the case of the hand-held mixer advertisement, a kind of infomercial that frankly 'masquerades as non-commercial programming such as an objective news report.' This infomercial demonstrates the mixer crushing a pineapple into pulp, but in subsequent tests it didn't work, and the Federal Trade Commission extracted a $550,000 settlement from the producers of the program. The newer infomercials are distinguished both by the absence of a hard sell and by a linking of direct selling with retail distribution. The goal of the newer type of infomercial is only to get the viewer into a store. Thus, the new breed of infomercial is more subtle and indirect in its presentation of the sales pitch.

The growing appeal of the infomercial has infiltrated the travel industry, which sees these presentations as a way of targeting specific groups with particular types of vacation possibilities (Cooper, 1993, p. 69). Advocating the new respectability of the infomercial, the National Infomercial Marketing Association (NIMA) claims that it is working hard to 'raise the level of integrity in the industry' and to 'make sure the customer is not deceived' (Richmond, 1993, p. A7). As an indication of its new status and respectability, infomercials now commonly use celebrities, like Cher and Dionne Warwick, and have high production values – up to $500,000 (Richmond, 1993, p. A7). To guard against the bad publicity and lawsuits that have plagued infomercials, the industry has formed a marketing body to promote its growing respectability.

According to the publisher of the *Infomercial Marketing Report*, 'Infomercials guard against mislabeling now by identifying the fact that they are a product pitch three times each half hour – at the beginning, middle and end' (Richmond, 1993, p. A7). This indicates that the infomercial has now become a more sophisticated kind of presentation that uses state-of-the-art advertising techniques. Although the goal of the new infomercials is still basically to sell a product, they now attempt to do this in a less obviously deceptive way that avoids patently false claims and adheres to quality control rules.

8. Educational and Print Formats

In the infomercial, there is a shift from a news program or talk show format to advertising for a specific product. Another comparable type of shift can be seen in the kind of case in which videotapes are brought into the school system, supposedly for educational purposes, and that turn out to be commercial messages produced and paid for by companies who are advertising a specific product. This type of argumentation is based on a dialectical shift from what is supposedly a kind of pedagogical dialogue, which presents information or educational material to students, but exploits a gradual shift (or *glissement*) to advertising a product. An example of this format was presented in a '60 Minutes' report on 10 October 1993.

Case 8.4
A so-called learning aid, called 'Gushers, Wonders of the World,' is a videotape that is supposed to teach children about geothermic phenomena. Samples of a sugary fruit snack called 'Gushers' were supplied to schools along with the videotape, with the suggestion that they be distributed to students during the program. The program bridged the gap between its geothermic content and its product by recommending that the teacher discuss how these fruit snacks gush when a student bites into them, and then compare this effect to the gushing of geothermic phenomena, like volcanic eruptions. After parents discovered that these candy products were being promoted and distributed to their children in the schools, they were understandably upset.

Another comparable example cited by '60 Minutes' concerns a sex education videotape seen in 3,000 schools in 1992. Called 'Considering Condoms,' it turned out to be a promotion for a particular brand of contraceptives. Following are other examples covered in the '60 Minutes' report.

Case 8.5
Another case involves a 'lifetime learning kit' which was distributed

to students and that turned out to promote telephone credit cards to teenagers. In another case, a video called 'Scientists and the Alaska Oil Spill: The Wildlife, the Clean-up, the Outlook,' produced by the public relations department of Exxon, claimed Exxon had successfully cleaned up the environmental mess from the oil spill. It was offered free to more than 10,000 science teachers around the U.S. When it was shown to one seventh grade science class, a twelve-year-old student commented to her teacher, 'We've just seen a commercial.' Even though the teacher suggested that scientists should be trusted because they are working for humanity, the students still 'wouldn't buy into it.'

It appears that even elementary school students have a well-developed ability to recognize this type of dialectical shift and to see that it is deceptive. Clearly they see that the argumentation is not what it appears to be and that, despite the allegedly information-presenting or educational type of format, the argumentation is really designed to be a commercial to promote or sell a particular product. We might tend to use the terms 'bias' or 'propaganda' in describing this particular kind of case. Such terms would be appropriate since they imply that there is an underlying dialectical shift in the argumentation that is inherently deceptive, in the sense that the dialogue is ostensibly of one particular type at the outset but subtly shifts towards quite a different type of dialogue during the sequence of argumentation.

In print formats, we also see a similar kind of dialectical shift of presentation of argumentation. Lee gives as an example the so-called magalogue, a catalogue advertising products that has a magazine-like layout (1993, p. 69). Characteristics that give the format the appearance of a magazine are flashy layouts, high-gloss paper, slick writing and trendy stories, as well as four-colour advertising. This type of publication is really a kind of hybrid that is designed to promote or sell a specific product. One case given by Lee is a biannual publication of the Sony Corporation called *Sony Style*, which costs $4.95 an issue and features articles on topics like 'freedom of speech' and 'information overload.' These articles, however, turn out to be advertisements that urge readers to buy specific products, like a cordless telephone or a new floppy disk. Implicit in this kind of argumentation is a dialectical shift, because the appearance of the publication leads readers to expect what they are familiar with in the format of a magazine. The articles in a magazine have various functions: to present information, to tell an interesting

story, or to discuss some controversial topic. But in the case of the magalogue, the magazine format is used as part of a deceptive tactic to mask
a sales pitch for a specific product. In this kind of case, the dialectical
shift exploits the reader's expectations that a certain type of publication
will have certain types of goals, and it is only as the buyer reads an article that there is a gradual shift towards a different type of dialogue during the sequence of argumentation.

9. Contextual Evidence for Retrospective Evaluation

The basic principle in evaluating argumentation as reasoning used for a
communicative purpose is to look backwards, where a dialectical shift
has occurred, in order to judge the argumentation by the standards
appropriate for the type of dialogue that the participants were supposed
to be engaging in at the outset. But this raises a practical question. How
do we know in a given case what type of dialogue the participants were
supposed to be engaged in at the outset? In the case of infomercials, the
evidence is to be found in indications of the format of the presentation,
typically found at the beginning phases of the sequence of the argumentation stage. For example, if the presenter of the argument is dressed in a
certain way and talks in a certain way, consistent with the appearance of
an anchor on a news format – if he or she is sitting at a desk and all the
other familiar aspects of a news broadcast are present – then the
viewer's expectation is that this is an information-presenting dialogue
of some sort. This type of format triggers the customary expectation that
the program is the familiar kind of news broadcast that all of us have
been watching for years, that it is a distinctive and well-defined type of
program.

In other cases, the initial format suggests the venue of a talk show.
Several participants are introduced, a topic is set for the discussion, and
participants take turns arguing back and forth. Again, this is a kind of
context that is very familiar to TV viewers. It suggests that a persuasion
dialogue or debate is under way.

Another example is the appearance of the magalogue, which suggests
a format of presentation of argumentation that we have come to expect
from a magazine, which contains news or articles that discuss controversial topics in the form of a persuasion dialogue. Once the reader gets
into a specific article, it becomes apparent that there is a *glissement*, or
gradual movement, towards a sales pitch. But initially the magalogue
bears all the appearances of the familiar magazine format. It is this ini-

tial appearance that sets certain expectations in place, customary expectations that are aroused by a particular style of format.

The deceptive trick of the infomercial is the gradual shift away from this initially perceived format towards a different type of dialogue. Once the reader's or viewer's interests and expectations are captured, set in motion by the format he initially perceives, the presumption is that he will continue reading the article or watching the program without perceiving the gradual shift or worrying about it. Even if he senses it, the hope is that this awareness will not prevent him from paying attention to the argumentation contained in the later stages of the sequence.

If we were to judge that such a sequence of argumentation is purely a sales pitch – an instance of advocacy dialogue to promote a particular product or to get readers to buy it – then there might be nothing wrong with this argumentation *per se*. For advocacy dialogue, or a sales pitch to sell or promote a product, is in itself not an inherently fallacious or deceptive kind of argumentation. However, if such an advocacy dialogue purports to be something else – some other type of dialogue with quite different goals than those based on the messages it gives during the initial stages of its presentation – then there is more to worry about from the critical point of view of evaluating the argumentation. In such a case, the argument could be perfectly reasonable in itself, as an advance from premises to conclusions. But when it is viewed in context in light of how the argument should properly be used in a normative framework of dialogue, there may be a very good basis for criticizing the argument for being deceptive and/or fallacious in certain respects.

10. Obstruction of Goals by Dialectical Shifts

In a case where there has been a dialectical shift during a sequence of argumentation, a dialectical evaluation of the argument begins by reconstructing the profile of dialogue, and then tries to determine the point in the profile where the shift occurred (see Figure 8.1). In the case of a gradual shift, it may not be a single point in the profile that indicates the shift, but rather a longer sequence where the two types of dialogue are mixed, or alternate back and forth.

The next step in the evaluation is to judge whether the second type of dialogue is embedded in the first, or whether the shift involves two dialogues that are functionally related. The shift might simply be an adventitious one, where the one dialogue is not embedded in the other. The second dialogue might begin as an interruption in the first one, and the

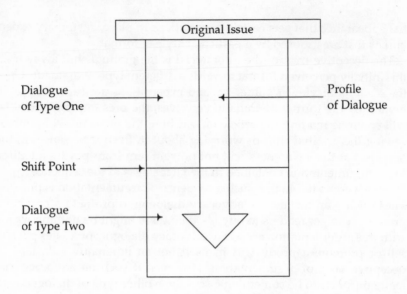

Figure 8.1 Dialectical Shift Point in an Argument

two dialogues are not functionally related at all. Or even worse, from the point of view of normative evaluation of a sequence of argumentation, the shift might involve the second dialogue actually displacing the first. Here the second dialogue blocks progress towards the goals of the first type of dialogue, and does not contribute in any constructive way to the argumentation in the first dialogue.

In evaluating a particular case, much depends on whether a dialectical shift is licit or illicit; that is, the retrospective evaluation depends on whether the shift is appropriate, whether it is properly agreed upon by the participants, and whether it is announced by the arguer in an appropriate way. If such a dialectical shift during a sequence of argument is concealed by one party, so that it functions as a tactic of deception against the other party, then it is the kind of illicit shift that functions as an obstruction to the goals of the initial type of dialogue. It is this kind of shift in argumentation that we should be worried about from the critical point of view of logic. For it is this tricky tactic of deception in argumentation that, in many cases, is identified with informal fallacies – tricky sophistical tactics that are obstacles to good reasoning.

In many cases of argumentation containing traditional informal fallacies, the dialectical shift in the sequence of argumentation is less visible than it is in infomercials. Moreover, in many of the cases featured in logic textbooks, not enough context of dialogue is presented in short examples to give very clear or decisive evidence that a dialectical shift has occurred. The interesting thing about the infomercials as case studies of dialectical shifts is their relative transparency. They trade on an identifiable, if gradual, dialectical shift. Our expectations about the type of dialogue we are engaged in during the initial phases of argumentation are relatively clear and well defined. During the later stages, there is plenty of evidence that there has been a gradual shift to a sales pitch and that a new normative framework for the argumentation has been set in place. This shift is clearly identifiable in the school case where the twelve-year-old student immediately recognized the video presentation as a commercial. Most of us have watched thousands of commercials, and our ability to identify this type of message is quite skilled. Hence, in the case of the infomercials, there is a relatively clear and definite dialectical shift from one recognizable type of dialogue to another.

In other cases, the dialectical shift is less pronounced, less sharply definable because the discourse is more of a mixed nature. We turn to examining these cases in the next chapter. Interesting questions remain. What type of dialogue is a sales pitch? We have suggested that it is some kind of advocacy dialogue. But what exactly is advocacy argumentation? The problem, as we will see in chapter 9, is that, although a sales presentation initially seems to be a clear case of a persuasion dialogue, this type of argumentation is somewhat complex, and is both narrower and wider in certain respects than the normative model of persuasion dialogue would indicate.

9

Mixed Discourse

Applying any of the six normative models of dialogue to any particular case of argumentation presents special problems for the new dialectic. In many cases, a text of discourse containing argumentation exhibits evidence that the speakers are engaged in several types of dialogue mixed together. But an evaluation of the argument depends on what type of dialogue the speakers are supposed to be engaged in. Yet the goals of one type of dialogue are quite different from, or even incompatible with, those of another type.

This phenomenon of mixed discourse presents a special problem when certain conventional types of speech exchanges which we tend to think of as univocal or homogenous really turn out to be composite from the point of view of our typology. The problem is not insurmountable, but it demands special sensitivity and qualifications when evaluating an argument in a text of discourse in a given case.

'Mixed discourse' may be defined as a text of discourse in which there is more than one of the normative models of argumentation during the same prolonged sequence of argumentation. In other words, a case of mixed discourse does not involve a dialectical shift from one type of dialogue to another, but is an instance of argument where two or more types of dialogue are both present over the same course of argument.

1. The Case of Question Period

As we noted earlier, the political debate is a good example of a type of discourse that frequently tends to be mixed. Since there are many different kinds of political debate that occur in conversation, it may be useful here, for purposes of an example, to focus on discourse in two particular formats of parliamentary debate.

Question Period in the Canadian House of Commons takes place five times a week when Parliament is in session. The purpose of Question Period is to allow opposition members to ask government ministers for information or to press for action on matters of current concern to the Canadian public (Franks, 1985).

According to the *Beauchesne's Parliamentary Rules and Forms* (1978), oral questions should be asked 'only in respect of matters of sufficient urgency and importance as to require an immediate answer.' Other rules state that a question should not require an answer involving a legal opinion, and a question should not require a lengthy or detailed answer, nor should it raise a matter of policy too large to be dealt with as an answer to a question. Another rule states that a question must be brief and should not be itself an expression of opinion. Another requires that answers to questions be as brief as possible. The purpose of a question is to seek information; therefore, questions should not be hypothetical, and they should not attack the respondent or cast aspersions on him or her. These rules make it clear that Question Period, as a parliamentary institution, does have a clearly stated purpose, and does have specific rules to determine what sorts of questions and replies are considered appropriate and legitimate.

The Speaker of the House is responsible for ensuring that the rules are followed, and is supposed to intervene only if a questioner or an answerer violates one of the rules (Franks, 1985). However, in practice, the Speaker tends to be permissive, intervening only when the violation is severe enough to obstruct the discussion in a serious way.

Judging from the statement of aims in *Parliamentary Rules and Forms*, the type of dialogue in Question Period is supposed to be either infor-mation-seeking or a deliberation type of dialogue oriented to pressing for action on a current problem. However, if we examine the transcripts of these debates in Hansard, the argumentation seems more like quarrel-some eristic dialogue, where one party attacks and tries to discredit the other.

Case 9.1 is a typical example of a loaded and complex question posed during Question Period (Hansard, 5 February 1986).

Case 9.1 The Economy: Exchange Value of the Dollar
LEADER OF THE OPPOSITION: Mr. Speaker, my question is directed to the Minister of Finance. He will know that, although the Canadian

dollar was up marginally this morning, the crisis is far from over. While he has adopted in this House the attitude of blaming everyone else for his problem, he must recognize that he, as the fiscal adviser to the Government, has the sole responsibility of dealing with this matter. Will he today, Wednesday, February 5, tell this House what he is going to do to solve the dollar crisis?

MINISTER OF FINANCE: Mr. Speaker, this Government takes full responsibility for the economic policies we brought in. We are proud of them and we think they are doing the job. I will tell the Hon. Member the sort of things we have been doing which are contributing to our economic strength. This is clearly evidenced by the fact that 1,000 jobs have been created every day since we came into office.

We initiated our program with the November economic statement. This set out in a very clear way the sum total of our economic policies. We brought in policies to increase investment, both foreign and domestic. We brought in policies to invigorate the energy sector and the small business community. We have followed a ...

MR. SPEAKER: Order, please. I hope questions and answers will be shorter than yesterday.

LEADER OF THE OPPOSITION: I have a supplementary question, Mr. Speaker. The answer does not relate to the question, so I will rephrase it, in French this time.

The Minister of Finance has the authority to solve the problem. What concrete step will he take to put an end to the Canadian dollar crisis?

MINISTER OF FINANCE: Mr. Speaker, the Hon. Member, a former Minister of Finance, says, to use his words, that my response was not relevant to the question. He asked what we are going to do to introduce a degree of stability into the Canadian dollar as well as strengthen the Canadian economy. For him to say that shows that he fails to understand the effect of the policies we have brought in and their impact on job creation, investment, housing starts, and inflation. All of these things are very, very clear.

If he cares to read not what I say but what expert economists have to say, he will see that they say the economy is strong and on the right track. They say they do not understand why there is a weakness in the dollar in the face of the strength in our economy and the fact we are taking action on the deficit, something which is long overdue after 10 years of mismanagement.

In the exchange in case 9.1, Minister of Finance Wilson objects to Opposition Leader Turner's description of the situation as a 'crisis,' and instead of giving an answer to the question, he offers some general remarks on government policies. Turner then complains that the reply is not relevant to the question he asked. Wilson, in his reply to this move, continues to criticize the implication of the original question, that there is an economic crisis, and cites the expert opinions of economists to back the claim that 'the economy is strong and on the right track.'

In case 9.1, the objection to the reply on grounds of irrelevance is highly localized in nature. Turner objects that Wilson's reply to his question is not relevant, in the sense that it does not answer the question. The problem of relevance in case 9.1 may be contrasted with the kind of problem of relevance encountered in case 7.2, where Kim Campbell was attacked for having smoked marijuana, an attack that occurred in the middle of a lengthy parliamentary debate on the Northumberland Strait Crossing Act. In case 7.2, the nature of the problem of relevance is quite different: in the midst of a long debate on a particular bill, there is a sudden internal shift to the topic of marijuana smoking and also a dialectical shift to the quarrel indicated by the *ad hominem* attack on a specific person, an attack that is not really related to the bill being discussed. Similar assessments of the failure of relevance in the tuna fish case, cited in chapter 7, could be made.

In case 7.2, the failure of relevance is global in nature. There is a lengthy sequence of argumentation on a bill that is supposed to be the issue, and then a sharp and sudden shift to an *ad hominem* attack. In case 9.1, the failure of relevance is much more local in nature. The perceived problem is that a specific reply fails to answer the question that immediately preceded it in the dialogue. Such aggressive and partisan questions, and evasive replies that fail to give a direct answer, are typical of the argumentation in Question Period (see Walton, 1988b).

Judged from the normative perspective of the information-seeking or deliberation types of dialogue, the argumentation in Question Period is largely a failure. The arguments seem to be full of fallacies, like irrelevant *ad hominem* arguments, evasive replies, and cases of the fallacy of many questions.

2. The Problem of Fallacies in Political Discourse

During Question Period, questioners frequently ask aggressive, loaded questions which use *ad hominem* argumentation to attack government ministers. And government ministers frequently give evasive replies, fail to answer a question altogether, or respond with equally vitriolic *ad hominem* attacks. Examples of argumentation of this kind are representative of the kinds of examples that informal logic textbooks cite and criticize for their fallacious arguments. Anyone who examines the Hansard transcript of the debates in the House of Commons will not have to look far to find striking examples of arguments traditionally identified with informal fallacies like *ad hominem* arguments, appeals to authority, complex questions, *ad baculum* arguments, arguments from ignorance, and so forth. All of the main twenty-two or so traditional major fallacies are abundantly represented.[1]

This abundance of fallacies raises a theoretical question for the evaluation of argumentation. Is it appropriate to criticize these cases of texts of discourse from Hansard as fallacious arguments? It seems that it is, or should be, at least in some cases. Indeed, students in informal logic should be encouraged to take an example from a text of discourse in Hansard, and evaluate whether that argument is fallacious using whatever standards the students have learned. The problem is that most students would judge a political discourse in a debate from Hansard by the standards for a critical discussion. For example, if a student were to say that an argument is irrelevant, or that a question is a loaded or complex question of the type identified as fallacious in logic textbooks, then these examples would be judged to be cases of fallacies, on the grounds that certain rules of the critical discussion are being violated. But is this a reasonable approach given that, as we have already seen, political discourse tends to be mixed discourse, a kind of argumentation that involves several different types of dialogue during the same sequence of argument?

We know that political argumentation is generally based on negotiation, in the form of interest-based bargaining by those who stand to gain or lose by legislation and by those who represent them. These days, in particular, we are familiar with so-called advocacy groups who make it clear that they are negotiating for the benefits or 'rights' of their particular group. If this is generally so, can we deny that political debate is partly a negotiation type of dialogue?

In many instances, it is also hard to deny that political debate, even the kind encountered in Question Period, is argumentation that is frankly eristic in nature. One party representative attacks another, quite often with *ad hominem* arguments, alleging that the other side is guilty of bad character for veracity, and using that to try to refute its arguments on an issue.

3. Political Debate as Mixed Discourse

The debate itself has been classified as a mixed type of argumentation involving both the persuasion type of dialogue and the eristic type in Woods and Walton (1982) and Walton (1989a). Ostensibly, the purpose of questioning in Question Period is to ask for information or to press for action on matters of concern to the Canadian public. This suggests that the discourse in Question Period should be an instance of information-seeking dialogue, or a kind of action-directed deliberation type of dialogue, or a combination of both.

However, we would not want to rule out that a sequence of argumentation in Question Period, like any argumentation in political debate, involves negotiation as well. In fact, Question Period is a mixed type of dialogue which has elements of five normative models of dialogue contained within its argumentation (Walton, 1992d, 94–5). These five normative models are: (1) information-seeking dialogue, because the basic purpose of a question is to ask for information; (2) action-producing dialogue, because the second stated goal of Question Period is to press for action on urgent issues; (3) eristic dialogue, because Question Period should allow for partisan, adversarial exchanges to some degree and, in fact, does so (Franks, 1985); (4) critical discussion, because questioning of assumptions and logical clarifications and rebuttals should be allowed where appropriate; and (5) negotiation, because political debates are always real conflicts of interest and are based on bargaining between interest groups.

Although the ostensible purposes of argumentation in Question Period are to solicit information and press for action, if we examine Hansard carefully, it seems that the actual practices of Question Period are quite different from these stated goals. In many cases, what is evident is an attacking mode in the questioning and defensive counter-attacking postures are evident in the answering. These aggressive tactics suggest that the argumentation in Question Period is better seen as a quarrel or eristic type of dialogue. We normally expect participants in political debate to attack each other in an adversarial way; this is called the 'bear pit' aspect of political debate (Franks, 1985). We expect our political representatives to engage in a kind of challenging combat with their opponents. It would be naive to expect any kind of political debate to be exactly like a critical discussion or carefully reasoned information-seeking type of dialogue, or to meet the kind of standards of clarity and rigour that we expect, for example, of a philosophical discussion. To some degree, then, the bear pit type of argumentation is tolerated and accepted in the democratic multiparty system. That seems to be part of its rationale in a democracy.

The same point was made in chapter 8 with respect to the *ad hominem* attack on Kim Campbell in case 7.2, which involves a lengthy debate on a specific bill (not an argument in Question Period). If an *ad hominem* attack on an officeholder's character is a relevant kind of argumentation in a political debate – as surely it is, in some instances – how can it be judged, according to the new dialectic, that the attack on Kim Campbell for having smoked marijuana is fallacious because it is irrelevant? The answer is to be sought in the requirement imposed by the new dialectic, that each argument must be judged on its merits on a case-to-case basis, as evaluated in a context of dialogue. And a parliamentary debate on a bill, like the Northumberland Strait Act, is (presumably) supposed to be a persuasion dialogue (or a deliberation, insofar as a decision to take action is involved), and is supposed to be a discussion of that issue, as opposed to being a quarrel about a different issue.

Generally, there is an expectation within western democratic political theories that there should be at least some elements of the critical discussion, or at the least the persuasion type of dialogue, in political debate, as well as elements of the deliberation and information-seeking types of dialogue, where these other types are embedded in the persuasion dialogue. This expectation is expressed in the following principle, a form of rationalizing assumption for political discourse. Political debate is only regarded as worthwhile and constructive in a western democratic political system if, to some extent, it represents a reasonable type of argumentative discussion which has some tendency to seek out the truth of a matter, or at least to have the truth somehow emerge from the discussion, and is based on information about the relevant facts, and leads to prudent decisions based on this information.

4. Evaluating Arguments in Political Discourse

If this rationality assumption about political debate is reasonable, then it is conditionally permissible to evaluate a political debate, like that in Question Period, from the point of view of a critical discussion or persuasion type of dialogue. It is not that we expect the debate to be a critical discussion in every respect, but rather that, in making criticisms of some of the lapses of argumentation or logical shortcomings, we can adopt the stance of viewing the discourse for these evaluative purposes from the point of view of the normative model of a critical discussion. Such an evaluation then takes the form of a conditional interpretation to the effect that, if we can interpret the speakers as engaging in a critical discussion, then we can say that their arguments commit such and such a fallacy.

This approach to evaluation seems legitimate as long as we are aware that the discourse also has other functions, and that viewing it as a critical discussion is not the only possible interpretation, or the exclusive interpretation that is legitimate. If the critical discussion is not the only interpretation that is allowed, then this leaves the person accused of committing a fallacy a way out. He can always say, 'Well, this is a political debate and it's supposed to be at least partly an eristic type of dialogue in which we engage in strongly adversarial argumentation on behalf of our political party and against our opponents, and so it is really naive of you to accuse me of committing a fallacy by saying that I violated some rule or requirement for a critical discussion.' The conditional interpretation as a way of evaluating an argument as fallacious, then, is conditional in the sense that it doesn't pin down the fallacy in an absolutely decisive way and leaves an arguer some legitimate avenues open for rebuttal. Ultimately, the question of whether a fallacy has been committed or not then depends on the prior question of what type of discourse is the proper context of this argument. The question is one of making a retrospective evaluation of which normative model applies to this particular case.

Moreover, in the case of Question Period and political debates generally, there is another complicating factor. Any real case of argumentation in everyday conversation occurs in a cultural and institutional setting called a 'speech event,' in which particular rules and requirements may apply.[2] For example, in the case of argumentation in Question Period, there is a set of rules and the Speaker of the House functions as a kind of referee of the debate who enforces these rules and makes rulings where difficulties in the debate arise. In judging an argument in a particular case, it could be a mistake not to take these particular rules and requirements for the speech event into account.

An eristic argument thought to be fairly acceptable within the context of a political debate could be judged inappropriate by a logic student who applies standards appropriate for a critical discussion. For example, a question that makes an aggressive *ad hominem* attack on the respondent, or a reply that doesn't answer the question and gives some irrelevant argument in response, could be judged fallacious by a logic student on the grounds that these arguments are inappropriate and contrary to the goals of a critical discussion. On the other hand, the same *ad hominem* attack, or the same evasion tactic, might not be seen as obstructive enough by the Speaker of the House to merit asking the participant to refrain from personal attack or to get back on track. Even so, the evaluation made by a logic student, concluding that the argument is a fallacious *ad hominem*, or a fallacy of relevance, should be seen specifically as a conditional evaluation made from a particular critical point of view.

Moreover, as a practical matter, it would be better if political debates were more often expected to meet a higher standard of reasoned discourse. For example, in the tuna scandal case outlined in chapter 7, Sheila Copps gets carried away with her own rhetoric, and deviates into other issues instead of responding to the deliberations on the particular bill under discussion. A government member rises on a point of order, claiming that the remarks made by Copps are not relevant to the bill being debated. Copps insists her remarks are relevant, even though it is clear from the viewpoint of persuasion dialogue that they are not (and from the point of view of deliberation). The Speaker then intervenes with a request that Copps get back to the bill. This does not deter her, however; she goes on insisting that her remarks are relevant. So how can we deny that they are in some sense relevant, even if they are not relevant if we judge the argumentation from the point of view of persuasion dialogue?

This kind of problem is a serious obstruction to political debate. The low quality of argumentation and the tendency to commit fallacies means that Question Period does not function well as a type of argumentation exchange. These heated exchanges during Question Period are televised, and respect for political debate in the House of Commons has no doubt declined as more and more evidence of this poor quality of argumentation has been broadcast to the public.[3]

Eristic dialogue, to some degree, is a legitimate part of political debate. But if it begins to appear to observers that the quarrel is becoming too predominant, leaving little room for persuasion dialogue or deliberation to play a significant part in political debate, there will be further erosion of public respect for parliaments and congresses as institutions. This is a practical problem, but the theoretical problem posed here is that political debate is generally a mixed type of discourse, and, therefore, it is somewhat artificial to evaluate the argumentation in political debate by exclusively using the standards of one normative model, like the critical discussion. However, it is permissible to base an evaluation on a conditional interpretation, provided it is clear what is being done, and the proper evidence concerning the contextual nature of the discourse is brought forward and identified. In logic, this question has to do with the problem of pinning down a fallacy (see Hamblin, 1970). A new dialectic-based solution to this problem is presented in chapter 10.

5. The Case of Sales Dialogue

Another common type of argumentation that is inherently difficult to analyse, because it involves mixed discourse, is sales dialogue. Let us consider a particular type of instance. A couple who is engaged in the process of buying a new car walks around a car showroom, looking at different cars. A salesman approaches and a conversation begins. At first, the couple asks the salesman questions about the features of the different models of cars. Then the salesman begins to ask questions about the couple's requirements for a car, and gradually, the discussion centres on one type of car or on a particular car that the couple is interested in. If the couple is interested in buying a car that is on the lot, then the salesman and the couple start to negotiate on price. At this stage, if the salesman gets an offer, he takes the offer to the dealer for approval, and a three-way negotiation begins, where the salesman acts as a kind of intermediary between the dealer and the buyer. Buying a new car is a familiar kind of ritual, and the conversational exchange that takes place generally goes through these particular phases.

According to Kaiser, a car sales type of conversation exchange passes through ten stages (1979, pp. 88–9).

1. Enquiry by telephone or in person;
2. Reception;
3. Specification (customer's requirements: 2nd hand car, use motive, consumer category);
4. Agreement on customer's requirements;
5. Presentation of offer by demonstration with stationary vehicle and on test drive. Coverage of needs and requirements thorough discussion, possibly distribution of promotional material, minimizing short-comings;
6. Point by point agreement between customer's needs and the offer is demonstrated and confirmed;
7. Final agreement with closing motivation;
8. Financial and other arrangements;
9. Delivery;
10. Follow-up conversations (in person or by telephone).

This process proceeds from 'finding out about the needs of the customer and defining his aims' to moving towards a contract or agreement (p. 83). At least, this is how it is represented from the salesman's point of view. From the customer's point of view, the dialogue proceeds from collecting of information about the product to a decision on how to comparatively judge the worth of the product in light of the alternatives available and the customer's needs and resources.

Initially, it is easy to categorize this type of argumentation exchange as a persuasion dialogue, but there are difficulties with this interpretation. When the couple first enters the showroom, the dialogue seems more like an information-seeking type of conversational exchange where the couple asks the salesman questions and he tries to provide answers. The couple asks, for example, 'What kind of mileage does this car get?' or 'Does it have anti-lock brakes?' or 'What kind of servicing do you have?' Here the salesman performs the function of an informed source, and he may even be seen as an expert, since we presume that he has been trained to be knowledgeable about the cars that he is selling. However, we consider him to be a biased sort of expert because we know that his goal is to sell a car. So we are sceptical, to some degree anyway, about what he says, and do not take his word as the final answer on the questions asked.

As we move towards the main argumentation stage of the conversational exchange, the salesman's side of the dialogue could correctly be described as a kind of persuasion dialogue. His goal is to persuade the couple to buy a car from his lot. His objective, in other words, is to sell a car at a price that is favourable to the dealer.

According to Kaiser, the salesman should avoid 'biting counterarguments' that tend to inhibit the development of the conversation, and instead concentrate on eliciting the opinions and interests of the customer. Using empathy, which Kaiser describes as 'making our own thoughts the thoughts of the other,' the salesman should 'loosen up the opposition' by asking 'concluding questions,' instead of pushing ahead with hard-edged arguments (p. 91).

This interpretation suggests that the salesman could be engaged in a kind of persuasion dialogue that requires empathy, and that uses the commitments of the customer as premises that form the basis of the argumentation. But it also suggests that the style of argumentation is different from that of, say, persuasion dialogue in a philosophy seminar or a court of law, where the persuasion argumentation has a harder edge.

Unlike the salesman, the couple looking to buy a car does not seem to be engaged in persuasion dialogue. The couple is not trying to persuade the salesman to become committed to any particular proposition. Later, at the negotiation stage, the couple is trying to get the salesman to accept an offer, but that is at a later stage. During the earlier stage, the salesman is still trying to persuade the couple either to buy a car or that buying a car from his lot would be a good idea. But are the potential buyers themselves engaged in a persuasion dialogue with the salesman?

One hypothesis is that the potential buyers are not trying to persuade the salesman of anything. They are just trying to collect enough information to reach an intelligent decision. In other words, they are really engaged in a deliberation type of dialogue in which they are trying to decide on a prudent course of action, whether it would be a good idea for them to buy a particular car or to buy a car from this dealer.

Another hypothesis is that the couple is engaged in a kind of persuasion dialogue with the salesman, because as potential buyers they are asking critical questions, to see whether the salesman's opinions are acceptable or not. For example, the couple may argue that *Consumers Report* says something different from what the salesman says, or that another dealer says something different. In this respect, then, it does seem that the two sides are engaged in a conversation that could be called a persuasion dialogue. Moreover, it is possible for a persuasion dialogue to be about the advisability of a course of action, so that we could describe the conversation as a kind of persuasion dialogue where the salesman has the objective of persuading the couple that buying a particular car would be a good idea, and the couple is asking the question whether buying this particular car would be a good idea.

On the other hand, this interpretation is somewhat questionable because it may be unrealistic and somewhat unfair to expect the argumentation of the salesman to meet standards appropriate for a critical discussion or another type of persuasion dialogue. When potential buyers enter the showroom, they are naturally sceptical about anything a salesman might say, because they know that the salesman is biased since his job is to sell cars. They also know that he is likely to be paid on commission and, by selling more cars, he increases his income. They would be somewhat naive if they didn't know this and take it into account in evaluating his arguments. Therefore, a case can be made that judging the salesman's arguments by the standards appropriate for a persuasion dialogue might be too high a requirement.

We should be reminded here of the difficulties of classifying advocacy advertisements (see chapter 4). The salesman's argumentation should be classified as a species of commercial speech, because he is making an offer of something for sale. In this respect, it would be simplistic to categorize the salesman's argumentation as the kind of critical discussion appropriate for advocating a point of view on some issue of controversy in ethics or public policy, where a commercial transaction is not directly at stake.

On balance, it seems best to hypothesize that the salesman's argumentation is a mixture of persuasion dialogue (of a certain sort) and commercial speech of a kind that could be best classified as a species of negotiation dialogue. We should note also that there are dialectical shifts at different stages of the process.

6. Evaluating Fallacies in Sales Dialogue

This question of what type of dialogue is involved in a sales conversation has practical implications because logic textbooks tend to say that fallacies are committed in sales dialogue. For example, Hurley cites a case in which a used car salesman sells a car to a woman, but fails to tell her that the odometer had rolled around twice and that the engine had two cracked pistons and a burned valve (1991, p. 149). Hurley claims that the salesman's argument in this case commits the fallacy of suppressed evidence, where an argument presents evidence for a conclusion but ignores stronger evidence that supports a different conclusion. In this case, we can say that the salesman lied about the mileage and failed to give important information about the engine and, therefore, that he has acted unethically. Also, lying about mileage is considered a crime in most jurisdictions. But has he committed a logical fallacy, in particular, the fallacy of suppressed evidence?

This type of criticism, pointing out that a fallacy has been committed, imposes a requirement on the salesman's argument that it must 'tell the whole truth,' so to speak. His argument must not omit relevant evidence. He has an obligation in the context of the dialogue to present all the relevant evidence, or enough of it so that no stronger evidence supporting any other conclusion is left out. This is actually quite a high standard for an argument to meet in order to be nonfallacious. Leaving out relevant evidence could be an indicator of bias, or it certainly is a good indication that the argument is weak and incomplete. But is the defect a serious enough one in context that we are justified in saying that the salesman has committed a logical fallacy? After all, the salesman is supposed to be engaged in advocacy for his particular point of view, and the buyer should know that.

If the buyer goes to a mechanic or to some service that inspects vehicles for their roadworthiness, then the mechanic has an obligation to meet the standard of completeness of evidence. He is expected to search out defects, such as cracked pistons or a turned-back odometer, and to report this to the person who consults him. But should this same standard, which would be appropriate for an advice-giving type of expert consultation, be imposed on the salesman who is selling the car? Should we say that the salesman commits the fallacy of suppressed evidence if he leaves any of these things out in his sales presentation to the buyer? Some would say that such a requirement is too high to impose on a sales presentation because the salesman is not supposed to be, nor do we expect him to be, a consumer advocate who presents all the evidence or all the strongest arguments on both sides. We expect the salesman to be somewhat biased and to present strong evidence on his side – that is, evidence that supports the thesis that it would be a good idea for the buyer to purchase this particular car. We know that the salesman and the dealership he represents are in business to sell a product, and we know in advance, therefore, that they are an interest or advocacy group with a particular bias.

We do hold car dealerships ethically and legally responsible for meeting certain standards, and they are legally required to report problems such as odometers that have been tampered with. But it is another question whether we should say that their arguments have committed logical fallacies if they fail to mention all evidence on both sides in a balanced way. Some people would say that this is just too high a requirement and that, to some extent, this sales dialogue type of argumentative exchange between a buyer and a seller should not presume a requirement that both sides have to tell the other side everything they know or give all the evidence that they have. Instead, these people would say that there should be some room in such an exchange for the principle of 'buyer beware,' and that there should be a presumption generally that both sides have an interest in a particular outcome.

Moreover, Hurley's way of defining the fallacy of suppressed evidence presents a requirement on argumentation that is even too strong to represent a critical discussion or persuasion type of dialogue. Even the persuasion type of dialogue is adversarial, in that each party is tries present the strongest arguments for his own thesis. Each has an obligation, or burden of proof to meet, and this means using arguments that will adequately meet this burden of proof. However, there is no require-ment in a critical discussion that an arguer must present evidence that supports a different conclusion than the one he is advocating. In a criti-cal discussion, there is division of obligations: one side presents his arguments and gives the strongest arguments for them, and the other side presents her arguments and gives the strongest arguments for them. There is no obligation for either party to include stronger evi-dence that supports the thesis of the other side or to point out that such evidence exists.

Thus, while the standard of presentation of evidence required by Hur-ley might be appropriate for a type of dialogue like the inquiry or the information-seeking dialogue, it appears to be too strong to be appropri-ate for persuasion dialogue. Even if such a standard were appropriate for persuasion dialogue, it is not altogether clear that the salesman's argumentation in the type of case we are considering should be required to meet all standards for persuasion dialogue. As we have seen, the kind of advocacy argumentation that the salesman is engaged in, according to the familiar requirements of this kind of encounter, is a mixed type of dialogue. Not only is it a mixed type of dialogue, but there are also dia-lectical shifts as the argumentation proceeds. At first, it appears to be more of an information-seeking dialogue. Then, it moves into something more like a persuasion dialogue, at least in certain respects. And finally, there is the final stage in which the conversation turns to a negotiation dialogue. Thus, evaluating the argumentation in this typical type of case turns out to be a more subtle task than initially expected, because the normative framework argumentation of the conversation is quite com-plex in a number of ways.[4]

7. Argumentation in a Legal Trial

Another type of argumentation that appears to involve several types of dialogue in its normative framework is the legal argumentation that we find in a criminal trial. At first, the context of argument seems to be that of a persuasion dialogue, since the criminal trial is based on the burden-of-proof principle. The prosecution must prove guilt beyond reasonable doubt, and in order to win, the defence needs only to cast doubt on the prosecution's case.[5] Thus it seems initially that the argumentation in a criminal trial fits the model of persuasion dialogue quite well, but there are a couple of complicating factors.

One factor is that a judge or jury decides the outcome, and such a determination does not necessarily represent the standard of rationality that would be appropriate for a critical discussion. In fact, judges and juries are often convinced by arguments that would, from a logical point of view, be considered fallacious (See Waller, 1988).

Another factor is that the legal system has its own special rules of evidence which are used to evaluate the argumentation in a criminal trial (Degnan, 1973). These rules govern what constitutes evidence, how that evidence may be presented, and how participants in a trial situation should judge that evidence to be strong or weak. There are also legal rules governing whether the introduction of evidence or a line of questioning can be considered relevant in a trial. It is the function of the judge to rule on such matters of relevance. There are also procedural rules in a criminal trial covering the sorts of questions that can be asked and the sorts of replies that can be given. In short, the speech event of the criminal trial involves a knowledge of special rules pertaining to a given jurisdiction that govern how argumentation is to be allowed into the proceedings and how it is to be judged once it is put forth as part of a trial. Some of these legal rules of evidence are interesting with respect to traditional categories of argumentation that are said to be fallacious in logic textbooks.

For example, impeachment, which is the process of discrediting the testimony of a witness with facts that question his veracity, is regarded as a legitimate type of argumentation in a criminal trial, within limits. This form of personal attack, which in logic is called *ad hominem* argumentation, can be used by a cross-examining attorney to attack the character of a witness and can lead to the rejection of the witness's testimony. Among the forms of impeachment argumentation recognized by Degnan are the following: first, showing that the witness has previously made statements that are inconsistent with his statements on the witness stand; second, showing that the witness is biased for one side or the other; third, showing the general bad moral character of the witness; and most particularly, fourth, showing that his character for veracity is bad (1973, p. 908).

These four types of impeachment argumentation methods correspond to the four distinctive kinds of *ad hominem* arguments recognized by logic textbooks as fallacious.[6] Interestingly, however, these legal rules of evidence indicate that such *ad hominem* arguments are regarded, in principle, as legitimate in the context of a criminal trial. If such arguments are carried too far in a trial, they will be regarded as illegitimate.[7] This would be indicated in a particular case by the judges objecting to or excluding such an argument. However, in general, such *ad hominem* arguments are regarded as reasonable, or not fallacious, in the context of a criminal trial, and this observation has very important implications for any analysis of the *ad hominem* fallacy in logic. It also shows that, in certain key respects, argumentation in the normative structure of the criminal trial is evaluated in a distinctively different way than it is in the critical discussion. Although the criminal trial as a framework for argumentation is similar to a persuasion dialogue in certain respects, these special rulings indicate that there is no exact one-to-one correspondence or equivalence between the two normative frameworks of argumentative discourse.

In another kind of argumentation allowed in the criminal trial, expert witnesses are brought in to express specialized opinions on technical matters that the judge or jury would otherwise have difficulty understanding (Degnan, 1973, p. 908). For example, a medical expert is called as a witness to give his opinion on how a brain concussion was caused by a blow that fractured a victim's skull (Degnan, 1973, p. 908). This type of argumentation corresponds to what is traditionally called the *argumentum ad verecundiam* in logic.[8] It also suggests that expert consultation dialogue is subjoined to the argumentation in a criminal trial.

We can also see that the sequence of argumentation in a criminal trial typically goes through several distinctive phases. An appeal to pity, for example, might be appropriate at the sentencing stage of the trial, once the defendant has admitted guilt. But the same type of appeal-to-pity argument might be considered inappropriate or even fallacious at the earlier argumentation stage of the trial, when guilt is yet to be determined. Such an evaluation would apply particularly at this earlier stage if the appeal to pity were used in an attempt to distract the jury from evidence, to avoid having the defendant answer a question, or to win the sympathy of the jury without really addressing important issues. Used at this stage, the appeal to pity could be judged to be fallacious on grounds of irrelevance.

Another interesting aspect of the kind of argumentation in a criminal trial is the notion of plea bargaining. The purpose of having a criminal trial is to determine guilt on the basis of relevant evidence and the strongest arguments put forward by both sides – a procedure that has dominant elements of a persuasion type of dialogue. An alternative to a trial is plea bargaining, which is a process of negotiation. In plea bargaining, the defence attorney offers a confession of guilt from his client if the judge agrees to give the defendant a reduced sentence for that type of crime. In the plea-bargaining process, the two sides agree to make a deal in order to save the time and expense of a trial. Here there is a shift from the trial or persuasion dialogue argumentation to a negotiation, and the outcome is decided by a process of negotiation or bargaining.

In short, then, while the argumentation used in a legal trial seems to have many aspects of persuasion dialogue – and perhaps can be usefully evaluated using that model of dialogue – in practice, it is a more complex type of discourse that involves other types of dialogue, and it must always be evaluated in relation to special factors that are characteristic of this speech event. Although it can be appropriate in some cases to talk about fallacies in the argumentation in a trial, special care is needed in judging such cases.

8. Pedagogical Dialogue

Another mixed type of discourse is pedagogical dialogue, which involves a teacher giving instruction to a student on some subject. In our classification, pedagogical dialogue seems to be primarily a type of information-seeking dialogue. However, aspects of the expert consultation dialogue are definitely involved in the pedagogical dialogue as a special subspecies of information-seeking dialogue. We presume that the instruction falls into a particular domain of knowledge and that the teacher is an expert in this field.

Although argumentation does occur in pedagogical dialogue, it more characteristically includes explanations. And this is one of the difficulties of evaluating argumentation in pedagogical dialogue: it is difficult to determine in a particular case whether a given sequence of reasoning is meant to be an argument or an explanation. In some cases, the same sequence of reasoning can fulfil both purposes in the given text of discourse (Govier, 1987).

The difference between information-seeking dialogue and pedagogical dialogue is that pedagogical dialogue transfers knowledge to the student, not just information. In other cases of pedagogical dialogue, what is passed along is a practical skill or a way of doing something in a skilled or efficient manner. For these reasons, it is tempting to classify pedagogical dialogue as a type of expert consultation dialogue, but it is not exactly the same thing. Giving somebody advice on how to do something is different from trying to teach them how to master a discipline or a skill, and it is perhaps this more general aspect of pedagogical dialogue that characterizes it as a distinctive type of discourse. In the new dialectic, pedagogical dialogue is classified as a subspecies of information-seeking dialogue which shares some common properties with expert consultation dialogue, although its purpose is somewhat different.

Aristotle includes didactic arguments as one of the five kinds of arguments he distinguishes in *On Sophistical Refutations* (165a38–165b12). Didactic arguments are 'those which reason from the principles appropriate to each branch of learning and not from the opinions of the answerer (for he who is learning must take things on trust)' (165b2). This account of didactic arguments makes an interesting point that seems to be characteristic of pedagogical dialogue generally – namely, in pedagogical dialogue, the information that is conveyed to the student is based on a curriculum, that is, some textbook or account of a given body of knowledge is used. So it is not a straight transfer of information or advice from the one party to the other; rather, it conveys some systematic body of information in a textbook, or the like, which has been written by an expert in a domain of knowledge.

Lectures and textbooks that convey the findings in a field are a familiar way to pass along information to students. However, another aspect of pedagogical dialogue, the Socratic aspect of questioning which involves elements of persuasion dialogue in some cases, has rightly been given a place of prominence by education theorists like Kaiser: 'The best known active teaching method is the teaching conversation which develops through questioning' (1979, p. 63). The use of questioning techniques allows the instructor to adapt the knowledge being taught to the understanding of the students. There is an important comparison with persuasion dialogue here. What is important for the teacher is to use empathy to focus on the commitments and level of understanding of his or her individual students, so that a maieutic effect on the student's dark-side commitments is part of the criterion by which we judge the success of the dialogue.

Kaiser advocates the following methods for developing good questioning techniques in pedagogical dialogue: (1) avoidance of 'long-winded' and jargon-ridden formulation of questions; (2) avoidance of unclear questions, where a question is based on a presupposition that the student is uncertain about or that is not known by the student; (3) avoidance of questions that are grammatically awkward or too complex to appear inviting to the student (pp. 65–6). In general, Kaiser thinks that a good conversational exchange in pedagogical dialogue must exhibit sequences of connected questions: 'the questions should be built onto each other, which means that the next question has to take into account the answer of the question preceding it' (p. 66). What is indicated here as part of the normative model of pedagogical dialogue is that the question-reply sequence should be relevant, and that the sequence of questions itself should exhibit a constructive relevance, each one being built on the previous sequence.

Aristotle also cites another characteristic applicable to pedagogical dialogue, namely, that this type of argumentation exchange concerns the principles appropriate to a branch of learning (*On Sophistical Refutations*, 165b10). What is conveyed, then, is the knowledge in a special discipline, with the methods and principles characteristic of that discipline. This means that the normative characteristics of good pedagogical dialogue will vary somewhat from discipline to discipline. Even so, certain features, like those cited above, are common to all fields. In the new dialectic, pedagogical dialogue does have certain distinctive characteristics that distinguish it fairly clearly from the other types of dialogue that we have analysed so far.

In the new dialectic, pedagogical dialogue is a subspecies of information-seeking dialogue, and it is similar to another subspecies of information-seeking dialogue, namely, expert consultation dialogue. One difference between pedagogical and expert consultation dialogues is that the former is generally based on a curriculum that has the goal of conveying a systematic body of knowledge, whereas the latter is typically focused on helping someone to solve a particular problem, or giving someone enough information to take action on some decision that requires an expert opinion.

But pedagogical dialogue and expert consultation dialogue are similar in that both, while mainly information-seeking in nature, involve subdialogues where critical questioning, testing and examining of the expert's opinion is usefully embedded in the main dialogue. Thus both involve dialectical shifts, and tend to be mixed types of discourse in practice.

9. Aristotle's Five Types of Arguments Revisited

The four other types of arguments that Aristotle classified are: dialectical arguments, examination arguments, contentious arguments, and demonstrative arguments. Demonstrative arguments, as noted in chapter 3, are very similar in their leading characteristics to arguments in the type of dialogue we have called the inquiry. Examination arguments are defined by Aristotle in *On Sophistical Refutations* (165b5–165b7) as 'those which are based on opinions held by the answerer necessarily known to one who claims knowledge of the subject involved.' This exchange sounds like a kind of argumentation we have typified as occurring within the expert consultation type of dialogue, and in chapter 8, it was analysed as an embedding of a persuasion dialogue in an expert consultation dialogue. Contentious arguments, as shown in chapter 7, are comparable to the use of argumentation we have characterized as taking place within an eristic dialogue.

This leaves us with what Aristotle called dialectical arguments. Are these comparable to arguments in persuasion dialogue? It seems that they are in some respects, but not all and that, in Aristotle's conception of dialectical arguments, they might fit as a subspecies of arguments in persuasion dialogue. According to Aristotle in *On Sophistical Refutations* (165b3–165b5), dialectical arguments are 'those which, starting from generally accepted opinions, reason to establish a contradiction.' According to Evans, Aristotle distinguishes between demonstrative argument and dialectical argument by means of the following criterion. The demonstrative syllogism 'starts from what is primary and true' as its premise. In contrast, the dialectical syllogism takes its start from *endoxa* which refers to opinions that are generally accepted or presumed to be true by the majority or the wise (1977, p. 77).

However, some other important differences between demonstrative and dialectical arguments are also cited by Aristotle in *On Sophistical Refutations*, and these differences are very interesting for us, because we can also ask whether they serve as additional characteristics that help us to distinguish between persuasion dialogue and Aristotelian dialectic as distinctive normative frameworks of argumentation. The first difference cited by Aristotle is that dialectic proceeds by interrogation (172a20). Therefore, Aristotle concludes, dialectic is not inquiry or demonstration, because the goal of a demonstration is to prove something and, Aristotle continues, any type of dialogue where the goal is to prove something must refrain from continual questioning – that is, the basic premises and principles (axioms) cannot be subject to continued questioning and possible retraction as the dialogue proceeds.

Another difference has to do with specialized subject matter. Aristotle writes in *On Sophistical Refutations* that dialectical argument 'has no definite sphere, nor does it demonstrate anything in particular' (172a15). And later he writes that 'a man could possess dialectic without any scientific knowledge because it is possible to have dialectical argumentation between two parties, neither of whom has any specialized scientific knowledge of a subject' (172a18). Aristotle concludes, 'Clearly therefore the art of examination is not knowledge of any definite subject, and it therefore follows that it deals with every subject; for all the arts employ certain common principles' (172a29). In other words, Aristotle concludes that everyone, including those people who do not have specialized knowledge of a scientific field, make some kind of use of dialectic.

Aristotle's remarks are very interesting in light of our classification of the different types of dialogue. However, we should be reminded once again that Aristotle is not engaged in the process of classifying contexts of argumentation or normative models of dialogue in which argumentation takes place. He sees himself as classifying different types of arguments. So our project here and what Aristotle sees himself doing appear to be inherently different projects. Even so, there are some interesting comparisons that can be made.

When Aristotle stresses that dialectic is characterized by questioning, and that this provides its fundamental contrast with demonstration (which is a kind of argument that needs to refrain from continual questioning), this is very reminiscent of how we earlier defined the key distinction between inquiry and persuasion dialogue. This criterion concerns the central problem of retraction, namely, that the inquiry is meant to be a type of dialogue in which the need for retraction is minimized or, if possible, eliminated. Whereas in persuasion dialogue, a certain amount of retraction is necessary, as noted in chapter 2. Persuasion dialogue is characterized by questioning where there is doubt or a conflict of opinion; hence, changing our mind or retracting propositions in persuasion dialogue is to be expected in many instances and cannot be excluded entirely. On the other hand, the problem is that, in persuasion dialogue, if retraction is allowed too permissibly, then the questioner will not have enough of a fixed base of commitments to pin down the answerer's position firmly enough to accomplish the goal of persuasion. In the inquiry, by contrast, it is important that commitments not be continually retracted or subject to continued questioning, because the whole aim of the inquiry is to fix a base of premises firmly to begin with, so that these can be used to advance, in a linear or branching way, towards conclusions that can be established firmly on the basis of these premises.

In short, it seems that Aristotle's distinction between dialectical argument and demonstrative argument does correspond fairly well to the basic defining distinction we made earlier between the inquiry and the persuasion type of dialogue. However, not too much should be read into this, because Aristotle's notion of dialectical argument seems to be quite highly specialized in relation to his own views on logic, in which the syllogism has a place of central importance. Also, there are many exegetical problems in determining exactly what Aristotle means by dialectical argument in his different works, as shown by Hamblin (1970), Evans (1977), Hamlyn (1990), Bolton (1990), Devereux (1990), Smith (1993), and other commentators.

10. Aristotle on Dialectical Argument

According to Hamblin, Aristotle is not sure whether dialectical and examination arguments are two distinct kinds or represent only one kind of argument (1970, p. 59). And Hamblin notes that, in different places, Aristotle makes each a subclass of the other. Hamblin quotes Aristotle's *Topics*, which defines dialectical argument as a process of criticism or an 'ability to raise certain difficulties on both sides of a subject,' which will enable us to 'detect more easily the truth and error about the several points that arise' (101a34b). This account makes dialectical argumentation sound very similar to what we have called persuasion dialogue.

Also, as noted earlier, Aristotle contrasts dialectical arguments with demonstrative arguments, and states that dialectical arguments start from premises that are not known to be true, whereas in demonstrative arguments, the reasoning starts from premises that are 'primary and true.' This contrast makes Aristotle's notion of dialectical argument seem very similar to the kind of argumentation that occurs in persuasion dialogue in the new dialectic. Also, when Aristotle writes that dialectical argument is possible between two parties, neither of whom has specialized scientific knowledge of a subject, this too sounds a lot like what is called persuasion dialogue in the new dialectic.

However, some other characteristics Aristotle attributes to dialectical argument make it seem like a more specialized or different type of dialogue in relation to persuasion dialogue. According to Hamblin, Aristotle's model of dialectical argument is 'the skill of the speakers in Plato's most mature dialogues' (1970, p. 60). This skill is, according to Hamblin, 'the result of a long training in move and counter-move' (p. 60). Hence, it seems that, for Aristotle, dialectical argumentation is a kind of specialized skill in which a person can become a sort of expert even though the subject matter of it is universal. If so, then it seems that what Aristotle calls dialectical argument is not as broad a category as we have in mind in defining persuasion dialogue as a normative framework of argumentation.

Also, Aristotle's main positive defining criterion of dialectical argument is that it is based on *endoxa* as premises, propositions accepted as reputable by the majority or the wise (see chapter 1). This criterion, however, is not essential to persuasion dialogue as defined in the new dialectic. What is essential to argumentation in a persuasion dialogue is that a successful (useful) argument by one participant must be based on premises that are commitments of the other participant. Typically, in a critical discussion about some controversial topic of public policy or ethical values (like the dialogue on tipping), *endoxa* represents commonly used and important kinds of premises. But such a premise base is not essential to argumentation in a persuasion dialogue. A persuasion dialogue can be about a subject where *endoxa* are not used as premises. Here, then, is a key difference between persuasion dialogue and Aristotelian dialectic.

One of the main problems in understanding what Aristotle means by dialectical argument is determining exactly what the purpose of it is supposed to be. According to Devereux, the function of dialectic in Aristotle's philosophy is not clear, even though he devotes a whole treatise, the *Topics*, to the subject. Devereux surveys the array of conflicting interpretations on the question:

The array of views on this question held by recent commentators is nothing short of bewildering. Some argue that Aristotle retains the Platonic conception of dialectic as *the* method of philosophical inquiry; not only is it the preferred method in dealing with subjects that do not admit of scientific demonstration, e.g. ethics and metaphysics, but even in the sciences it provides the only possible justification for their first principles and undergirds our confidence in scientific procedures and methods. At the other extreme are those who contend that Aristotelian dialectic is a rule-governed method of discussion whose aim is simply to increase one's ability to argue effectively on both sides of a question. According to this view, dialectic has no concern for getting at the truth and has no role in a properly philosophical or scientific inquiry. (1990, p. 264)

Devereux also cites a more moderate position between these extreme views, represented by Bolton (1990). Bolton argues that the purpose of dialectic is to train the participants to argue effectively on any topic, on the basis of what seems plausible, without being concerned with the truth or falsity of their premises or conclusions.

Bolton also surveys many conflicting views of Aristotelian dialectic which have been defended by specialists in Greek philosophy. His analysis cites Aristotle's assumption that some premises can be more *endoxon* than others, and builds on this assumption to articulate a basic principle laid down by Aristotle to govern dialectical argument used in 'testing and inquiry' (p. 205). In the *Topics*, Aristotle writes: 'The one who reasons correctly [as a result of questioning] establishes his set thesis on the basis of things which are more *endoxon* and more intelligible [than the thesis itself]' (159b8–9). This principle is reminiscent of the principle that is the kind of plausible reasoning typically used in persuasion dialogue: a plausible argument proceeds from premises that are more plausible to a conclusion that was less plausible before the plausible argument was brought to bear on it (Walton, 1992b). Bolton sees this principle of plausible reasoning as characteristic of the kind of peirastic use of dialectic that has concern for truth as part of its goal. His linking of the principle with dialectic as a knowledge-based enterprise is made through his argument that Aristotle sees scientific evidence as based on our actual practices of justification and, hence, as 'the deepest or most *endoxon* of beliefs' (p. 225).

According to Bolton's account of the goal of dialectical argument in Aristotle, peirastic dialectic is concerned with truth because, according to Aristotle in *Sophistical Refutations* (165b3–165b4), premises in peirastic arguments used to examine the first principles of a science are necessarily known by the respondent, an expert in a domain of knowledge who professes to have knowledge in a scientific field. Bolton sees the principle of plausible reasoning cited above as characteristic of the reasoning used in the peirastic type of dialectical argument. Devereux, however, questions this assumption, stating that there are no signs that Aristotle means to apply this principle 'to a particular type of dialectic rather than to dialectical discussions in general' (1990, p. 269). As Devereux sees it, the evidence in the *Topics* for a special type of dialectic 'adapted for use in scientific and philosophical inquiry is rather skimpy and of dubious value' (p. 270). So Devereux and Bolton disagree on what the goal of Aristotelian dialectic is supposed to be.

Does Aristotle think that the purpose of dialectic is to train participants to argue effectively on both sides of an issue, on the basis of what is plausible, without being concerned with the truth? Or does he think that the purpose of dialectic could go towards the truth (or knowledge) through a peirastic examination of first principles of science? Aristotelian commentators simply do not agree on which of these conflicting views of dialectic is correct.

In the new dialectic, the purpose of persuasion dialogue is to increase maieutic insight on an issue. And this insight, to use Locke's words from *An Essay Concerning Human Understanding*, does not 'bring knowledge' or 'help me ... to the reception of truth,' but it can 'dispose' a participant 'for the reception of truth.' Thus persuasion dialogue, of the kind defined in the new dialectic, may be (in certain respects) more like Socratic dialectic than Aristotelian dialectic.

It seems that Aristotle thinks of dialectical argument more as a technique of argument, rather than as, what the new dialectic calls, a normative framework of argumentation. Therefore, trying to compare our pragmatic framework for argumentation with Aristotle's classification of several different kinds of argument is artificial and somewhat misleading – like comparing apples and oranges. But it is tempting to make comparisons, even at the risk of distorting or misinterpreting Aristotle's intentions, given that some of the distinguishing characteristics that he cites for different types of argumentation also seem to be useful and revealing indicators for distinguishing between the different types of dialogue that we have identified.

When we use the word 'dialectical,' we mean it in the sense of the new dialectic, which is an extension of the sense used by Hamblin (1970; 1971) and also roughly corresponds to the sense used by the so-called pragma-dialectical school of argumentation.[10] Here, 'dialectical' refers to argumentation as a sequence of verbal exchanges between two parties within a goal-directed normative framework that defines the purpose of the exchange. Aristotle uses the word 'dialectical' in a much more specialized sense to refer to something that we would classify as a subspecies of persuasion dialogue. However, it is worthwhile to repeat once again that such a comparison may be inherently misleading, in the sense that Aristotle sees himself as defining different types of arguments, whereas the new dialectic proceeds by defining different characteristic types of normative frameworks in which argumentation occurs and can be evaluated critically with respect to how it has been used in that context.

These terminological and philosophical differences are worth some further comment (see Walton, 1990b, pp. 414–7). Aristotle frequently uses the word 'reasoning' where we would use 'argument,' and vice versa. An ambiguity in Aristotle's concept of demonstration might be explained, in our terms, as a dialectical shift. In one sense, demonstration can be seen as simply an inquiry. But, in other cases, what Aristotle thinks of as a demonstration can be seen as a kind of information-giving dialogue where the results of the inquiry are presented to a new audience. What Aristotle really means by demonstration, by dialectical argument, or by the other types of arguments he distinguishes, are problems of interpretation best left to specialists in Greek philosophy. But it is interesting to note that, although our project of defining different contexts of dialogue for argumentation appears to be novel and even radical from a twentieth century point of view, this project would not have seemed at all out of place in the ancient world, and particularly within the framework of the study of techniques of argumentation and the analysis of fallacies that Aristotle presents in the *Topics* and *On Sophistical Refutations*.

10

The Dialectical Method of Evaluating Arguments

The new dialectic provides new foundations for logic as an applied discipline. At the same time, the new dialectic provides a basis for new methods that can be used to identify the existence of arguments in a given case, as opposed to explanations and other speech acts. And it also provides new methods for evaluating arguments as correct or incorrect in a given case.

Very often arguments are spread out over a whole paragraph, speech, chapter, or other longer discourse. In this case, the argument may be a long chain, composed of several subarguments. Generally, the first step is to identify the ultimate conclusion of the argument, the thesis, contention, or interest that is the subject of dispute, which the proponent of the argument is obliged to prove or has agreed to argue for. Whether his premises are rightly said to be dialectically relevant depends on their relationship to this conclusion. A fallacy of irrelevance (*ignoratio elenchi*) occurs if propositions are fairly judged to be not relevant to that conclusion in the context of dialogue. Such a failure of relevance can be particularly deceptive, as we have seen, if there has been a shift to a different type of dialogue. Many *ad populum* and other emotional appeals can be evaluated as failures of dialectical relevance in argument, as the textbooks often suggest.

Another feature of extended dialogue is that questions and answers should be evaluated in sequences, in their relationship to each other and to the ultimate conclusion of the dialogue. An answer to a question can be locally irrelevant to the question it was a reply to. But its global relevance to the ultimate conclusion at issue can also be questioned.

As noted in chapter 1, much of the current method of evaluation used in the applied parts of existing logic courses is tied to the concept of fallacy. The implications of the new framework for evaluation of arguments in context proposed in the preceding nine chapters for the study of fallacies is briefly sketched in this chapter. The intent is not to analyse all the fallacies, but to make selective remarks on the few major fallacies introduced in chapter 1 to indicate how the new pragmatic approach leads to a new view of the concept of a fallacy, which will be much more useful than the one currently advocated in the logic textbooks.

1. Argument Evaluation

To get an idea of what sort of concept of evaluation is appropriate to the study of fallacies and other criticisms of opinion-based reasoning in natural language, first we need to appreciate the kinds of tasks and skills that are important in applying the new dialectic to cases of arguments. The best place to begin is with the concept of an argument criticism.

The basic argument criticism is that of weak argument, which means that the conclusion is not strongly enough supported by the premises. However, the question of when given support is strong enough in an argument depends on burden of proof. Therefore, a critic of argument also must ask how strong an argument needs to be in order to prove its point. This depends on the goal of the dialogue and the particular context of dialogue. How strong an argument needs to be depends on its purpose in a dialogue, and that, in turn, implies a burden of proof – a level of support required for the argument to be successful. This aspect of the new dialectic is a novel approach, given the usual assumption of the logic textbooks that any argument that is weak can be declared fallacious – for example, if it fails to be deductively valid.

Whether an *ad ignorantiam* argument is reasonable or not depends on the burden of proof. For example, if the issue of a deliberation is whether a passenger aircraft is safe enough to be flown with a larger number of passengers, then any reason for doubt may be strong grounds for the presumption that the aircraft is not safe.

Two other factors which can only be determined by the context of a particular corpus of dialogue are also very important in dialectically evaluating arguments. One is the requirement of evidential priority. In some contexts of dialogue, certain propositions are to be taken as established premises. Then any new conclusions can only be established by appeal to these prior and better-known premises. In a dialogue where evidential priority is a requirement, like an inquiry, circular argument is fallacious. If there is no requirement of evidential priority that can be determined from the context of the dialogue, circular arguments are permissible, and should be judged as benign or vicious on a case-by-case basis.

The second factor is the arguer's position, defined by his commitment set. If a circumstantial *ad hominem* allegation has been made, then whether or not it can be substantiated depends on the arguer's position. We determine the arguer's position by looking over the given corpus of dialogue, and citing evidence for the arguer's commitment to any propositions that may not be consistent with his conclusions. The first step in evaluating an *ad hominem* criticism is to sort out the set of propositions alleged to contain the circumstantial inconsistency. Then the job of evaluating consistency or inconsistency can be undertaken. As we have seen, this job requires a dialectical evaluation of an arguer's commitments in a given context of dialogue.

Once we have clearly identified the propositions in the reasoning in an argument, precise methods for evaluating the reasoning as deductively valid or invalid, or as inductively strong or weak, can be applied. However, many other important questions about the adequacy of the argument may remain which can only be answered by carefully examining the corpus of the given argument to determine the context of dialogue.

In assessing an argument used in a context of dialogue, the speech acts in the dialogue can be paired as question-reply argumentation. In this type of dialogue, the participants take turns asking and replying to questions, and this sequence provides a local context for the argument.

Another important characteristic of dialogue is that there is a sequence of moves (messages) in a certain order directed towards a global goal or issue. In argumentative dialogue, chains of arguments are linked together, and even at the local level of dialogue, the subarguments are directed towards a global issue.

Studying criticisms of relevance and fallaciousness by constructing more complicated dialogue systems to take the complexities of everyday argument into account is 'a complicated and arduous task' (Krabbe, 1992, p. 277). Fortunately, as Krabbe notes, 'There is ... a shorter way than that of trying to define a full-fledged system.' This is the method of profiles of dialogue, as described in previous chapters, in the different types of dialogue. According to Krabbe, profiles of dialogue are 'tree-shaped descriptions of sequences of dialectic moves that display the various ways a reasonable argument could proceed' (p. 277). Thus, at a more localized level, a sequence of moves can be modelled by a profile. However, as we have stressed in presenting the different types of dialogue of the new dialectic, such a profile always needs to be evaluated as being embedded in a longer, global context of dialogue.

The sequence of arguments globally moves towards a final stage or outcome of the dialogue called a goal. The goal defines a successful outcome of good dialogue. Every dialogue starts from an initial situation (initial position) and, according to rules of procedure agreed to by the participants, moves from the initial position through a sequence of moves towards the goal or outcome. Shorter sequences of rule-governed moves can, in some cases, be shown to be instances of the use of argumentation techniques. The uses of these techniques are woven through the thread of argumentation that holds a dialogue together as relevant discourse.

In this book, we have not concentrated on the task of identifying these argumentation techniques (see Walton, 1996b). But the different types of dialogue identified form a framework that allows us to judge whether these argumentation schemes are being used correctly to contribute to a communicative goal.

Another problem with identifying arguments is that it is sometimes difficult to pin down and verify what the premises are supposed to be. The *ad populum, ad baculum*, and *ad misericordiam* fallacies can take place where emotions are used to disguise the lack of good premises to support the conclusion. Equivocation can take place where ambiguity introduces too many premises so that what appears to be an argument is in fact a confusing multiplicity of arguments.

Another kind of case where there seems to be no premise but where there may be a fallacy is the case of question-asking. Question-asking seems innocent because there appear to be no affirmative propositions being advanced, and consequently no argument. But questions have presuppositions, which are propositions. And, as we saw in chapter 5, certain types of aggressive questions do have conclusions, so to speak, because they attempt to force a proposition on anyone who answers the question.

Once the argument has been identified (its premises and conclusion), the next step is to evaluate how the reasoning has been used in the argument to contribute to the goals of dialogue the participants are supposed to be engaging in. To give a general framework to show the reader how to go about this process of argument evaluation, and what to look for, we propose a four-step method of argument evaluation.

2. The Four-Step Method

This section presents a general framework, in the form of a four-step method, for evaluating whether an argument in a given case is being used reasonably or not. In the sense of the new dialectic, 'used reasonably' means contributing to the goal of the type of discourse which the argument is supposed to be a part of. This method is still very general, and needs to be supplemented in further research by an analysis of argumentation schemes and common fallacies.

Following is a five-point check-list that can be used to begin the process of identifying the argument.

STEP I: IDENTIFYING THE ARGUMENT

1. What is the conclusion? What are the premises?
2. Are there too few premises? Check for omissions of relevant premises.
3. Is it a question that needs attention? What are the presuppositions? Should the presuppositions of the question be acceptable to the respondent?
4. Is there ambiguity – too many premises? Check for equivocation. Is the conclusion unambiguously indicated?
5. Is it an enthymeme? Identify missing (unexpressed) premises.

But before the process can go very far, the roots of the local argument have begun to branch out into a larger context of argument. For example, there may be more than one conclusion, and then sequential (pragmatic) methods of argument reconstruction must be brought to bear. Thus we need to add a sixth point to our check-list.

6. What is the ultimate conclusion? Analyse the sequence of reasoning. Are there points where relevance of a line of argument are open to question?

This point has taken us into considerations of the context of dialogue, and to analyse the argument more fully, we need pragmatic methods at the global level.

STEP II: IDENTIFYING CONTEXTS OF DIALOGUE

1. What type of dialogue is it? Is it a persuasion dialogue, a quarrel, an

inquiry, a negotiation of interests, an information-seeking dialogue, a deliberation, or a mixed type of discussion?

2. What are the goals of the dialogue? How do they establish relevance?
3. Expand the analysis from point 6 of step I (above) to include the formulation of the global conclusion. What is the issue of the dialogue?
4. Have there been any dialectical shifts during the sequence of argumentation? Are they licit or illicit?
5. Is there a requirement of evidential priority? That is, do the premises have to be established as being better known (more plausible) than the conclusion?
6. What can be known about the positions (commitments) of each of the arguers involved? How have these changed significantly over the course of the dialogue?

Once the argument has been identified, then specific criticisms can be raised or evaluated. If a specific criticism has already been brought against the argument, then the criticism can be evaluated. Or, in other cases, the argument evaluator may see that a certain specific criticism of the argument would be appropriate.

Identifying the argument in the first two steps is often a difficult job. But evaluating a criticism is inherently more difficult because every argument has two sides. Thus, every criticism also tends to have two sides. In many cases, there is something to be said both in favour of and against a criticism.

The third aspect of argument analysis requires an identification of the specific segment of the argument subject to criticism. It can be a localized part of a large argument, or a globally extended sequence of argumentation. Then the next step is the assessment of the burden of proof that is required to make the argument successful in meeting its goal in the dialogue. This means identifying whether the reasoning in the argument is deductive, inductive, or a use of presumptive reasoning.

STEP III: BURDEN OF PROOF

1. What is the burden of proof? Give evidence from corpus.
2. Is it a deductive argument? Check for missing premises.
3. Is it an inductive argument? Check for inductive errors or missing premises.

The burden of proof imposes an obligation on a participant in an argument: he must give a strong enough argument to meet the burden in order for his argument to be judged successful in persuading the other participant or audience in the case of a persuasion dialogue (or otherwise to fulfil the goal of a dialogue). Burden of proof is also affected by the type of argument used in a given case. Freeman (1992) gives an excellent account of how to distinguish dialectically deductive, inductive, and other (presumptive) kinds of arguments, based on the kind of 'warrant' the argument is supposed to have.

On which side does the burden of proof fall in an argument? One general rule is the old maxim that he who asserts must prove. Generally, at the global level of argument, each participant must prove his thesis. But even at the local level, any assertion advanced by an arguer brings with it a burden of proof. The other side can challenge such an assertion, and need not accept it until the burden of proof is discharged by the first party.

4. Is it a presumptive argument? Check for missing premises in appeals to authority.
5. Are presuppositions of questions loaded or multiple? Check for unduly aggressive questioning in a dialogue.

At this point, specific criticisms can be raised or evaluated, including the following.

STEP IV: EVALUATION OF CRITICISMS

1. Arguments against the person
2. Questionable use of emotional appeals
3. Question-asking or answering criticisms
4. Relevance
5. Circular arguments
6. Appeals to authority
7. Loaded definitions or terms
8. Equivocation
9. Slippery-slope problems
10. Deductive errors
11. Inductive errors
12. Questionable causal arguments

This organization of a four-step method of analysis is based on the view that often we are confronted with a particular argument at the local level which first needs to be identified. Then we might proceed through the second and third steps to the fourth step of considering the global context of dialogue. However, the method is not meant to be applied in a purely mechanical sequence. In some cases, it might be better to start at the fourth step in order to get a sense of perspective. If we are confronted with a longer sequence of argumentation, say, a whole article or even a book-length argument, our initial job may be to work at the fourth step. The problem here may be that the corpus is so large that we need to pare down the details and try to grasp the main thrust, the most important line of argument to concentrate on.

In using this four-step method, a critic of argument has to use his judgment in ordering the sequence of steps appropriate for the analysis of the particular case. Yet the four-step method does provide a general perspective that can be used to check off the various considerations that might be overlooked in judging how an argument has been used in a context of dialogue.

3. Evaluating Dialectical Relevance

One of the difficulties of teaching formal logic in the past has been our inability to define a concept of relevance that is useful and can be applied to the evaluation of argumentation in everyday cases of conversational exchanges. Relevance logic and other formalistic kinds of criteria have been devised, but these formalistic criteria have not been very useful in helping us evaluate fallacies and other kinds of failures of relevance that are important when we criticize an argument for being faulty on grounds of irrelevance (see Walton, 1982).

The problem can be posed by a classic case from Copi (1982, p. 110). A legislator rises to speak in favour of a particular proposal for housing legislation in a legislative debate, but his whole argument is directed towards the conclusion that all the people should have decent housing. Supposedly, the fault of relevance in this case is that nobody in the legislature disagrees with the conclusion that all the people should have decent housing. It's just that this is not a very useful premise to prove that the proposal under consideration is a good one, one that ought to be voted for and that is better than any competing proposals which might come along. But the problem is that the legislator's argument that all the people should have decent housing is relevant to the proposal for housing legislation under consideration. It is topically relevant in the sense that both considerations are about the question of housing. However, we can also say that the legislator's argument is not materially relevant in the sense that it presents enough evidence or any evidence of the right kind that would change anybody's mind in the legislative debate. So here we have to look at relevance from a dialectical point of view. Presumably, the legislators are engaging in a deliberation on whether they should vote for this bill, and whether this bill is a practical solution to the housing problem, one that would be an intelligent course of action in the given situation. But in this context of deliberation, the legislator's argument that all the people should have decent housing is not dialectically relevant, in a way that is comparable to the argument used in the Northumberland Strait debate in case 7.2. It is not an argument that bears on, or could be used to resolve, the issue of the deliberation in the debate one way or the other. In this pragmatic and dialectical sense, then, it is not a materially relevant argument. To evaluate a case like this, we have to look at the goal of the housing legislation, and then evaluate the legislator's argument in relation to the sequence of practical reasoning that would be useful in this type of deliberation to achieve the goal. We are not given very much evidence from the context of dialogue by Copi in this case, but from the information we are given, it seems that the legislator is simply engaging in pettifoggery, in the sense that his speech about all people needing decent housing is simply a digression or diversion. It is meant to have some popular effect on the voters, but is not a serious material contribution to the deliberation, which is the type of dialogue he should be engaging in.

The problem with irrelevance of argumentation in a deliberative type of dialogue is not that it is inherently harmful in what it does, but that it wastes time that could be devoted to other arguments that thoroughly explore both sides of the issue. In a successful deliberation, the strongest arguments for both sides should be presented and their merits weighed and evaluated by the participants. However, if the arguments are dialectically irrelevant, if they go off on tangents and digressions and make points that are not useful in the deliberation, then this weakness can undermine the goal of the deliberation, which is to arrive at an intelligent decision on what to do based on strong evidence showing that one course of action is more prudent than another possible course of action which is also being considered.

The new dialectic gives us a way of evaluating dialectical relevance, and many other faults and failures of argumentation that relate to relevance, a way that is not purely a function of the logical form of a particular argument – that is, a localized set of premises and a conclusion. Instead, the focus is on the dialectical context in which the argument has been used in a given case, and the presumption is that the argument has been used for some purpose, as a means of fulfilling some goal of a type of dialogue or a conversational exchange that the two parties are engaged in. The approach of the new dialectic, then, is based on Grice's insight that, underlying any argument, there are conversational postulates indicating what is a collaborative move in a conversational exchange at any particular stage of that conversation between the two parties. One of Grice's maxims is 'be relevant,' but he does not tell us exactly what constitutes success or failure in conforming to this maxim in a given case (1975, p. 68). The problem with Grice's proposal is that he does not make it specific enough as a method that can be applied to actual cases of conversational argument by indicating the different types of dialogue or conversational exchanges that people generally engage in, in common examples of argumentation. There are different types of conversational exchanges, and there can be shifts from one type of dialogue to another during a sequence of argumentation. In order to evaluate whether an argument in a particular case is relevant or irrelevant, reasonable or fallacious, and so forth, it is necessary to determine whether the argument has been put forward in a deliberation, for example, as opposed to a negotiation or persuasion dialogue or other type of dialogue. For the goals and the rules for each type of dialogue are quite different.

4. Evaluating a Case for Relevance

In the new dialectic, the question of whether an argument is dialectically relevant in a given case needs to take six kinds of factors into account. The first factor is the type of dialogue. If it is a critical discussion, then the argument needs to be judged as relevant or not in relation to the issue of the critical discussion. However, an argument that is relevant in a critical discussion might not be relevant in another type of dialogue, for example, in a negotiation or an inquiry.

The second factor is the stage the dialogue is in. An argument or other kind of move, like a question, that was relevant at one stage of the dialogue may not be relevant at a later or earlier stage.

The third factor is the goal of the dialogue. Relevance is generally determined by the goal of the type of dialogue in question. If the type of dialogue is supposed to be that of a critical discussion, then it is supposed to resolve a conflict of opinions between two parties. This conflict is the issue of the discussion, and an argument or other move in a case will be relevant insofar as it materially bears on this issue – that is, insofar as it can be used to advance the line of argument on one side or the other of this issue.

The fourth factor is the type of argument that is involved. In Walton (1996b), many different types of arguments (or forms of argument), other than the traditional inductive and deductive types, are defined. These types of arguments are said to be presumptive in the sense that their function is to affect a balance of considerations in a dialogue exchange of argumentation between two parties. For example, if an argument takes the form of an appeal to expert opinion, then whether that argument is relevant or not will depend on the argumentation scheme for the argument from expert opinion. This argumentation scheme has several distinctive premises. One postulates that the speaker is citing some person or source that is said to be authoritative in a given field or domain of knowledge, and the second premise says that the proposition being advocated as true falls within this domain. So whether or not an argument is relevant in a given case will depend on that argumentation scheme. And if a reply to an argument is to be judged relevant or irrelevant in a given case, then that judgment will depend on the types of critical questions that are appropriate for that argumentation scheme. In Walton (1996b), sets of critical questions for each of these various argumentation schemes are identified. The critical questions define the appropriate kinds of replies for that argumentation scheme as used at some point during the sequence of argumentation in a type of dialogue.

The fifth factor is the prior sequence of argumentation in the given case. Our judgment about whether an argument is relevant or not in a given case depends on what sequence of argumentation has gone before in the dialogue. Thus, in a given case, if there is textual evidence of the prior sequence of argumentation indicating, for example, the commitments of an arguer, this text will be an important source of evidence of relevance or irrelevance in evaluating the case.

The sixth factor is the institutional or social setting of the particular case which imposes particular constraints or rules on what is acceptable in a conversation. For example, if the argument is part of a legal trial, then there will be specific legal rules that will define what is considered relevant in that particular case. Or if an argument is part of a political debate in a legislature, then there will be rules of procedure which the Speaker of the House is supposed to enforce, and these rules of procedure will affect, at least from the point of view of the legislative debate, whether a particular argument is considered relevant. So from the point of view of the new dialectic, it is somewhat debatable the extent to which we should take these special contexts and social settings and disciplines into account in evaluating arguments. It is possible, for example, that we might evaluate a debate in a legislature from the point of view of a deliberation, without worrying too much about the procedural rules of legislative debate. On the other hand, we can't ignore these social or institutional rules in some cases, because they can have an important effect on whether a line of argument is appropriate or relevant in that particular situation. So this sixth kind of evidence is a factor that needs to be taken into account to some extent, in at least some cases of the kinds of arguments that are typically evaluated in logic textbooks.

Thus when we evaluate an argument with respect to whether it is dialectically relevant or not, or whether it commits certain informal fallacies or not, using these six sources of evidence, we are evaluating it from the communicative, pragmatic, and dialectical point of view of the new dialectic. Evaluating it from this point of view, the argumentation is seen as an organized sequence of connected moves that are (generally) questions and replies taking place in a dialogue exchange between two parties. Adopting this communicative framework of evaluation means that we do not see an argument simply as a localized set of premises and a single conclusion and that we do not evaluate it in relation to some appropriate logical form, like *modus ponens*. Instead, we are evaluating the argument dynamically as a contribution to a longer sequence of argumentation which is aiming towards some goal that is appropriate for a type of dialogue that the two participants are engaging in. Whether the argument is correct or not, and whether it is relevant or not, will depend not only on what type of dialogue the participants are supposed to be engaged in, but also on what particular stage and move of the dialogue this particular argument is supposed to be made at.

When applying these different types of dialogue to particular cases as normative frameworks for evaluating argumentation, it is important to be aware of the dialectical shifts, or changes from one type of dialogue to another, that can occur during the same sequence of argumentation. For example, the use of *ad hominem* argumentation is one sign that there could be a shift from a persuasion type of dialogue to a quarrelling type of dialogue, and it may be very important for someone who is evaluating the argument to be aware of the existence of such a shift. An interesting type of case of a deceptive shift of this type (examined in chapter 8) is the so-called infomercial, which has the format and appearance of news presentation or talk show. But as the argumentation goes on, it becomes clear that it is really a commercial advertisement, a form of commercial speech to sell a particular product (Cooper, 1993). The tricky dialectical aspect of these infomercials is that they tend to exploit the viewer's initial expectation that he is watching some conventionally recognizable type of dialogue, like a news or talk show that is presenting information, or that has a reporting or interviewing format. But it becomes clear, over the sequence of argumentation, that the program is really an advertisement. Thus, the infomercial is specifically designed to exploit this deceptive shift from the one type of dialogue to the other. Some infomercials, as we saw in chapter 8, have all the trappings of a news show, like expert panelists, breaks for commercials, closing credits, and so forth.

In evaluating particular cases for relevance, an assessment should be based on the kind of conversation that the participants were originally supposed to be engaged in. Each of these types of a dialogue has a goal, and an argument that is used in the context of one of these types of dialogue can be evaluated as correct or incorrect insofar as it contributes to the goal of the dialogue using the appropriate types of arguments. Each type of dialogue has four stages, and it is important to realize that any argument or move in a dialogue needs to be evaluated in relation to the stage of the dialogue, as well as the type of dialogue in which it is being used. The four stages are the opening stage, confrontation stage, argumentation stage, and the concluding stage. These terms are self-explanatory, but it should be noted that the issue or problem that the dialogue is supposed to resolve or address is stated at the confrontation stage, and that the main stage, where the arguments on both sides are presented, is the argumentation stage.

5. Fallacies, Blunders, and Errors

It is important to distinguish between the meaning we are giving to the term 'fallacy' in the new dialectic and the meaning the term has traditionally had in logic textbooks. In the new sense, a fallacy is a type of move in dialogue or argumentation sequence that often goes wrong or is used wrongly in a tricky, deceptive way in a dialogue exchange. In the traditional sense, a fallacy is a particular argument in a given case that we, as critics, think is wrong because it is an instance of a particular type of inference or argument.[1] In the traditional sense, a fallacy is a general type of argument pattern or form that is presumed to be generically wrong. In the new dialectical sense, a fallacy is a particular instance of an argument that is, in principle, a legitimate kind of argument, but that has been used wrongly in a particular case, according to the normative standards of dialogue appropriate for that case.

Overlooking this distinction can be problematic because the type of argument technique 'baptized' as the 'fallacy' can be used correctly in a particular case. To tell whether or not an argument is fallacious in a particular case requires judgment, putting a burden of proof on the would-be critic to cite specific details of the text of discourse as evidence to back up his charge.

Johnson (1987) has rightly characterized fallacies in the first sense as general types of argumentation techniques that are worth 'baptizing' and watching out for because they are dangerous, that is, relatively powerful and commonly used. The practical reason for studying fallacies is to become aware of and analyse standard techniques that can be used both effectively and deceptively in argumentation in order to improve our capacity to deal with them constructively. It is a matter of improving and refining existing critical skills of argumentation.

It is important to distinguish between fallacies and other less serious kinds of errors and faults of argument. A fallacy is a serious, underlying, systematic type of error that is so bad – often because it involves the use of a sophistical tactic to unfairly get the best of a partner in dialogue – that it calls for strong refutation as an argument malpractice.[2] When a proponent of an argument is accused of committing a fallacy, there is a strong weight of presumption against him which requires a vigorous response. There is also a burden of proof placed on the critic to back up her charge that a fallacy has been committed with solid evidence from the text and context of discourse.

Less serious errors of good argument practice are blunders and weak or flawed arguments. A violation of a rule of reasonable dialogue can be a blunder rather than a fallacy. For example, a circular sequence of reasoning can be confusing, or even violate a rule of the type of dialogue it was advanced in, yet it might not be a *petitio principii* fallacy. The blunder might be just a weak or inept argument from the proponent, and not a sophistical tactic or tricky argument that poses a danger to the respondent's side of the dialogue (see Walton and Batten, 1984). Many blunders in argumentation are violations of rules of dialogue, which amount to superficial misdemeanours or misunderstandings of one sort or another rather than systematic and serious errors or sophistical tactics that should be classified as fallacies. In such cases, we can have an incorrect (or poorly substantiated) argument that is not a fallacy.

According to van Eemeren and Grootendorst, all violations of the rules of a critical discussion are incorrect moves, and these incorrect moves 'correspond roughly to the various kinds of defects traditionally referred to as *fallacies*' (1987, p. 284). A fallacy, for van Eemeren and Grootendorst, is defined as a violation of a rule of critical discussion, a type of dialogue where the goal is to resolve a conflict of opinions. For example, their first rule is: 'Parties must not prevent each other from advancing or casting doubt on standpoints' (p. 284). (This earlier version should be compared with the later version cited in chapter 2.) Both *argumentum ad baculum* (putting pressure on an opponent) and *argumentum ad hominem* (using personal attack on an opponent) are said to be fallacies that correspond to violations of this rule of critical discussion. But is violating the rule equivalent to, or the same as, committing one of these fallacies? It seems not, because there is one rule but two quite distinctively different fallacies cited as violations of the rule. Indeed, virtually any of the major informal fallacies could be cited, in some case or other, as an argument technique used in a such a way that it violates this rule.

It was a great advance and a refreshing break with tradition to link fallacies with violations of rules of reasonable dialogue. But, unfortunately, there is no simple one-to-one correspondence between individual fallacies and violations of rules of dialogue. Violating a rule of reasonable dialogue is a necessary, but not a sufficient, condition for calling a move in argumentation a fallacy. Moreover, there are other kinds of dialogue than the critical discussion, like negotiation and information-seeking types of dialogue, that are context of dialogue in which fallacies are committed. Sometimes also the dialectical shift from one type of dialogue to another is important to recognizing and evaluating an argument as fallacious.

Despite these criticisms of van Eemeren and Grootendorst's classification or theory of fallacies, their pragma-dialectical approach has been enormously valuable and beneficial in putting proper stress on the careful and systematic interpretation and analysis of the given text of discourse in a particular case. Their dialectical approach of viewing the evaluation of fallacies as a problem of applying normative models of dialogue to given cases of a text of discourse has helped move the field of fallacy study forward from where Hamblin left it.

The framework of question-answer dialogue advanced by Hintikka (1981) involves formal dialectical models with precise rules for the asking and answering of questions. Rescher (1976; 1977) proposes models of dialogue using presumptive inferences which shift back and forth on the basis of burden of proof. The approach of van Eemeren and Grootendorst is less formalistic and more general, but focuses on one particular type of reasoned question-reply dialogue, the critical discussion. Hamblin (1970), Barth and Krabbe (1982), and Walton (1984) construct formal systems of dialogue with the intention of modelling fallacies as breaches of the formal rules that constitute a particular structure of interactive reasoning.

My current impression from interacting with other researchers in argumentation is that they are willing to accept this working presupposition that many of the major informal fallacies are breaches of rules of reasonable dialogue. Research now needs to go beyond this stage in order to pinpoint how each of the individual fallacies functions precisely as an important kind of violation of one or more rules in different cases. But to do this, the concept of fallacy needs to be enriched even further, to see how each fallacy functions as an effective technique of unfairly gaining a victory in argumentative dialogue by exploiting concealed and deceptive shifts from one type of dialogue to another.

Fallacies are best seen as good arguments that have been misused, or used badly or inappropriately, in a context of dialogue. Many of the classical examples of fallacies cited by the traditional logic textbooks are arguments that are reasonable when interpreted as defeasible arguments meant to shift a burden of presumption in a dialogue.[3] Often these arguments are weak and, therefore, open to critical questioning and qualifications, but they are basically arguments that do make some legitimate contribution to the argumentation sequence of a dialogue. But they are not fallacies in the sense of being vitiating errors or arguments that can be strongly refuted as worthless or completely wrong.

A fallacy is a misuse or misexecution of an argumentation technique and, as such, it obstructs the legitimate goals of dialogue in the given argument. It is not just a blunder, or an incidental violation of a rule of reasonable dialogue. Rather, it is a use of argument that is at odds with the context of dialogue, an underlying systematic error or a tricky, deceptive technique that is used to get the best of a partner in dialogue unfairly – often by shifting to another type of dialogue altogether.

The study of fallacies has a normative element, a tactical element, and a practical element. The normative element requires that a fallacy be understood as an incorrect argument, a serious, systematic violation of a rule of dialogue. The tactical element of fallacy is its use as a sequence of moves in a smooth pattern as a technique of argumentation. The practical element stresses that the fallacy is an effective device of argument, one we need to be warned about encountering in everyday argumentation. The fallacy is a deceptive use of argumentation that takes unfair advantage of a speech partner in a verbal exchange where two parties reason together. It is an argument that is not what it seems to be on the surface. The explanation for this aspect of its deceptiveness lies in the concept of a dialectical shift.

6. Fallacies and Dialectical Shifts

Each of the major fallacies briefly outlined in chapter 1 is a powerful tactic, a persuasive argument that is commonly used in argumentation in everyday reasoning of all kinds. The fact that such arguments are so persuasive is partly a function of their being reasonable arguments in many cases. What makes them go wrong? Certain types of fallacies have been classified primarily as fallacies of relevance, and these are the ones we will focus on (see Walton, 1992c; 1995).

Whether an *ad hominem* argument is reasonable or fallacious in a particular case depends on the context of dialogue. An attorney's allegations about the bad moral character of a witness he is cross-examining in court can be a reasonable kind of *ad hominem* argumentation. But in a scientific inquiry, criticizing a scientific argument by attacking the moral character of the scientist could be inappropriate and fallacious.

The *ad hominem* argument is well suited to the goal of the quarrel, which is to air personal grievances by attacking the moral character of an opponent. The *ad hominem* can be a reasonable argument in a critical discussion, but it often goes wrong by causing the argumentation to shift into a quarrel, as the exchange becomes more heated and personal. In such a case, the *ad hominem* fallacy occurs because the argument was originally supposed to be a critical discussion, and quarrelling is a very poor and inefficient way of carrying out the goals of a critical discussion, which are sometimes blocked altogether.

The relationship between the *argumentum ad hominem* and the quarrel is one of typical association rather than a necessary or inherent connection. One of the best clues or signs of the shift from the critical discussion to the quarrel is the *ad hominem* argument. In the reverse direction, the *ad hominem* argument can often be best explained, analysed, or evaluated as an argumentation tactic that is effective in getting the best of an opponent in argument by revealing the underlying shift to the quarrel.

If we define a fallacy as a violation of a rule of critical discussion (van Eemeren and Grootendorst, 1984), then the personal attack in the Lorenzo case (see chapter 8) is not an *ad hominem* fallacy, or any other sort of fallacy. Can an argument that shifts from a negotiation dialogue to a quarrel be a case of the fallacy of *ad hominem*? This is an interesting question. In our analysis, an argument that takes place in the context of a dialectical shift from a negotiation dialogue to a quarrel can definitely be said to be an instance of the *ad hominem* fallacy, precisely on these grounds. But not everyone would agree.

When the bias type of *ad hominem* attack is used in a critical discussion, the allegation is that the respondent has illicitly and covertly shifted to a negotiation dialogue, that she is only making a pretence of looking at both sides of the issue with an open mind towards the evidence, and that from the outset she intended to push her own side for personal gain. For example, suppose that in a critical discussion on the issue of acid rain, one party accuses another of being a major stockholder in a coal company.[4] The *ad hominem* attack alleges that her mind was made up, that she never really (honestly) entered into the critical discussion at all. Generally, with this type of *ad hominem* argument, an alleged shift from one context of dialogue to another is involved.

The bias type of *ad hominem* argument is not necessarily fallacious. It depends on how it is used in relation to the type of dialogue the participants are supposed to be engaged in. For example, if the participant in the acid rain discussion had concealed her relationship with the coal company, and posed as a scientific observer who was objectively looking at the evidence on both sides of the issue, the other party's revelation of the relationship could be a reasonable allegation of bias.

Another fallacy involving dialectical shifts is the *ad baculum*. A negotiation type of dialogue typically involves threats and appeals to force or sanctions. However, if the context is supposed to be that of a critical discussion, the same kind of argumentation that was appropriate in the negotiation context then becomes fallacious. A fair consideration of the arguments on both sides of an issue is very important in a critical discussion. In this context, the use of the *ad baculum* argument is always highly suspicious and tends to be at odds with the discussion, because it is a way of closing off the free expression of a participant's point of view.

Generally, threats and appeals to force or fear violate the rules of a critical discussion because this is an open type of dialogue in which participants are obliged to give each other a fair chance to raise questions or bring forth arguments. Too often, such appeals or threats are ways of bringing pressure to bear in a way that is meant to choke off arguments or inhibit free discussion of an issue. Much depends, however, on how the *argumentum ad baculum* is defined. Must it be a threat? Or are appeals to fear (scaremongering) that are not threats also included?

The most subtle and effective type of *ad baculum* argument is the indirect type, which is overtly a warning and covertly a threat, for example, 'My advice is for you not to do that, or it could be very dangerous for you and your family – the men in my union are hard to restrain, and they are vicious brutes when you do something they don't like.' In a given case, this speech act could be a threat, and it would be very important for the respondent's survival for him to recognize and interpret it correctly. The key to evaluating whether such cases are fallacious or nonfallacious is to analyse the underlying dialectical shift correctly. A warning might be legitimate in negotiation dialogue, for example, but if there is an underlying, covert threat, the *ad baculum* argument could be a contravention of the rules of dialogue, and could rightly be judged fallacious.

In other cases, the dialectical inappropriateness of the *ad baculum* argument may be obvious to everybody, but it does not matter. For example, suppose we are having a critical discussion on some issue and you make a threat that I know is a credible one, in the sense that I know you are in a position to carry it out effectively. I will be affected by the action you threaten to take, and I am likely to comply by carrying out the course of action you are proposing. Even though I realize that the argument (threat) is irrelevant in a critical discussion, I may, nevertheless, nominally accept the conclusion you are advocating in the critical discussion because of some threat you have made (Woods, 1987). Even though I see that your threat is irrelevant in the context of the critical discussion, nevertheless, the threat is effective if it causes me to act in a certain way or to agree, or to appear to agree, with the view you are arguing for. Here, the *ad baculum* works because there is a shift from the critical discussion to a deliberation type of dialogue; you are, in effect, arguing that a particular conclusion would be prudent for me because if I don't carry out this action, then you will ensure that something bad happens to me.

The *argumentum ad verecundiam* is usually treated as a fallacy, but many appeals to expert opinion in argumentation are quite reasonable as arguments, provided the context of dialogue is appropriate. (See the analysis of Hitchcock, 1992, pp. 264–5, and the range of different kinds of cases evaluated in Walton, 1989a, chapter 7.) Generally, with *ad vere-*

cundiam argumentation there are four participants and three contexts of
dialogue involved – in other words, it is a mixed dialogue situation. For
example, two primary participants are engaged in a critical discussion,
and the first party accuses the other of not paying sufficient attention to
an expert opinion that he has brought forward to support his line of
argument. What is presupposed here is that a secondary dialogue
exchange has taken place between the first party and some third party –
an expert source who has been consulted by the first party. The first
party is alleging that his opponent in the critical discussion has not been
properly respectful of the expert authority, that the opponent is immod-
estly saying, in effect, that he 'knows better' than the expert. The first
party is therefore appealing to a fourth-party audience, arguing that
they should not take the arguments of this opponent seriously since he
is so immodest and unwise to think that he knows better than the
experts. Thus, the third context of dialogue is the dialogue between
some fourth-party wider audience and the two original participants
who are in a contest to persuade this audience.

The expert consultation dialogue can be embedded in the critical discussion in a way that positively supports the goals of the critical discussion. In the critical discussion on the issue of whether nuclear reactors
are good or bad, for example, the discussion might not have been so
intelligent and revealing without input from expert opinions included
in embedded subdialogues.

The fallacy of many questions is also very sensitive to contexts of dialogue. The question 'Have you stopped cheating on your income taxes?'
would be nonfallacious if posed by a cross-examining attorney to a person who previously admitted that she had cheated on her income tax in
the past. In another context, asking this question would be rightly
judged fallacious. Whether it is fallacious or not depends on the context
of dialogue in a particular case, as evaluated by the profile of dialogue
used in chapter 5. In particular, it depends on the prior commitments of
the respondent in the prior sequence of the dialogue in the given case, as
judged by comparing the profile of dialogue to the sequence of dialogue
exchanges in the actual case.

The distinction between the fallacy of begging the question and the
nonfallacious use of circular argumentation also depends very much on
the context of dialogue. In an inquiry there is always a requirement of
evidential priority, which means that the premises must be better established than the conclusion that is to be proved from them. In this context, the use of circular argumentation goes strongly against the goals of

the dialogue. The inquiry is supposed to move forward from firmly established premises, and not circle back to stages already covered. In a different context, like that of a negotiation or a critical discussion, however, a circular argument could be evidence of confusion or a blunder. In some cases, therefore, a critic would not be justified in calling it a fallacy.

All the criticisms of argument that are identified with traditional fallacies depend on requirements that are highly sensitive to a context of dialogue. The criticism that an argument begs the question, in particular, depends on the requirement of evidential priority. While that requirement may or may not be present in a persuasion dialogue, it is mandatory in an inquiry. To see whether the requirement is present in any particular argument, not only must the critic look at the evidence from the text, but he must also have some grasp of the type of dialogue that is involved.

7. Fallacies Reconceptualized in the New Dialectic

As a method, the new dialectic shows how traditional fallacies have been superficially and wrongly portrayed in the standard logic textbooks. Because they are all addressed to a specific subject, these powerful tactics of persuasion have been treated with considerable mistrust and suspicion, and have traditionally been labelled 'fallacies' or 'sophistical refutations.' Though these suspicions are sometimes fully justified, it is a central thesis of this book that these kinds of arguments are in many cases useful, appropriate, and correct methods of arguing from premises based on the assent of participants in a reasonable discussion. Although they all have a subjective aspect, and should give way to scientific evidence drawn from 'objective facts' when it is available, these three kinds of argument have an important place when objective evidence is insufficient to resolve a disputed issue. In these cases, they can prepare the way for the open-minded reception of objective evidence, when it becomes available, by clearing away fallacies, biases, and weak arguments.

To understand these three kinds of argumentation, we have to become familiar with their use as techniques of argument that are commonly brought to bear as tactics to gain assent or as devices to win an argument when reasoning with others. These three argument techniques share four distinctive features: they are explicitly directed to the commitment of a partner in dialogue; they take advantage of limitations of that partner's knowledge; they are used as devices to swing the weight of presumption to one side of an argument on a controversial issue where conclusive evidence is hard to come by; and they contrast with arguments and proofs drawn from probability or external experimental evidence drawn from 'the nature of things themselves' (as Locke puts it). All three methods of argument are essentially dialectical, in that they are directed towards reasoning with another person in an exchange of information in dialogue by suiting the argument of one party to the special position, knowledge base, or state of opinions of the other party.

There are three especially important themes that link *argumentum ad hominem*, *argumentum ad verecundiam*, and *argumentum ad ignorantiam*. First, all three kinds of argumentation characteristically come into prominence in situations of incomplete knowledge where, for one reason or another, access to external facts that would settle a conflict of opinion is lacking. Second, all three kinds of argumentation become decisive and necessary ways of arriving at a conclusion where there is a need to take a position, to act, or to make a decision, despite constraints that make objective knowledge of the issue uncertain. And third, all three kinds of argumentation use presumption to arrive at a provisional conclusion by deploying existing presumptions in a discussion or dialogue format.

The first of this trio is the argument based on the use of expert opinion to make a point. With the advent of expert systems, we have come to accept systematized extraction of expertise from human experts as a highly useful technology.[5] These practices have produced a new climate of respect for the use of expert advice as a legitimate kind of reasoning. However, the appeal to authority in argument (usually the authority of expertise), which is often identified with the *argumentum ad verecundiam*, is classified as a fallacy by logic textbooks. This traditional attitude, which arose out of the distrust of appeals to authority that was characteristic of the Enlightenment and the rise of scientific method, took it for granted that authority-based argumentation should not be counted as serious evidence for a conclusion. It became an accepted presumption that authority-based argumentation was subjective and, hence, too prone to bias, error, and fallacy to contribute to knowledge in an inquiry.

The second type of argument is directed towards the person of the dialogue partner. This can take the various forms cited in chapter 1. The first subtype uses the character of the other party as its premise; this is the so-called abusive or direct *ad hominem* argument. As we have seen, it can be a reasonable type of argument in the cross-examination of the testimony of a witness in court.

Another subspecies of *ad hominem* argument is the circumstantial variety. Characteristic of this type of argument is the use of an opponent's concessions in dialogue as an instrument of his defeat by turning them back against his own argument. This tactic exploits an arguer's previous declarations, actions, or personal circumstances that seem to run contrary to his line of argument, and thereby, weaken his case by suggesting that his personal advocacy of his own argument is somehow questionable or insincere. In some cases, this device of personal attack appears to be a kind of negative variant of the *ad verecundiam*. The suggestion that an opponent in argument is a liar or hypocrite undermines his credibility as a reliable source of opinions.

The third technique involves one party presenting his own conclusion in an argument as a presumption that immediately requires the other party's assent, since the other party has not presented (sufficient) evidence to refute this conclusion. Known as the argument from ignorance (*argumentum ad ignorantiam*), this tactic argues that if the opponent in a dispute lacks the knowledge to prove that a proposition is false, then he should, for the sake of argument, accept that proposition as a presumption that is true.

This third technique has also traditionally been held to be a fallacy, on the assumption that it is generally an error to draw a conclusion on the basis of ignorance. For failure to prove the negation of a proposition does not necessarily provide positive proof that the proposition is true. A participant's failure to prove, in some cases, might only demonstrate his ignorance.

On the other hand, we often have to decide on a course of action, even where knowledge and proof are lacking. In such cases, intelligent guesswork and plausible presumption might be better ways of deciding what to do than deciding on whim, for example, or by flipping a coin. When we have to rely on presumptive reasoning alone, in the absence of definite or conclusive knowledge, being guided by the stronger presumption is an intelligent way of reasoning. In such cases, failure to disprove a proposition by any available basis of reasoning for refuting it might be a good reason to accept the proposition, tentatively, as a basis for proceeding.[6] Thus, although the *argumentum ad ignorantiam* has traditionally been held to be a logical fallacy, there are some grounds for thinking that it is a reasonable kind of argument for drawing a tentative conclusion to assent to an opinion in a situation characterized by the absence of conclusive knowledge for acceptance or rejection.

What can be said about all three kinds of argument is that they are less than perfect, even though they are widely used in the practices of persuasion in discussions of many kinds. And although they are prone to exploitation, error, and abuse, they also have legitimate and powerful uses in the practical politics of reasoning with another participant in dialogue on controversial issues where the lack of definite, objective, or conclusive knowledge leaves room for debate. Although all three kinds of techniques are directed to the other person's knowledge-base or position in an argument and, therefore, are successful or not depending on his concessions on an issue, they do have a legitimate function in guiding an arguer to press ahead with or to rebut presumptions on an issue of contention in response to previous moves in the dialogue. And they also have a legitimate dialectical function as techniques of argumentation that can be used to reasonably shift presumption in order to persuade another party in a dialogue, or to contribute to goals of other types of dialogue. The legitimacy of all three kinds of argument is recognized in legal principles of evidence, where expert testimony is accepted as a kind of evidence, where burden of proof requires a presumption of innocence and proof of guilt is not 'beyond reasonable doubt,' and where evidence of character and previous concessions or actions can be used in cross-examining a witness.

We have seen how all three of these assent-producing techniques are powerful and inherently interesting as tactics of persuasion, and how they have legitimate uses in other reasoned contexts of dialogue. We have also seen how we can be deceived by these techniques in some cases when a dialectical shift occurs. In such a case, the argument seems to be reasonable because its use is appropriate in the particular type of dialogue that appears to be present in a given case. But if the participants are really supposed to be engaged in another type of dialogue, a fallacy may occur. Even more important, we have put forward clear procedural guidelines that enable a participant in argument, or a critic of an argument, to distinguish between the fallacious and the legitimate instances of their use in a given case.

Thus, Locke's brief but fascinating description of the *ad ignorantiam, ad hominem*, and *ad verecundiam* types of arguments – in chapter 14 of his *Essay Concerning Human Understanding* – as acceptance-based arguments that are not necessarily fallacious can be viewed as an inherently dialectical account, in the sense of the new dialectic. It is the dialectical nature of Locke's account of these arguments that reveals them so clearly and perspicuously when viewed in light of the new dialectic. But this is also undoubtedly what made them so obscure to the generations of commentators who turned them into the standard treatment of fallacies. By contrasting these three types of argument with the type of argument he called *ad judicium*, Locke opened the way to distinguishing between the persuasion dialogue and the inquiry. And he also put his finger on the purpose of persuasion dialogue as a use of arguments that 'dispose ... me for the reception of truth,' even though (unlike those in the inquiry) they do not 'help me ... to the reception of truth.'

8. Dialectical Advice for Using These Arguments

The *ad hominem, ad verecundiam,* and *ad ignorantiam* are closely related to each other because, as Locke noted, they all veer towards the fallacious or objectionable in argumentative dialogue, when one party uses one of these techniques to press ahead too aggressively in an attempt to prevail by forcing the other party into silence. But they are closely related to each other in additional ways. In ethotic argumentation, the *ad hominem* can overlap, in some cases, with the *ad verecundiam.* And all three types of argumentation techniques are knowledge-based tactics that exploit the knowledge (or ignorance) of another party in a communicative dialogue situation.

But there is an even more fundamental relationship. As fallacies, both the *ad hominem* and *ad verecundiam* can be viewed as subspecies of the type of argumentation technique that is characteristic of the *ad ignorantiam.* Both the former types of techniques are methods of shifting the burden of proof as one party tries to close off a dialogue in his favour by exploiting his opponent's relative ignorance – ignorance that stems from the lack of decisive, objective evidence. I have examined this relationship in *Informal Logic* [1989a, p. 165] where the basic *ad hominem* fallacy was recognized as being fundamentally a species of *ad ignorantiam* fallacy, and in *Informal Fallacies* [1987, p. 200] where the *ad vercundiam* was recognized as an argument from ignorance which exploits a situation where objective (direct, scientific) evidence to resolve a controversy is lacking.

The *argumentum ad ignorantiam* is, therefore, fundamentally important to the study of reasoned dialogue not only because it underlies the structure of both the *ad hominem* and the *ad verecundiam,* but also because it is an expression of the concept of burden of proof in argumentative dialogue. All plausible argumentation that is expressed in dialogue on controversial subjects (where existing knowledge does not determine the issue) is basically argumentation from ignorance. What we are underlining here is simply that much argumentation in everyday conversations is plausible reasoning, based on a presumption of uncertainty, where there is a lack of existing evidence sufficient for closure of dialogue. The conclusion of this type of reasoning, therefore, character-istically has the status of a presumption that is determined by the burden of proof appropriate for the given context of dialogue.

The lesson that applies to all three kinds of argumentation – the *ad hominem, ad verecundiam,* and *ad ignorantiam* – is that the context of dia-logue has to be right in order for the argument to be effective. Other-wise, it can turn out to be unconvincing, or even demonstrably fal-lacious in the worst cases. All three of these kinds of argumentation gen-erally tend to be appropriate and useful in cases of dialogue where knowledge is incomplete within a practical framework of discussion. By contrast, in the context of a scientific inquiry where plenty of experimen-tal or mathematical evidence is relevant and facts can be definitely established, these subjective kinds of argumentation can be clearly irrel-evant. For example, in a discussion about the verification of a scientific hypothesis in nuclear physics, attacking the character of the scientist who advanced the hypothesis amounts to an irrelevant and fallacious *ad hominem* argument.

The *argumentum ad ignorantiam* expresses the concept of burden of proof in a situation of incomplete knowledge, and so it is perfectly appropriate in this type of situation. But it becomes clearly less appro-priate where the standards of success of an argument in a context of dia-logue require well-established knowledge to back up a claim. Thus, in politics or discussions of moral values, where empirical facts are not decisive in settling a dispute, the *ad ignorantiam* is a powerful technique of argumentation, often appropriately employed with great success. Shifting the burden of proof in these cases is one of the most potent and legitimate techniques for attacking one point of view or defending the other side of an argument.

Similarly, in a persuasion dialogue where scientific knowledge is rele-vant but scientific facts are not directly accessible within the practical constraints of the discussion – for example, in a panel discussion of the safety of nuclear reactors as a source of power – the *ad verecundiam* can be an all-powerful method of argumentation. Indeed, the whole argu-ment can rightly hinge on how to interpret and judge the opinions of experts in domains of knowledge relevant to the subject of the dispute.

Thus, the first piece of practical advice is to use any of these three kinds of argument – and to defend against them – only where the con-text of dialogue is appropriate for their effective use. And the corollary advice is to forbear from using them where the context of dialogue is not right. A second corollary piece of advice is to strongly attack an *ad hominem*, *ad ignorantiam*, or *ad verecundiam* argument where the context of dialogue is not right, by pointing out the irrelevance of the argument in that context.

This practical advice is particularly important if we plan to use the personal or so-called abusive type of *ad hominem* attack on an arguer's veracity or moral character. We should ask ourselves whether character is relevant to the discussion before launching into this type of attack, since it can easily backfire. We can be accused of mudslinging and lowering the level of debate; even worse, our opponent can reply, *tu quoque*, using the same kind of *ad hominem* argument back against us. This makes the danger of a dialectical shift, or descent to the personal quarrel, a real possibility. If two participants in a discussion are aiming at convincing a third-party audience, an *ad hominem* display can have the opposite effect by lowering the credibility of both discussants. In the case of political argumentation, character evidence is often relevant. Because of the mixed nature of political discourse, it may be hard to prove that it is not relevant.

With the bias type of *ad hominem* attack, context of dialogue is equally important. There is nothing wrong with advocating a single point of view in the context of a persuasion dialogue. Indeed, it is the goal of persuasion dialogue to successfully advocate one side of a disputed issue. The criticism of bias comes to the fore, however, when an arguer professes to be undertaking a neutral or scientific inquiry, which requires examining all the evidence available on both sides of the issue. If disinterested inquiry is the professed aim, then a one-sided advocacy, if it can be convincingly demonstrated, becomes a devastating criticism of the participant's credibility. Hence, the context of dialogue is absolutely crucial in sorting out accusations of personal bias in an argument. The opening and confrontation stages of an argument provide important sources of evidence here. Announcements at the beginning of an argument that this is an inquiry can later be used very effectively to back up criticisms of personal bias, should passionate advocacy of one side of the issue become pronounced in the argumentation stage. The criticism of bias involves weighing textual evidence from the whole context of dialogue by comparing performance in one stage with goals professed during another stage of the argument.

Any argument that is based only on the passionate advocacy of one side of the issue can be very vulnerable to criticism of bias. Hence, it may be the nature of the issue itself that indicates a proper context of dialogue for argumentation, and thereby sets up a profile or standard for judging the bias in an argument.

We should remember, however, that not all bias is so bad that it can be called fallacious or a case of the bias type of *ad hominem* fallacy. The fallacy comes in cases where the bias is part of a systematic tactic of *ad hominem* argumentation which uses the allegation of bias as part of a personal attack on an arguer.

9. Evidence Required to Support a Dialectical Evaluation

With these methods used by the new dialectic, the nature of the evidence required to evaluate an argument differs significantly from the old traditional view of logic based on the formal deductive model. According to the requirements of the new dialectical way of evaluating an argument, what is centrally important is the context of discourse in which the argument is situated within a broad text of discourse. It could be a few lines, a page, or a whole book. In many of the kinds of cases that we study in logic courses, it's not possible to look at an abundant amount of evidential detail. What we need to provide are case studies that are based on a broader text of discourse – that is, case studies that are more realistic than the typical kinds of cases that are studied now and that are not so detailed that they overwhelm the confines of our pedagogical situation.

Certain kinds of evidence from the text of discourse are particularly important. The commitments of the respondent and the proponent, as known from the text of discourse, are often crucial in determining whether a fallacy can be properly said to have been committed in a particular case. An obvious instance is the straw man fallacy, which is typically defined as the distortion or exaggeration of an opponent's position in order to make it appear unbelievable or easy to destroy. For example, someone is refuting an environmentalist by claiming that his argument requires the world to be 'a pristine place with no imperfection or human habitation or industry.' In order to analyse this case of the straw man fallacy, or a case where the straw man fallacy has allegedly been committed, we have to take a close look at what the environmentalist's stated position was in the prior sequence of argumentation. We have to quote, if possible, from the environmentalist's own description of his position or from his response to cross-questioning by the other party. Only then can we fairly evaluate whether or not a straw man fallacy has been committed in this case. So the straw man fallacy very clearly shows that a collection of evidence of an arguer's commitments is a required part of evaluation.

In this new viewpoint on the concept of fallacy, a fallacy is, first, an argument or a move in an argument that takes place between two parties; second, a move or argument that falls short of some standard of correctness or appropriateness for such a move; third, a move or argument that is used in a type of dialogue in which the two participants are supposedly engaging; fourth, an argument that is used as above and that appears to be correct, but, that under the surface, is incorrect; and fifth, an argument or a move in argument of the above type that poses a serious obstacle to the realization of the goal of the dialogue in question (Walton, 1995, p. 255). According to this definition, a fallacy is not necessarily, in all cases, a fallacious argument. For example, a question can be a fallacy, as in the fallacy of the complex question. However, a fallacy generally is an argument or a move used in argumentation, so that in the case of the fallacious complex question, the question is used in an argumentative exchange to try unfairly to get the best of the other party.

For example, if someone asks, 'When did you stop cheating on your income tax returns?' this question could be used in a fallacious way. But it depends on the context of a dialogue for the particular case being studied. If this question were asked of a witness or a defendant in court who had previously admitted to cheating on his income tax returns, then it is appropriate to ask when he stopped cheating on his income tax returns. In this context, asking such a question would not be fallacious. However, in another case where the person being questioned has not admitted to cheating on her income taxes, asking this question poses a difficulty because a direct answer requires citing a time at which the respondent stopped cheating on her income tax returns. So the respondent can't give a direct answer to the question without incriminating herself, that is, without agreeing to presuppositions within the question that would be incriminating to her side of the dialogue. In a case like this, the respondent has to question the question, or even more strongly, to rebut the presumptions inherent in the question. So in this kind of case, we say that asking such a question could be fallacious, in the sense that it is an inappropriate move at a particular point in the sequence of argumentation in the stage of a dialogue, if the questioner hasn't already secured the respondent's commitment to the proposition that she has cheated on her income tax at some point in the past. If the questioner has not secured this commitment, then asking this question with the expectation of getting a direct answer would be too aggressive an approach. It would frustrate the respondent's ability to get a fair hearing, to make it known that she never admitted to cheating on her income taxes at all. So in this sense, the asking of such a question, even though it isn't an argument, is an argumentative move in a dialogue that blocks or interferes with the proper sequence of question-reply responses needed to complete the dialogue successfully. It interferes with the respondent's ability to give a straight answer, and in this sense, it could be evaluated in a particular case relative to the text and context of the dialogue for the case as a fallacious move or a fallacy.

In most cases, however, the kinds of arguments that have traditionally been designated by the textbooks as informal fallacies are, in fact, types of arguments (like the *ad hominem* argument) that have an argumentation scheme representing the form of that argument. But when we say that argument has been used in such a way that a fallacy has been committed, we do not just mean that the argument has been insufficiently supported so that one of the premises hasn't been justified, or something of that sort. To call the argument fallacious is a stronger criticism, implying some kind of serious underlying error, or a use of the argument as a sophistical tactic to try unfairly to get the best of the other party. Very often, arguments like the *ad hominem, ad baculum,* and other typical kinds of arguments associated with fallacies are extremely powerful in ordinary conversational exchanges, and may be used to try to prevent the respondent from taking a meaningful part in the subsequent dialogue by asking further questions or by making challenges. This is the kind of case in which it is appropriate to call such an argument fallacious because it is a sophistical tactic, and not just a blunder or a violation of a rule for a type of dialogue.

Thus, according to the new theory, when we evaluate an argument like an *ad hominem* argument or an *ad baculum* argument, first we identify the argumentation scheme for that type of argument, and then ask whether the argument meets the requirements for the argumentation scheme. If this test is passed, the next question is whether the premises of the argument have been supported adequately enough so that the argument shifts a weight of plausibility towards the conclusion, making it necessary for the respondent to give a reply, unless he decides to accept the argument.

The first question focuses on the structure of the argument. Is the inference from the premises to the conclusion of a legitimate type? On the second question of whether the premises are adequately supported, we can say that a conclusion is justified to the level of the requirements needed for that type of argument as used in that context. If the premises are not adequately justified by the right kind of evidence in a given case, we can say that the argument is weak or not sufficiently justified in relation to the requirements of burden of proof appropriate for that type of argument and context. But if an argument is weak or not sufficiently justified to make the conclusion acceptable, it does not necessarily follow that the argument is fallacious. On the contrary, there are lots of arguments that are weak but not fallacious. For an argument to be shown to be fallacious, it has to exhibit a serious and underlying structural kind of error or the use of a sophistical tactic of deception of a baptizable and recognizable type. And the bottom line criterion of whether the argument is fallacious, as opposed to being merely weak or insufficiently justified, is whether it interferes with the goals of the dialogue in which the argument was used in a given case. So the difference here is between an argument that merely fails to contribute anything material (or enough support that is material) to the dialogue, by providing sufficient reason to accept the conclusion, and the other type of case where the use of the argument is of such a nature that it interferes with the dialogue in some systematic way. These are the methods used in the new dialectic to determine whether an argument or a move in argumentation, in a particular case, is fallacious or not.

10. Prospects for the New Dialectic

What is important in evaluating arguments using the new dialectic is the identification of the type of dialogue that the participants are supposed to be engaged in and the commitments of the participants, as revealed through their speech acts as verbal exchanges in the dialogue. But commitments are not beliefs or motives (psychological entities) of the participants (see Hamblin, 1970, p. 257). Commitments are inserted into the commitment stores of the participants in a dialogue by virtue of the rules of dialogue. Whether an argument is judged fallacious or nonfallacious in a given case, then, is a matter of judging the commitments of both the proponent and respondent as revealed by their performances in a context of dialogue. As shown above, this task of evaluation requires the assessment of a lot of evidence.

The use of the new dialectical method of collecting evidence to support an analysis of argumentation will not be popular with everyone because it places a serious burden of proof on the would-be critic. He can no longer simply declare, 'That's an *ad hominem* argument, therefore, it's fallacious,' or 'That's an appeal to authority, therefore it's a fallacy.' Since the use of these argumentation techniques are sometimes reasonable in a type of dialogue, it is incumbent upon the critic to show why they are fallacious in a particular case. This puts a serious burden of proof on the critic to support a charge of fallaciousness by citing evidence of two types: textual evidence from the given text of discourse in a particular case; and contextual evidence showing the type of dialogue involved, including the existence of dialectical shifts.

The problem with evaluating arguments from the perspective of the new dialectic is that so many of the examples in the standard textbooks give too little of the context of the argument. Because of this, we are forced to make a conditional evaluation based on assumptions about how the argument is being used by a proponent to make some point in a context of dialogue. If the textbook examples of the various fallacies included longer arguments, where the context of dialogue is more fully filled out, then students could examine a text of discourse in a pragmatic way to identify the sequence of moves made by the two parties, as well as other important parts of the evidence, including the commitments of the two parties, how these commitments have been retracted, and so forth.

This dialectical point of view, however, tends to make the analysis of fallacies more difficult. We can no longer take a dismissive approach to the fallacies, arguing, for example, that because such-and-such is an *ad hominem*, we can automatically discount it as fallacious. Instead, we have to examine arguments on a case-to-case basis. If we identify an *ad hominem* argument, then we have to identify not only the argumentation scheme corresponding to it, but also the critical questions that can be used to reply to it. We must also try to get a good global picture of the sequence of argumentation. In such a case, it is also very useful to know more about the argument's source, whether it comes from a textbook, a newspaper article or an editorial, or a commercial advertisement. These factors are extremely important in evaluating the argument dialectically. A commercial speech from an advertisement has to be evaluated differently than an argument used in a political debate or in a philosophical discussion because the purpose of the argument is different, as are the methods used to achieve that purpose.

Teachers of critical thinking courses might find this new approach to analysing arguments, which requires a broad collection of evidence from the text and context of discourse, somewhat daunting. A strong attraction of the old way of analysing fallacies is that we could dismiss arguments as straw-man fallacies or *ad hominem* fallacies without collecting any (or much) evidence to support the evaluation. Now, in order for case studies to be convincing, we have to make a serious effort to collect and systematically evaluate the evidence that can be gleaned from the text of discourse in a given case. This new approach not only implies more work, but also implies a serious effort to build case evaluations on a theory of argument evaluation which will enable a student or user to systematically carry out evaluations in particular cases.

It has been evident to many scholars in speech communication that the use of dialectical methods of argument evaluation is useful and even necessary to properly study rhetoric. However, in a critical thinking course, the goal is to study not effective persuasion, how to actually persuade audiences, but how to critically evaluate arguments as strong or weak, fallacious or nonfallacious, once we have the text of discourse of the argument at hand. For this purpose, we can apply the evidence-collecting methods of the new dialectic in order to judge, on the basis of the textual evidence given, whether the requirements for a correct use of argument in relation to a given normative model of dialogue are met. This type of evaluation may not always be useful when reacting or responding immediately to an argument, but it is extremely useful for arriving at a reasonably careful critical evaluation of an argument.

One of the primary uses of the new dialectic is to show people how to avoid common errors and fallacies in arguments. But the influence that will lead more directly to the acceptance of the new dialectic as a normative model of argumentation is its adoption in the field of computer science, especially in Artificial Intelligence, in the field of human-computer interactions (developing user-friendly computers), and in the use of computers to assist group deliberations and argumentative dialogues. Researchers working in these fields of application are already paying serious attention to dialectical models of argumentation.[8] Among the most encouraging developments is the work in the new field of computational dialectics, and the use of dialectical techniques of argumentation for modelling reasoning in medical diagnosis and treatment. An example of this research is the use of concepts of argumentation theory like 'balance of evidence' to model judgments of risk assessment in order to build a carcinogenic risk adviser to warn of the danger of chemical compounds in causing cancer (Krause and Fox, 1993–4).

The term 'computational dialectics' was introduced by Gordon to define 'the study, within Artificial Intelligence, of the theory, design and implementation of systems which mediate discussions and arguments between agents, artificial and human' (1995, p. xi). In Gordon's work, a formal dialectical model of argumentation, called the Pleadings Game, is applied to the arguments and counterarguments used in civil pleading in a court of law. It is in such research projects in Artificial Intelligence and computational dialectics that the new dialectic will find its acceptance in mainstream logic as a framework for new methods of evaluating arguments.

Notes

Chapter 1

1 In particular, we refer to *On Sophistical Refutations* here, but throughout the treatment of the concept of dialogue as a framework of argument in this book, many references will be made to Aristotle's other works.
2 See Johnson and Blair, 1985.
3 See also the classifications and analysis in Walton, 1992b.
4 See also Walton, 1987.
5 Ibid.
6 See Walton, 1991.
7 See Kneale and Kneale, 1962, p. 7; see also Irwin, 1988, p. 7.
8 Kneale and Kneale, 1962.
9 Byrne, 1968.
10 Hamblin, 1970, p. 31.
11 See Walton and Batten, 1984.

Chapter 2

1 I thought for some time I had invented the term 'persuasion dialogue,' but found that the term had been used by Armar A. Archbold in a working paper on dialogue modelling. Archbold defines 'persuasion' as 'the successful or unsuccessful attempt by a speaker (the persuader) to change an interlocutor's (the persuadee's) factual or evaluative beliefs so as to increase their congruence with the beliefs of the persuader, or with beliefs the persuader does not hold but wants the persuadee to adhere to, by means of the production of arguments – an attempt which meets with some resistance on the part of the interlocutor' (1976, p. 1). This definition of persuasion dialogue

accords fairly well with our own, except that it is expressed in terms of belief, as opposed to ours which is expressed in terms of commitment.

2 Walton and Krabbe, 1995.

3 Walton, 1988a; 1992b.

4 The root is the Greek word *maieutikos*, meaning 'skill in midwifery.' Socrates adapted this term to refer to his role as a participant in dialogue who brings new ideas to birth by questioning a respondent.

Chapter 3

1 See Woods and Walton, 1978; and Walton and Batten, 1984. This conception of the inquiry, using directed graph theory as a model, is further developed in Walton, 1991.

2 Ibid.

3 See the account given in Hamblin (1970, p. 76) where propositions in an Aristotelian demonstration are described as having a 'peck-order.'

4 Ibid.

5 We refer to the famous Cartesian method of beginning with 'indubitable' axioms and then proceeding in geometrical fashion to deduce logical consequences from these axioms in an ordered progression.

6 See section 7.

7 This aspect of testability has frequently been emphasized in writings in the philosophy of science on the use of experimental methods in science.

8 According to Krabbe (1982, p. 177), the Barth and Krabbe interpretation is a different intuitive interpretation of constructive (intuitionistic) logic from the Kripke interpretation.

Kripke intends the nodes (elements) H, H' of a set K (of a *model structure*) to represent (possible) *evidential situations* of *ours*. Further, he suggests that we read HRH' as follows: in situation H *we* may, as far as we know, advance to situation H'.

In [Barth and Krabbe] on the other hand, the elements d, d' of the set D (corresponding to Kripke's K) in a *dialectical structure* represent *possible dialectical situations* of a specifiable *dialectical subject*, and dRd' is read accordingly. An evidential situation is characterized, at least partly, by the set of sentences verified or verifiable by *us* in that situation. Hence the 'values' assigned to sentences (by a model) represent the predicates *'verified'* and *'not verified.'* A dialectical situation is characterized, at least partly, by the set of sentences upon which positive agreement has been reached by a dialectical subject in that situation. Therefore the 'values' assigned to sentences (by an interpretation/valuation) are these:

A, for *Agreement*

N, for *Non-agreement*

There is no reason why there should be just one acceptable intuitive interpretation for any particular structure of semantics. Adoption of the dialectical interpretation does not commit one to a *rejection* of Kripke's own 'monological' interpretation: the plausibility of both interpretations can be independently criticized.

Using Krabbe's terminology, the Kripke interpretation could be described as monological, as opposed to the Barth and Krabbe interpretation, which could be called dialectical.

Chapter 4

1 This, in fact, appears to be the view expressed by van Eemeren and Grootendorst (1984; 1992), who identify argumentation with a type of persuasion dialogue called the critical discussion.
2 As noted in section 9, the concept of making an offer is important to any type of commercial speech generally, where a transaction or exchange of money, goods, services, or interests, is an important part of the goal of the dialogue.
3 See chapter 1, section 4.
4 Empathy is especially important in our own account of the normative structure of negotiation, which is different in certain important respects from that given by Fisher and Ury.
5 See Walton, 1990a.
6 See chapter 6.
7 See chapter 8 for a systematic study of dialectical shifts.
8 See chapter 7.
9 See chapter 1, section 4.

Chapter 5

1 See Hamblin, 1970, pp. 270–1; and Walton, 1984, pp. 52–62.
2 For many comparable cases of this type analysed in detail, see Walton, 1989b.
3 This is the *tu quoque* type of *ad hominem* argument mentioned in chapter 1, section 4.
4 In other words, the kind of reasoning used by the expert to arrive at a conclusion is, or may be, quite different in nature from the kind of reasoning used by the layperson to draw a conclusion from what the expert says.
5 Forsyth, 1984.

Chapter 6

1 The case of conflicting basic goals would make the dialogue a hybrid between persuasion dialogue and deliberation – a species of mixed discourse.
2 See von Wright, 1972.
3 Slipping between the horns and grasping one of the horns are not the only ways of attacking a dilemma. A third form of attack is that of constructing a counter-dilemma. However, this form of attack requires elaborate preparation, and is a more sophisticated form of attack which is not as commonly used as the other two more direct forms.
4 At least, in the simplest type of case.
5 This concept of abstraction is familiar in recent work in Artificial Intelligence and expert systems. See Forsyth, 1984; or any recent work on robotics and Artificial Intelligence.
6 See chapter 3, section 3.
7 This is a good point of contrast with persuasion dialogue.

Chapter 7

1 Such a move could perhaps rightly be evaluated as a fallacious and irrelevant *ad hominem* attack in a critical discussion, for example.
2 Surprisingly (for current readers) the concept of the quarrel was regarded as highly important to logic – in the broad sense of evaluation of arguments used in everyday discourse – when the subject of logic was founded.
3 A quarrel is like a thunderstorm which comes upon us somewhat unexpectedly, whether we like it or not.
4 The notion that the quarrel is characterized by argumentation that drops the usual restraints of politeness is very important. Following Grice (1975), the concept of reasoning together in collaborative conversation is all based on maxims and presumptions of politeness.
5 See chapter 1. The *ad baculum* is a leading fallacy in this connection. Quarrels typically involve threats.
6 Here we do not attempt to conduct a historical or exegetical inquiry into what Plato really meant by 'dialectic.' This is best left to the specialists.
7 The exception here would be Schopenhauer (1851), who elevated eristic dialogue to the status of primary normative model of dialogue for the evaluation of arguments.
8 This would appear to be comparable to what we have identified as practical reasoning.

9 See note 4.
10 See chapter 1, section 5.

Chapter 8

1 Much of this material originally appeared in Walton, 1992c, 137–40.
2 John Schwartz, Erik Calonius, David L. Gonzalez and Frank Gibney, Jr., 'A Boss They Love to Hate,' *Newsweek*, 20 March 1989, 20–4.
3 Ibid.

Chapter 9

1 Some cases of political debates in Hansard that relate to traditional fallacies have been studied in Walton, 1989.
2 See Van Eemeren and Grootendorst, 1984, p. 38.
3 The media tend to televise the segments that show colourful emotional outbursts, like *ad hominem* attacks.
4 To give an idea of how hard the logic textbooks are generally on both sales dialogue and advertising when it comes to alleging that these arguments commit fallacies of various kinds, we should recall the analysis of the *ad populum* fallacy given by Copi and Cohen (1990, p. 103) quoted in chapter 4, section 9.
5 The thesis that the argumentation in a trial can be evaluated by the model of the critical discussion is advocated by Feteris, 1989.
6 See chapter 1, section 4.
7 Waller, 1988.
8 See chapter 1, section 5.
9 This type of syllogism has important implications for the analysis of both the *ad populum* and *ad verecundiam* fallacies. Aristotle's account suggests that both appeal to popular opinion and appeal to expert opinion could in many instances be reasonable kinds of arguments (in the right context).
10 See van Eemeren and Grootendorst, 1984; 1992.

Chapter 10

1 Hamblin, 1970.
2 Walton, 1995.
3 Walton, 1992b.
4 See the acid rain case, in chapter 4, section 8.
5 Forsyth, 1984.

6 Walton, 1992b; 1996a.
7 According to Nuchelmans (1993), there are two lines of historical development of the *argumentum ad hominem*, both going back to passages in Aristotle. Nuchelmans's first type of argument is the Lockean type of *ad hominem* argument, a type of *ex concessis* argument that uses a respondent's commitments to get him to accept a conclusion. The second type is the kind of personal attack that is characteristic of the *ad hominem* fallacy (especially the abusive type) as treated in the modern textbooks. Our description of the circumstantial type of *ad hominem* argument would be a subspecies of the Lockean type, where a circumstantial inconsistency of commitments is cited.
8 As indicated in the proceedings of the Bonn Conference on Practical Reasoning (see Gabbay and Ohlbach, 1996).

References

Andreas, Steve. 1992. 'Embedding the Message.' *The Family Therapy Networker*, May/June, 59–62.

Archbold, Armar A. 1976. 'A Study of Some Argument-Forms in a Persuasion-Dialogue.' In *Working Papers in Dialogue Modelling*, vol. 2, edited by James A. Levin and Armar A. Archbold. Marina del Rey: Information Sciences Institute.

Aristotle. 1928. *The Works of Aristotle Translated into English*, edited by W.D. Ross. Oxford: Oxford University Press.

– 1955. *On Sophistical Refutations*. Translated by E.S. Forster. Loeb Classical Library Edition. Cambridge, Mass.: Harvard University Press.

Aristotle. 1968. *The Nicomachean Ethics*. Translated by H. Rackham. Loeb Classical Library Edition. Cambridge, Mass.: Harvard University Press.

Barnes, Jonathan. 1980. 'Aristotle and the Method of Ethics.' *Revue Internationale de Philosophie* 34, 490–511.

Barth, E.M., and E.C.W. Krabbe. 1982. *From Axiom to Dialogue*. New York: De Gruyter.

Barth, E.M., and J.L. Martens. 1977. '*Argumentum Ad Hominem:* From Chaos to Formal Dialectic.' *Logique et Analyse* 77–8, 76–96.

Beardsley, Monroe C. 1950. *Practical Logic*. New York: Prentice-Hall.

Berg, Jonathan. 1991. 'The Relevant Relevance.' *Journal of Pragmatics* 16, 411–25.

Black, Max. 1946. *Critical Thinking: An Introduction to Logic and Scientific Method*. New York: Prentice-Hall.

Blair, J. Anthony. 1992. 'Premissary Relevance.' *Argumentation* 6, 203–17.

Bolton, Robert. 1990. 'The Epistemological Basis of Aristotelian Dialectic.' In *Biologie, Logique et Métaphysique chez Aristote*, edited by Daniel Devereux and Pierre Pellegrin, 185–236. Paris: Editions du Centre National de la Recherche Scientifique.

Brinton, Alan. 1985. 'A Rhetorical View of the *Ad Hominem*.' *Australasian Journal of Philosophy* 63, 50–63.

- 1986. 'Ethotic Argument.' *History of Philosophy Quarterly* 3, 245–57.
- 1987. 'Ethotic Argument: Some Uses.' In *Argumentation: Perspectives and Approaches*, edited by Frans H. van Eemeren, Rob Grootendorst, J. Anthony Blair, and Charles A. Willard, 246–54. Dordrecht: Foris Publications.

Broad, William, and Nicholas Wade. 1982. *Betrayers of the Truth*. New York: Simon and Schuster.

Bronniman, Werner. 1988. 'Agonistic Elements in Dialogue Exchange.' *Bulletin CILA* 48, 88–93.

Byrne, Edmund F. 1968. *Probability and Opinion*. The Hague: Martinus Nijhoff.

Colford, Steven W. 1992. 'Bell Atlantic Weds Sitcom: Infomercial.' *Advertising Age* 63, no. 46, 8.

Collingwood, R.G. 1939. *An Autobiography*. Oxford: Oxford University Press.

Collins, Harry. 1992. 'Anyone Can Make a Mistake.' *The Times Higher Education Supplement*, 20 March, 16.

Cooper, Jim. 1993. 'Infomercials Welcomed Back into Ad Fold.' *Broadcasting & Cable*, 24 May, 69.

Copi, Irving M. 1982. *Introduction to Logic*. 6th ed., New York: Macmillan.

Copi, Irving M., and Carl Cohen. 1990. *Introduction to Logic*. 8th ed. New York: Macmillan.

Crain News Services. 1993. 'Infomercials Hawk Cars.' *Automotive News*, 25 Jan. 26.

Dascal, Marcelo. 1977. 'Conversational Relevance.' *Journal of Pragmatics* 1, 309–28.

Degnan, Ronan E. 1973. 'Evidence.' *Encyclopaedia Britannica*, vol. 8. 15th ed.

Devereux, Daniel. 1990. 'Comments on Robert Bolton's *The Epistemological Basis of Aristotelian Dialectic*.' In *Biologie, Logique et Metaphysique chez Aristote*, edited by Daniel Devereux and Pierre Pellegrin, 263–86. Paris: Editions du Centre National de la Recherche Scientifique.

Donohue, William A. 1981a. 'Development of a Model of Rule Use in Negotiation Interaction.' *Communication Monographs* 48, 106–20.

- 1981b. 'Analyzing Negotiation Tactics: Development of a Negotiation Interact System.' *Human Communication Research* 7, 237–87.

Dreyfus, Hubert L., and Stuart E. Dreyfus. 1986. *Mind Over Machine*. New York: Free Press.

Epstein, Richard L. 1979. 'Relatedness and Implication.' *Philosophical Studies* 36, 137–73.

- 1990. *The Semantic Foundations of Logic*. Vol. 1: *Propositional Logics*. Dordrecht: Kluwer.

Evans, J.D.G. 1977. *Aristotle's Concept of Dialectic*. London: Cambridge University Press.

Felscher, Walter. 1986. 'Dialogues as a Foundation for Intuitionistic Logic.' In

Handbook of Philosophical Logic, vol. 3, edited by D. Gabbay and F. Guenther, 341–72. Dordrecht: Reidel.

Feteris, Eveline T. 1989. *Discussieregels in het recht. Een Pragma-dialectische Analyse van het Burgerlijk Proces en het Strafproces* (Rules for discussion in law: A pragma-dialectical analysis of the civil process and the criminal process). Dordrecht: Foris Publications.

Fisher, Roger, and William Ury. 1991. *Getting to Yes*. 2nd ed. New York: Penguin.

Flowers, Margot, Rod McGuire, and Lawrence Birnbaum. 1982. 'Adversary Arguments and the Logic of Personal Attacks.' In *Strategies for Natural Language Processing*, edited by Wendy G. Lehnert and Martin H. Ringle, 275–94. Hillsdale, N.J.: Lawrence Erlbaum Associates.

Forsyth, Richard, ed. 1984. *Expert Systems: Principles and Case Studies*. London: Chapman and Hall.

Franks, C.E.S. 1985. 'The "Problem" of Debate and Question Period.' In *The Canadian House of Commons*, edited by John C. Courtenay, 1–19. Calgary: University of Calgary Press.

Fraser, Alistair, G.A. Birch, and W.F. Dawson, eds. 1978. *Beauchesne's Parliamentary Rules and Forms*. 5th ed. Toronto: Carswell.

Freeman, James B. 1992. 'Relevance, Warrants, Backing, Inductive Support.' *Argumentation* 6, 219–35.

Fritz, Gerd, and Franz Hundsnurscher. 1994. 'Formale Dialogspieltheorien.' In *Handbuch der Dialoganalyse*, 131–52. Tubingen: Max Niemeyer Verlag.

Gabbay, Dov, and Hans-Jürgen Ohlbach, eds. 1996. *Practical Reasoning*. Proceedings of the International Conference on Formal and Applied Practical Reasoning in Bonn, Germany, 1996, Lecture Notes in Artificial Intelligence. Berlin: Springer.

Garfield, Bob. 1992. 'Bell Atlantic's Sitcom Should Fall on Deaf Ears.' *Advertising Age* 63, 52.

Gay, Katherine. 1992. 'Interview Questions that Dig Deeper.' *Financial Post*, 24 February, S22.

Gordon, Thomas F. 1995. *The Pleadings Game: An Artificial Intelligence Model of Procedural Justice*. Dordrecht: Kluwer.

Govier, Trudy. 1983. '*Ad Hominem*: Revising the Textbooks.' *Teaching Philosophy* 6, 13–24.

– 1987. *Problems in Argument Analysis and Evaluation*. Dordrecht: Foris Publications.

Graham, Michael H. 1977. 'Impeaching the Professional Expert Witness by a Showing of Financial Interest.' *Indiana Law Journal*. 53, 35–53.

Grice, H. Paul. 1975. 'Logic and Conversation.' In *The Logic of Grammar*, edited by Donald Davidson and Gilbert Harman, 64–75. Encino: Dickenson.

Grover, Mary Beth. 1990. 'Step Right Up Ladies and Gentlemen.' *Forbes*, October, 43–4.

Gulliver, P.H. 1979. *Disputes and Negotiations*. New York: Academic Press.

Gumperz, J.J. 1972. 'Introduction.' In *Directions in Sociolinguistics: The Ethnography of Communication*, edited by J.J. Gumperz and D. Hymes, 1–25. New York: Holt, Rinehart & Winston.

Guthrie, W.K.C. 1981. *A History of Greek Philosophy*, vol. 6. Cambridge: Cambridge University Press.

Hamblin, C.L. 1970. *Fallacies*. London: Methuen.

– 1971. 'Mathematical Models of Dialogue.' *Theoria* 37, 130–55.

Hamlyn, D.W. 1990. 'Aristotle on Dialectic.' *Philosophy* 65, 465–76.

Hansard: Debates of the House of Commons (Canada). 'Northumberland Strait Crossing Act.' 14 June 1993, 20729–44.

Harrah, David. 1984. 'The Logic of Questions.' In *Handbook of Philosophical Logic*, vol. 2, edited by D. Gabbay and F. Guenther, 715–64. Dordrecht: Reidel.

Hintikka, Jaakko. 1981. 'The Logic of Information-Seeking Dialogues: A Model.' In *Konzepte der Dialektik*, edited by Werner Becker and Wilhelm K. Essler, 212–31, Frankfurt am Main: Vittorio Klostermann.

– 1987. 'The Fallacy of Fallacies.' *Argumentation* 1, 211–38.

Hintikka, Jaakko, and Esa Saarinen. 1979. 'Information-Seeking Dialogues: Some of Their Logical Properties.' *Studia Logica* 38, 355–63.

Hitchcock, David. 1992. 'Relevance.' *Argumentation* 6, 251–70.

Hurley, Patrick J. 1991. *A Concise Introduction to Logic*. 4th ed. Belmont: Wadsworth.

Infante, Dominic A., and Charles J. Wigley. 1986. 'Verbal Aggressiveness: An Interpersonal Model and Measure.' *Communication Monographs* 53, 61–9.

Irwin, Terence. 1988. *Aristotle's First Principles*. Oxford: Clarendon Press.

Jacobs, Scott, and Sally Jackson. 1992. 'Relevance and Digressions in Argumentative Discussion: A Pragmatic Approach.' *Argumentation* 6, 161–76.

Jennings, Nicholas R., and Michael Wooldridge. 1995. 'Applying Agent Technology.' *Applied Artificial Intelligence* 9, 357–69.

J.F. 1990. 'Infomercials: Can Viewers Tell the Difference?' *Broadcasting* 118, no. 6, 61–2.

Johnson, Paul E. 1983. 'What Kind of Expert Should a System Be?' *The Journal of Medicine and Philosophy* 8, 77–97.

Johnson, Ralph H. 1987. 'The Blaze of Her Splendors: Suggestions about Revitalizing Fallacy Theory.' *Argumentation* 1, 239–54.

Johnson, Ralph H., and J. Anthony Blair. 1985. 'Informal Logic: The Past Five Years, 1978–1983.' *American Philosophical Quarterly* 22, 181–96.

Johnstone, Henry W. 1959. *Philosophy and Argument*. University Park: Pennsylvania State University Press.

– 1978. *Validity and Rhetoric in Philosophical Argument*. University Park: Dialogue Press of Man and World.

Jonsen, Albert R., and Stephen Toulmin. 1988. *The Abuse of Casuistry*. Berkeley: University of California Press.

Kaiser, Artur. 1979. *Questioning Techniques*. Pomona: Hunter House.

Kamlah, W., and P. Lorenzen. 1967. *Logische Propädeutik: Vorschule des vernünftigen Redens* (Logical propaedeutic: Pre-school of reasonable discourse). Mannheim: Hochschultaschenbücher-Verlag.

Kapp, Ernst. 1942. *Greek Foundations of Traditional Logic*. New York: Columbia University Press.

Kennedy, George. 1963. *The Art of Persuasion in Greece*. London: Routledge and Kegan Paul.

– 1980. *Classical Rhetoric and Its Christian and Secular Tradition from Ancient to Modern Times*. Chapel Hill: University of North Carolina Press.

Kerferd, G.B. 1981. *The Sophistic Movement*. Cambridge: Cambridge University Press.

Kneale, William, and Martha Kneale. 1962. *The Development of Logic*. Oxford: Clarendon Press.

Kotarbinski, Thadée. 1963. 'L'éristique – Cas Particulier de la Théorie de la Lutte.' *Logique et Analyse* 6, 19–29.

Krabbe, Erik C.W. 1982. *Studies in Dialogical Logic*. Ph.D. diss., University of Groningen.

– 1992. 'So What? Profiles of Relevance Criticism in Persuasion Dialogues.' *Argumentation* 6, 271–83.

– 1996. 'Dialogue Logic and Formal Dialectics.' *Fundamentals of Argumentation Theory*, edited by Frans H. van Eemeren et al., 246–73. Mahwah, N.J.: Erlbaum.

Krause, Paul, and John Fox. 1993–4. 'An Argumentation-Based Approach to Risk Assessment.' *IMA Journal of Mathematics Applied in Business and Industry* 5, 249–63.

Kripke, Saul. 1965. 'Semantical Analysis of Intuitionistic Logic I.' *Formal Systems and Recursive Functions*, edited by J.N. Crossley and M. Dummett. Amsterdam: North-Holland.

Lambert, Peter D. 1990. 'Congress Looks into Infomercials.' *Broadcasting* 118, no. 22, 66.

Lascher, Edward L. 1994. 'Assessing Legislative Deliberation.' In *Kennedy School of Government: Faculty Research Working Paper Series*. Cambridge: Harvard University.

Lee, Charles S. 1993. 'Books of Their Own.' *Newsweek*, 1 Nov. 69.

Levine, Joshua. 1993. 'Entertainment or Deception?' *Forbes*, 2 Aug. 102.

Locke, John. 1961 [1690]. *An Essay Concerning Human Understanding*, edited by John W. Yolton. 2 volumes. London: Dent.

Lorenzen, Paul. 1969. *Normative Logic and Ethics*. Mannheim: Bibliographisches Institut.

Mackenzie, J.D. 1980. 'Why Do We Number Theorems?' *Australasian Journal of Philosophy* 58, 135–49.

Mackenzie, J.D. 1980. 'The Dialectics of Logic.' *Logique et Analyse* 94, 159–77.

Manor, Ruth. 1981. 'Dialogues and the Logics of Questions and Answers.' *Linguistische Berichte* 73, 1–28.

– 1982. 'Pragmatics and the Logic of Questions and Assertions.' *Philosophica* 29, 45–96.

Marchionini, Gary. 1995. *Information Seeking in Electronic Environments*. Cambridge: Cambridge University Press.

Massey, Gerald J. 1975. 'Are There Any Good Arguments that Bad Arguments Are Bad?' *Philosophy in Context* 4, 61–77.

Mickleburgh, Rod. 1993. 'Controversy Dogged Inquiry from Outset.' *Globe and Mail*, 3 Nov. A5.

Middleton, Kent R. 1991. 'Advocacy Advertising, the First Amendment and Competitive Advantage.' *Journal of Advertising* 20, 77–81.

Nuchelmans, Gabriel. 1993. 'On the Fourfold Root of the *Argumentum ad Hominem*.' In *Empirical Logic and Public Debate*, edited by Erik C.W. Krabbe, Renée José Dalitz, and Pier A. Smit, 37–47. Amsterdam: Rodopi.

Pascal, Blaise. 1966 [1659]. 'Reflections on Geometry and the Art of Persuading.' In *The Essential Pascal*, edited by Robert W. Gleason, 297–327. New York: New American Library.

Picard, André. 1993. 'Blood Concentrates Still Suspect.' *Globe and Mail*, 23 Nov. A1–A2.

– 1996a. 'Truth About Tainted Blood May Never Be Known.' *Globe and Mail*, 25 Jan. A4.

– 1966. 'Red Cross Challenges Krever.' *Globe and Mail*, 23 May, A1.

Plato. 1961. *Collected Dialogues*, edited by Edith Hamilton and Huntington Cairns. New York: Random House.

Proctor, Robert N. 1965. *Cancer Wars: How Politics Shapes What We Know and Don't Know About Cancer*. New York: Basic Books.

Putnam, Linda L., and Tricia S. Jones. 1982. 'The Role of Communication in Bargaining.' *Human Communication Research* 8, 262–80.

Rescher, Nicholas. 1964. *Introduction to Logic*. New York: St Martin's Press.

– 1976. *Plausible Reasoning*. Assen-Amsterdam: Van Gorcum.

– 1977. *Dialectics*. Albany: State University of New York Press.

Richmond, Ray. 1993. 'A World of Soloflex and Psychic Friends.' *Globe and Mail*, 19 Nov. A7.

Robinson, Richard. 1953. *Plato's Earlier Dialectic*. Oxford: Oxford University Press.

Sacks, Harvey, Emanuel A. Schegloff, and Gail Jefferson. 1974. 'A Simplest Systematics for the Organization of Turn-taking for Conversation.' *Language* 50, 696–735.

Saunders, Doug. 1996. 'Public Inquiries Too Lengthy, Far-Ranging, Critics Charge.' *Globe and Mail*, 24 June, A6.

Schelling, T.C. 1960. *The Strategy of Conflict*. Cambridge: Harvard University Press.

Schopenhauer, Arthur. 1951 [1851]. 'The Art of Controversy.' In *Essays from Parerga and Paralipomena*. Translated by T. Bailey Saunders, 5–38. London: Allen and Unwin.

Sextus Empiricus. 1933. *Outlines of Pyrrhonism*. Translated by R.G. Bury. Loeb Classical Library Edition. Cambridge: Harvard University Press.

60 Minutes. 1993. 'Readin', Writin' and Commercials.' CBS News 26, no. 4 (10 Oct.), 13–20. Livingston, N.J.: Burrelle's Transcript Service.

Smith, Robin. 1993. 'Aristotle on the Uses of Dialectic.' *Synthese* 96, 335–58.

Sperber, Dan, and Deidre Wilson. 1986. *Relevance: Communication and Cognition*. Cambridge: Harvard University Press.

Stegmüller, Wolfgang. 1964. 'Remarks on the Completeness of Logical Systems Relative to the Validity-concepts of P. Lorenzen and K. Lorenz.' *Notre Dame Journal of Formal Logic* 5, 81–112.

Tannen, Deborah. 1994. 'The Triumph of the Yell.' *Globe and Mail*, 28 Jan. A17.

Tindale, Christopher W. 1992. 'Audiences, Relevance and Cognitive Environments.' *Argumentation* 6, 177–88.

Tully, James. 1988. 'Governing Conduct.' In *Conscience and Casuistry in Early Modern Europe*, 12–71. Cambridge: Cambridge University Press.

20/20. 1990. 'It's Really a Commercial.' ABC News. Transcript of Show #1039, 12–17. New York: Journal Graphics.

Unger, Tom. 1992. 'Gain the Winning Edge at the Negotiating Table.' *PC Magazine*, 26 May, 455–6.

U.S. Supreme Court. 1983. *Bolger v. Youngs Drug Products Corp.*, 463 U.S. 60.

van Eemeren, Frans H., and Rob Grootendorst. 1984. *Speech Acts in Argumentative Discussions*. Dordrecht: Foris Publications.

– 1987. 'Fallacies in Pragma-Dialectical Perspective.' *Argumentation* 1, 283–301.

– 1992. *Argumentation, Communication and Fallacies*. Hillsdale, N.J.: Lawrence Erlbaum Associates.

van Eemeren, Frans H., and Tjark Kruiger. 1987. 'Identifying Argumentation Schemes.' In *Argumentation: Perspectives and Approaches*, edited by Frans H. van Eemeren et al., 70–81. Dordrecht: Foris Publications.

von Wright, G.H. 1972. 'On So-Called Practical Inference.' *Acta Sociologica* 15, 39–53.

Waller, Bruce N. 1988. *Critical Thinking*. Englewood Cliffs: Prentice-Hall.

Walton, Douglas N. 1980. 'Why is the *Ad Populum* a Fallacy?' *Philosophy and Rhetoric* 13, 264–78.

– 1982. *Topical Relevance in Argumentation*. Amsterdam: John Benjamins Publishing.

– 1983. 'Enthymemes.' *Logique et Analyse* 103/4, 395–410.

– 1984. *Logical Dialogue–Games and Fallacies*. Lanham: University Press of America.

– 1985. *Arguer's Position*. New York: Greenwood Press.

– 1987. *Informal Fallacies*, Amsterdam: John Benjamins Publishing.

– 1988a. 'Burden of Proof.' *Argumentation* 2, 233–54.

– 1988b. 'Question-Asking Fallacies.' In *Questions and Questioning*, edited by Michel Meyer, 195–221. Berlin: Walter de Gruyter.

– 1989a. *Informal Logic*. Cambridge: Cambridge University Press.

– 1989b. *Question-Reply Argumentation*. New York: Greenwood Press.

– 1990a. *Practical Reasoning*. Savage, Md: Rowman and Littlefield.

– 1990b. 'What is Reasoning? What is an Argument?' *Journal of Philosophy* 87, 399–419.

– 1991. *Begging the Question: Circular Reasoning as a Tactic of Argumentation*. New York: Greenwood Press.

– 1992a. *Slippery Slope Arguments*. Oxford: Oxford University Press.

– 1992b. *Plausible Argument in Everyday Conversation*. Albany: State University of New York Press.

– 1992c. *The Place of Emotion in Argument*. University Park: Pennsylvania State University Press.

– 1992d. 'Questionable Questions in Question Period.' *Logic and Political Culture*, edited by E.M. Barth and E.C.W. Krabbe, 87–95. Amsterdam: North-Holland.

– 1992e. 'Types of Dialogue, Dialectical Shifts and Fallacies.' In *Argumentation Illuminated*, edited by Frans H. van Eemeren et al., 133–47. Amsterdam: SICSAT.

– 1992f. 'Which of the Fallacies are Fallacies of Relevance?' *Argumentation* 6, 237–50.

– 1995. *A Pragmatic Theory of Fallacy*. Tuscaloosa: University of Alabama Press.

– 1996a. *Arguments from Ignorance*. University Park: Pennsylvania State University Press.

– 1996b. *Argumentation Schemes for Presumptive Reasoning*. Mahwah, N.J.: Lawrence Erlbaum Associates.

Walton, Douglas N., and Lynn M. Batten. 1984. 'Games, Graphs and Circular Arguments.' *Logique et Analyse* 106, 133–64.

Walton, Douglas N., and Erik C.W. Krabbe. 1995. *Commitment in Dialogue*. Albany. State University of New York Press.

Walton, R.E., and R.B. McKersie. 1965. *A Behavioral Theory of Labor Negotiations*. New York: McGraw-Hill.

Woods, John. '*Ad Baculum*, Self-Interest and Pascal's Wager.' In *Argumentation: Across the Line of Discipline*, edited by Frans H. van Eemeren et al., 343–9. Dordrecht: Foris Publications.

– 1988. 'Buttercups, GNP's and Quarks: Are Fallacies Theoretical Entities?' *Informal Logic* 10, 67–76.

– 1992. 'Apocalyptic Relevance.' *Argumentation* 6, 189–202.

Woods, John, and Douglas Walton. 1974. '*Argumentum Ad Verecundiam*.' *Philosophy and Rhetoric* 7, 135–53.

– 1976. '*Ad Baculum*.' *Grazer Philosophische Studien* 2, 133–40.

– 1977. '*Ad Hominem*.' *The Philosophical Forum* 8, 1–20.

– 1978. 'Arresting Circles in Formal Dialogues.' *Journal of Philosophical Logic* 7, 73–90.

– 1982. *Argument: The Logic of the Fallacies*. Toronto: McGraw-Hill Ryerson.

– 1989. *Fallacies: Selected Papers, 1972–1982*. Dordrecht: Foris Publications.

Wooldridge, Michael, and Nicholas R. Jennings. 1995. 'Intelligent Agents: Theory and Practice.' *Knowledge Engineering Review* 10, 115–52.

Wright, Larry. 1995. 'Argument and Deliberation: A Plea for Understanding.' *Journal of Philosophy* 92, 565–85.

Younger, Irving. 1982. 'A Practical Approach to the Use of Expert Testimony.' *Cleveland State Law Review* 31, 1–42.

Yankelovich, Daniel. 1991. *Coming to Public Judgment*. Syracuse: Syracuse University Press.

– 1992. 'A Widening Expert/Public Opinion Gap.' *Challenge* May/June, 20–7.

Index

Acid rain case, 121–2

Ad hominem argument, 137, 192, 193, 206, 233, 256, 261; irrelevant, 221

Ad hominem attacks, 113, 182, 192, 194, 201, 206, 221–2, 226; abusive, 271; aggressive, 225; bias type, 262, 271

Advertisement: advocacy, 124

Advice seeker: obligation of, 32

Agents, 152–3, 175; ability to criticize, 166; actions of, 164; discretion of, 157

Agreement: wise, 101

Andreas, Steve, 141

Answer: direct, 140–2, 147–9; indirect, 140

Antilogic, 188

Antiphon, 15

Appeal: to authority, 266; emotional, 22, 245; to expert opinion, 20, 27; to pity, 22, 234; psychological, 123

Arguing from ignorance, 20

Argument, 178; adversary, 192; *ad baculum*, 116, 262, 263; circular, 9, 75, 246; contentious, 11, 13, 33, 238; deductively valid, 41, 60–1, 160–1; defeasible, 260; demonstrative, 11–12, 237; dialectical, 10–11, 14–16, 20, 238, 240; didactic, 11; eristic, 14; examination, 11, 13; *exetastic*, 13; evaluation (four step method of), 249; from authority, 27; from consequences, 158–9, 164, 168–70, 174, 202; from negative consequences, 116, 159; from plausibility, 15; from positive consequences, 159; identification, 249–50; implicit, 170; inductive, 61; irrelevant, 111, 205; *peirastic*, 13; presumptive, 26; probative function of, 41–2; purpose of, 85; retrospective evaluation of, 205; slippery slope, 161; sophistical, 13–14; threat-posing, 116; type of, 255; to ignorance (see *argumentum ad ignorantiam*); to the best explanation, 86; valid, 9; weak, 246, 258. *See also* individual argument

Argumentation: commitment-based, 105; irrelevance of, 253; prior sequence of, 255; sophistical, 9

Argumentation course case, 103–4

Argumentation schemes, 41, 255, 274; critical questions for, 255

Argumentation themes, 44
Arguments from Ignorance, 25–6
Argumentum (*see also* Fallacy): *ad baculum*, 23, 259; *ad consequentiam*, 176; *ad hominem*, 18, 24, 102, 182, 185, 202, 259, 266, 268–70; *ad ignorantiam*, 18, 25, 246, 266–70; *ad judicium*, 18–19, 269; *ad misericordiam*, 22; *ad populum*, 21; *ad verecundiam*, 18, 27, 145, 234, 263–4, 266, 267, 268–70
Aristotle, 15, 22, 32, 33, 34, 36, 78, 146–7, 195, 236–7; advocated reasoned argumentation, 189; classification of arguments, 4, 8, 11; concept of a fallacy, 15; deliberation, 34, 239; demonstration, 77, 239; dialectic, 240–1; fallacies distinguished by, 10; logic, 3, 14; practical reasoning, 155–6
Artificial intelligence, 98, 277–8
Assertions, 55, 251; clarification of, 148; initial, 96; set of, 54
Assumption, 60
Attack: emotional, 143; personal, 20, 24, 102, 118, 179, 182–5, 187, 192, 193, 202, 233, 262, 267
Axioms, 12, 238

Bargaining, 101; distributive, 103, 109, 112; integrative, 103–4; intraorganizational, 103; unionmanagement, 32
Barnes, Jonathan, 15
Barth, E.M., 5, 75, 84, 94–8, 260
Beacon Expert Systems, 120
Bear Pit, 206, 223
Beardsley, Monroe C., 87–91, 97; stages of an inquiry, 89, 97
Berg, Jonathan, 64, 128

Bias, 213, 229, 231, 233, 271–2; indicator of, 230
Bicycle path case, 199–201
Bicycle to work case, 157–8
Birnbaum, Lawrence, 192
Black, Max, 87–9, 91
Blair, J. Anthony, 65
Blunder, 112, 258
Bolton, Robert, 241–2
Bronniman, Werner, 192
Brouwer, L.J., 69
Burden of proof, 162, 231, 246, 268–70; assessment of, 250–1; critic's, 258, 275–6; defined, 30; initial, 39; positive, 38; shifting, 269

Campbell, Prime Minister Kim, 182–3, 206, 221, 224
Casuists, 16
Celebrities, 211
Cement case, 102, 116, 200, 202
Child-custody disputes, 113
Cloak case, 156, 165, 174
Cognitive environment, 62
Cohen, Carl, 123
Collingwood, R.G., 79–80, 90
Commitment, 141, 255, 275; affirmation of, 142; agent's, 157; communication of, 108; compromises in defining, 120; concept of, 31; darkside, 48, 52, 53, 54, 56, 58, 59, 62, 107, 120; disinclined to take on, 44; extracted, 50, 51; implicit, 107; incurring, 109; making a, 38; in negotiation dialogue, 106, 108, 115; process of testing, 119; retraction, 45–6, 70, 84–5, 107, 109, 164, 165, 168; roots of, 58; ruling on, 52; set, 28, 31, 39, 50, 51–2, 61, 62, 164, 165, 247; sharpened, 56; store, 40, 45–6,

55, 109, 129, 275; tracking, 40; to truth, 108

Concessions, 100–1, 110; explicit, 102; set of, 54

Conflict: resolution of, 47, 57–8

Context of dialogue, 252

Conversation, 6

Copi, Irving M., 123, 252–3

Copps, Sheila, 194

Critical discussion, 6, 110, 146, 148; complex, 47; defined as a dialogue, 48; four stages of, 47; goal of, 57; and persuasion dialogue, 48; purpose of, 47; simple, 47; violation of rules of, 262

Critical thinking, 20

Criticism, 166; evaluation of, 251

Culture of critique case, 179–80

Cumulativeness, 70, 73, 85

Dascal, Marcelo, 35, 64, 67

De sophisticis elenchis, 18, 33

Debates: deliberative decision-making, 172; parliamentary, 142, 182–3; political, 25, 150, 172, 173, 194, 206, 218, 222, 223, 224

Deception, 205

Degnan, Ronan E., 233

Deliberation dialogue: compared to the inquiry, 167; critical questions, 155; defeasible nature of, 167; eleven dynamic aspects of, 164; ethical aspect of, 166–7; flexibility of, 168; global, 174; goal, 152, 154, 163, 164, 165; initial situation, 151; joint, 151, 153; political, 169; schemata, 154–5; seven-step sequence of, 171–2; stages of, 162–3

Demonstration, 32, 243; scientific, 167

Déplacement, 201

Descartes, René, 79

Devereux, Daniel, 241–2

Dialectic, 239, 243; defined, 6, 187–8, 190; historical development of, 12

Dialectical argumentation, 189

Dialectical evaluation, 215

Dialectical subject, 95

Dialectically irrelevant, 206, 208, 253

Dialecticians, 187

Dialegesthai, 10

Dialogue, 6; advocacy, 215; classes of, 31; concept of, 29; context of, 49; defined, 3, 30, 34; deliberation type of, 34; eristic, 33; exchange, 96; goal, 30, 34, 254, 257; move in, 34; negotiation, 32; patient-physician, 32; profile of, 138, 141; rule violation in, 259; stages of, 30, 254, 257; type of, 254. See also individual dialogues

Dialogue on tipping, 37–8, 48, 58–9, 66, 241

Didactic arguments, 236

Dilemma, 153; constructive, 160

Discovery, 20

Disjunction and negation, 83

Divorce-mediation dispute, 201

Donohue, William A., 114; fourteen rules for distributive bargaining, 109, 112

Dreyfus, Hubert L., 144

Dreyfus, Stuart E., 144

Eastern Airlines strike, 202

Eikotic, 15

Embedding, 60, 204, 209. See also Shift

Empathy, 228

Endoxa, 15, 22, 147, 238, 241–2

Enlightenment, 16

Enthymeme: defined, 60; solving the problem of, 61

Equivocation, 248

Eristic: defined, 14, 181–2, 187–8

Eristic dialogue, 226; adversarial nature, 186; closed attitude of, 187; five identifying characteristics of, 196; goal of, 181; key characteristic of, 186; subtypes of, 195

Erlangen School, 83–4

An Essay Concerning Human Understanding, 18, 243, 268

Euclidean geometry, 12, 80

Euthydemus, 181, 188

Evans, J.D., 238

Evidence: relevant, 97, 234

Evidential priority, 246

Examination arguments, 237

Expert: biased, 228; critical examination of, 147; defined by five characteristics, 143; opinion, 266; paradox of expertise, 145; stages of, 144

Expert consultation dialogue, 148, 234, 235, 237, 238, 264

Explanation, purpose of, 85–6

Fallacies, 10, 176–7; committing, 115, 191; emotional, 21–2; informal, 176, 274; sophistical tactics type, 8, 178

Fallacy, 60; *ad baculum*, 115, 248; *ad misericordiam*, 248; *ad populum*, 123, 248; of begging the question, 26–7, 258, 264; defined, 257–61, 273; elements of, 260–1; of irrelevance, 66, 113, 245; of irrelevant conclusion (*ignoratio elenchi*), 63; of many questions, 26, 90, 138, 221, 264, 273; of relevance, 110, 123, 226; of suppressed evidence, 230–1; sophistical tactics type, 26; straw man, 27, 272–3. *See also* Argument; *Argumentum*

Feedback, 164

Felscher, Walter, 95–6

Fisher, Roger, 32, 101–2, 106, 116–19; four maxims of principled negotiation, 102–3, 202; notion of negotiation dialogue, 107; solution to deadlock, 120

Flowers, Margot, 192

Foundationalism: view of science, 78–80

Freeman, James B., 251

Fritz, Gerd, 5

From Axiom to Dialogue, 95

Fulton, Jim, 182–3

Games: CAVE, 52; CAVE+, 52; CBV, 51–2, 61; complex, 50; economic-oriented, 104; formal games of dialogue, 31; -like exchange, 83; negotiation, 104; Obligation, 14; Pleadings, 278; theory, 104; zero-sum, 103–5, 112

Garfield, Bob, 210

Generalizations, 156, 164; universal, 167

Glissement, 201, 206, 212, 214

Goal, 57–8, 248; global, 247; of human cognition, 128; main, 39

Gordon, Thomas F., 277–8

Grice, H. Paul, 5, 59, 67, 126, 254; concept of argumentation, 57; cooperative principle of, 63; irrelevance, 64; maxims, 5, 126, 192, 197

Grootendorst, Rob, 6, 31, 49; commitment sets, 50; critical discussion, 59, 260; fallacy defined, 259; intersubjective testing procedure, 203–4;

premises, 61; rules of, 48–9, 53; violation of rules of a critical discussion, 259

Grover, Mary Beth, 210

Gulliver, P.H., 111

Gumperz, J.J., 198

Guthrie, W.K.C., 13

Hamblin, C.L., 6, 9–10, 13, 28, 30, 91, 240, 243, 259–60; basic type of dialogue structure, 74; concept of commitment, 40, 43, 45, 50, 51, 56; dialogues, 53; framework for analysis of fallacies, 5; games of dialogue, 31–2, 52; on Locke, 18; open type of system, 54; problem with argumentation model, 51

Harrah, David, 136

Heuristics, 67

Heyting, A., 69

Hintikka, Jaakko, 5, 127, 129; framework of question-answer dialogue, 259–60

Hitchcock, David, 19, 149

Hundsnurscher, Franz, 4

Hurley, Patrick: on dilemmas, 160–1; standard presentation of evidence, 232; used car case, 230–1

Hypotheses: evaluating, 90; main, 88; vague, 91

Ignoratio Elenchi, 21. *See also* Fallacy (of irrelevance)

Implicature, 67–8

Income tax case, 137–40, 199, 264, 273–4

Inconsistencies, 40

Infante, Dominic A., 185

Inference, 67, 156; chaining of, 36, 43, 156; deductive, 88, 156; logical, 111;

plausible, 15–16; practical, 154–5; presumptive, 260

Infomercial Marketing Report, 211

Infomercials, 208–10, 257; evolution of, 211; goal of, 211–12; transparency of, 217

Information-presenting dialogue, 209, 214

Information-seeking dialogues, 5, 43, 133, 157, 163, 172, 208; advice-solicitation, 32, 43; asymmetrical, 127; goal of, 31, 135; opening stages of, 126; preceding a deliberation dialogue, 175; versus pedagogical dialogue, 235

Initial situation, 248

Inquiry, 32, 46, 167, 239, 264–5, 271; abstract normative model, 92; common-sense, 85; cumulative method of, 82; defining characteristics of, 70; empirical, 81; goal of, 70, 93, 98; legal, 82–3; linear function of, 74–5; property of cumulative argumentation, 75; public, 81, 84, 88, 93, 94; purpose of, 86; scientific, 32, 240; sequence of argumentation in, 72–3; shift between argument and explanation, 86; stages of, 33, 81, 85, 87, 89–90, 92, 97, 98

Interview, 31; celebrity, 131; employment, 130; media, 131, 134; provocation in, 132, 199

Irrelevance, 147, 196. *See also* Relevance

Irwin, Terence, 77

Issue, 38

Jackson, Sally, 113, 118, 201, 202

Jacobs, Scott, 113, 118, 201, 202

Jennings, Nicholas R., 153

Jesuits, 16
Johnson, Ralph, 65, 143, 258
Johnstone, Henry W., 10, 25
Jones, Tricia S., 104–5; four dimen-
   sions of commitments, 108
Jonsen, Albert R., 16

Kaiser, Artur, 130–1, 227–9, 236
Kamlah, W., 83–4
Kapp, Ernst, 12
Kennedy, George, 15–16
Kerferd, G.B., 181
Key words, 133–4
Kneale, Martha, 10, 13
Kneale, William, 10, 13
Knowledge, 165; accumulation, 76.
   See also Commitment set
Kotarbinski, Thadée, 191
Krabbe, Erik C.W., 5, 46, 48, 54, 55, 56,
   75, 83–4, 94–8, 247, 260; enthy-
   memes, 62; tree-shaped descrip-
   tion of moves, 247–8
Krever Inquiry, 91–2
Kripke, Saul, 69, 72, 98; model of
   intuitionist logic, 72–5, 78; model of
   the argumentation of an inquiry,
   83, 95
Kruiger, Tjark; *argumentum ad conse-
   quentiam*, 176

Lascher, Edward L., 169–70, 172
Lee, Charles S., 213
Legal cases, 25, 233, 268; plea bargain-
   ing, 234–35
Levine, Joshua, 211
Locke, John, 243, 268–9
Lockean analysis, 24, 27
Logic, 3, 16; deductive, 80, 161; formal,
   7; intuitionistic, 69, 72–4, 83, 95, 98;
   Middle Ages, 14; syllogistic, 14

Logical Dialogue: Games and Fallacies,
   43, 50, 51
Logical propaedeutic, 83
Lorenzen, Paul, 5, 83–4; -style strips,
   95
Lorenzo case, 202, 262
Lyne, Andrew, 71

Mackenzie, J.D., 5, 80
Magalogue, 214
Manor, 149
Mary, Peter, and William case, 127–8,
   175
McGuire, Rod, 192
McKersie, R.B., 112; classification of
   subtypes of negotiation dialogue,
   103; integrative bargaining, 105;
   view of commitment in negotiation
   dialogue, 107, 114, 115
Meno, 187
Mexican War case, 176
Middleton, Kent, 124
Mixed Discourse (dialogue), 201, 264
Modus Ponens argument, 169–70, 256

Negotiation, 172, 229, 234–5; business, 184; labour, 103; political, 222;
   principled, 117
Negotiation dialogue, 232; compared
   with persuasion dialogue, 108; confrontation stage, 110, 112; goal of,
   100–1, 118; goal of participant in,
   101, 105; initial situation, 101; irrelevant move in, 112; multiple interests in, 107; normative goal, 101
Nichomachean Ethics, 34, 166–8
Normative frameworks for evaluating argumentation, 256
Northumberland Strait Crossing Act
   case, 182–3, 206, 221, 223, 253

Nuchelmans, Gabriel, 18

On Sophistical Refutations, 10–11, 13, 166, 189, 190, 236, 237, 238, 243
On the Movements of Animals, 156
Opinion polls, 22
Outlines of Pyrrhonism, 42

Parliamentary Rules and Forms, 219
Pascal, 16, 17
Pedagogical dialogue: good questioning techniques in, 236; as subspecies of information-seeking dialogue, 237
Peirastic, 146
Perastikoi, 13
Persuasion dialogue, 31: defined, 48, 279–80 ch2n1; dual view of, 56; goal of, 31, 37; maieutic function of, 58; notion of commitment in, 39; permissive persuasion dialogue (PPD), 54, 55–8, 60, 204; presumptions in, 39; relevance in, 42, 43; rigorous persuasion dialogue (RPD), 54, 55–6, 204; rules of, 40; types of goals of, 38
Petitio principii. See Fallacy of begging the question
Phronesis, 169
Plato, 12, 13, 14, 181, 190
Plausible Argument in Everyday Conversation, 37, 58
Positions, 102
Posterior Analytics, 14, 76–8
Praxiology, 191
Principia, 79
Principle of preservation, 84
Prior Analytics, 14
Priority, 77; evidential, 77
Point of view, 49

Premises, 76, 156, 238; base, 241; as commitments, 64; dialectically relevant, 245; disjunctive, 161; goal, 154; implicit, 60; initial, 12, 75; knowledge, 175; means, 154; missing, 60, 63; nonexplicit, 61–2, 63; in peirastic arguments, 242; unexpressed, 49
Presumption, 67, 134; defeasible, 135; normal, 135; weight of, 59
Presupposition, 140
Principle of excluded middle, 74
Probative function, 64
Proctor, Robert N., 162
Proof: standard of, 32
Propaganda, 213
Propositions, 39; conditional, 52; mapped set of, 73; pair of, 38; probatively relevant, 64; simple, 52; topically relevant, 64; verified, 94
Public opinion polls, 171
Putnam, Linda L., 104–5; four dimensions of commitments, 108

Quarrel, 14, 118, 178, 226; cathartic effect of, 34, 179, 185; characterized by, 194; contrast with persuasion dialogue, 186; goal of, 33, 184, 261; group, 186–7, 196; indicators of, 185; initial situation of, 184; natural, 196; participant's goal of, 178–9; pretence in, 195; purpose of, 33; successful, 186; staged, 196; staged intellectual, 190; typified by, 33
Question Period, 219–23; purpose of, 223; quality of argumentation in, 226; set of rules in, 225
Question-asking, 248
Question-Reply Argumentation, 52, 247, 260

Question-reply relationship, 35
Question-reply sequence, 149, 237
Questions, 236–7; aggressive, 221, 248; and answer technique, 188, 189; argumentative aspect of, 137; bad, 131 ; conditional, 136; critical, 155, 159, 229, 255, 260, 276; deliberative, 136; hypothetical, 136, 165; implicit, 152; loaded and complex, 219, 221; negative-suggestive, 130; traps, 130; tricky, 140; why, 129; yes-no, 129, 137–8, 149

Reasoning, 11, 243; abductive, 97; based on warranted assertability, 69; circular, 74–6, 80, 258; contentious, 13–14, 190; decision-making, 151; defeasible, 41; deductive, 16; deductively valid or invalid, 247; dialectic, 12, 19, 76, 200; general rules of, 167; genuine, 189; goal-directed, 129; identification of, 250; logical, 90, 124; mathematical, 69; non-monotonic, 41; plausible, 242; practical, 34, 106, 108, 111, 136, 152, 153, 155–6; 173–4; premissary, 65; presumptive, 163; probable, 16; scientific, 78–9, 162; sequence of, 43, 82, 89; statistical, 162; syllogistic, 11, 76–7; use of, 248
Rescher, Nicholas, 176, 260
Red herring, 63
Relevance, 175; of an argument, 174; concept of, 67–8, 252; conversational, 128; definition of, 35, 127, 176; determining, 174–5; dialectical, 63, 110; evaluating argumentation for, 97; failure of, 147, 177, 194, 197, 221, 245, 252; in inquiries, 97, 98; judgments of, 68, 149; lack of, 22,

194; link of, 183; local, 149; method for deciding, 66–7; in negotiation dialogue, 110; in persuasion dialogues, 42, 63; probative dialectical, 64–5; seven factors to judge, 65–6; topical, 64
Republic, 188
Retraction, 239; in scientific argumentation, 71–2
Rhetoric, 15, 168
Rhode Island case, 169–71, 173–4
Rigorous persuasion dialogue, 5
Robinson, Richard, 14, 187–8
Rules: of argumentation, 40; commitment, 109; of critical discussion, 59, 262; dialectical, 47, 53; of dialogue, 263, 275; for distributive bargaining, 112; of evidence, 233; for gaining commitment, 114; lack of, 182; of PPD (permissive persuasion dialogue), 55; of persuasion dialogues, 59–60; of politeness, 3; presumptive, 109; procedural, 233, 248; of public inquiry, 94; of reasonable dialogue, 260; of relevance, 255–6; of RPD (rigorous persuasion dialogue, 57; RDS (rule in CB game), 51–2; structural dialogue, 109; turn-taking, 109; win-loss, 32

Saarinen, Esa, 127
Sales pitch, 209, 214–15; dialectically irrelevant, 208
Sanctions, 114
Schwartz, Bryan, 94
Scientific argumentation, 71, 78; ideal model of, 80
Scientific research, 80, 162–63
Sextus Empiricus, 42
Shift, 67, 119, 184; deceptive, 191, 257;

degeneration, 188; detectability of, 198–9; dialectical, 116–17, 149, 232, 259, 271; external, 200; from a critical discussion to a deliberation dialogue, 263; from deliberation to an information-seeking dialogue, 163; from dialectic argument to eristic, 188; from an expert consultation dialogue to persuasion dialogue, 204; from an information-seeking dialogue to a peirastic type, 199; from an inquiry to a criminal trial, 93; from negotiation to an information-seeking dialogue, 117; from negotiation to critical discussion, 202; from negotiation to quarrel, 118; from PPD to RPD, 55–6, 62; from a quarrel, 197, 202; illicit/licit, 176–7, 200, 216; to a quarrel, 25, 192, 256, 261

Socrates, 188; aspect of questioning, 236

Sophist, 15–16, 27, 181, 190–1

Sophist, 188

Sophistical dialogue, 190

Sophistical refutations, 3–4, 15, 265

Sophistical Refutations, 14, 242

Speech acts, 45

Speech event, 225

Sperber, Dan, 127–9, 135, 175

Strategies: distancing, 44; loophole, 45; separating, 44

Straw-man argument, 193

Structuring: attitudinal, 103

Syllogism, 12, 14, 76, 166; dialectical, 238

Tactics, 20, 22–3, 26, 148; aggressive, 178, 223; argumentation, 102, 180, 195; calculated, 196; commitment,
115; of deception, 138, 195; deceptive tricks, 197, 214–16; evasion, 226; fallacious, 22; knowledge-based, 269; legitimate, 115; in negotiation dialogues, 107; scare, 23; sophistical, 27, 112, 181, 216, 258, 274–5; straw-man, 196; threats as, 115; of trapping a respondent, 26

Tannen, Deborah, 179, 192–3

Tautology, 161

Terms: loaded, 142

Thesis, 39, 42; opposing, 44

Threats, 23, 192, 262; covert, 263; in a critical discussion, 23; direct, 114; indirect, 114; in negotiation dialogue, 23, 113; relevant, 116

Tindale, Christopher W., 62

Topical Relevance in Argumentation, 35

Topics, 11, 13–14, 166, 168, 240–4

Toulmin, Stephen, 16

Tree structure, 72–3, 75, 95, 98–9, 138, 248

Tu Quoque, 185, 201, 271

Tuna scandal case, 206; lack of relevance, 194

Tutiorism, 163

Ury, William, 32, 101–2, 106, 116–19; four maxims of principled negotiation, 102–3, 202; notion of negotiation dialogue, 107; solution to deadlock, 120

van Eemeren, Frans H., 6, 31, 49; *argumentum ad consequentiam*, 176; commitment sets, 50; critical discussion, 59, 260; fallacy defined, 259; intersubjective testing procedure, 203–4; premises, 61; rules of, 47–8,

53; violation of rules of a critical discussion, 259
Verbal aggressiveness scale, 185

Walton, Douglas N., 46, 48, 54, 55, 56, 73, 112, 144, 223, 255, 260; classification of subtypes of negotiation dialogue, 103; enthymemes, 62; integrative bargaining, 105; presupposition, 140; view of commitment in negotiation dialogue, 107, 114, 115
Wigley, Charles J., 185

Wilson, Deidre, 127–9, 175; account of relevance, 135
Wisdom: practical, 34
Woods, John, 73, 144, 223; criticizes account of relevance, 135
Wooldridge, Michael, 153
Wright, Larry, 152

Yankelovich, Daniel, 171

Zeno of Elea, 13